Colonial Effects

Colonial Effects

The Making of National Identity in Jordan

Joseph A. Massad

COLUMBIA UNIVERSITY PRESS   NEW YORK

COLUMBIA UNIVERSITY PRESS
Publishers Since 1893
New York   Chichester, West Sussex

Library of Congress Cataloging-in-Publication Data
  Massad, Joseph Andoni, 1963–
    Colonial effects: the making of national identity in Jordan /
    Joseph Andoni Massad
      p. cm.
    Revision of author's thesis.
    Includes bibliographical references and index.
    ISBN 0-231-12322-1 (cloth : alk. paper) — ISBN 0-231-12323-X
    (pbk. : alk. paper)
      1. Jordan—Politics and government—20th century.   2. National state.
    3. National characteristics, Jordanian.   4. Jordan—Ethnic relations.
    5. Postcolonialism—Jordan.   6. Jordan—Armed Forces—Political activity.
    7. Culture and law.   I. Title.

    JQ1833.A58 M37 2001
    956.9504'3—dc21   2001028017

Casebound editions of Columbia University Press books
are printed on permanent and durable acid-free paper.
Printed in the United States of America

c 10 9 8 7 6 5 4 3 2 1
p 10 9 8 7 6 5 4 3 2

For my parents,
Jacqueline T. Hallaq
and
Andoni Y. Mas'ad 'Arbid

Contents

Acknowledgments

This book began as a dissertation. I have enjoyed thinking about, researching, and writing it in ways I did not anticipate. When I embarked on this intellectual journey, I thought that I already knew many of the answers to the questions I was posing. In the process, I realized that I knew only few of them, and even then not adequately. I have learned much from this project, not only about nationalism and Jordan but also about myself as a subject of both. It is through working on this project that I came to understand how I became a *Palestinian Jordanian*. My hope is that this book will serve to explain the process through which the Jordanian people came to see "ourselves" the way "we" do.

I have been helped and guided by many colleagues, friends, and family members in the years since this project began. I would like to begin by thanking Lisa Anderson, my professor and advisor, for believing in this project and for supporting it despite her initial misgivings about its unorthodox methodology. Her trust in me strengthened my resolve to proceed and finally to complete this project. Although I was not his student, Timothy Mitchell gave me much of his time and attention. His careful reading of the dissertation chapters and his attention to the historical material as well as my theoretical approach made me rethink a number of contentions I had initially made. His interventions made the final version much richer. I thank him for his support and intellectual engagement.

From Edward Said, I learned much of what I know about culture, representation, and empire. I began reading Edward Said when I was a freshman in college. I only met him eight years later. His work has had the greatest influence on my intellect and my work. His help and support in and out of class went beyond the call of duty. To him, I owe much gratitude, both professional and personal.

My mother has had and continues to have the greatest influence on my life. I have learned much from her about the importance of knowledge and education, about inequality between women and men and between the poor and the rich, about commitment and respect, and most of all about love. I would never have been able to pursue my university education were it not for her personal and financial sacrifices (and those of my father and sisters).

From my father I learned to love languages. Although he learned English and French at school, he taught himself Italian so well that he speaks it as fluently as he speaks Arabic. When my sisters and I were children, my mother and father (both of whom were 1948 Palestinian refugees who, along with their families, fled the Palestinian city of Jaffa to escape advancing Zionist forces, losing all their belongings in the process) would always tell us "we do not have wealth to bequeath to you, only education. Even if we had money to bequeath to you, you would spend it. Education, however, will remain with you forever." This dictum is shared by many Palestinian refugees rendered penniless by the loss of their country and homes.

My mother always dreamed of obtaining a university education, a dream that remains unfulfilled. To make it up to herself, she moved heaven and earth to ensure that her children would go. My father's pride in his children's academic accomplishments is always manifest. Like my mother, he did not have a chance to obtain a university education.

During my stay in Amman in 1994 and 1995, and during subsequent visits in 1996 and 1997, I received much love and support from my sisters, Suzie, Roula, and Rania, and my nephew and nieces, Samer, Dina, and Nadine. I thank them all for their patience and love.

The intellectual engagement and friendship of Muhammad Ayyub and Jihad Yahya kept me sane at many different moments. Even after I left Amman, Jihad helped procure documents for me that I needed and did not have. The loving friendship I received from Salam ʿArif Al-Rubayʿi sustained me throughout that period. All three provided me with much-needed companionship, forming with my family a support system without which Amman would have been a much lonelier place. I thank them all.

In my research efforts, I was helped by a number of people in Amman. I would like to thank Nahlah Abu-Khalaf and Camelia Hattar from the Center for Strategic Studies at the University of Jordan for facilitating contacts and for their professional support despite institutional constraints. I would also like to thank Dr. Nufan al-Humud of the Center for Manuscripts (Markaz al-Watha'iq) at the Library of the University of Jordan for his research help. 'Abdullah Damdam of the microfilm center at the library of the University of Jordan was tireless in his efforts. He helped me locate many newspaper issues that otherwise would have been impossible to find. His help was truly exemplary. I owe him much gratitude. My research experience was made less lonely by Marc Lynch, who was conducting his own research at the same time in Amman. We shared our high and low points in conducting research, as well as many a bus ride from the University of Jordan.

I would like to thank Dr. Ma'n Abu Nuwwar for sharing with me his recollections as well as his research material, and Dr. Ma'ruf al-Bakhit of the Jordanian Arab Army's General Headquarters (al-Qiyadah al-'Amah) for facilitating my access to the library of the Army's Department of Spiritual Guidance (Maktabat Al-Tawjih Al-Ma'nawi).

Rana William Ziyadat, the librarian at Maktabat al-Tawjih al-Ma'nawi, was generous with her time and with extra books from that library. Hani Hurani was also generous with his time and with the publications of the New Jordan Studies Center. I thank them both for their support. My cousins Ninette 'Arbid and Amin Batshun were very generous with me personally and professionally. The thousands of copies they made for me at their business were offered not only free of charge but with a loving and supportive smile. I will always be grateful to them.

Many thanks to Mu'nis al-Razzaz and Suhayr Al-Tall, with whom I had many informative and lively conversations. Suhayr has been a role model in many ways. Her intellectual acuity, commitment to justice, and political activism on behalf of Jordanian women in general, and on her own behalf as a Jordanian woman, are inspirational. I would like to thank her for her friendship and generosity.

I also would like to thank Buthayna Jardanah of *Nadi Sahibat Al-A'mal wa All-Mihan* for her time and help in giving me access to the *Nadi*'s library. My thanks to the Jordanian Women's Union for the documents and conference papers they provided me. Riccardo Bocco is a friend and a colleague. His support and critical insight have helped improve many parts of the manuscript. I thank him for all the support he has given me.

While writing in New York, I received the help of many friends, not all of whom lived in that city. From Washington, D.C., Lamis Jarrar, Lana Shekim, and Nour Barakat gave much love and support. Our long-distance telephone bills testify to that. José Quiroga has supported my doctoral career from the beginning. His loving support, friendship, and advice were always a source of encouragement. He helped me move to New York from Washington, D.C., easing my transition difficulties to a city I had held in awe. Kouross Esmaeli provided much love and support. His political intransigence matched mine in ways he might not know. Ella Habiba Shohat and Magda al-Nowaihi were a great source of support and friendship, both personal and political. Ali Razki and Susan Scott-Kerr gave me much love and support *and* excellent food. I thank them all.

Since my first years in college at the University of New Mexico, a number of people have played a role in changing the way I apprehend the world. Marcos Paz, Liza Martinez, Lori Rudolph, and Madeline Aron taught me much about "America." Philip Farah was the first to teach me what politics and intellectual life are. Despite our many political and intellectual differences since that "inaugural moment," I remain indebted to him for introducing me to a world of which I knew very little. Beth Kaimowitz has the sharpest intellect of anyone I know, as well as the most passionate commitment to justice. From her, not only did I learn how to answer certain questions but also how to reformulate the questions altogether, and how to interrogate the terms that the questions deploy. I am a much richer person for having known them all.

The friendship, love, and intellectual engagement of Neville Hoad made writing and thinking through this book a challenging and pleasurable exercise. His sharp intellect and wit have kept me constantly on my feet. His intellectual imprint can be found on every word of this book. He has graciously read and reread more versions of chapters than I (or he) care to remember. Without his insights, this book would have looked very different.

Special thanks are owed to Kate Wittenberg and Peter Dimock of Columbia University Press, whose support was crucial for the publication of this book. Marjorie Wexler's highly non-interventionist copyediting made the publishing process enjoyable. I thank her for all her efforts. I would also ike to thank the manuscript's anonymous readers for their insightful comments.

My research in Jordan was funded by a fellowship provided by Columbia University's Department of Political Science and a number of summer travel grants provided by Columbia University's Middle East Institute. I thank them both for trusting in my project. An earlier version of Chapter 1 was published in *Le Royaume Hachémite de Jordanie: Identités sociales, politiques de développement et construction étatique, 1946–1996*, edited by Riccardo Bocco and published (2001) in Paris by Karthala and in Amman and Beirut by CERMOC.

Introduction

        The object of this study is the production of national identity and national culture within Jordan as both a typical and an atypical post-colonial nation-state. Recent studies of nationalism describe the nation as "invented"[1] or "imagined,"[2] by intellectuals and/or political elites who are producers of, or produced by, the political discourse of nationalism.[3] In this study, I am more interested in whether *institutions* play a role in the production of colonial and postcolonial national identity and culture. More specifically, I examine whether two key state institutions, law and the military, assist in the production of the nation. Do these institutions contribute to the identification of people as "nationals"? Do they play any role in the production of ideas and practices that come to constitute "national culture"? In posing these and other related questions, what I am proposing is not a general or generalizable theoretical model for the study of nationalism but rather a general and generalizable mode of inquiry.

    Law and the military were central institutions set up by the colonial powers in the colonies. They replaced existing juridical and military structures, or introduced them to societies that did not have them before. Both law and the military retain their colonial markings as European institutions established to serve the colonial state. As Frantz Fanon has shown, however, once national independence is achieved, the new nation-state elites replace their colonial masters in administering the same institutions that were used to control them.[4] Furthermore, the postcolonial state, as Partha Chatterjee states, has "expanded and not transformed the basic institutional arrangement of colonial law and administration, of the courts, the bureaucracy, the police, the army, and the various technical services of government."[5] Colonial institutions and epistemology are thus adopted and adapted to the national condition. Instead of serving European colonialism, law and the military come to serve national independence, or its state representatives.

To study national identity and culture through these colonial institutional mechanisms, we must begin by understanding the general role these institutions play in governance within the postcolonial nation-state and their inception under colonial rule. As a background, I will discuss the major theoretical contributions dealing with questions of law, military, and discipline, and with nationalist ideology and its relationship to questions of cultural tradition and modernity. I will also provide a brief history of Jordan from 1921 to the present.

Law, Military, and Discipline

In his studies of the transformation of western European state power in the modern period, Michel Foucault speaks of the development of modern government. For Foucault, western European state rule was initially based on law on which sovereignty itself was founded. Any illegality was an affront to the power of the sovereign, which had to be redressed with corporeal punishment as public spectacle. With the emergence of penal reform, discipline emerged as the art of managing the population "in its depths and details." Its object was "not to punish less, but to punish better; to punish with an attenuated severity perhaps, but in order to punish with more universality and necessity; to insert the power to punish more deeply into the social body."[6] Foucault asserts that the "point of application of the penalty is not the representation [as in public executions as spectacle], but the body, time, everyday gestures and activities; and the soul, too, but in so far as it is the seat of habits. The body and the soul, as principles of behaviour, form the element that is now proposed for punitive intervention."[7] This does not lead to a restoration of the "juridical subject who is caught up in the fundamental interests of the social pact, but the obedient subject, the individual subjected to habits, rules, orders, an authority that is exercised continually around him and upon him, and which he must allow to function automatically in him."[8] According to Foucault, discipline has not necessarily replaced previous modalities of power, "it has infiltrated the others, sometimes undermining them, but serving as an intermediary between them, linking them together, extending them and above all making it possible to bring the

effects of power to the most minute and distant elements. It assures an in-
finitesimal distribution of power relations."[9]

Government, which emerged in the eighteenth century, was to become
the new form constituting the state's function.[10] Foucault describes modern
"governmentality" as constituting this triangle of "sovereignty–discipline–
government."[11] For Foucault, indeed, "if it is true that the juridical system
was useful for representing, albeit in an inexhaustive way, a power that was
centered primarily around deduction and death, it is utterly incongruous
with the new methods of power whose operation is not ensured by right but
by technique, not by law but by normalization, not by punishment but by
control, methods that are employed on all levels and in forms that go beyond
the state and its apparatus."[12] Foucault insists that power in the modern
period controls not necessarily by *repressing* individuals but by *producing*
them in the first place as subjects subjected to power.

Foucault seems to be echoing Antonio Gramsci's notion of *hegemony*.
Unlike Foucault, who overstresses production at the expense of repression,
Gramsci describes the modern state's techniques of controlling the population as both coercion *and* hegemony. Hegemony is that "which the dominant group exercises throughout society . . . on the other hand of 'direct
domination' or command exercised through the State and 'juridical' government." Hegemony, for Gramsci, has the central function of producing
"[t]he 'spontaneous' consent given by the great masses of the population to
the general direction imposed on social life by the dominant fundamental
group." As for coercive power, Gramsci describes it as a state apparatus that
"legally" imposes "discipline on those groups who do not 'consent' either
actively or passively. This apparatus is, however, constituted for the whole
of society in anticipation of moments of crisis of command and direction
when spontaneous consent has failed."[13]

Although Foucault contends that a productive disciplinary power has "infiltrated" repressive juridical power, he proceeds in a way that indicates that
productive discipline has indeed *overtaken* the repressive rule of law. In
doing so, Foucault underestimates the importance of law in the organization
of state repression. Nicos Poulantzas correctly states that Foucault's approach
treats the state's repressive apparatuses as "mere parts of the disciplinary
machine which patterns the internalization of repression by means of normalization."[14] Although, in line with Foucault, disciplinary power's infiltration of juridical power has reconstituted law as a series of productive and
normalizing tactics, law is also constituted by a repressive technique engineered to penalize those who remain outside the norm. One could even

contend that production and repression as techniques of control are fully imbricated in each other. Disciplinary and juridical production implies disciplinary and juridical repression. To produce the new, the old has to be repressed. The very production of a normalized subject requires the production of its *other*, the "abnormal," whose abnormality has to be *repressed* and buried to reveal the normal as essence.

In this study, I examine whether the nation-state's repressive apparatuses, especially law and the army, are indeed parts of a disciplinary machine as they are *also* parts of a juridical one. Does the juridical itself acquire the double function of production and repression? Weber contends that the modern state has a monopoly of the *legitimate* means of coercion and physical violence, and that this coercive ability is organized in a "rational-legal" manner. I demonstrate how the nation-state also acquires a monopoly over the *legitimate means of discipline*, which is then generalized through the institutions of law and the military across the surface of society. Schools and the media, through which education is institutionalized, also become favorite channels for enforcing disciplinary normalization of the population, although both remain subservient to the juridical power of the state. I take Gramsci's initial contention as operative for the nation-state. Hegemonic methods are used unless they fail to be effective with the subjects of the nation-state, in which case coercive methods are used. I take Foucault's notion of discipline, or the set of practices, rules, habits, and orders that it generates for the purpose of normalizing and controlling the population, as central for the maintenance if not the continual reproduction of the hegemony of the state and its nationalist ideology. I will rely on Foucault's important contribution of the *productivity* of disciplinary regimes.

Unlike Foucault, however, and in line with Poulantzas, in this study I show how the nation-state governs through a disciplinary-juridical dyad, which is both *productive and repressive,* formative and destructive. In the course of our examination of the journey traversed by what becomes national identity and national culture, these repressive and productive mechanisms are shown to be working hand in hand, destroying what exists and forming what is new. More important, through their control of the time and space of the nation, they formulate the *new* as that which has always *been*. This is accomplished not only within the confines of the law and the military but also by these institutions' generation of processes of cultural production that overflow into society and other state institutions. It is these cultural productions that augment the juridical and military strategies to which they owe their very existence.

Law and the military, however, are not always the servile instruments of political elites. They do not only translate decisions made by these elites. These institutions develop an independent momentum that produces outcomes not necessarily envisioned by state elites and that lie outside their immediate control. Law and the military, which play their designated repressive role, prove to exceed their control mandate by playing a *productive* role not initially envisioned by those who deployed them. They set new demarcations on who is and who is not a "national," what is and what is not "national culture." They come to constitute and produce the subjects and the categories they seek to discipline and/or repress. Moreover, the strategies through which these subjects are produced generate a range of processes outside the realm of the military and the law, which carry their production to the realm of national culture. It is these series of productions and their repressive correlates that I study.

Tradition and Modernity

Nationalism is ideology. However, as Louis Althusser emphasizes, "Ideology always exists in an apparatus . . . and its practice, or practices. This existence is material."[15] One of the most obvious ideological underpinnings of anticolonial nationalisms is the combining of modernization and tradition. While one of anticolonial nationalism's dual goals is the achievement of technological modernization in the Western sense, its other goal is the assertion of a traditional national culture.[16] As Chatterjee has argued, for nationalism to achieve its dual goals, it divides the world into two domains, "the material and the spiritual. The material is the domain of the 'outside,' of the economy and of statecraft, of science and technology, a domain where the West had proved its superiority and the East had succumbed. . . . The spiritual, on the other hand, is an 'inner' domain bearing the 'essential' marks of cultural identity. The greater one's success in imitating Western skills in the material domain, therefore, the greater the need to preserve the distinctness of one's spiritual culture."[17]

In the Arab East, as in the rest of Asia, national identity was the site of negotiating not only East and West as conceptual anchoring categories, but, as importantly the foundational ruse of gendered citizenship. The respective responsibilities of men and women to the nation emerged as cornerstones of nation-building in the colonized world just as they had been and continue to be in European countries.[18] I examine how national identity conceives of masculinity in defining nationalist agency. The category of masculinity itself is shown to be embedded in a temporal schema, whose telos is European modernity; a geocultural schema, whose core is urbanity at the expense of the countryside and the desert; and a class schema, organized by bourgeois economics replacing previous rules of property and ownership. In examining masculinity within nationalist philosophy, my objective is not to describe the unfolding of a masculine-based nationalism but rather to show the process through which masculinity itself, *and* femininity, are lived within the modality of the nation-state—indeed, how masculinity and femininity are nationalized.

In accordance with liberal ideology, the colonial state sets up the binary of the public and the private. Chatterjee claims that nationalists "operated in a field constituted by a very different set of distinctions—those between the spiritual and the material, the inner and the outer, the essential and the inessential. That contested field over which nationalism had proclaimed its sovereignty and where it had imagined its true community was neither coextensive with nor coincidental to the field constituted by the private/public distinction."[19] This is partially true. It proves to be quite inaccurate, however, when describing the realm of the juridical. It is within the law that the material/spiritual, the outer/inner, the modern/traditional, male/female distinctions are divided into the realms of the public and the private. The arena of law becomes one where modernity and modern European codes can adjudicate matters of statecraft and the economy while religious and local "traditions" adjudicate matters of sexual and family relations and culture. In the case of Jordan, for example, European legal codes were to run the public sphere (inhabited by modern urban men), while religious laws (Muslim and Christian) and Bedouin customary laws (until 1976) were to run the private (inhabited by women and the Bedouins who constitute parts of the "inner", the "traditional," and the "spiritual" essence of the nation).

Benedict Anderson claims that Asian and African nationalist intellectuals "imagined" their nations by imitating the already existing "modular" forms of nationalisms in Europe and the Americas. Chatterjee criticizes Anderson's contentions by asserting that if "nationalisms in the rest of the world have to choose their imagined community from certain 'modular' forms . . . what do they have left to imagine?"[20] Indeed, for Chatterjee, since nationalists adopt European models of the "material," it is in the spiritual realm that they can be imaginative: "Here nationalism launches its most powerful, creative, and historically significant project: to fashion a "modern" national culture that is nevertheless not Western. If the nation is an imagined community, then this is where it is brought into being. In this, its true and essential domain, the nation is already sovereign, even when the state is in the hands of the colonial power. The dynamics of this historical project is completely missed in conventional histories in which the story of nationalism begins with the contest for political power."[21]

I am in agreement with Chatterjee on this point, although with some reservations. Whereas nationalists are agents in the construction of national culture, or what Chatterjee calls the "spiritual," this domain is hardly "sovereign" or independent from productive colonial machinations. The colonial state, through its institutions, is, in fact, instrumental in the production of national culture. Colonial economic relations, the military, colonial schools, law, are in fact *repressive* of a range of cultural material and *productive* of another. Nationalists later adopt the colonial cultural product as "traditional," with no reference to its colonial genealogy of repression and production. From repressing existing cultural practices to producing "traditional national" dishes and music, clothes, personal grooming, flags, and sports, colonial institutions are central. Chatterjee is correct in asserting that the nationalist attempt is to *dress* these products up as traditional and modern simultaneously, without implicating them in the *Western* modern project. It is in doing so that the nationalists manifest their agency, an agency they had initially shown in their refusal of the racial/cultural hierarchical epistemology within which colonialism had imprisoned them. However, in putting this project into effect, the nationalists' combining of European and existing gender, religious, and aesthetic (in short, "cultural") norms does not result in cultural syncretism; rather it is a process whereby European norms *sublate* (*aufheben*) traditional ones. The new cultural norms are modern inventions dressed up in traditional garb to satisfy nationalism's claims of a national culture for which it stands. This new culture, however, is not so much *traditional* as it is *traditionalized*.[22]

The military is especially important in this regard. In schooling its soldiers in the art of warfare, the colonial state also introduces them to a new way of apprehending the world, a new epistemology, underlain by the *modern* colonial order and that of the nation-state. This epistemology is maintained with little variation on the assumption to power of anticolonial nationalists. Whereas the anticolonial nationalist struggle questions the colonial hierarchy of Europeans and non-Europeans by according "Orientals" and Africans agency, it fails to question the colonial epistemology of governance. Traditional sociological and political science approaches to the military have been limited to its "praetorian" role, to its role in the formation of modern states, or to its "politics" in relation to the state, political society, and civil society.[23] Samuel P. Huntington, for example, defines praetorianism "in a limited sense" as "the intervention of the military in politics."[24] He discerns this "phenomenon" within states in Latin America, Asia, and Africa. Alfred Stepan, on the other hand, seeks to uncover the different roles played by the military under authoritarianism and democracy and its relationship to other state agencies and society at large.[25] What these approaches fail to account for is the *productive* role of the military: how the military *produces* politics rather than how it is related to it or what "its" politics actually are. What kind of repressive techniques underlie the military's *productivity* of identities and practices? And what kind of productive techniques underlie its *repression* of identities and practices? In constituting itself as a machine of coercion and discipline, the military represses existing forms of being and produces a new species of citizen-nationals that permeate the rest of society. In the context of the modern nation-state, these militarized citizen-nationals impart to the rest of society, through a variety of mechanisms (media, official propaganda, schools, family, military conscriptions, songs, music), new cultures and traditions that are identified as "national." Following Timothy Mitchell, the military as a state organ is indeed as permeable as are other state agencies and society itself more generally.[26] This permeability between society and the army, between the realm of the civic and the realm of the military, is what facilitates the normalization of society that had begun within the military. Here, I am referring not only to the generalizability of the military's disciplinary function to schools, universities, hospitals, sports clubs, and the family, but also to the generalizability of the specific normalization of citizens within the military—as nationalist agents defending the nation—to the rest of society at large.

Historical Moments

Examining the roles of state organs, such as law and the military, in the fashioning of a postcolonial national identity reveals national identity to be a non-essence, a product overdetermined by a variety of mechanisms and discourses of which it is the effect. It also reveals it to be a dynamic entity. Its *self* and its *other* change according to different historical moments.

In analyzing how bourgeois revolutions and hegemony are achieved, Antonio Gramsci identifies three historical moments of the "relation of forces" whose resolutions are determinative of the outcome of political struggles. The first is that of the structure of the economy, "objective, independent of human will"; the second is "the relation of political forces"; and the third is "the relation of military forces."[27] In studying Indian nationalist thought, Partha Chatterjee adapts Gramsci by positing three moments in its development, the moment of departure (that of its encounter with post-Enlightenment thought), the moment of manoeuvre (that of mobilization), and the moment of arrival ("when nationalist thought attains its full development").[28] As I am studying the role of state agencies in the production of national identity, I have chosen a different set of historical moments that are definitional of that identity. Like Chatterjee, I am not positing a teleological model of ascending evolutionary stages. I am positing these moments as transformative moments that are at times, but not necessarily always, historically discontinuous.

The first moment is the colonial moment. This is the moment when colonialism establishes a state-framework on a colonized territory/country, either replacing an existing state structure or inaugurating one where it had not existed before.[29] This inaugural moment establishes the political, juridical, administrative, and military structures of the colonized territory/country, effectively rendering it a nation-state (laws of nationality, governance, and citizenship are codified, borders and maps are drawn up, bureaucratic divisions and taxonomies of the territory and the population are imposed, conscription and/or induction of colonized men into colonial military structures is established). This moment constitutes a radical discontinuity with what existed before the colonial encounter.

The second moment is the anticolonial moment. This is the moment when the struggle against colonial rule becomes generalized and hegemonic, leading to the ultimate establishment of national independence. This is also the moment when the administrative colonial framework is adopted by the colonized to set up their independent nation-state. The nationalist representatives of the colonized will oversee the colonial state's institutions, which are now in the service of the postcolonial independent state. This moment is discontinuous from the previous one in that it overthrows the existing discursive and material structure of colonial governance. The nation-state and its apparatuses are now staffed and run by anticolonial nationalists for the benefit of the nation and not colonialism. However, as far as the techniques of governance are concerned, there is almost complete institutional continuity. The colonial structure of governance survives the "rupture" unscathed.

The third moment is that of the expansion and contraction of the nation. Here, I am referring mostly to the territorial and demographic expansion and contraction of the nation-state through annexation or loss of territory (including India, Indonesia, Jordan, Israel, Saudi Arabia, North and South Yemen, Morocco, Pakistan, Ethiopia) or the incorporation and/or denationalization of sectors of the population. However, this moment also includes the expansion of the rights accorded to citizen-nationals to groups that have hitherto been denied such rights (women, certain ethnic groups and classes). As a result, this moment might in reality be a series of historical moments during which these expansions and contractions took place.

The fourth moment is the moment of internal implosion, generally characterized by civil war or revolution calling for an identitarian redefinition of the nation-state itself or for secession from it (a moment experienced by a large number of postcolonial nation-states but not necessarily all).

Although the first moment is also the first chronologically, the next three do not necessarily follow a chronological order. Expansion and/or contraction of a country can take place before or after independence from colonialism. Civil wars and revolutions can also take place under colonial or postcolonial rule. Therefore, with the exception of the colonial moment, the remaining three moments follow no systematic chronology, but all remain central definitional moments of national identity. In the course of this study, I identify the transformation in law, the military, political rights, and cultural discourse in the context of these historical moments.

The self that constitutes national identity and the other to which it is opposed also change depending on the historical moment. Whereas the period between the colonial and anticolonial moments is generally characterized by the constitution of a national self that is opposed to the colonials, this schema changes, especially after the end of colonialism. Whereas colonial *divide et impera* policies can and do bear fruit during the colonial period and continuing after it (India is a case in point), most of them are articulated in the postcolonial period where the constitution of a national-self that is no longer besieged by an *external* colonial other now organizes itself against an *internal* other (ethnic groups, groups from different geographic regions in the country, religious groups, racial groups, language groups, political groups). Examples include Cambodia, Sri Lanka, Rwanda, Burundi, Sudan, Ethiopia, Nigeria, Indonesia, Iraq, Jordan, Pakistan, India, Lebanon, and so forth.

Jordan's Historical Moments

A cursory perusal of recent books written about Jordan reveals titles such as *The Jordanian Character*,[30] The Political History of East of the Jordan in the Mamluk Period,[31] and *Jordan in History: From the Stone Age until the Establishment of the Emirate*.[32] The intent of this book is to narrate the story through which Jordan came to *acquire* a history in the Stone Age or in the Mamluk period and how Jordanians came to have a specific national "character."

Before 1921, there was no territory, people, or nationalist movement that was designated, or that designated itself, as Transjordanian. Transjordan as a nation-state was established in the wake of World War I, in 1921, by the British and the recently arrived Hijazi Amir 'Abdullah. This was Transjordan's colonial moment, its very inaugural moment. The British replaced the few existing state structures left by the Ottomans, and the small, short-lived regional governments that regionalists had established in 1920 to 1921 during the interregnum period following the end of Ottoman rule and the beginning of British rule. The first decade of rule was characterized by the British and the Amir's attempts to set up a governmental structure, an army, a police force, and a bureaucracy followed by the establishment of laws that began to be decreed in 1927. Transjordan's first constitution was set up in 1928, as the "Organic Law," concomitant with many other laws governing every aspect of life in the new state. Also, Transjordan expanded demographically and geographically through the annexation of an area extending in the south from Ma'an to 'Aqaba, which had been part of the Hijaz before. Several changes of the bureaucratic guard and of the institutional framework of the army and the police took place during the first decade. Moreover, several popular uprisings against encroaching state institutions and against the age of the nation-state were staged. Some of them targeted the bureaucracy and political apparatus, which was wholly staffed by people from outside the newly designated borders of the country. They were all defeated by the might of British military force and/or the will and diplomacy of the Hijazi Amir. It is the institutional establishment of the state, especially its juridical and military organs, that, as we will see, was detrimental to the production and repression of identities and cultural practices within the newly demarcated borders. During this period, a Jordanian nativist self developed that was opposed to an assortment of non-native others (the British, the Amir, and the Hijazi, Syrian, Palestinian, and Iraqi bureaucrats and politicians).

Consolidation of state power proceeded apace in the 1930s through coercion and co-optation of local elites, whose resistance to the non-representative state in the late 1920s and through the mid 1930s was crushed or neutralized by different means and through the recruitment and subjugation of the hitherto recalcitrant Bedouin population, constituting almost half the nascent country's population. Anticolonial uprisings took place in the second half of the 1930s in solidarity with the neighboring Palestinians who were revolting against the British and the Zionist project. These were also crushed. The 1940s saw major changes in the country. The war years were profitable to Transjordan's merchant class, a majority of whom had Syrian and Palestinian origins. Transjordan's mostly Bedouin army, the Arab Legion, acquired an international role through intervening in Iraq and Syria on behalf of the British government, and a domestic one of disciplining the Bedouin population itself through its integration into state structures. Transjordan itself was transformed from a mere mandated emirate into an independent kingdom in 1946 with its ruling amir declaring himself king. Independence, however, was nominal, as the country's army continued to be led by a British officer and the country continued to depend on massive British subsidies. The very name of the country, Transjordan, which had been invented by British parliamentarians after World War I, was changed to the Hashemite Kingdom of Jordan. This was not accompanied by anticolonial revolts on the part of the populace but was rather the result of international changes following World War II and local diplomatic pressure by the amir and his politicians. The newly independent country experienced even more radical transformations before the decade was over. It had expanded to include central Palestine, the largest chunk of Palestinian land that the Zionists did not conquer, and a large Palestinian population consisting of the natives of central Palestine (which was renamed the West Bank), and the refugees expelled from the part of Palestine that became Israel, more than tripling the population. This was the second time that Jordan had expanded geographically and demographically. The 1925 and 1948 to 1950 expansions constitute an important moment in the country's history as the country's physical boundaries and demographic constitution were transformed in ways detrimental to its national identity and culture.

The 1950s saw more radical transformations. ʿAbdullah was assassinated in 1951. His son Talal assumed the throne for a brief period, followed by regents who ruled the country until Talal's son, Husayn, came of age in 1953, at which point he was enthroned. The state had begun to Jordanize the Palestinian population and territory through co-optation and manipulation and at times coercion. An anticolonial current overtook the country in the mid 1950s, demanding complete independence from the British as well as democratic reforms. Influenced by the anticolonial rage in the Third World more generally and the recent anticolonial triumphs in neighboring Arab countries, the movement acquired immense momentum, so much so that for a time the young King Husayn was swept by its zeal. Jordan's anticolonial moment was ushered in then and culminated in the expulsion of General John Bagot Glubb, the British head of the army, in March 1956. The anticolonial momentum did not subside following Glubb's departure and the "Arabization" of the army. Democratic reforms as well as Jordan's realignment in international politics were the big items on the agenda of the anticolonial nationalist movement. The king and his coterie of family and friends worried that the tide might sweep the monarchy away. With the help of the British and the Americans, a palace coup took place in 1957, putting an end to the liberal experiment and releasing a tide of political re-pression under which the country lived for the next three decades, if not to the present. Jordan's anticolonial moment also had many implications for its national identity and national culture. It is during this historical moment that the Jordanian self was radically opposed to the colonial British other.

The 1960s brought even more changes and transformations to the coun-try. While Palestinian-Jordanians were now represented in government and among the country's economic elite, the Palestinian poor living in refugee camps were continuing to agitate to end their exile. The 1967 War with Israel cost Jordan the West Bank, forcing its *de facto* demographic and geo-graphic contraction. The rise of the Palestine Liberation Organization (PLO) in 1964 and that of the Palestinian guerrilla movements after the 1967 War challenged the Jordanian government's claim that the West Bank and the Palestinian population it acquired are now Jordanians for whom it alone can speak. Moreover, the guerrillas began to encroach on the country's very sovereignty. The situation exploded into a civil war between the Jor-danian army, which includes Palestinians, and the Palestinian guerrillas, which include Jordanians. This is the country's moment of implosion, which proved crucial for national redefinition. Much of the country's elite, includ-ing the Palestinian-Jordanian elite, backed the regime. The guerrillas were defeated and a major campaign of Jordanization, which had already been in existence before the Civil War, went into full swing after it. The other of the Jordanian was no longer the external British colonialist but an internal other, namely, Palestinian Jordanians. The merchant class, which had few Transjordanians, lost much of its political power to the strong bureaucracy, the mainstay of Transjordanians of settled origins. The army, in Transjordan-ian hands since Arabization, continued to be the major force at the disposal of the regime. Discriminatory policies against Palestinian-Jordanians (con-stituting more than half the population) became increasingly institutional-ized: there was less government representation, less employment in the public sector, fewer academic opportunities, and less access to public funds. The private sector, the mainstay of Palestinian power, continued to favor Palestinians in its employment practices.

The country, however, saw a constitutional expansion of rights through the normalization of citizens. Women were granted the vote in 1974, and the Bedouin population, living under Bedouin customary laws and quasi military/police rule since 1929, were normalized by the cancellation of these laws in 1976, finally equating the Bedouins and women with male urbanites juridically, as far as political and civil rights were concerned. The country was stabilized and its economy began to improve as a result of increasing remittances from its labor migrants in the Gulf states, from foreign aid from Arab Gulf states and the United States, and from land speculation, which skyrocketed by the end of the decade.

The 1980s brought yet more transformations. Jordan's economy began to teeter on the edge of collapse by mid decade. The Palestinian Uprising in Jordan's West Bank was not only questioning the Israeli occupation but also the very Jordanianness of the West Bank, whose Palestinianness was being asserted more strongly than ever. With the PLO increasingly recognized as the only political representative of the revolting Palestinians, Jordan's king "disengaged" from the West Bank, effectively giving up the territory *de jure*. Its Jordanian population was soon denationalized with the same peremptory power that 'Abdullah had nationalized them almost four decades earlier. The country's expanding moment had come full circle through this con-traction. Moreover, the governing arrangement itself was to be transformed with the inauguration of a liberalized period in 1989, leading to parliamen-tary elections and the expansion of liberties that were still as restricted as they had been since the Palace coup of 1957.

The 1990s ushered in a new liberal age that opened up pent-up frustra-tion on the identity issue. Transjordanian exclusivists began agitating for a more Transjordanian-only Jordan, bringing to the political battlefield anti-Palestinian frustrations that had been growing and made more legitimate by the regime since the Civil War. Some of these essentialist claims are also questioning the Jordanianness of the royal family itself.

This study intends to describe and analyze the processes through which peoples and territories that were constituted as a nation in 1921 came to accept this designation and within a few decades began to agitate for political rights based on it. How did the peoples and the territories that the British and the Hijazi amir captured in 1921 become Jordanian is the main question that this book seeks to answer

This book, however, is not *only* about how Jordanian national identity and culture are historically contingent, resulting from colonial and postcolonial state institutions that actively produce and repress identifications and practices, it is *also* about how national identity and culture in general are produced. The Jordanian case is especially illustrative of these processes because of its more recent constitution as a nation-state and the clear markings stamped on it by its architects, markings that are less visible in other postcolonial settings. Although Jordan is not unique in the postcolonial world, it is one of the less common cases: "Outsiders" conceived of its borders and identity; they led its national army well after independence; people whose roots within existing memory lie outside the new borders of the country, ruled and continue to rule it; its population consists in its majority of people whose geographic "origins" within living memory are located outside the borders of the nation-state (this does not refer only to Palestinian Jordanians, but also to Syrian-Jordanians, Hijazi-Jordanians, Egyptian-Jordanians, Iraqi-Jordanians, Lebanese-Jordanians, Turkish-Jordanians, Circassian-Jordanians, Kurdish-Jordanians, Chechen-Jordanians, and Armenian-Jordanians); the country has a large dependence on foreign money to support its resource-poor economy; and claims are put forth by neighboring powerful states on its very identity (Israel, Saudi Arabia, and Nasirist Egypt, to list the more prominent ones historically), or on parts of it (the West Bank and Palestinian Jordanians) by a strong nationalist movement (namely, the PLO). It is in the context of this wide array of factors that Jordanian nationalist discourse has a more difficult time stabilizing the terms and essences it posits than the nationalist discourses of other postcolonial nation-states. Whereas Jordanian national identity is no more "imagined" or "invented" than other national identities, its more recent exclusivist defenders have a harder battle to wage than their counterparts elsewhere in the world. It is this characteristic of the Jordanian case that makes it more clearly illustrative of nationalization processes that are better dissimulated elsewhere, and thus it allows the exposure of such dissimulation.

This study is not intended to tell the whole story of how national identity is produced, nor does it imply that law and the military are the only factors relevant to the production of national identity and national culture. Due to the absence of any examination of these institutions in recent studies of nationalism, the contribution this study makes to the debate lies in its demonstration that law and the military are *central* to the production of the nation and are generative of other discourses that infiltrate other state agencies and society at large in their defining of national culture.

The first two chapters examine the juridical production of national identity and national culture. I look at laws of nationality, election laws, and civil laws, as well as at the organization of law itself into three separate realms:

European codes, religious codes, and Bedouin customary law. The third and fourth chapters examine the military's production of national identity and national culture. I examine the role of the British in organizing a population that resisted the order of the nation-state, and their transformation, through repressive and productive techniques, not only into obedient citizen-nationals but also into defenders of the new order. I also examine the impact colonial legacy had (and has) on anticolonial nationalists. Chapter 4 also presents a lengthy but needed diplomatic history of politics within the military and of politics between the military and the regime. A fifth chapter discusses the juridical, military, and political aspects of the relationship between Palestinian Jordanians and Transjordanians, and its productive and repressive impact on Jordanian national identity and national culture. This is important as it reveals how disciplinary strategies used by the colonial and postcolonial state organize national identity by identifying its self and its other. This chapter will also include diplomatic history, especially as relates to the PLO and its relationship to the Jordanian State and regime. I will end by examining the current nationalist discourse in Jordan and its increasingly exclusivist and essentialist claims. Throughout the five chapters, the discussion will center not only on the law and the military but also on the important discourses on national identity that both institutions generate outside their institutional rubric and that spill over into other state agencies and society at large. These discussions (e.g., music, food, sports, tourism, archeology) are not extraneous to our examination of law and the military; rather, they are the effects of the different processes generated by the law and the military, albeit processes that exceed their institutional boundaries.

Throughout the book, you will notice that I identify the geographic origins and the religious and ethnic backgrounds of people. This is done deliberately. As contemporary Jordanian nationalism adheres to a set of essentialist markers that are geographically, ethnically, and at times religiously constant, and that it claims "constitute" Jordanian identity, my identification of people's backgrounds is intended to interrogate that claim. The elements that constitute today's Jordanian national identity and Jordanian national culture and the backgrounds of individuals who uphold the essentialist character of Jordanian identity are much more varied geographically, ethnically, and religiously than the guardians of contemporary Jordanian nationalism would like to believe. Drawing attention to people's varied "origins" then is itself an argument against an essentialist notion of national identity.

When applied to different national contexts, this mode of inquiry will not result in the same outcome that it does in the specific case of Jordan. As each national context is particular, the mode of inquiry I am proposing will elicit different results in each case. Its strength then is in asking a new set of questions that prevailing methods have not asked and in explaining specific outcomes that as of yet have not been explained adequately. This is not to say that the case of Jordan (and indeed of every country) is so specific that we cannot use it to illustrate other cases. It is simply asserting that this mode of inquiry does not seek to "normalize" all nation-states under the banner of one model. It does, however, aim to pose important questions of how nation-states *in general* impose their modality where one had not existed before. Jordan's case is in fact generalizable insofar as the colonial institutional and philosophical legacy that Jordan inherited from British colonialism is one that is shared by many nations in Asia and Africa. What is specific is the outcome these institutions produced (or produce) in each national context. What follows then is not a study of nationalist movements or necessarily of nationalist thought in the colonial world. It is a study of how the state, colonial and postcolonial, participates in the *identification* of the nation, and the role it plays in the production of national identity and culture, which nationalist thought adopts as objective essences.

1 Codifying the Nation

Law and the Articulation of National Identity in Jordan

It has become commonplace to theorize nationalist discourses of the colonial and anticolonial varieties as aiming to produce national identities as essences that transcend time and space that are internalized by national subjects.[1] This view, however, does not consider how these identities are codified in the laws of nation-states and is generally oblivious to the importance of the juridical in its constituting of nationalism. This chapter will explore the juridical dimension of national identities. Arguing that nationalist discourse and juridical discourse subsume each other while simultaneously maintaining a certain separateness, this chapter will attempt to demonstrate how the law produces juridical national subjects. Unlike nationalist discourses that posit national identities as anterior to them, as immutable essences of which nationalist discourse is a mere effect, the juridical discourse of the nation-state will be shown to enact nonessentialist national identities that are deployed, changed, and rescinded by the law. Whereas juridical discourse claims the status of the juridical subject as prediscursive, and in that it is similar to nationalist discourse, unlike the latter it posits national identity as an effect of the law, not its precedent. All postcolonial national identities are anchored in the laws of nation-states. This chapter will demonstrate, however, that while the juridical secures the precepts of nationalism by *interpellating* subjects as nationals, it simultaneously reveals nationality as a fiction to be molded and remolded by the law.[2] Moreover, this chapter will argue that the juridical is not a mere repressive manifestation of the political, but that it also plays a central *productive*, albeit regulatory, role: it produces and regulates identity.

The importance of laying down the law and applying it through enforcement is key to understanding how modern states operate internally vis-à-vis their subagencies, the bureaucracy, the military, and political institutions (the executive, the legislative, and the judicial), and externally vis-à-vis the territory over which the state reigns and the people this territory encompasses. As Louis Althusser has pointed out, however, the law is part of both the "repressive state apparatus" and the "ideological state apparatus"; it plays a unique double role.[3] Althusser's distinction is a variation roughly corresponding to what Antonio Gramsci calls "civil society" and "political society." Gramsci's civil society is where popular consent is produced noncoercively through what he termed *hegemony*.[4] What is important in discussing the state in its national guise (i.e., the nation-state itself) is how the institution of law, as a repressive and ideological apparatus (or, as Gramsci would have it, one that produces conformity through hegemonic and coercive means), is needed to guarantee control over time and temporality more generally—not only time as present and future but, just as importantly, time as past—over space and spatiality more generally—not only of identifying territory as national or foreign but also rendering it juridically governable—and over people as normalized juridico-national subjects. In this vein, Jacques Derrida states that the "the founding and justifying moment that institutes law implies a performative force . . . not in the sense of law in the service of force, its docile instrument, servile and thus exterior to the dominant power but rather in the sense of law that would maintain a more internal, more complex relation with what one calls force, power or violence."[5] The law's ability to structure the time and space of the nation-state, and to delimit the nature of the bodies of nationals, is therefore of utmost importance when discussing how nationalist discourses formulate national identities and how these identities are codified into law, whereby, following Derrida, *the juridical is always internal to the national project* and not an external manifestation servile to it. The very act of codification by the nation-state is part of the foundational moment of nationalization. Codification then is the productive act of identifying subjects as national.

Through juridical fiat, the law of nation-states defines and limits the time of the nation, its space, and its subjects. However, not only is the law interested in the identification of time as national time, space as national space, and the interpellation of subjects as nationals, but just as central to the definitional coherence of these categories (as we will see when we examine Jordanian laws of nationality later) is the law's ability to identify time as non-national (as foreign, as colonial, and as postcolonial), space as non-national (as colonized, as occupied), and to interpellate and thus identify subjects as non-nationals (as foreigners). Sharing Derrida's understanding that "[n]either identity nor non-identity is natural, but rather the effect of a juridical performative"[6] is imperative in this context. Law, then, in a nation-state enacts the foundational differentiation of all the categories that it interpellates as binaries. It enacts *not* identity but difference *tout court*. However, the two components of this binary hold asymmetrical valences manifested in the law's enumeration of rights and duties corresponding to them. To accommodate this asymmetry, which the law itself enacts, the two juridical subjects—the national and the foreigner—are inscribed through different categories of law. Juridical power in its ideological role, then, as Foucault has taught us, does not only repress and punish, it also *produces* the juridical subjects over whom its power is distributed. As a productive power, the law's ideological instrumentality is the object of interest not only of state architects but just as importantly of the architects of nationality.

In the case of Transjordan, the first manifestation of a nationalist discourse propelled by the state was evidenced in the transformation of the state into one that rules juridically. This was accomplished through the enactment of a series of laws in the 1927 to 1928 period culminating in Transjordan's Organic Law (al-Qanun al-Asasi, or the Basic/Foundational Law)[7] in 1928. In the extra-juridical societal realm, this was preceded by several Transjordanian uprisings in the early 1920s asserting nativism against the non-native Mandatory-Hashemite state. Moreover, the time of the enactment of these laws by the Mandatory-Hashemite state coincided with a highly mobilized anticolonial nationalist movement whose identity was still in flux, but whose other (i.e., British colonialism) was clear. It was not until decades later, however, that a full-fledged Jordanian nationalism articulated itself (although the 1920s uprisings were renarrated by some Jordanian nationalists as nationalist moments) dialogically and in conjunction with the juridical discourse of nationality.

Crucial to this inquiry about the role of law in nation-building is the question of national identity and of nationalist agency, as they are differently constituted within nationalist discourse and in the laws of nation-states. Although the specifics of national identity and nationalist agency may differ according to the discourse within which they are formulated, they are constituted through similar operations. Whereas national identity is constituted through interpellation by nationalist discourse and the definitional fiat of nationality law, nationalist agency is produced through a combination of interpellation and performativity. By national identity, I mean the set of characteristics and markers (territorial origins, patrilineal or matrilineal ancestral origins, religion, race, gender, class, language) that nationalist thought sets as the prerequisites to having a certain national identity as that identity is defined by nationalist thought itself. Nationalist agency refers to the abilities and the will to perform a set of acts and practices aimed at achieving nationalist goals, as those (the abilities, the acts, the practices, and the goals) are defined by nationalist discourse and the laws of the nation-state. A national is someone who is identified by nationalist discourse, and its corollary, nationality law, as a "national" in a monological operation of interpellation. In this operation of interpellation, the national is the object of nationalist discourse and the subject of the law. The nationalist agent, however, is someone who identifies as, and who is identified by nationalist discourse as, part of the nation, and one whom nationalist discourse considers to be a possessor of the aforementioned abilities and will based on criteria set by nationalist discourse. Thus the agent functions as both object (interpellated) and subject (performer). Laws of the nation-state base themselves on this dialogical discursive identification to interpellate nationalist agents as performers. In this vein, Homi Bhabha[8] states,

> [The] people are not simply historical events or parts of a body politic. They are also a complex rhetorical strategy of social reference where the claim to be representative provokes a crisis within the process of signification and discursive address. We then have a contested cultural territory where the people must be thought in a double-time; the people are the historical "objects" of a nationalist pedagogy, giving the discourse an authority that is based on the pre-given or constituted historical origin or event; the people are also the "subjects" of a process of signification that must erase any prior or originary presence of the nation-people to demonstrate the prodigious, living principle of the people as that continual process by which the national life is redeemed and signified as a repeating and reproductive process.

The foundation of Transjordan as a state in 1921, although a hesitant act by its architects, the British and the Hashemites, was to be made permanent through the enactment of a series of laws culminating in the Organic Law of 1928 authorizing the new state in its territorial and temporal claims and in its control of the bodies over which it rules. This chapter will concern itself only with the Nationality Law,[9] which was enacted alongside the Organic Law in 1928, and its juridical journey of amendments, nullifications, and reenactments through the present. Nationality Law is important not only for its foundational regulation of who is a national and who is not, but also for its ever-continuing role in reorganizing the nation's temporal, spatial, and corporeal borders. Nationality Law is conscious of its very productivity of "the people." "But this people does not exist . . . *before* this declaration, not *as such*."[10] Still, the very act of interpellation is a reproductive performance, of giving birth to the people *as* nation. Who is interpellated as a Jordanian, however, undergoes many variations in the journey of this law for the next eight decades. The occurrence of such variations is commensurate with the redefinition of Jordan spatially and of Jordanianness temporally. In this context, the role of law is not necessarily one that deals with questions of justice, but rather with the self-referential questions of legality, of juridicality. As Derrida asserts, "in the founding of law or in its institution, the . . . problem of justice will have been posed and violently resolved, that is to say buried, dissimulated, repressed. Here the best paradigm is the founding of the nation-states or the institutive act of a constitution that establishes what one calls in French *l'état de droit*."[11]

The Prehistory of Juridical Postcoloniality

As anticolonial nationalism is derived from the European Enlightenment and post-Enlightenment Romantic thought, so are the laws demarcating nationhood in the now independent former colonies derived from the laws of European nations. Jordanian Nationality Law is hardly an exception in this regard. Jordan's Ottoman and British colonial legacy, as will be demonstrated later, defined not only its legal system but also the juridical epistemology governing Jordanian nationality from the outset and through the present.

Whereas most legal experts and political historians trace Jordanian nationality laws to the Ottoman period and to the Treaty of Lausanne severing the country from its erstwhile sovereign, they have not, surprisingly, connected Jordanian nationality laws from the 1920s to the present with the laws of the British Empire; this is especially surprising as the articles on nationality in the Treaty of Lausanne itself are highly influenced by British nationality laws.[12] The inhabitants of what became Transjordan were indeed governed before 1924, the effective application date of the Treaty of Lausanne (concluded in 1923 between the Ottomans and the Allies), by the Ottoman Nationality Law of 1869,[13] itself the culmination of the 1839 *Gül-*

hane decree and the 1856 *Hatt-i Humayun* decree, which were attempts to Westernize Ottoman law as part of the Tanzimat Reform. Ottoman laws enacted during the Tanzimat period were influenced by and borrowed from the French and the Italian codes and judicial practice.[14] The Treaty of Lausanne stipulated in its article 30 that "Turkish subjects habitually resident in territory which in accordance with the provisions of the present Treaty is detached from Turkey will become *ipso facto*, in the conditions laid down by the local law, nationals of the State to which such territory is transferred."[15] It should be emphasized that the Treaty of Lausanne gave the choice to those (over eighteen years of age) who desired to remain Turkish citizens to do so, to those who chose another nationality to have the right to reapply for the Turkish nationality within two years of the effective date of the Treaty, and to those who belong to a different "race" from the majority of the population of the territory of which they are resident to apply for the nationality of the country whose majority is of their same "race" in accordance with the laws of that country.[16]

As for the British Nationality Law (much of which was lifted verbatim into the Nationality Law of Transjordan) in existence at the time of the establishment of the British Mandate over and the creation of Transjordan, its modern form, which emerged in 1844 and was elaborated on in 1870,[17] took shape in the British Nationality and Status of Aliens Act of 1914[18] and its amendments of 1918.[19] As the forthcoming comparisons will show, almost everything that came to constitute juridical Jordanian national subjectivity was lifted verbatim from these British laws. This palimpsestic operation has been the most successful in concealing itself and in not being revealed by Jordanian nationalists to this very day. Whereas the influence of Islamic Ottoman judicial practice and of the Westernized Ottoman Tanzimat is readily accepted, insofar as the Ottomans are not conventionally considered culturally "other," the "original sin" of British colonial contamination of what Jordanian juridical nationality constitutes, is conveniently erased out of the genealogy of juridical and nationalist memory.

It is interesting to note here that British colonial officials were not even certain that a separate Transjordanian nationality should be created at all. In 1922, a correspondence between several British colonial officials discussed the options of granting the people of "Trans Jordania" a separate nationality or simply, as Winston Churchill insisted, to consider them as "Transjordanian Palestinians." The matter was ultimately settled in favor of the "separate Transjordan Nationality."[20] The very name of the territory had in fact already been debated a year earlier during British parliamentary debates in April 1921. Mr. David Ormsby-Gore, a former assistant secretary of the Middle Eastern Committee, suggested that the very name of the country be made "Belka." It was explained to him that Belka "was the name of one district only. The whole territory was at present known officially as Trans Jordania." [21] Even the Amir ʿAbdullah was not sure which name the territory should have—a national one, *Sharq al-Urdunn* or East of the Jordan, or a more inclusive Arab nationalist one. Upon setting up his government in 1921, he named it the Government of *Mintaqat Al-Sharq Al-ʿArabi*, or the Government of the Territory of the Arab East, a name that was used alongside *Sharq al-Urdunn* until the late 1920s.

The Nationality Law of 1928 was not the first attempt to define Jordanians juridically. The first attempt to do so had taken place a year earlier through the enactment of the Law of Foreigners (or Aliens).[22] Following the 1914 British Nationality Law, the 1927 law defines Jordanians in similar terms to the 1928 law and defines a foreigner as "everyone who is not Jordanian." However, there are a number of exclusions from the category of "foreigner" that the law insists upon, namely, those in the service of the Transjordanian Mandatory government, any individual in the service of His Majesty's (Britain's king) naval, land, or air forces, or anyone in the employ of British political, colonial, or consular agencies, and other nonhonorary consular employees. Whereas the Law of Foreigners will not apply to those excluded, it is unclear if laws dealing with nationals do, or indeed if those excluded can be juridical subjects of the Transjordanian state at all! In fact, the British government was so concerned with this matter that it included a provision for it in the 1928 Agreement between the British government and the amir. In article 9 of the agreement, it is asserted that "no foreigner shall be brought before a Transjordanian Court without the concurrence of His Britannic Majesty." This article further stipulates that the amir undertake to "accept and give effect to such reasonable provisions as His Britannic Majesty may consider necessary in judicial matters to safeguard the interests of foreigners."[23] Moreover, under the terms of the agreement, foreigners could not be "brought to trial before Transjordan courts without the consent of the British Resident."[24] This differs substantially from the 1914 British Nationality Law, which stipulates in its article 18 that an "alien shall be triable in the same manner as if he were a natural-born British subject."

The essentialist/anti-essentialist feature of nationality law is the very core of the law. The law's Orwellian instrumentality in rewriting and renarrating the nation will be shown to be crucial for the law's ability to *present* (in both temporal and spatial senses) the nation, in every act of rewriting and renarrating, as a seamless continuity with no ruptures. This is done "not by suppressing all differences, but by revitalizing them to itself in such a way that it is the symbolic difference between 'ourselves' and 'foreigners' which wins out and which is lived as irreducible."[25] This presentation is the effect of the symbiotic relationship that juridical nationalist discourse and popular nationalist discourse cohabit. Any questioning, however, of the ruptures prevalent in the law itself as regards the question of nationality, is coded in popular nationalist discourse as a subversive attempt to rupture the nation itself, indeed as national treason.

National Time

Nationalism's obsession with temporality (confused as historicity) is related more to establishing a collective memory for itself and its subjects than to inscribing itself in history (which is of secondary import). The importance of this collective memory is crucial to the project of interpellating people as identical. To conjure up identity among people is to suppose it not to be self-evident; it is to counter an apparent *difference*, which nationalism does by "revealing" identity as the organizing principle of "the people" who until recently had thought of themselves unconnected, non-identical—in short, different.

National time is a double time. This double time, however, is a synchronous one. The nation's commitment to the preservation of a traditional national culture carried through from the past and its project of technological modernization as the present goal to be achieved in the future place the nation on a synchronic temporal continuum, whereby the nation simultaneously lives its traditional past, its present emergence, and its future modernity as one unmediated moment. It is the nation's subjects who are interpellated differentially to signify these different temporalities of the nation—tradition and modernity.[26] In an anticolonial setting, national time then involves deploying a counter-memory, one that challenges not only the apparent difference it acknowledges but as importantly the active colonial denial of its subjective identity.

The attempt of nationalist movements to "retrieve" the memory of the "nation" was analogized by Freud to a person's childhood memories. "This is often the way in which childhood memories originate. Quite unlike conscious memories from the time of maturity, they are not fixed at the moment of being experienced and afterwards repeated, but are only elicited at a later age when childhood is already past; in the process they are altered and falsified, and are put in the service of later trends, so that generally speaking they cannot be sharply distinguished from phantasies." Freud[27] proceeds to explain how nations come to write their histories:

> Historical writing, which had begun to keep a continuous record of the present, now also cast a glance back to the past, gathered traditions and legends, interpreted the traces of antiquity that survived in customs and usages, and in this way created a history of the past. It was inevitable that this early history should have been an expression of present beliefs and wishes rather than a true picture of the past; for many things had been dropped from the nation's memory, while others were distorted, and some remains of the past were given the wrong interpretation in order to fit in with contemporary ideas. Moreover people's motive in writing history was not objective curiosity but a desire to influence their contemporaries, to encourage and inspire them, *or to hold a mirror up before them* [emphasis added].

This is exactly how historical memory as mirror *identifies* the nation's subject by unifying its fragmented self. It is through this national identificatory mirror that the "national" is imaged/imagined as a category that assimilates all different experiences into it as one and the same. Memory/counter-memory is a crucial instrument for nationalism. Identifying time as national or foreign is then imbricated in the core project of identifying nationals and foreigners.

Before 1921, the area that became Transjordan was under several Ottoman regional jurisdictions, including areas in southern Syria, Palestine, and the northern Hijaz (all of which, like Transjordan, were divided into *wilayas* and other subdivisions). Much of Jordan's official history[28] examines the pre-state period retrospectively, as if the creation of the Jordanian state had been inevitable. Jordan's pre-state population is described as highly "divided," "lawless," having no "central" authority, and plagued by internecine rivalries, a condition which could be remedied, the historians suggest, only by the arrival of the Hashemite Amir 'Abdullah, who "unified" the "country" both demographically and territorially. The British, on the other hand, describe the territory and people of what became Transjordan as ungovernable. Due to the inability and disinterest of the Ottoman state to administer (what became) Transjordan effectively, the "population," the British concluded, was unaccustomed to obedience to central authority. Setting up a governmentalized state should render the "population" governable and ensure the attainment of specific colonial political and economic goals. By governmentality, I take Foucault's definition as operative: "the ensemble formed by the institutions, procedures, analyses and reflections, the calculations and tactics that allow the exercise of this very specific albeit complex form of power, which has as its target population, as its principal form of knowledge political economy, and its essential technical means apparatuses of security."[29]

In the waning days of the Ottoman Empire, the contest for control of the region heated. Upon Ottoman withdrawal, the area that became Transjordan was the staging area for the takeover of Syria in 1918 by 'Abdullah's brother, Faysal. In accordance with the British and French Sykes-Picot agreement of 1916, the French soon evicted Faysal from Syria. His Arab nationalist supporters retreated to the area that later became Transjordan. The end of Ottoman rule had left that area with no imperial authority able to subdue the Arab nationalists or control the trade routes. The British, therefore, elected to install Faysal's brother, 'Abdullah, as ruler of a new entity, Transjordan, hoping to appease the Arab nationalists after Faysal's loss of Syria, and to prevent opposition that might have arisen to direct colonial rule. Although 'Abdullah made alliances both with and against various tribes and families among the population, he and the British realized (for varying reasons, not all of them shared by the two parties) the need to "unify" the region and provide it with a new political identity as a separate state. The British were at the time much concerned with ensuring the safety of the Zionist project in Palestine, and they saw the existence of a vassal regime in Transjordan (legitimating itself under the banner of Arab nationalism) as ensuring that no opposition would arise there to that project. Although much has been written about the Zionist–Hashemite relations and the *state*-building efforts of the Hashemites, little is available about the *national* project that was put in motion upon the creation of the Transjordanian state.[30]

For the British and the Hashemites, the (initially ambivalent) creation of the Transjordanian state, however, involved the simultaneous creation of a nation to constitute this state. Unlike most other nation-states whose formation is preceded by a nationalist movement or a sense of national identity, Transjordan experienced no such transformations. In fact, there was no country, territory, people, or nationalist movement called Transjordan or Transjordanians prior to the establishment of the nation-state. The Transjordanian state, as a result, (albeit ambivalently at first) embarked on a number of policies, some of which intentionally aimed at fostering a sense of nationhood, while others unintentionally elicited an unwelcome nationalist reaction by the subject population. For example, on the one hand, the very presence of the British and Hashemites as rulers aided by a bureaucracy and a military staffed by people from outside the area of Transjordan (Palestinians, Syrians, Hijazis, Iraqis, and British) unwittingly produced a strong nativist reaction against the new rulers and their state structures at several moments in the first decade of the state; on the other hand, the deliberate act of creating Transjordan as a nation-state that was juridically defined, territorially and demographically, as having a national identity created the sense of unity of the people of what became Transjordan, albeit a fateful unity of being subjects of the new state and its laws.

The new Transjordanian state faced a number of revolts in the first decade after its establishment, the more important of them being the al-'Adwan rebellion in 1923. Shaykh Sultan al-'Adwan was not only a tribal chief but also the ruler of much of the Balqa' region in northern Transjordan, which included other tribes such as Bani Hasan, Bani Hamidah, the Da'jah, al-Balqawiyyah, and al-'Ajarmah. The arrival of 'Abdullah and the close alliance he built with the Bani Sakhr tribe, considered as al-'Adwan's traditional rivals, enraged Shaykh Sultan. Equally important, however, was al-'Adwan's anger over the staffing of the government bureaucracy with outsiders to the exclusion of educated locals. It should be noted that some of the locals had already occupied bureaucratic positions in the Ottoman administration. Whereas the presence of some of the *Istiqlali* nationalist leaders (members of the anti-Ottoman pan-Syrian nationalist *Istiqlal* party who had fled Syria after their defeat by the French) in the country was not opposed, the importation of mercenary employees from neighboring areas, whose sole purpose was financial gain, angered many in Transjordan. Al-'Adwan was not alone in his disenchantment. A number of educated men and intellectuals made common cause with him. Prominent among those was Jordan's foremost poet, Mustafa Wahbah Al-Tall, who coined the slogan "Al-Urdunn Lil Urduniyyin," or "Jordan for the Jordanians," as an assertion of nativist rights against their usurpation by outsiders. The government at first responded by reconstituting the cabinet, and in the process they appointed the Transjordanian 'Ali al-Khulqi as minister of education, as a gesture to meet the demands of the rebels. The new cabinet put forth a ministerial plan that included the "preference for the appointment of qualified members of the area [Abna' al-Mintaqah], over others, to [government] positions."[31] This, however, did not placate al-'Adwan and his supporters among the local intelligentsia. The government, not wanting to appear weak, arrested prominent local intellectuals, including Al-Tall, and accused them of plotting to overthrow the government. British military force, including the air force, was used to quell the revolt, which was defeated soon after.[32] Sultan al-'Adwan and his supporters fled to Syria, and those caught were arrested.[33] The common fate experienced by the 'Adwanis and the intellectuals under the new state introduced a sense of native unity against outside usurpers and a unity of purpose aimed at giving native Transjordanians their legitimate rights of ruling themselves. In a few decades, this moment of nativism would be appropriated by Jordanian nationalists for a new type of exclusivist nationalism.

Whereas Transjordan was established as a political entity ushering in a new temporality (post-Ottoman, Arab, and independent), encompassing a specified geography (with shifting boundaries) and population (with shifting composition), the juridical establishment of Jordanian identity did not come about until the enactment of Nationality Law in 1928, in which those who became the Jordanian people were interpellated, transformed, and produced through juridical fiat. Nationality Law was enacted at the same time as Transjordan's Organic Law, which through border demarcations identified the territory over which the new state was distributed as "Transjordanian."[34] This new juridical discourse established the geographic specifications of the country and instituted a binary of nationals and foreigners through a retro-active application of the law to 1923. Therefore, according to this juridical discourse, although Jordanian nationality was produced through a new legal discourse instituted in 1928, juridical power can be enacted in such a way as to apply itself to past times, establishing jurisdiction over not only who is Jordanian in the present and who becomes so in the future, but as importantly who was considered Jordanian in the past. The period from 1923 to 1924 is important because it was then that the Treaty of Lausanne was signed (July 22, 1923) and made effective (August 30, 1924). In this treaty between Turkey and the allies, Turkey relinquished control over Transjordan, and the Ottoman Nationality Law (enacted in 1869) that had applied to that country was rendered no longer in effect. This period also coincided with the deportation of many Syrian Arab nationalists who were the regime's lieutenants for its first two years in power,[35] and it came after the postwar population movements and settlements had subsided.[36]

It is important to stress that the very interpellation of people as "Jordanian" or "foreign" is accomplished through the law's reflective functionality as mirror. If juridico-national subjects are to be subjected to the law that produces them, they must view their very production in the law as mirror re-

flections, as well as establish their very reproducibility through juridical duplication. In this process of duplication, in which a national recognizes all
other nationals as duplicates of the law's mirror reflection and on that basis
recognizes the foreignness of those who are juridically reflected as such,
misrecognition (*méconaissance*) becomes a logical impossibility. In this specular economy of identification, recognition is established as the basis of
identification of nationals and foreigners, as the very basis of juridical existence (and this is *the only* allowable existence) in the modality of the nation-
state.

The political context of these juridical initiatives was the agitation for
representativity by native Transjordanians, who had also called for a constitutional structure, and for an end to the British mandate, but not for an end
to the recently constituted nation-state. Whereas the first nationalist party
(albeit of the Qawmi variety) in the country was the pan-Syrian *Istiqlal* whose
members were purged and exiled from Transjordan by the British and the
amir in 1924, Hizb al-Sha'b (or the People's Party) was established in 1927
as the first *Transjordanian* party. Party founders were mostly Transjordanians, some of whom had been imprisoned by the government during the
al-'Adwan revolt. Their program included the assertion of the country's independence as well as equality among its people.[37] The party called on the
government to include it in talks with the British and to set up a representative and responsible parliament. Following the Transjordanian-British
agreement of February 1928 and the refusal of the government to reevaluate
its position despite massive demonstrations in April, May, and June 1928,
the party decided to convene a General National Congress (Mu'tamar Wa-
tani 'Am) to represent the country and speak for it. The congress convened
at the Hamdan Cafe, downtown Amman, in July 1928, and it was attended
by over 150 prominent personalities and Shaykhs in the country. The congress
issued the Jordanian National Charter (Al-Mithaq Al-Watani Al-Urduni) identifying Transjordan as "an independent sovereign Arab country" and demanding the establishment of a constitutional government. The charter
also rejected the principle of the British Mandate except if it meant "an
honest technical assistance in the interest of the country." In opposition to
legislation that would allow Zionists to purchase land in the country, the
charter also asserted that "any exceptional legislation that is not based on
the principle of justice and the general welfare and the real needs of the
people is hereby considered nullified." Thus, the congress confirmed the
juridical creation of the nation-state by the British and the Hashemites. It
questioned only the governing arrangement of the new nation-state and

not its modality. The charter was submitted to the amir, who in turn submitted it to the British. The British rejected all the demands and claimed
that the country's people "have not yet proved their competence in learning
how to administer [the country]." In the meantime, a number of laws were
enacted to limit political activity. The Crime Prevention Law was enacted
in September 1927 allowing the government to arrest anyone whom it considered a security threat, and the Law of Collective Punishment and the
Exile and Deportation Law were enacted in August and October 1928, respectively. These laws were used to harass and repress the nationalist opposition (and to expel members of the Bani 'Atiyyah tribe in 1932),[38] but they
were also used to *produce* a sense of national unity among the opposition as
subjects of the same laws of the same nation-state. The government moved
in to close down a number of newspapers (including *Al-Shari'ah, Sada Al-
'Arab, Al-Urdunn,* and Mustafa Wahbah Al-Tall's *Al-Anba'*). The opposition
persisted and sent more delegations to speak with the British High Commissioner. They objected to the election law and to the new dictatorial laws
that limited people's freedoms. When they did not receive any concessions,
the People's Party and their supporters boycotted the elections of 1929 and
convened the Second National Congress in March 1929. This time, they
forwarded their demands to the League of Nations instead of to the British.
Around the same time, fissures within the party were becoming obvious as
some of its members decided to run for the boycotted elections. This led to
the emergence of a new nationalist party in April 1929 calling itself the Party
of the Executive Committee of the National Congress (ECNC).

The new party was able to attract members of the People's Party as well
as members of the National Congress. The ECNC proved to be the most
nationalist in its demands. Its members, who included Transjordanians as
well as Syrians, Iraqis, and Palestinians, pledged that their task would be to
realize the demands put forth in the National Charter. The ECNC continued to exist until 1934. It published a newspaper (*Al-Mithaq*), which was
suppressed soon after, while its leaders, including Subhi Abu Ghanimah
and 'Adil Al-'Azmah, were in the forefront of opposing the Mandatory government and the amir on a number of issues including land sales to Zionists.
Under their tutelage, three more congresses were convened (in May 1929,
March 1932, and June 1933). The ECNC sought to change the system of
governance through peaceful and "legitimate" means. Its agitation among
the people of the country was opposed not only by the Mandatory authorities
and the amir, but also by large land-owners who were supporters of the amir
(but not necessarily the British). To oppose the nationalists, the land-owners

formed their own party, Al-Hizb Al-Hurr Al-Mu'tadil (or the Free and Moderate Party), in June 1930, which did not last long. Other land-owners, including Christians and Circassians as well as Bedouin tribal leaders, formed
their own party in March 1933, which they called the Party of Jordanian
Solidarity (Hizb al-Tadamun al-Urduni). This party called for the "defense
of the being of the children of Transjordan, the attainment of their rights
. . . and the dissemination of modern education."[39] Their exclusivist Jordanian nationalism was in stark contrast to the inclusivist Jordanian *Arab* nationalism of the ECNC. The Party of Jordanian Solidarity stipulated in article 36 of its Founding Charter that membership in the party is limited to
those who settled in Transjordan before 1922.[40] This party also did not last
long, as it represented only its members, with little if any popular following.
Its claims of who the real Jordanians are, however, were to be upheld by
Jordanian nationalists decades later. The fact that Transjordan existed only
for a few months before the 1922 date, and that it did not then include the
southern third of the country (which was annexed in 1925), did not figure
in the calculations of these exclusivist nationalists. For them, the juridical
procedures that were used to create Transjordan itself in 1921 and its expansion in 1925 were to be appropriated into their nationalist discourse,
erasing their juridical genealogy.

When these parties failed to defeat the ECNC (whose popularity
stemmed from its relationship to the first National Congress), many of their
members formed a rival party claiming the same descent as the ECNC (i.e.,
from the National Congress, which they renamed the General Jordanian
Congress). Their new rival party, which they set up in August 1933, was
called the Party of the Executive Committee of the General Jordanian People's Congress. They attempted to delegitimize the National Congress party
and the congresses it had held since the original break in 1929. The National
Congress Party continued its activities opposing the draconian measures
taken by the new prime minister Ibrahim Hashim (of Palestinian origin and
an ally of the amir) against the opposition. The leaders of the party were
soon scattered, some going into exile. Both parties ceased to exist by the end
of 1934.[41]

The importance of all these parties, be they anticolonial or not, is that
they accepted the modality of the nation-state as providing the spatial limits
of their political organization. Unlike the Istiqlalis, who were pan-Syrian
nationalists calling for the unification of all of Greater Syria, these parties
sought to fight the colonial presence or to uphold the existing colonial arrangement of Mandatory rule within the existing modality—that is, the

nation-state. These political developments demonstrate how the juridical and political establishment of the Transjordanian state in 1921 had already become internalized in society less than a decade after its initial inception.

National Space

The Organic Law acting as the country's first constitution identified territory as Jordanian. This was carried out through demarcation, whereby those areas included in the new nation-state were Jordanized and those that were not were interpellated as foreign. Territory acts as a malleable entity, expanding and contracting according to the law. Whereas (Trans)Jordan expanded in 1925 and 1948, it contracted in 1988 (there were also some minor border rectifications with Saudi Arabia in 1965[42]). These expansions and contractions were building on the core territory of 1923 identified as Jordanian in 1928, and can in no way constitute a threat to the nationalization project. This core has not been affected by subsequent contractions. It serves to secure the nation's territory as an essentially national space. In this new signifying economy, "the 'external frontiers' of the state have to become 'internal frontiers' or—which amounts to the same thing—external frontiers have to be imagined constantly as a projection and protection of an internal collective personality, which each of us carries within ourselves and enables us to inhabit the space of the state as a place where we have always been—and always will be—'at home'."[43]

The nation-state, however, was interested not only in nationalizing territory through demarcation of borders and the requisite cartographic representations of these demarcations, but also in reparceling the territory internally. This process of reparceling involved the introduction of a new taxonomy and a new conceptualization of land; it signaled an epistemological break with previous conceptions of space. This was produced through an extensive process of surveys, censuses, land registration, privatization, transfer of property, confiscation, and decommunalization, which were initiated in the late twenties and continued through the early fifties. This micro-arrangement of the national space, although colonially planned to alter class relations in the country, served to nationalize that space by subjecting it to a systematic administration by Mandatory state officials and by subjecting it to the laws of the new nation-state. The process of nationalizing the internal space of the nation-state, through the conversion of communal property into bourgeois forms of property,[44] was part of the same process of demarcating its borders in relation to foreign space while simultaneously subjecting that space to the law. John Bagot Glubb, the head of the Arab Legion (Jordan's army) from 1939 to 1956, observed that the "establishment of law and order resulted in the rich becoming richer and the poor growing poorer. . . . The establishment of public security deprived the farmer of the power to threaten the usurer with violence."[45] In short, nationalizing space and rendering it juridically governable was one and the same process.

According to Michael Fischbach, what the British-Hashemite land program (which was put into effect beginning in the late twenties) in Transjordan managed to do was to "enforce a British conceptualization of law and private property in the country and reduce or eradicate indigenous social aspects of land-owning, such as holding land in unpartitioned joint ownership."[46] This macro- and micro-management of land produced space as nationally cohesive while erasing previous ruptures. Equally important was the reorganization of social ties among the population of Jordan through this radical reorganization of space. The nation-state seeks to territorialize identity and is therefore hostile to kinship ties that cross the newly established national territory. As Frederick Engels explains, "The state distinguishes itself from the old gentile organization firstly by the division of its subjects on *a territorial basis*. The old gentile bodies, formed and held together by ties of blood, had, as we have seen, become inadequate largely because they presupposed that the gentile members were bound to one particular locality, whereas this had long ago ceased to be the case. The territory was still there, but the people had become mobile. The territorial division was therefore taken as a starting-point and the system introduced by which citizens exercised their public rights and duties where they took up residence, without regard to gens or tribe. This organization of the citizens of the state according to domicile is common to all states."[47]

In a country where the inhabitants had tribal and family links that crossed the invented national boundaries (to Palestine, Syria, Iraq, Egypt, Lebanon, the Hijaz, Armenia, and the Caucasus), the reorganization of identity had to be territorialized. It is through this new epistemology of space that the Transjordanian state sought to define Jordanian nationality juridically.[48] Blood ties had to be superseded by territorial contiguity and residency. Engels adds, "Only domicile was now decisive, not membership in a lineage group. Not the people, but the territory was now divided: the inhabitants became, politically, a mere appendage of the territory."[49] In the case of Transjordan, as in other nation-states, the new juridically defined national space becomes a seamless whole with no internal ruptures. The only ruptures that exist are the new ones created by the law, namely, those that secure the new juridical binary—that is, ruptures that inhabit the border securing the discreteness of national space and separating it from foreign encroachment.

This, however, needs to be contrasted with extra-juridical popular nationalism. As evidenced by the Party of Jordanian Solidarity in the early 1930s and its contemporary extensions, Jordanian exclusivist nationalists reject the criterion of residency as a basis to establish Jordanianness, substituting instead the notion of origin. Only those who can claim the national space as the originary space from which they hail can claim Jordanianness as an identity. It is unclear if certain historical moments preceding 1921 or 1922 act as thresholds for this definition. An added dimension is Jordan's inscription in a pan-Arab nationalism that renders it a part of a unified Arab nation, both demographically and geographically, although not juridically (the Arab League, as the major official arm of state-sponsored pan-Arab nationalism, has no juridical power over the internal affairs of member states).

National Territory and Paternity

The establishment of paternity as the source of nationhood has been enshrined in British nationality laws since the nineteenth century. In the exemplary case of Britain, as Francesca Klug demonstrates, "women were only allowed to reproduce the British nation on behalf of their husbands. They could not pass their nationality to their children in their own right."[50] In fact, British women who married outside the nation lost their British nationality, as did their children. On the other hand, the children of British men and non-British wives would be automatically British, as would the non-British wives. Some of these laws were changed in 1981 and 1985, when British women won the right to transfer their citizenship to their own children born abroad.[51] It is the former British model that was transported to the colonies.

As a simulacrum of British law, Transjordanian Nationality Law adheres to the same epistemology.[52] On the one hand, the law interpellates individuals as Jordanian (as in article 1 and article 6), whereby "all Ottoman subjects who were living habitually in Jordan on August 6, 1924 are considered as having *acquired* the nationality of Transjordan (East of the Jordan), whereby 'living habitually in East of the Jordan' includes any person who took up habitual residence in East of the Jordan for twelve months prior to August 6, 1924" (article 1), and whereby any person, "regardless of where

he was born," whose father is Transjordan-born or had been naturalized at
the time of that person's birth is considered Jordanian (article 6a). It is important to note that the territory of Transjordan that the law defines in article
20 is that of the country in 1928, which the law applies retroactively in
considering nationality applications. Following this Orwellian move, the cities of Maʿan and Aqaba and the area between them (previously part of the
kingdom of the Hijaz), which were annexed in June 1925, are identified by
the 1928 law as having been Transjordanian in 1923, which is the originary
moment of the law's application, and their populations are thus defined as
having lived in the territory of Transjordan when at that time they were in
fact Hijazis living in Hijazi territory. The law never tackles this issue except
in its territorial demarcations of Jordan's borders, in which the inclusion of
Maʿan and Aqaba is dealt with matter-of-factly. In doing so, juridical nationalist discourse provides a genetic account of the nation-state and its people, whose interpellation is treated as a *fait accompli*.

Jordanian nationality, the law asserts, can be established by a combination
of two processes: interpellation, which acts as a monological process in
which the state interpellates its own subjects as juridical nationals; and
choice, which acts as a dialogical process in which the state interpellates
subjects as nationals or foreigners juridically and in which these subjects
have to "choose" between these two juridical identities—thus granting limited agency to juridical subjects, although both of their choices are imposed
by the state that had already erased any outside to the binary. This strategy
is made evident in several articles of the law (see articles 2, 3, and 5). These
articles specify that every person who has acquired Jordanian nationality
according to the law can as an adult "choose" another nationality (articles
2 and 3). In the case of Ottomans born in Transjordan, the law, in conjunction with the Treaty of Lausanne, asserts that upon reaching adulthood
they can choose to become Jordanian (article 5).[53] An important feature of
this law is the deadline regulation. All deadlines included in this law precede
its very enactment by at least two years. This, it seems, is the law's insistence
on its ability to create *faits accomplis*.

Jordanian nationality, following Ottoman and British nationality laws,[54]
is interpellated through two principal ways: paternity or *jus sanguinis*, and
(residency in Transjordan's) territory or *jus soli*. As for paternity, it is interesting that being born to a Jordanian father whose Jordanian nationality was
established through naturalization or "birth" is one of the two criteria for
interpellating subjects as Jordanian, especially so since the rest of the law
gives no indication that being born in Jordan has any currency in establish-

ing Jordanian nationality. The only exception is article 5, whereby birth in Jordan has to be supplemented with other criteria to have any currency in establishing Jordanian nationality [one has to be an Ottoman, who reached adulthood, who submits a written request before August 6, 1926, to become Jordanian, and whose request is approved by the Chief Minister (*Ra ìs al-Nuzzar*)]. In fact, article 9 of the 1954 Nationality Law,[55] which replaced the 1928 law, upholds this criterion and explicitly states that the "children of a Jordanian [in the masculine] are Jordanians irrespective of where they were born."

The law, however, has a contingency plan for those cases in which paternity cannot be determined. In 1963, the Law of Nationality was amended to accommodate those "born in the Hashemite Kingdom of Jordan to a mother who holds Jordanian nationality and to a father with an unknown nationality or without nationality, or if the paternity of the father was not legally established," and those "born in the Hashemite Kingdom of Jordan to unknown parents.[56] The *Laqit* [illegitimate child] in the Kingdom is considered to have been born in it unless otherwise proven."[57] Note how the absence of a nationalized father is rendered equivalent to the absence of the father *tout court*. Paternity, it would seem, has to be a juridical category to have national agency. As in British law,[58] in the absence of such a nationalized paternity, women and territory (birth) can become agents of nationality as substitute (albeit secondary) fathers. Whereas territory has to be supplemented with paternity, where the latter can be established as always already nationalized, territory can perform its function as a national agent independently in the father's absence. As for women, this is the only time that their maternity can be co-opted as substitute paternity in conjunction with territory (birth), and in that substitutive role, both are endowed with juridical agency. However, since the law accords territory the independent role of substitutive paternity in the absence of a nationalized father, it is unclear why women are endowed with the contingent agency of substitutive paternity in the first place. A child born in Transjordan to a non-nationalized father can be nationalized by appealing to the territory's substitutive paternity irrespective of whether the child has a nationalized mother. It would seem, then, that this contingent agency that women/mothers are granted as substitute fathers is at best supplementary and at worst gratuitous.

The operative criterion in this law besides paternity is residency in the territory of Transjordan, a residency that has to satisfy certain temporal specifications directly related to the establishment of Transjordan as a nation-state. Here, residency is constrained by time. Therefore, it is being present

in what the law creates as "the national space" at what the law establishes as
a specific "national time" that functions as a prerequisite to establishing
nationality. The establishment of nationality however, as already discussed,
can be carried out by direct interpellation by the state through the nationality
law, or by a combination of interpellation and a new juridically constituted
choice in which the subject (a new legal fiction in itself) "chooses" her or
his position in relation to this national space as being an "outsider" or an
"insider"—a national.[59] Those who choose the former will in fact have to
move within 12 months outside the geographic boundaries of the nation-
state (article 4).

Nationalizing Non-nationals

Whereas paternity and residency establish nationality, they also establish
non-nationality—foreignness. Residency, however, as a dynamic changeable
condition, can also be the catalyst for the transformation of foreigners into
nationals. The section of the law that questions essentialist notions of nationality and opens it up to include erstwhile foreigners is the section on
naturalization, or *tajnis* (literally, nationalization), the conditions for which
are outlined in the law. It must be noted that naturalization does not necessarily depend on the subject's choice (although it also does that in specific
cases); it can also be imposed through direct interpellation by the law. Consistent with other aspects of the law, naturalization affirms the law's view that
nationality is not an inherent essence; rather, it is a juridical category that
can be acquired or lost, imposed or withdrawn.

Article 7, stipulating normative health and ability, states that only applicants who are not "disabled" can apply for naturalization, provided they
satisfy the following conditions: a two-year residency in the country prior to
the application, a good character, intention to reside in the country, and
knowledge of the Arabic language. The first of these conditions, residency,
can in fact be waived by the chief minister if the case is considered to have
special circumstances that would serve "the public interest" and if it is approved by his highness the amir. According to the 1928 law, a naturalized
citizen will be considered Jordanian in all facets of life (article 9). These
conditions are lifted (with minimal variation) verbatim from the 1914 British
law.[60]

The word *'ajz* (or disability, incapacitation, or incompetence) refers to a
married woman, a person under age, a mad person, an idiot, or any person

who is not competent before the law. The term and its definition are also borrowed in their entirety from British law.[61] The word *'ajz* was replaced in 1954[62] by the term *loss of [legal] competence*, which refers to an underage person, a mad person, an idiot, or any person who is not legally competent. Although married women were dropped from this category, their legal standing was not changed in relation to this law (see details later).

In the wake of the establishment of Israel and the Jordanian takeover of central Palestine at the end of the war, King ʿAbdullah signed an addendum to the 1928 Law of Nationality. The 1949 addendum[63] affirms that "all those who are habitual residents, at the time of the application of this law, of Transjordan or the Western Territory administered by the Hashemite Kingdom of Jordan, and who hold Palestinian nationality, are considered as having already acquired Jordanian nationality and to enjoy all the rights and obligations that Jordanians have" (article 2).[64] It is unclear, however, if the new Jordanians are interpellated as native Jordanians or were simply interpellated as naturalized Jordanians, especially so because the Palestinian territories had not been legally annexed to Jordan yet and therefore were not considered Jordanian territory at the time of the mass nationalization of their population. It is also unclear if there are distinctions in the way the Palestinians were Jordanized—for example, would native "West Bankers" be considered native Jordanians, whereas Palestinian refugees from the part of Palestine that became Israel, whether now resident in the West or East Bank, would be considered naturalized? Or would all the Palestinians belong to the same category, native or naturalized? This is important because the annexation of central Palestine did not take place until a year later, in April 1950, and because the part of Palestine that became Israel was never under Jordanian sovereignty, nor was it ever claimed officially as Jordanian territory. The distinction between nationalized and native is also important because the law of nationality has different stipulations for each category (more on the Palestinian dimension in chapter 5).

These laws were amended in 1954. The Law of Jordanian Nationality, which replaced all former laws related to the question of nationality, stresses that Jordanians are those who became Jordanians in accordance with the Nationality Law of 1928 and the addendum Law of 1949. In addition to adding new stipulations for naturalization, this law adds one more criterion designed to include and exclude different categories of people. On the one hand, article 3 of this law wants to include those Palestinians (holding Palestinian nationality before May 15, 1948) who arrived in the country after the enactment of the 1949 law (whether from Israel or the neighboring Arab countries to which they fled or had been expelled), while simultaneously excluding application of this law to Jews who before the war resided in those parts of Palestine that came under Jordanian jurisdiction. It must be noted that the 1949 addendum did not exclude Jews. As Transjordan did not have any Jewish population, the exclusion of Jews in 1954 was an attempt to thwart Zionist efforts for colonial settlement in Jordan and Zionist claims for Jewish-owned lands in the country, which were being asserted in the fifties.

The new features of the 1954 law, however, are the new conditions for naturalization and the introduction of a new important legal category— namely, the category of Arab.[65] This was done in the context of the increasingly popular unionist Arab nationalism spearheaded by the Ba'th party and Egyptian President Jamal 'Abd al-Nasir. According to this law, an Arab who resides in Jordan and has resided there for 15 consecutive years has the right to acquire Jordanian nationality provided "he" give up his original nationality in accordance with his country's laws (article 4). This is to be contrasted with the naturalization of non-Arabs, whereby, in addition to being legally competent, they must satisfy the conditions of only four years of habitual residence, not having been convicted of crimes (that violate "honor or morals"), intention to reside in the country, knowledge of Arabic (reading and writing[66]), and a good reputation (article 12). This article was amended in 1963, whereby the non-Arab applicant must "be of sound mind and that he not have a deformity rendering him a burden unto society," and that "he have a legitimate way of earning a living provided he not compete [Muzahamat] with Jordanians in skills that a number of them have." These new stricter conditions for naturalization, compared to the 1928 law, were responding to the increasing mid-fifties tenor of anti-British sentiment opposing King Husayn's flirtation with the British-sponsored Baghdad Pact and the presence of British officers in the Jordanian Arab army (see chapter 4). In addition, the issue of Arab nationals had to do with Jordan's signing in 1953 of an Arab League agreement with other member states over the national status of the citizens of these countries in relation to each other.[67]

The term *Arab* was used for the first time in the 1952 Jordanian constitution in defining the state's supranational identity: "The Hashemite Kingdom of Jordan is an independent Arab state."[68] The constitution also defines the country's cultural, religious, and linguistic identities: "Islam is the state religion and Arabic its official language."[69] This definition of the state's identity differs from that elaborated in the 1946 constitution, wherein Jordan was simply defined as "an independent sovereign state, with Islam as its religion"[70] and Arabic as its official language.[71] The 1928 Organic Law also defined Transjordan only territorially, with no reference to ethnicity in its definition of the state.[72] However, the Organic Law did stipulate that the state religion was Islam[73] and that the official language of the state was Arabic.[74] The 1952 constitutional identification of the state as Arab was responding to the rising tide of Arab nationalism, the ideas of which were supported by Jordan's King Talal, under whose brief reign the 1952 liberal constitution was enacted. Note that what is being defined in the constitution is not the Jordanian nation but rather the Jordanian state. It is unclear if the latter is reducible to the former or if the latter is metonymically deployed to represent the former. Such a privileging of Arabic, Arabness, and Islam, however, the 1952 constitution asserts, cannot be used to exclude non-Arabs or non-Muslims, or non–Arab Muslims, from having nominally equal rights and duties: "Jordanians are equal before the law with no discrimination among them in rights or duties even though they may differ in race, language or religion."[75] This is in keeping with the 1946 constitution (which prohibits discrimination on the basis of "*origin*, language or religion"[76]) and the 1928 Organic Law (which prohibits discrimination on the basis of "*race*, language or religion [emphasis added]"[77]), both of which treated non-Muslims and non-Arabic-speakers as equal despite the privileged definitional power of Islam as the state religion and Arabic as the official language of the state. In this constitutional narrative, the non-Arab but Muslim Circassians and Chechens, the Arab Christians, and the non-Arab non-Muslim Armenians (Christian) are equal citizens before the law. More importantly, since the Law of Nationality makes no reference to ethnicity or religion, their membership in the Jordanian nation is ostensibly on the same legal footing as Muslim Arab Jordanians, although the Arabic language as regards the question of naturalization of non-Jordanians remains privileged at the expense of non-Arabic-speaking non-Jordanians (but not non-Muslims) and in favor of Arabic-speaking ones. Here again, the lines between access to citizenship and nationality are blurred, indicating further that these two categories are conflated by the law.

Returning to the Law of Nationality, it should be noted that an Arab must have resided in the country for 15 years before becoming eligible to acquire Jordanian nationality, whereas a non-Arab need have resided for only four years in the country to satisfy the law's eligibility criteria. However, all these legal details can be overcome if his majesty the king chooses to grant Jordanian nationality to anyone he deems meritorious of it. Article 5 states, "It is up to his majesty the king, based on the Council of Ministers' delegation, to grant Jordanian nationality to any foreigner who chooses in a written petition Jordanian nationality provided he give up any other nationality that he may hold at the time of the petition."[78] In 1963, in an increased atmosphere of government repression and fear of pan-Arab nationalist infiltration, the law was amended. The amended law continued to grant an Arab resident in the country for 15 years the right to acquire Jordanian nationality. However, it imposed the conditions that "he be of good repute and good conduct and that he not be convicted of any honor or moral crime," that "he have a legitimate way of earning a living," that "he be of sound mind and not possess a handicap rendering him a burden unto society," and that "he swear allegiance and loyalty to his majesty the king before a justice of the peace"[79]—the last condition being of utmost importance to ensure the political loyalty of new citizens (Bedouins had to submit to similar criteria as far back as 1928[80]). Here, to become Jordanian, an Arab had to pledge allegiance and loyalty not to Jordan, as the new homeland, but to the king, as the two are conflated as one.

In line with the anti-essentialist stance of nationality law, not only can foreigners become nationals if they satisfy certain performative criteria, nationality itself as a jealous identity that refuses to coexist with any other is made more pliable. Until 1987, Jordanian nationality laws asserted that persons living in Jordan could be only Jordanian or foreign, but the new international economic and political order changed this dictum. The 1987 amendment to Nationality Law allows Jordanians to inhabit the binary on which the very essence of the nation-state was initially built—that is, to become dual-nationals, or foreign *and* national. The new category is not that of a foreign-national or national-foreign citizen; rather, when the law grants a person dual nationality, it recognizes the chameleonic nature of this new postmodern identity; the dual-national will be Jordanian in Jordan and a national of the second country of nationality when she or he is in that country. It is Jordanian laws that will apply to the Jordanian dual-national when in Jordan, not "the law of foreigners." This change in the law had been discussed since 1984 as the Jordanian state sought to have its expatriate citizens invest in the country, as Jordan's ailing economy needed many injections of foreign capital to sustain itself. To facilitate this and to induce expatriate investors, the Jordanian government organized annual conferences for Jordanian expatriates (mostly those who live in the Persian Gulf states) in Amman. These conferences, which began meeting in the summer of 1985, and which continued for a few years thereafter, proved to be a failure, although one of the demands of expatriates (namely, dual nationality) finally materialized in 1987.[81] This is one more example of the productive quality of the juridical.

In contradistinction to the previous legal stipulation of Nationality Law that all naturalized Jordanians will be equal in "all facets of life," the amendments enacted in the 1987 law introduce within that law, for the first time in Jordan's history, restrictions on the citizenship rights of naturalized Jordanians. Article 6 of the 1987 law asserts that "a person who acquires Jordanian nationality through naturalization is considered Jordanian in all aspects except that he cannot occupy political and diplomatic positions and public positions that are specified by the Council of Ministers, and he cannot become a member of Parliament until at least ten years had elapsed since his acquisition of Jordanian nationality. He also does not have the right to nominate himself to municipal, village councils or to vocational unions until at least five years had elapsed since he had acquired Jordanian nationality." What is interesting about these stipulations is that this is the first time they were listed as part of nationality law as opposed to election law. According to the 1960 election law,[82] which contradicted the existing Nationality Law, one had to have been a (male) Jordanian who, if naturalized, had to have been Jordanian for at least five years to be eligible to run for Parliament. In the 1986 election law, a naturalized citizen has to have been Jordanian for at least ten years before she or he becomes eligible to run for Parliament.[83] The 1987 amendments to the Nationality Law simply incorporated some of the provisions made in the election law of the year before, thus removing the existing contradiction between the two laws. It needs to be asserted that this law was enacted at the moment when Jordanian popular nationalist discourse and its increasingly exclusive claims had become hegemonic.

The juridical expansion of the Jordanian nation-state, demographically and territorially, which took place in 1949, was not a unique moment in Jordan's history. A similar demographic expansion took place in 1969, whereby members of the "Northern Tribes" resident in the northern territories that were annexed to Transjordan in 1930 also became "Jordanian."[84]

Losing Nationality: The Law Giveth and the Law Taketh Away

Consonant with the anti-essentialist epistemology of Nationality Law, whereas Jordanian nationality can be acquired, it can also be lost. As in

British law, the conditions of loss of nationality are listed as the acquisition of the nationality of a foreign country by choice (although a person could reinstate his nationality if he were to return to Transjordan and reside there for one year—see article 14). Whereas all Jordanians (Arab and non-Arab) have the right to give up their nationality and acquire that of another country, Arab Jordanians can do so only with the approval of the council of ministers if their new nationality of choice is non-Arab. If the new nationality they want to acquire is Arab, then no such approval is necessary (see articles 15, 16, and 17 of the 1954 law). Another condition leading to loss of nationality is joining the civil, military, or royal services of a foreign country without the permission of the Jordanian government, and refusing to quit that service when requested to by the Jordanian government, or joining the service of an enemy country. To this article was added one more condition in 1958, whereby a Jordanian can lose "his" nationality "if he committed or attempted to commit an act considered dangerous to the state's safety or security."[85] This section was added immediately after the government's 1957 antidemocratic coup that instituted martial law and suspended the constitution.[86] Note the performative aspect of this amendment, whereby political loyalty to the state is rendered a condition of nationality. In this case, citizenship and nationality are conflated as one. As far as the law is concerned, the two are imbricated in each other so much that a person cannot inhabit one without inhabiting the other. Citizenship and nationality, the law asserts, constitute an identificatory dyad that cannot be disaggregated. This condition for nationality is designed to circumvent Jordan's 1952 constitution. Whereas most rights accorded Jordanians in the 1952 constitution are restricted by the caveat "according to the law," article 9 of the constitution is explicit and unwavering in its stipulation that "the deportation of a Jordanian from the Kingdom is not allowed." Since the constitution defers all matters of nationality to Nationality Law, the preceding amendment circumvents this by denationalizing Jordanians as a precursor to deportation. The constitution's commitment against the deportation of citizens, it must be noted, was a new innovation countering the 1928 Exile and Deportation Law.[87] That law stipulated that "if the Legislative Council were convinced that any person behaves in a manner dangerous to security and order [Nizam] in East of the Jordan, or seeks to provoke enmity between the people and the government in East of the Jordan, or between the people and the Mandatory state, then it would be allowed that the Legislative Council order that such a person be deported from East of the Jordan to the place decided upon by the Executive Council, for the period it deems appropriate."[88] Unlike the

1957 amendment, the 1928 law did not seek the denationalization of the deportable citizen, as the Organic Law did not have the liberal provisions of the 1952 constitution. In the first case of its kind, however, the Jordanian government of 'Abd al-Ra'uf al-Rawabdah, backed by King 'Abdullah II, contravened the constitution by deporting four Palestinian Jordanian Islamists to Qatar in the fall of 1999. The four are suing the government from their exile on the basis of this constitutional violation.

Whereas the preceding laws were finally amended in 1987 to allow Jordanians to hold dual nationality, the 1988 Jordanian disengagement from the West Bank was one that denationalized over 1 million Jordanians resident in that part of the kingdom (see chapter 5).[89] This sudden contraction of the nation-state was officially described as a boost to Palestinian nationalism. Jordanians of Palestinian origin resident in what is known as the East Bank were assured by King Husayn that the fate of their compatriots across the river would not befall them.[90]

Women and Children

These stipulations on who is Jordanian apply to all adult males and all adult unmarried females, the masculine pronouns used in the law notwithstanding. The law, however, has different regulations for married women and underage children, who are grouped together in the law under the heading, The Naturalization of Married Women and Under-Age Children (see chapter three of this law). This category is also borrowed verbatim from British law.[91]

The only acceptable national status of married women—be they of premarital Jordanian or foreign nationality—is that of their husband, irrespective of the husband's nationality. The 1928 law is explicit on this matter. Echoing the words of British Nationality Law,[92] it is asserted that "the wife of a Jordanian is Jordanian and the wife of a foreigner is a foreigner." According to the law, "a woman who has acquired Jordanian nationality through marriage has the right to give it up within two years of her husband's death or of the breakup of the marriage." Moreover, "a woman who lost her Jordanian nationality through marriage has the right to retrieve it . . . within two years of her husband's death or of the breakup of her marriage" (article 8). This categorical denationalization of married Jordanian women and the commensurate nationalization of foreign women married to Jordanians (irrespective of their choice) is changed in amendments in 1961[93] and 1963.[94]

These new amendments stipulate that the wife of a Jordanian is Jordanian and the wife of a foreigner is a foreigner, except that "a Jordanian woman who marries a non-Jordanian[95] can keep her nationality until she obtains his country's nationality according to his country's laws," and "a foreign woman who marries a Jordanian can keep her nationality if she so wishes, in which case she must declare her wish to do so in written form submitting it to the Minister of the Interior within one year[96] of the date of her marriage, and will henceforth be treated according to the Law of Foreigners and its related regulations." A new section was added in 1963 stating that "a Jordanian whose husband acquired the nationality of another country or who acquires the nationality of another country due to special circumstances can keep her Jordanian nationality." These laws were amended to rectify the situation of those Jordanian women who married outside the nation only to find themselves stateless overnight, as they could not obtain their husband's nationality immediately. Thanks to this amendment, women were protected against statelessness and were no longer full followers of, or fully dependent on, their husbands.

After much lobbying by women in the country, the 1987 amendment[97] finally allowed Jordanian women to keep their nationality after having married a non-Jordanian, or to hold dual nationality, their original nationality and that of the husband. Moreover, "a Jordanian woman whose husband acquires the nationality of another country *can keep* her Jordanian nationality [emphasis added]." As for foreign women who marry Jordanians, whereas they were no longer automatically nationalized by Jordanian law, their access to Jordanian nationality became subject to stricter conditions. If these foreign women were of Arab nationality, then they would qualify for Jordanian nationality after a three-year residency in the country. If they held foreign non-Arab nationality, there is a five-year residency requirement. These foreign women also can keep their nationality in addition to acquiring Jordanian nationality.[98] It would seem that this new law accords married Jordanian women more rights as independent citizens than as followers of (or dependents on) men, and considers Jordanian men's rights to recruit new nationals through marriage not a condition sufficient unto itself. Men's rights now have the function of agency in transmitting nationality when supplemented with residency inside the territory of Jordan. The law also took care of the matter of national reproduction by clarifying (article 11, law of 1954) that if a foreign widow or divorcée marries a Jordanian, "her children before that marriage do not acquire Jordanian nationality because of such marriage only."

Whereas, following British law,[99] article 10 of the 1954 law takes away a Jordanian man's children's nationality in accordance with his loss of it ("If some person has lost his Jordanian nationality, his under-age children will also lose it although they will have the right to retrieve it in a petition to that effect that is submitted within two years of reaching legal age"), the 1963 law nullifies this article by allowing the children to keep their Jordanian nationality until they reach legal age, at which point they will have to make a choice (amendment to article 10). The 1987 law gave children (along with married women) the right to keep their Jordanian nationality regardless of what their fathers might do with theirs. Article 10 was nullified and rewritten as follows: "An underage boy whose Jordanian father acquires the nationality of a foreign country can keep his Jordanian nationality."[100] Here the "boy" is ostensibly a stand-in for the "ungendered" universal.

Until the 1987 changes, juridical power in Jordan not only denationalized women who marry or married outside the nation, and citizens whose political views it deemed dangerous to the state (not the nation), it could also unilaterally denationalize *whole sections of the population* with as much impunity as it could nationalize them into it in the first place, as was the case with the inhabitants of the West Bank. The denationalization of women who marry outside the nation (as it is juridically defined), of political opponents, and of other sectors of the population for political ends is in fact a violation of article 15 of the United Nations Universal Declaration of Human Rights. Whereas, after 1987, women who marry outside the nation, and children, can no longer be denationalized based on the earlier criteria, political opponents (men or women) and many Palestinian Jordanians (men, women, and children) can be stripped of their nationality by the law.

The juridical nation is then an elastic entity expanding and contracting while maintaining a central territorial core (the Transjordan of 1925) and a central demographic core (those interpellated in 1928 and their descendants, unless they are politically disloyal to the state or if they are women who marry outside the juridical nation). Thus, it would seem that the ontological conception on which nationalism's claims rest is conceived differently by popular nationalist discourse and juridical nationalist discourse. In popular nationalist discourse, the time of the nation is infinite — it has always existed and will always exist; it is an eternal time. In juridical nationalist discourse, however, the time of the nation is finite — it has a beginning and an end, at least as far as part of the nation is concerned. Whereas the law stipulates that territory and people became Jordanian in 1923, it also specifies that Jordanian territory and people ceased to be Jordanian in 1988 (as is the

case with the West Bank territory and people). Whereas the law's conception
of territory as national territory is transient, popular nationalism's conception
of it is permanent and fixed—Jordan exists today in the way it has always
existed. Whereas the law tells us that the Jordan and Jordanians of 1923 are
not the same Jordan and Jordanians of 2000, popular nationalism acknowledges no such ruptures.

Where, then, is this symbiosis between the popular national and the juridical national located? I would suggest that it is at the genetic moment of
every interpellation, of every retelling of the (hi)story of the nation that the
juridical national and the popular national meet. Nationalist Jordanians (including Jordanian Islamists) who are questioning today the constitutionality
of the 1988 denationalization of the West Bank are not relying on Jordanian
nationalist thought preceding the juridical identification of central Palestine
(West Bank) as Jordanian (as no such claims were made before); rather, they
accept the juridical identification of the nation in 1949 to 1950 on which
they base their constitutional claims today. In fact, their nationalist claims
are secured by the juridical constitution of national land and people. Is it
then the territorially and demographically expansive juridical identification
that is subsumed within popular nationalist discourse? Even this proves a
hurried conclusion. Popular nationalism in Jordan traces its genesis to the
1920s. However, that moment of nativist mobilization was protesting the demographic expansion of the nation to include those from outside the territory
identified as Jordanian. Is it then juridical territorial expansion that is subsumed by the discourse of popular nationalism to the exclusion of the inhabitants? Perhaps! However, to determine if this is the case, we must identify these moments of intersection, of subsumption.

It is in the nationalist retelling of these moments that the intersection
occurs. Whereas the genetic moment of every national interpellation secures
the subsequent claims made by popular nationalism anchoring the political
and popular concept of the nation, every retelling of the story of the nation
becomes in fact a moment of sublation (incorporation *and* transcendence),
wherein the newly constituted Jordanian identity sublates its predecessor
in an interminable process, and whereby the new Jordanian identity is
reinscribed as the one that had always already existed as it does today. The
Hashemites established Transjordan based on anti-Ottoman Arab nationalist
sentiment, but through the law, the Mandatory-Hashemite state undermined
that sentiment by inscribing a new local one on the body politic of Transjordan. In response to Arab nationalist attack on the Arab nationalist cre-
dentials of the Hashemite state in the 1950s, new laws were enacted to limit

Arab access to Jordanian nationality (the 1954 and 1963 laws). Jordanian popular nationalism, which matured in the seventies and eighties in the wake of the Civil War of 1970, was to recite these moments as nationalist ones without any direct reference to these laws.

The effects of these laws are the anchor stabilizing Jordanian nationalist claims today. Whereas the Hashemite state, under the Mandate and after independence, produces Jordanianness through juridical power, the discourse of popular nationalism developed its own independent momentum, whether through the ideological state apparatuses (school, media, military, government bureaucracy) or through societal ones (family, business associations, labor and professional associations, social and athletic clubs, political parties, literature). In the political economy of signification, Jordan has many referents, popular-political and juridical. The nationalist discourse of the Jordanian state and that of Jordanian nationalists, as the rest of this book will show, shuttle between these referents, deploying one or the other, as a matter of expediency. It is crucial not only to identify the moments in which one referent is deployed at the expense of the other and vice versa, but also, as we will see in the remainder of this study, to identify the moments in which the meaning of Jordan can no longer be controlled by those deploying it, when Jordan assumes multiple referents that are imbricated in each other in such a way that they cannot be disentangled.

2 Different Spaces as Different Times

Law and Geography in Jordanian Nationalism

Anticolonial nationalism is structured around the dyad of modernization and tradition. These are conceived both as synchronic temporalities lived in the modality of the nation-state and as diachronic temporalities constituting the linear history of the nation. In the Jordanian case, as in all other nationalisms, the national subjects representing these two temporalities are conceived by nationalism based on considerations of space as geography. Women (those whom bourgeois nationalism constructs as inhabiting the domestic space) and Bedouins (those inhabiting the nonurban desert) are conceived as inhabiting a national time (that of traditional culture) different from men and urbanites (who inhabit the modern time of the nation). This epistemology anchors national subjects in a spatialized and temporalized essence, which then pervades all aspects of nation-state policies.

This chapter will address another dimension of juridical nationalism. In the case of Jordan, women and Bedouin men, unlike urban men, have a dual status in the law, whereas Bedouin women have a triple status. All women are considered ostensibly equal to all men in the civil code, whereas all of them are unequal (in terms of rights and duties) in the personal status law in relation to all men. All Bedouins are ostensibly equal in the civil code but are constituted as different through the application of tribal law. Bedouin women are equal to men in the civil code, unequal to men in the personal status law, and different from urbanites with the application of tribal law to them. The three realms of law in Jordan (civil, personal status, and tribal) reflect not only the spatial dimension of the different subjects of the nation, but more importantly the conflation of space with time that constitutes these subjects. This reading of the laws will be accompanied in this chapter by a study of the political history and philosophy of Jordanian nation-building as it intersects with and diverges from the juridical history and philosophy just outlined. This study shows that the initial basis of a resistant anticolonial nationalism that posits a national self against the colonial other has a very complicated account of what constitutes this national self, which influences every aspect of its project. It is in this vein that women, as residents of the private domestic sphere, and Bedouins, residents of the nonurban desert, signify, through their spatial locations, a temporal location, that of tradition, whereas men, considered as residents of the public sphere, and urbanites, through their spatial locations, signify the temporal location of modernity.

Different Species of Citizens: Women and Bedouins

The juridical journey of Westernization began in Ottoman times in the mid-nineteenth century, long before Jordan was conceived as a national idea. The split in Ottoman law following the Tanzimat was one of regulating that which was essential to modernizing the Ottoman Empire versus that which maintained its "traditional" cultural identity. The former, the realm of the economy (but not necessarily all aspects of property), or what Marx called "civil society," was to be governed by an adapted version of post-Napoleonic French and Italian legal structures. The latter, the realm of the social, was to be governed by a variety of laws inspired by the Shari'ah and Christian ecclesiastic dicta. When Transjordan was established in 1921, these two realms of the law were maintained. In fact, the first codified Ottoman family law enacted in 1917 continued to be applied in Jordan until 1947, a year after formal independence from the British and 28 years after the end of Ottoman rule, when the Temporary Family Rights Law was enacted.[1] This, in turn was replaced by The Law of Family Rights of 1951,[2] which was finally replaced by the 1976 Personal Status Law.[3] A project for a new law that has been in the making since the early eighties was shelved in favor of several other projects, the latest of which is still being drafted.[4] As of now, the latest project has been frozen and is yet to be submitted to Parliament for debate.

As for nomadic Bedouins, who were distinguished from some of the rural and urban populations also laying claim to tribal heritage, they were to be governed by a new set of laws as early as October 1924, when the Mandatory-Hashemite state enacted the Law of Tribal Courts, which was replaced by the Law of Tribal Courts of 1936.[5] This took place after the British government, on the recommendation of the Arab Legion's chief Frederick G. Peake, forced ʿAbdullah to accept the abolition of the semi-independent Tribal Administration Department (Niyabat al-ʿAshaʾir) headed by Sharif Shakir Bin Zayd in the summer of 1924,[6] and enacted new laws to control the Bedouins as early as October 1924.[7] The positions of Tribal Administration representative and deputy representative had in fact been established since the first Transjordan ministerial administration was set up on April 4, 1921, although the position of deputy (occupied by Ahmad Maryud) was abolished on February 1, 1923, and the position of representative (occupied by Shakir) was completely done away with on June 26, 1926, two years after the abolition of the Tribal Administration itself.[8] In this context, Peake proudly insists that "had not the British stepped into Trans-Jordan and the French into Syria there is little doubt that both countries . . . would soon have reverted to tribal rule and poverty." To achieve this important task, Peake set to work: "My policy was to raise a Force from the sedentary, or village, Arabs, which would gradually be able to check the Beduin and allow an Arab Government to rule the country without fear of interference from tribal chiefs."[9]

Also, the end of 1923 saw the Kuwait conference, in which Ibn Saʿud and the Transjordanian government were attempting to delineate their borders, which were finally agreed upon in the Hidaʾ agreement in November 1925, stressing that Hijazi and Transjordanian tribes (ʿashaʾir) cannot cross the border between the two countries without proper documents.[10] The issue as far as Bedouins were concerned was not only that their affairs would be run according to a different set of rules, but also that they needed to be territorialized, and in this they required special supervision and control. To achieve this, the government enacted the Law of Supervising the Bedouins of 1929 (or the Bedouin Control Law, as it is officially translated into English), updating it again in 1936.[11] These laws governing the Bedouins as a separate category of nationals and citizens were viewed as transitional, facilitating the integration of the Bedouins within the framework of the juridical nation-state. This, the Jordanian government felt, was achieved in 1976. That year, a law canceling all previous tribal laws including the Law of Supervising the Bedouins was enacted, thus ushering the Bedouins into the world of the nation-state as equal to and no longer a distinct species of citizen-nationals.[12]

As for women, the key constitutional article relevant to our topic is article 6 of the 1952 constitution, which stipulates that "Jordanians are equal before the law with no discrimination among them in rights or duties, even if they differed in race, language or religion."[13] Despite its specific qualifications and the absence of any mention of sex or gender, this article has been heralded as a point of departure for Jordanian feminist legal scholars. In fact, this stipulation of the equality of all citizen-nationals based on the preceding criteria had been asserted in the 1946 constitution as well as in the Organic Law of 1928.[14] Certainly, it is nationalism's commitment to bourgeois equality that is at stake in such a proclamation—an equality that will have to be extendible to include what nationalism had considered as initially marginal, but which now is making itself central. It is then in the realm of the civil code that women can ultimately be accommodated as equal citizens, or at least potentially equal, while maintaining their supposedly traditional "unequal" role through the codifications of the Personal Status Law.

In this constitutional narrative, feminist scholars argue, all citizens are considered equal in all aspects of civil life. For example, this equality is supposed to extend to holding public office (following article 22-1, article 42, and article 75-1), as all stipulations in that regard apply to all Jordanians. Despite its masculine form, the word "Jordanian" used throughout the constitution is considered by these scholars as a stand-in for the ungendered universal. However, this reading of the constitution is somewhat deceptive. Whereas there is no gender stipulation on who could hold public office in the constitution, election laws that were enacted in Jordan from 1923[15] through 1974, and in some cases until 1982, did not allow women to vote or run for national or local office. Despite proposed amendments to alter this anomaly, which were presented as early as 1955, thanks to the tireless efforts of Jordanian women activists, women were not granted the vote until the 1974 amendment, which was issued as a royal decree. Similarly, the 1955 Municipalities Law (law 29) did not allow women to run for municipal office or vote in municipal elections, a situation that was changed only in 1982 when an amendment to include women was enacted (law 22).[16] In fact, had the allegedly "ungendered" Jordanian acted in the constitution as encompassing both sexes, these laws would have been judged unconstitutional. The fact that no such case was ever brought to the attention of Jordan's courts testifies to that effect. However, the fact that women have been able to press some of their claims within the realm of citizenship exemplified in the civil code does not necessarily contradict the nationalist dictum placing them along a dual axis of tradition and modernity. Whereas women can be, and in some cases should be, modernized according to nationalist criteria, their "traditional" role in the private sphere must be preserved through the application of the Personal Status Law. It is thus that the modern postcolonial nation-state can remain true to its founding axioms.

In fact, the concept of full national citizenship has gone through a long journey of amendments and changes whereby there has been a considerable change in who is considered a full-fledged citizen-national. The 1923 law allows only men over twenty to vote, and only men over thirty with no criminal record, who speak and read Arabic, to run for Parliament. The only people exempted from the Arabic literacy condition are Bedouin tribal leaders. The 1928 law, in turn, introduced some changes.[17] The law defined a Bedouin as someone who belongs to one of the nomadic tribes that are listed in the law. These tribes are divided in turn into two geographic types: northern and southern Bedouins.[18] The law has different provisions for Bedouins and Hadaris (the sedentary population). Article 7 explicitly states that "every Jordanian (non-Bedouin) [both *Jordanian* and *non-Bedouin* are in the masculine] who has completed 18 years of age has the right to vote in primary elections. . . . " As for Bedouin representatives, article 16 stipulates that "two members representing the Bedouins should be elected. His Great Highness the Amir will appoint, in a published edict in the *Official Gazette*, two official committees of Northern Bedouins and Southern Bedouins, each of which comprising ten tribal leaders [mashayikh] with each committee electing one member." A special statute governed the workings of these committees.[19] By 1947, a year after independence, Jordanian lawmakers became more explicit as to what designated identities meant in the law. The 1947 electoral law defines a Bedouin as "every male member of the nomadic tribes."[20] The "election" of Bedouin representatives followed the same process as the 1928 law.[21] As for Hadaris, all Jordanian Hadari men over eighteen had the right to vote, unless they were serving a prison sentence, were sentenced to death, were foreclosed upon by a court, were declared bankrupt by a court, or were crazy.[22] Note that the range of normal citizenship excludes criminals, the mad, and failed capitalists who have been declared juridically propertyless.

The democratic opening in the mid-fifties facilitated the work of many feminists attempting to change the electoral law to allow women to vote and run for public office. After much agitation and organization—whereby a number of petitions signed and finger-printed by thousands of women were presented to Parliament—a ministerial decision, made with the prompting of Parliament, was issued on October 3, 1955, to allow women with elementary education to vote (a condition that did not apply to men).[23] But with the dissolution of Parliament by the king and the dictatorial cancellation of all parliamentary decisions that were made during the liberal period, the decision to grant literate women the vote was rescinded.

Soon after, the electoral law of 1960 was enacted. This law stipulated that only male Jordanians over twenty years of age could vote, and only those among them over thirty could run for public office.[24] These provisions included, for the first time in the country's history, Bedouin men, as the law made no reference whatsoever to separate Bedouin "elections" or appointments. This was the case, as the government felt that its sedentarization policies of the Bedouins had been largely completed in 1960.[25] This law also stipulated that all members of the Jordanian Arab Army, both officers and servicemen, could not vote.[26] It is interesting to note that a large percentage of Bedouin men serve in the army. Thus for Bedouin men, little would have changed, as at the moment they were finally allowed to vote, those among them serving in the military could not. Still, the integration of the Bedouins into juridical national citizenship, as at least partially "modernized," had just begun, despite the reality that they remained under special "supervision" by the state until 1976, when their integration into the world of the nation-state became complete.

In the mid-sixties, with the partial reopening of political life in the kingdom, King Husayn sent a letter to the prime minister asking that the matter granting women the vote should be studied.[27] Nothing came out of this. It was eight years later, on March 5, 1974, that the king sent another letter to the prime minister, issuing a royal decree, by which an amendment was attached to the 1960 electoral law granting all adult women the vote.[28] The amendment replaced the definition of Jordanian in article 2-a of the 1960 law as "every male person" with "every person whether male or female." The timing of this amendment was crucial for Jordan's international image, as the United Nations decade on women was going to commence with the 1975 conference in Mexico City, and Jordan was planning to send delegates. Also, in 1982, the Municipalities Law was amended to finally allow women to run for public office. Finally, a new electoral law was enacted in 1986 (with a few amendments in 1989) changing the age of voting citizens, both men and women, to nineteen years,[29] and maintaining the assertion that all active military personnel cannot vote.

Bedouins and National Citizenship

In Ottoman days, the government had very little control over the Bedouins of the area that became Transjordan. Administratively, since the mid-nineteenth century, the area was divided into the *Sanjaq* of ʿAjlun (first created in 1851), which was part of the Nablus governorate or *Mutasarrifiyyah* (part of Palestine today), the northern town of Ramtha and its environs, which were linked to the Sanjaq of Huran (part of Syria today), and the areas in the Jordan valley, which were part of the Tabariyyah (Tiberias) *Qaʾimmaqamiyyah* (previously part of Palestine and now part of Israel). Later, the entire *Sanjaq* of ʿAjlun was annexed to the Huran *Mutasarrifiyyah*, and the Balqaʾ district, with Salt as its center, became part of the Nablus *Mutasarrifiyyah* from 1882 to 1905 and was later annexed to the Karak *Mutasarrifiyyah* (in southern Jordan today), which was the district least connected to the central Ottoman authorities until its military reconquest in 1894, which rendered it under the authority of the Wali of Damascus.[30]

Nomadic Bedouins constituted almost half (46 percent) of the Transjordanian population in 1922, numbering 102,120 people out of a total of 225,350, according to the estimates of the Tribal Administration Department (Niyabat al-ʿAshaʾir). This estimate included all nomadic Bedouins within the 1921 to 1925 borders of Transjordan, thus excluding the area extending from Maʿan to Aqaba, which was annexed in 1925, and which includes one of the more major Jordanian tribes, the Huwaytat.[31] Due to the government's sedentarization campaigns, mainly through the Arab Legion, but also through the curtailment of Bedouin mobility within the country and internationally, the percentage of Bedouins in the country maintaining a nomadic lifestyle had decreased by 1943 to 35.3 percent (120,000 people), although the percentage of the Bedouins would have been higher in 1922 had the Bedouins of the Maʿan-to-Aqaba area been included. The 1946 census (which provides some contradictory figures resulting from the general classificatory confusion as to who was considered a Bedouin) put the percentage of the Bedouins to the general population to be 23 percent (99,261 people).[32]

As for governing the Bedouins, the Law of Supervising the Bedouins of 1929 was in effect a declaration of martial law, for the main executor of this ordinance was none other than the head of the Arab Legion, Transjordan's army. The law made provisions for a committee consisting of the head of the Arab Legion, the Amir Shakir Bin Zayd, a Hijazi cousin of the Amir 'Abdullah considered to be knowledgeable about things Bedouin, and a third person "elected" by the Amir 'Abdullah from among the non-nomadic tribal leaders who were also considered knowledgeable of the traditions of nomadic tribes. The "elected" leader would hold his position so long as the amir decreed.[33] The duties of this committee were to oversee the Bedouins and to establish full "surveillance" of their movements; to decide, when necessary, the place where the Bedouins should settle, with punishment (which includes fines and imprisonment) meted out to those who resist; to listen to grievances made by the Bedouins in accordance with the Law of Tribal Courts; to withdraw categorically, when it wishes, any case being deliberated before a tribal court; and to investigate any security breaches and mete out punishments to the guilty parties, including the sequestering and confiscation of property.[34] The head of the Arab Legion is designated as the executor of all decisions made by the committee, of which he is a member.[35] This law was enacted a year before the arrival of John Bagot Glubb, a British officer considered the foremost authority in pacifying Bedouin tribes, a job he had excelled at in neighboring Iraq in the preceding decade. Glubb, with the aid of these legal strictures, was able to use military conscription as the preferred method to control the Bedouin tribes, and to integrate them within the fold of the nation-state. His strategy, with the aid of a number of laws, proved most successful.

With the immense progress made by Glubb in integrating the Bedouins through the military (see chapter 3), a new law to supervise the Bedouins was enacted in 1936, replacing the old one. The most important feature of this law was the doing away with the three-member committee and dele-gating all the authority that it had had in the 1929 law to the person of the army chief, then occupied by Peake Pasha, or anyone to whom he delegates authority, in this case Glubb Pasha, who was to replace Peake in 1939 as the head of the Arab Legion.[36] This had resulted from the death of the Sharif Shakir Bin Zayd. Shakir, alongside Peake and Glubb, had been the main executor of all laws pertaining to the Bedouins until his death in December 1934, after which the British and their local officers took over all authority pertaining to Bedouins. In fact, in the five years following Shakir's death, 50 percent to 60 percent of the cases heard by tribal courts were settled by Glubb himself without any recourse to Amman.[37] Another not-so-minor fea-ture of this law was the discrepancy about which tribes were considered Bedouin in 1929 and which ones were considered so in 1936—as some were dropped from the list and others were added. This was mainly a result of the arbitrary system of classification used by ignorant administrators to determine who is and who is not Bedouin.[38] In fact, the Law of Tribal Courts enacted in 1936 designated the army chief as the Mutasarrif, or provincial governor, of the entire area encompassing nomadic tribes—that is, the non-urban and nonrural desert.[39] This situation persisted until 1958, two years after the expulsion of Glubb and the subsequent "Arabization" of the army, when a new law separating the police from the Arab Legion was issued.[40] Although the government's decision to separate the police from the army had taken place on July 14, 1956, almost two years earlier, it revoked that decision after the palace coup that ousted the nationalists from the cabinet and the army (see chapter 4).[41] Article 4 of the new law stipulated that the new head of public security would no longer be answerable to the head of the army but rather to the minister of interior, wherein all the authority over issues of internal public security (i.e., police work) previously exercised by the minister of defense was now within the purview of the interior minister, and similarly all police authority previously exercised by the head of the army was hereby transferred to the head of public security (Mudir al-Amn al-'Am). Article 2 of the new law specified that public security referred to supervising the Bedouins, tribal courts, and so forth. It was thus that from 1958 until 1976, the Bedouins were no longer living under martial law with the army running their lives; rather they were now living under the constant supervision and surveillance of the police as if they were criminal suspects.

In a country where the inhabitants had tribal and family links that crossed the invented national boundaries (to Palestine, Syria, Iraq, Egypt, Lebanon, the Hijaz, Armenia, and the Caucasus), the reorganization of identity had to be territorialized, especially in the case of the Bedouins who had little respect for nation-state jurisdiction. In addition, the internal reorganization and division of space into national administrative units, such as governorates (muhafazat), districts (alwiyah), provinces (aqdiyah), and cities, served to sedentarize nomadic Bedouins within the nation-state itself. Their mobility was being circumscribed not only on the international level but just as importantly on the *intra*national level. It is through this new epistemology of space that the Transjordanian state sought to define Jordanian national citizenship juridically. Blood ties had to be superseded by territorial contiguity and residency.

These series of laws were meant to achieve several things. On the one hand, as far as Bedouins were concerned, Bedouin law could become subservient to non-Bedouin interpretations. It could be organized, controlled, deployed when necessary, rescinded when necessary, while the whole apparatus remained under the jurisdiction of the non-Bedouin nation-state and its overarching juridical dicta, which had nothing to do with Bedouin tradition while at the same time claiming to represent it. Also, the Law of Supervising the Bedouins relegated the Bedouins to the space of the nation-state, as far as preventing them from being international entities crossing nation-state borders at will, and simultaneously nationalized the internal space to which they were relegated. This was achieved through prescribing settlement locales, forcing such settlement, or employment by the military. The latter served the multiple purposes of having the Bedouins police themselves in tune with nation-state laws—territorializing the Bedouins in more or less settled surroundings such as army camps (which could be mobile but whose ultimate authority was geographically fixed in the capital where army headquarters "al-Qiyadah al-'Amah" were/are located), or in cities and towns throughout the country. In addition, this law intended to nationalize the Bedouins through shifting their loyalties from the tribe to the military and ultimately to the nation-state that this military was supposed to protect.

The laws and policies followed by the Jordanian nation-state helped to destroy the Bedouin economy, transforming it into one completely dependent on the state. The criminalization of the Bedouin lifestyle and the juridically sanctioned penalties imposed on Bedouins who resist state-sponsored sedentarization policies led to the prevention of Bedouin raiding, and international crossing, and to the confiscation of the cattle and herds of resistors—which in conjunction with droughts in the late 1920s and early 1930s decimated Bedouin herds—with the state providing the Bedouins with alternative economic activity through the military mainly, but also through agricultural settlement and wage labor (mainly with the British-owned Iraq Petroleum Company[42]). It was thus not only the transplanting of the Bedouins from one geographic locale to another that ushered them from the realm of tradition to the realm of modernity, characterized by the juridical rule of the nation-state, but equally important was the transformation of all space within the nation-state through nationalization, land laws, reparceling of territory, and demarcation of internal provincial borders as well as external borders marking the frontier of the nation-state.

Moreover, the co-optation of the Bedouin leadership by the state went hand in hand with the integration of the rank and file within the nation-state economy. While the latter was enlisted in the Arab Legion's Desert Patrol, the leadership was incorporated within state structures—namely, the legislative council and the tribal courts. Unlike the rest of the population, who had elected representatives, with special quotas for ethnic and religious minorities, in accordance with the 1928 electoral law, the Bedouins had their designated seats filled by appointments made by the Amir 'Abdullah. As Abla Amawi observes, this electoral system, which was not based on proportional representation, benefits some sectors of society over others and ensures "a docile legislative body."[43] Whereas Jordanian Christians and Circassians received a disproportionately higher percentage of seats than their numbers would warrant, Bedouins, who constituted 23.4 percent of the population, were given a mere 12.5 percent of the seats.[44] Still, what this meant was that these appointments were made by the amir according to the shaykhs' loyalty to *him* and to the state and not based on popular will. Thus the appointed shaykhs were answerable only to the amir and not to their constituencies. In fact, tribal shaykhs were co-opted early on by the state through other means, namely state assistance in their agricultural endeavors, which was substantially higher than the meager assistance given to the rest of the tribes for cultivation. For example, a loan was granted to the paramount shaykh of the Bani Sakhr, Mithqal al-Fayiz, to assist him in cultivating his extensive landholdings. The reasons given for advancing the loan to al-Fayiz were to assist him in the transition period from nomadism to settled life and to "restore" his position within his tribe.[45] In addition, the state paid tribal shaykhs a salary of 240 Palestinian pounds a year to establish the state's control over their tribes. The shaykhs were also expected to maintain public order by ensuring the good behavior of their tribesmen "on pain of loss or reduction of salary."[46] Moreover, while many tribal shaykhs (or what Hani Hurani calls al-aristuqratiyyah al-qabaliyyah al-iqta'iyyah, or the feudo-tribal aristocracy) increased their landholdings as a result of the land settlement process launched by the state in 1933,[47] they also acquired more prestige and power within the tribes because access to state institutions went through them, especially recruitment into the armed forces.[48] Also, as already mentioned, tribal shaykhs served on tribal courts along with state officials giving them power in judicial matters.

No juridical changes in the status of the Bedouins were effected for a couple of decades after independence. In fact, without the changes in the electoral law of 1960 wherein Bedouins acquired the right to vote as the Hadari population could, previous laws remained operative until the seventies when the status of the Bedouins began to change both juridically and in the popular discourse of palace-planned nationalism. These changes followed the 1970 Civil War between the Jordanian army and the Palestinian guerrillas, which ended in the defeat of the latter during the Black September massacres in 1970 and their final defeat and expulsion from the country in July 1971. It was hardly a coincidence that the Council of Tribal Leaders (Majlis Shuyukh al-ʿAshaʾir) was set up on July 31, 1971, by royal decree, a few days after the final expulsion of the Palestinian guerrillas. King Husayn designated his brother, Prince Muhammad, as council president. The council included twelve to fifteen tribal leaders, all of whom were to be appointed by royal decree based on the recommendation of the council president (see articles 2 and 5).[49] The law stressed that an appointed member of the council must be Jordanian, a tribal leader, or a prominent tribal personality belonging to the tribes enumerated in the law, and that he not be ineligible to hold public office due to crimes or felonies (article 6-a, b, c). The official purpose for creating the council was to "elevate the living standards among the Bedouins, and to put into effect developmental, agricultural, health, and educational projects aiming at supporting the program of settling the people of the Badiyah [desert], and to provide them with a good living to which they are entitled and which is the duty of the state to provide them with, in order that they can perform their role of pushing the wheel of progress and construction in this struggling country."[50] In 1973, the council issued a statute (nizam) to unify tribal traditions, Tawhid al-ʿAdat al-ʿAshaʾiriyyah, wherein all nomadic and sedentary tribes or clans in the country would be governed by the same statutes and wherein all their disparate traditions would be nationally unified before the law.[51] This of course was part of the new government policy of unifying the Transjordanian population under one national identity after the challenge that the 1970 Civil War constituted to the country. Prior divisions between the Transjordanian population such as Bedouin and Hadari were proving counterproductive to the nationalist project of the state and palace. The government decided to cancel the Council of Tribal Leaders law in May 1973,[52] replacing it with an extra-juridical understanding between the country's tribes and the palace. This new understanding came to be known as Mahdar al-Qasr, or the Palace Convention, and it was signed on August 18, 1974. The convention was attended on the part of the state by Muhammad Hashim, the king's advisor on tribal matters; the head of the Jordanian Armed Forces General Habis al-Majali; the interior minister Ahmad Tarawnah; the head of public security (the police) Major General Anwar Muhammad; and the governors of all of Jordan's governorates and the heads of all police departments. As for the tribal side, Ahmad ʿUwaydi al-ʿAbbadi states that tribal leaders and experienced and prominent tribal personalities who are knowledgeable of tribal laws and traditions attended on behalf of the tribes.[53] The official purpose of the Mahdar was described as follows: "Based on the royal desire to crystallize conven-

tional tribal traditions among all the sectors of the esteemed Jordanian people, rendering them in a frame [characterized by] clear vision, those concerned in matters important to this dear family [i.e., the Jordanian people]
. . . are meeting to study all the important parts of tribal conventions [a'raf]
and to decide which of them is good and beneficial for public welfare and
amend what needs to be amended, and to look into what needs to be reviewed in order that tribal conventions be capable of catching up with the
times [muwakabat al-zaman] and proceed according to the needs of the
present."[54] It was the hope of those present that this would lead to the "cohesion of the Jordanian family."

A most interesting aspect of this Mahdar was those articles that dealt with
exempting members of the police and armed forces from being pursued by
tribal law or its executors. Thus, people who, on orders of their superiors,
might commit acts in defense of state security or state economic interests,
or to "impose state authority," and in doing so might use their weapons
against members of the tribes, may not be pursued by tribal law or its executors after they are released from military or police service, and no tribal
vendetta should be exacted from them or their families. Moreover, tribal
members of the armed forces may not take part or intervene in tribal affairs
and disputes.[55] Such a stipulation clearly defined the reach of tribal customary law. Whereas the state would impose a state-sanctioned version of tribal
law whose executors are state representatives, the reach of this law cannot
encompass the state itself or its representatives, even though (or especially)
if they are members of the tribes. This point is crucial in the modern nation-
state's ability to demarcate the borders between the traditional and the modern. Whereas the modern nation-state can and should include within it
"traditional" authority structures and practices, these are always already subsumed under the supreme authority of the modern state's laws to which they
will always be subservient. It is clear that this is not a case of intersection of
the traditional and the modern, but rather one of subsuming the traditional
by the modern, which in the process redefines the traditional according to
its modern criteria of governance.

These changes in the lives of Bedouins were taking place in the realm of
the law at the same time as state development planners were devising sedentarization schemes to end the nomadic lifestyle of the Bedouins. This
had been in operation since the Arab League convened several conferences
to debate the issue of Bedouin sedentarization and development (in Beirut
in 1949, in Cairo in 1950, and in Damascus in 1952). Other international
organizations that contributed to this discourse of development included the

United Nations Educational, Scientific, and Cultural Organization
(UNESCO), the World Health Organization, the United Nations Food and
Agriculture Organization, and the International Labor Organization.[56]
These organizations created a corps of Arab and European "development"
experts who devised plans for "developing" the Bedouins. As Riccardo Bocco
points out in his pioneering study, both groups shared the same epistemology
and philosophy: "Les préjugés des uns et des autres se renforcent mutuel-
lement."[57] The goal was to normalize the Bedouins and usher them into the
life of modern citizen-nationals.

In 1976, the government issued a law canceling all laws pertaining to the
Bedouins that had remained in effect until then, including the Law of Supervising the Bedouins and the Tribal Courts Law.[58] However, although the
government's decision to eliminate all juridical distinctions between male
Jordanians in 1976 was engineered as the final act of unifying all the Transjordanian population (wherein all male Jordanians, whether of Bedouin or
Hadari background, will be treated the same, and all female Jordanians, be
they of Bedouin or Hadari background, will be treated the same—thus maintaining unequal gender criteria), the Palace Convention, which does not
have the status of law, remained in effect.

On the political front, popular opposition to the special status of the
Bedouins was in evidence since the fifties, as the Arab Legion's mostly Bedouin soldiers and police were increasingly being relied on to suppress the
government's massive opposition. By the mid-fifties, nationalist and leftist
demands became so strong that the government conceded on joining the
British-sponsored anti-Soviet Baghdad Pact, and the king expelled General
Glubb and began the process of Arabizing Jordan's armed forces. It is in this
context that many among the Bedouins became politicized, joining nationalist and leftist parties, and began calling for abolishing the special status
accorded the Bedouins, seeing it as a manifestation of the British divide-
and-conquer strategy dividing a "unified" people. The non-Bedouin opposition also called for abolishing the special status of the Bedouins, as it saw
this as the reason that the Bedouin population remained shielded from the
rest of society, unaffected by political transformations, and thus remaining
a loyal instrument of repression used by the British and the Hashemite regime. After the palace coup in 1957, these voices were again silenced until
the eve of the 1970 Civil War, when the Bedouin regiments of the army
were used against the civilian population as well as the Palestinian guerrillas.

However, during the same period, new voices emerged from within the
newly created police apparatus set up by the state in 1956 and 1958, ren-

dering the police independent from the army. As early as 1959, the head of
Bedouin police proposed the amendment of the Bedouin Supervision Law
of 1936, wherein police powers would be augmented to increase the imprisonment of Bedouin offenders from one to five years, as well as to increase
the fines in that law from 40 Palestinian pounds to 200 Jordanian dinars,
commensurate with the criminal code applicable to the Hadari population.[59]
Moreover, the interior ministry itself had issued an order in 1962 to all the
administrative governors and heads of police departments to send the requisite recommendations necessary to "organize Bedouin traditions ['adat],"
especially in matters of murder, in ways that are compatible with the circumstances of the period.[60] In 1964, the head of the police of the city of
Karak (as well as the city's legislative council) recommended that a meeting
of the country's tribal shaykhs and judges be set up to "formulate new traditions ['adat] that are compatible with present conditions." He added that
Bedouin conventions are like the civil code in that they require changes
that are commensurate with the general changes taking place in the country.[61] Others expressed concern of the way tribal laws, which were juridically
applicable to nomadic Bedouins, were being used by non-nomadic village
and city folks of "tribal" backgrounds to resolve their conflicts (a practice in
existence for decades). Based on this, a recommendation to amend tribal
laws in such a way as to render them applicable to all the tribes (nomadic
and sedentary alike, which means all the Transjordanian Arab population
that traces its origins to the country within the post-1921 borders, but who
lived there before these borders were actually designated), and that all laws
pertaining to raids be nullified as they are irrelevant in the present period
where raids had disappeared.[62] A similar recommendation was sent by the
country's director of public security in 1966 expressing similar sentiments
about the *de facto* use of tribal laws to resolve conflicts pertaining to both
nomadic Bedouins and non-nomadic Hadaris with claims to tribal heritage.[63] He further recommended that a collection of Bedouin traditions be
"established" as a basis for a new tribal law and that the Law of Supervising
the Bedouins of 1936 be amended. In addition, he suggested a change in
the vocabulary used in these laws—for example, "raids," an anachronistic
term in the age of the nation-state, should be replaced with the more appropriate "breach of security," or "al-ikhlal bil-amn." These debates had
become so heated that in 1966 the Jordanian government recommended
the establishment of a separate Bedouin governorate. The recommendation
included twenty-two articles specifying the authorities of the projected governor. It is not clear why this recommendation arrived stillborn.[64] Within a

few months, however, the minister of interior issued an order to all governors in the country to consult with all prominent tribal personalities in their respective areas about tribal traditions and procedures, to "find and develop a new tribal law that is applicable to future living conditions."[65]

In the wake of the civil war and the increasing division between Palestinian Jordanians of post-1948 citizenship and Jordanians (irrespective of geographical origins) of pre-1948 citizenship—popularly (mis)understood as "Jordanians versus Palestinians"—the government saw more clearly the benefits of unifying the population under the new umbrella of the "one Jordanian family," or al-usrah al-urduniyyah al-wahidah. It was in this context that the government sought first to unify the "traditions" of all Jordanian tribes through the new council of 1971 and the *nizam* of 1973, finally consolidating it through a pact with the palace (the Mahdar). Once that was achieved as an understanding, there was no longer a need to have Bedouin-specific laws, which led the government to cancel them all in 1976 despite the opposition of many tribal leaders who wanted them only amended.

Soon after the 1976 law was issued, a large number of tribal leaders met to protest the government's decision to do away with tribal laws. Within two weeks of the cancellation of the law and in an attempt to redress the grievances of tribal leaders, King Husayn visited the headquarters of the Bedouin police (the only remaining exclusively Bedouin military outfit in the country) on June 9, 1976. Defending the government's decision, the king asserted, "We are Arabs and we shall not neglect our valuable traditions or our praiseworthy traits, which we have inherited from our noble and gallant ancestors. We have canceled the Laws of Supervising the Bedouins in order to allow for the future punishment of criminals before regular civil courts, which in turn will issue severe punishments and rulings wherein only the criminal will be punished for his crime, and not the group as a whole. And at any rate, the traditional conventions, which we hold dear and of which we are proud, will continue, and we shall remain beholden to them and shall not bypass them."[66] It is clear that the king and the government were making a selective distinction between what they considered proper Bedouin traditions—"which we hold dear"—worthy of being identified as "Arab" and hence preserved, and other traditions, which were protective of Bedouin practices deemed "criminal" by the state. For the state to normalize its conception of justice across a nationalized but still disparate population, it could not allow a Bedouin murderer to get off with only one year imprisonment (following tribal law, which calls for the material compensation of the aggrieved family by the family of the murderer, if not also for a counter vendetta

murder to redeem the initial murder), when a Hadari murderer could receive up to fifteen years of jail if not capital punishment for a similar crime.
But despite the cancellation of all tribal laws, the state preserved certain
vestiges and symbols of tribal culture within it, such as the directorate of
Bedouin police (Mudiriyyat Shurtat al-Badiyah).

Nationalist Tribalism or Tribalist Nationalism: The Debate

Since the 1920s, which saw the last instances of some Bedouin tribes'
disaffection with the Hashemite regime, the Bedouins and the regime have
coexisted peacefully and collaboratively, and they depended on each other
in vital matters of regime-survival as well as Bedouin socioeconomic and
cultural interests. This relationship went beyond using the Bedouins in international ventures to crush the enemies of the British Empire, as happened
in 1941 in Iraq and Syria, but more importantly to crush internal enemies
of both the Empire and the Hashemite regime. Such services were rendered
in the later 1930s when Palestinian guerrillas and their Transjordanian supporters were pursued and crushed by Glubb's Bedouin Desert Patrol. After
independence, and under Glubb's leadership, the same army was to be used
to crush the popular demonstrations of the 1950s, killing tens of citizens in
the process. Moreover, following the expulsion of Glubb and the palace
coup of 1957, the Bedouin regiments in the army continued to be deployed
in the country as executors of the palace-declared martial law. Finally, the
government was to rely heavily on the Bedouins to crush the Palestinian
guerrillas during the 1970 Civil War and the summer of 1971. It is this last
instance that was to shake the foundations of the Hashemite regime, which
had remained stable since 1957 through massive internal repression and
U.S. military and financial support.

This situation caused resentment among the Bedouins themselves, who
felt used by the government when it was in danger and ignored by it when
it felt safe. In fact, those of Bedouin background were not as politically
quiescent as is generally believed. In February 1974, a limited military mu-
tiny occurred in Zarqa' among the Bedouin members of the 40th armored
brigade, an elite force that until recently had been serving on the Syrian
front. The rebellion was triggered by economic duress caused by the increasing cost of living and soaring inflation. The government had recently
increased the wages of its civilian employees to cope with the situation, but
it neglected to do the same for the military. In response to this limited
rebellion, the king himself, who was abroad at the time, returned immedi-

ately to the country and promptly matched the civilian wage increase, thus ending this episode.[67] This mistake was never repeated: "Army salaries were raised several times between 1975 and 1981, with two pay hikes in 1980 alone."[68] Concomitant with Bedouin disaffection with the state, the Hadari population also understood that the government's ability to use the Bedouins as instruments of repression of the rest of society stemmed from their different juridical status in the country that shielded them from the functioning of "modern" society, and as a result they began calling on the government to integrate (normalize) the Bedouins into national life.[69]

This, however, coincided with a contrary trend, namely the increase of the cultural tribalization of society itself. Whereas Jordanians of settled backgrounds saw themselves as belonging to tribes, they did not see themselves as Bedouin. The Circassians and the Chechens, who had fewer cultural similarities to the Bedouins, decided to cash in on tribal affiliations and set up in 1979 a Circassian-Chechen Tribal Council to represent their interests in Jordanian society. This was the second attempt to portray Circassian and Chechen families as "tribes." The last attempt was the establishment in 1969 of a Circassian Tribal Council "mainly due to the political insecurity of the times." The council met only sporadically and then dissolved itself. The new Council was more inclusive, however, and it also included the Chechens.[70]

As for the Bedouin tribes, their anger was not fully placated by the king's explanations following the 1976 cancellation of tribal laws. They continued to simmer until October 1979, when they exploded on the streets of Amman with demonstrations by tribal leaders and former Bedouin army officers against what they claimed were wrongs done them by Prime Minister Mudar Badran's government (but not the monarchy) and its economic policy.[71] The economic duress the Bedouins were complaining about related to inflation and the increasing wage–price disparity. They called for "Jordan for Jordanians," both Bedouin and non-Bedouin, clearly excluding the Palestinians as a foreign body existing within the Jordanian nation and as responsible for their economic duress. It should be borne in mind that these were Jordan's most important economic boom years since independence.[72] This situation escalated in July 1983 into a confrontation between the Badran government and the Bani Hasan tribe in the north of the country. Members of the tribe clashed with security agents who were preventing them from fencing in some tribal land. This confrontation led to the arrest and imprisonment of dozens of Bani Hasan men.[73]

The government's new push for detribalization, launched in 1976, finally spilled over to Jordanian newspapers and threatened to spiral out of control. This was in the context of the March 1984 parliamentary by-elections. The question of tribalism, being the operative criterion by which votes were being solicited, elicited much hostility by political commentators and newspaper columnists.[74] This led the editors of Jordan's largest newspaper *Al-Ra'y* to request and obtain a government-issued order banning the advertising in Jordan's newspapers of all tribal deeds dealing with criminal cases (such deeds would include, for example, money paid to the aggrieved party by the criminal's tribe, in exchange for the tribe of the former to drop its case against the latter). Mahmud al-Kayid (of Jordanian tribal background) condemned tribalist "primitivism" and tribalist challenges to state sovereignty, which give the impression that "we do not live in this century,"[75] and 'Abd al-Latif al-Subayhi expressed his shock "in the face of a childish and ignorant/pre-Islamic [jahili] enthusiasm" leading him to pose the question, "Is this what our society wants at the end of the twentieth century?"[76] This precipitated responses and counter-responses, prominent among which was Ghassan al-Tall's response (al-Tall, of Jordanian settled origins, was a master's degree student at the University of Jordan, writing his thesis on aspects of tribal legal tradition) and Husayn Taha Mahadin's counter-response (Mahadin is a Jordanian of tribal origins). Al-Tall's response was swift in its attack on the anti-tribalists. He insisted that tribalism in Jordan was essential to any sense of nationalism in the country and posed the rhetorical question, "Can Jordanian society afford not to be a tribalist ['asha'iriyyan] society?"[77] Mahadin countered by pointing out al-Tall's confusion between tribalism as "descent" and tribalism as "role." He attacked al-Tall's temporal confusion between the era of tribalism and the era of nationalism, stating that "Ghassan's sociological error is his referring to 'tribalism' as 'national belonging and nationalist pride.' For he borrowed the contemporary concept of nationalism and attached it to an earlier period without realizing the *evolutionary* difference [between] this concept [and tribalism]." Al-Tall's confused and confusing account aside, the fact that nationalism and tribalism coexisted synchronically in modern Jordan seems to have escaped Mahadin's attention, because for him, they do not exist in coeval time at all. Tribalism, rather, existed in an allochronic time, albeit one that inhabits the same national space. The stress on "evolution" is not incidental but, as will become clear, *thematic*. This exposure of al-Tall's temporal confusion led Mahadin to dismiss the former's research as unscientific.[78]

The debate became so vociferous that the upper house of Parliament (Majlis al-A'yan, literally the council of appointees, as members of this chamber are not elected but appointed) began deliberating on how to abolish the remnants of tribal law and practice in the various departments of government. Newspaper columns were written condemning the remaining tribal traditions in the administrative sector of the government and calling in strong terms for eliminating all vestiges of tribalism in the country. Dr. ʿAbdullah al-Khatib, of Palestinian settled origins, in an article in the mass-circulation *Al-Raʾy* titled "We Applaud the Cancellation of Administrative Tribalism," stressed that tribal and administrative thinking are "contradic-tory."[79] However, he lamented the institutionalization of tribalism within the administrative apparatus, stressing that with the increase of education, one would normally expect tribalism to decrease, yet he marveled that, in the case of Jordan, "the situation is reversed: more education means being more ingrained in tribal practices." He further called for the enactment of laws that penalize tribalist thinking as well as nepotism in the administrative apparatus of the government, which he described as an "epidemic" or "*wa-baʾ*." The situation was exacerbated by the senate debate itself and the vote to eliminate all remnants of tribal legal practices that had persisted despite the 1976 cancellation of tribal laws. Former and future Prime Minister but current senator Zayd al-Rifaʿi (of Syrio-Palestinian origins) called on the government to abolish tribal laws "on the ground and not only in theory."[80] Al-Rifaʿi and many others saw these laws as contradicting Jordan's path to evolution (or "tatawwur"[81]) and progress (or "taqaddum"), not to mention the state's "modern laws and legislations." This situation, insisted al-Rifaʿi, had rendered "the gap between the legal, social, and cultural reality in our country and those tribal laws very wide . . . which is what had prompted the government to abolish them." Al-Rifaʿi stressed that there is a difference between tribes forming part of the "flesh" of Jordanian society and "tribalist practices." Whereas "we accord the tribes love and respect, we abhor and denounce [tribalist] practices." Justice minister Ahmad Tarawnah, (of settled tribal Jordanian origin) was more selective. Whereas he denounced "tribal traditions that burden citizens," he supported others that did not. Senator Jumʿah Hammad (of Palestinian Bedouin origin) stressed the difference be-tween tribal laws and tribal traditions denouncing the former and supporting the latter. The senate concluded its debate by passing a resolution to abolish all remaining tribalist practices, with one opposing vote, that of Hayil al-Surrur (of Bedouin Jordanian origins). Al-Surrur, who supported tribal tra-ditions, asserted that he would oppose tribal laws only in the event "an alternative" was devised, since the state's civil laws are not capable of dealing with tribal issues. Marwan Muʿashsher, a Christian Jordanian of settled tribal origins and a columnist in Jordan's English daily *Jordan Times* (who became the country's first ambassador to Israel in 1995), expressed his concern that the government's "implicit support for tribal practices are [sic] abundant in Jordan, and that they are followed not only by bedouins but also by many of urbanite, educated Jordanian families." He saw the "survival" of tribal practices as anomalous in the context of Jordan's recent transformations and compared them to neighboring countries like Saudi Arabia, where, according to him, they did not. He declared, "We have *evolved* from a desert confederacy of tribes to a modern country with a law and a constitution. If tribalism still has a place in the social contest of affairs, it certainly should be denied any such place in our legal conceptualisation of the country. Jordanians cannot be governed by dual, often contradictory laws" (emphasis added). He presented tribal affiliations as opposing national affiliation, and he stressed, "I wish to see people proud because they are Jordanians, not only because of their surnames." This, he felt, "is the major argument against tribalism." His call was a call that all citizens, "even though not born equal, should be treated as though they were, under the law, the one law."[82]

The situation became so heated that King Husayn himself intervened by sending a letter to Prime Minister Ahmad 'Ubaydat, which was published in all the daily newspapers. The king chastised those who denigrate tribal traditions and claimed pride in his own "tribal" heritage—the Hashim tribe—that produced none other than the Prophet Muhammad himself.[83] He added that whatever is being said about "the tribes, the clans, conventions and traditions" reflects on the king and his family as well. The king proceeded to attack the Jordanian press for allowing such attacks on tribalism to take place and threatened to close down newspapers that did not desist from such "irresponsibility."

Jordan's liberal minister of information Layla Sharaf (the Lebanese Druze wife of the late Prime Minister 'Abd al-Hamid Sharaf, who before getting married worked as a television announcer in Lebanon[84]) resigned in protest.[85] She had refused to publish the king's letter in the local press and submitted her resignation instead. The king accepted her resignation on January 28, the same day that his letter appeared in the newspapers. However, before submitting her resignation letter to the Prime Minister Ahmad 'Ubaydat (who also served formerly as head of the Mukhabarat), Sharaf forwarded copies of it to the local and international press.[86] Her letter was never published in Jordan. In it, Sharaf explained her position:

With all my idealism and simplicity, I thought I had the blessing for pursuing an information policy based upon *enlightening* the citizen on all issues that concern him, moving away from daily interference in his right to think and freedom of expression. I belong to the school of Abd al-Hamid Sharaf's [her late husband and a former prime minister] school which respects the Jordanian and Arab mind and believes in the freedom of the press as long as this freedom does not *endanger national security*. I have tried to achieve whatever little we could achieve, and this has had a positive impact on the local press and *its reputation outside*. But after a good initial response, the government has started to show impatience towards even the simplest forms of freedoms and all frank communications with the Prime Minister have disappeared, making it impossible for me to continue in this job [all emphases added].[87]

In light of these developments, Sharaf was to comment later, "We are a nation that has not decided on its identity."[88] It would seem that Sharaf failed to understand that questioning the Jordanian nation's constructed notion of the tribal origins of nationals does constitute an endangerment of "national security." Her valuation of the "enlightening" of citizens as a positive project seems to have missed the other part of nationalism's dyad, "tradition." For as much as "tradition" is traditionalized by nationalism, so is European "enlightened" modernity mythologized as the ultimate liberatory project, the less than democratic results of much of modern European history and political practice—toward not only Europeans but more importantly the rest of the world—notwithstanding. Sharaf, it would seem, had internalized the modernization project uncritically.

The state's initial effort to keep the Bedouins apart from the national body politic (1923 to 1976) and its subsequent attempt to integrate them in it (1976 to the present) have now combined to produce a new strategy. King Husayn's commitment to identifying Jordanian culture as tribal relied on these two strategies to accomplish its goal—namely, to render the country tribalized (or even Bedouinized) through sedentarizing the Bedouins, in that the Bedouins are seen as the carriers of Jordan's true and authentic culture and traditions, while the new tribalization/Bedouinization process of the Bedouin and Hadari populations is based on the state's reconfiguration of what Bedouin tribal culture actually is. Thus, the process of sedentarizing the Bedouins was constituted by the state's process of redefining their culture for them while continuing to identify it as Bedouin, and it set the new culture as the norm throughout society by identifying it as true "Jordanian culture." In this vein, Schirin Fathi observes, "By emphasizing the collectivity of tribes and integrating individual tribal identities into a broad category of tribal heritage—as has been the government's policy—tribalism may serve as a source of shared history and a national symbol."[89]

The government's sedentarization projects continued in the 1970s (after the Civil War) and were integrated in its 1970 to 1973 three-year plan and the 1975 to 1980 five-year plan.[90] Indeed, the process of sedentarization of the Bedouins was part of the process of nationalizing them by the state. Whereas Paul Jureidini and R. D. McLaurin argue that this was done through three separate processes, sedentarization, education, and communication,[91] the latter two are part of the process of sedentarization itself. It is sedentarization that allows access to education as well as to the media (especially television). The "Bedouins' " use of televisions, transistor radios, tape recorders, and more recently video recorders and satellite dishes (as in the Hadari community) makes this all too evident.[92] The fact that the Arabic word for sedentarization is *Tawtin*, literally "settling" or "giving a homeland," certainly helped the Bedouins conceive of Jordan as a w*atan* (homeland) rather than a *dirah* (tribal land). In fact, what transpired was the conflation of *watan* and *dirah* as one and the same. The popular song of the 1970s *Diritna al-Urduniyyah* (Our Jordanian Dirah) is a prime testimony to that conflation. A similar conflation took place between the notion of rab' (tribal members) and sha'b (people), as many "Bedouin" songs of the 1970s and 80s attest.

Law, then, did not only affect the juridical and political status of Bedouins in the country, but in doing so, it also generated other cultural productions consonant with its new definitions. One important cultural area generated by this juridical discourse was music and songs. Song had in fact become one of the central instruments used by the state to Bedouinize Jordanian culture. In the early to mid-1970s, Samirah Tawfiq, an unsuccessful Lebanese singer of Armenian descent, adopted a new genre of "Bedouin" song as her hallmark, marketing herself in Jordan. Her subsequent success and the success of her "Bedouin" genre (many followed in her footsteps) resuscitated her dying career and launched her as the quintessential "Bedouin" singer, not only in Jordan but also across the Arab world. Her ostentatious, gaudy dresses, which were supposedly inspired by Bedouin style, although they resembled nothing that Bedouin women, of any tribe, ever wore, added to her "Bedouin" aura. Her songs, in addition to *Diritna al-Urduniyyah*, included *Urdunn al-Qufiyyah al-Hamra'* ("Jordan of the Red Kufiyyah"), and many more "traditional" songs composed for her by the architects of Jordan's new cultural image. Other songs of the period included adulation to the young king and celebrations of the city of Amman. Amman, to which relatively few Transjordanians trace their origins, had to be centralized in the consciousness of the new Jordanian nationalism. Songs were sung for the king and for Amman not only by Jordanian singers (Salwa al-'As, of Palestinian origin and Jordan's earliest radio singer;[93] Siham al-Safadi, a Jordanian of Palestinian origin; and 'Abduh Musa, a Jordanian of gypsy origin, who played the Rababah and sang in a Bedouin tent (Bayt Sha'r) in full Bedouin regalia and Bedouin ambience), but also by foreign singers, prominent among whom were the Lebanese Fayruz and the Syrio-Egyptian Najat al-Saghirah.

In linking Jordanians to their newly asserted Nabatean origins, Fayruz and her Rahbani company went so far as to produce a very popular Broadway-style musical in the late seventies called *Petra*. *Petra's* narrative mixed history and fiction in telling the story of the Nabatean "anti-imperialist" struggle against Rome, the heroes of which were none other than the king and queen of Petra. The musical included songs about the all-sacrificing king (ostensibly of Petra but with an obvious reference to Jordan's King Husayn), which were met with deafening applause by the audience when the musical was performed in Jordan. *Petra*, in addition to celebrating the history of the Nabatean proto-Jordanians, also celebrated the recently invented national dish of Jordan, *mansaf*. *Mansaf* is said to have been eaten by the proto-Jordanians 2,000 years earlier. The Jordanians and their national symbols, it would seem, have always existed. Today, they and their king and queen are continuing in a living tradition that has survived for millennia. *Petra* continues to be shown on Jordan television periodically. As a metonym for all things Jordanian, the name Petra was adopted by the Jordanian state's official news agency.

Jordanian Culture in an International Frame

The redefining of Bedouin culture in accordance with nation-state criteria and its presentation as Jordan's quintessential living culture became increasingly important not only for domestic consumption but also in the realm of foreign relations. Karl Marx had an interesting insight in this regard. He stressed, "Civil society embraces the whole material intercourse of individuals within a definite stage of the development of productive forces. It embraces the whole commercial and industrial life of a given stage and, insofar, transcends the State and the nation, though on the other hand again, it must assert itself in its foreign relations as nationality, and inwardly organize itself as State."[94] Marx's insight, however, misses the importance of how, in addition to organizing itself as a state internally, civil society also asserts itself as a nationality inwardly as well as in foreign relations, and this is not specific to formerly colonized states but applies equally to colonizing states. The importance of Marx's insight here is in understanding that inwardly, nationality is always enforced and propelled by (although, contra Marx, never limited to) state power—which was the entity he was studying—and that in fact it should be understood as a primarily state project, whereas within the international system, civil society was marked by nationality. Whereas Marx's European historical examples led him to conclude, "The antagonism between town and country begins with the transition from bar-barism to civilization, from tribe to state, from locality to nation,"[95] our case shows how the tribe and the nation-state become mutually dependent on each other for their conceptual coherence as well as their institutional coexistence—be that in juridical or extra-juridical practice. As the Jorda-nian example demonstrates, tribes were legislated in and out of existence by the juridical power of the nation-state and its coercive apparatus. In this, the Jordanian example, *mutatis mutandis*, is not so much different from the colonial invention of tribes in many formerly colonized African countries.[96]

Still, whereas the 1970s was the decade to assert Bedouin culture as the basis for Jordanianness internally, the 1980s, in addition to continuing the same trend, became the decade to assert that identity internationally. This strategy was engineered to achieve multiple goals: defying Israeli claims that "Jordan is Palestine,"[97] distinguishing Jordan as a proud carrier of "ancient" Arab culture within the modern Arab world, and projecting an international marketing image for tourists of a modern country with an old *living* "tradi-tional" culture.

Continuing the British Mandatory policy of marketing the Bedouins for European tourists (see chapter 3), the Jordanian government launched simi-lar campaigns with an important and careful twist. Jordan, a modern country with a modern infrastructure that can accommodate European tourists, can offer the Bedouins as representatives of an ancient and noble but still living culture in their "traditional" surroundings. Tourism campaigns, which were stepped up in the 1970s and continue to the present, have offered the Bed-ouins and Petra as the true representatives of modern Jordan.[98] Whereas Petra is surrounded by an Orientalist mystique (especially for Israelis, who visu-alize Jordan as Petra and King Husayn, who are attached to unnecessary people, places, and cultures of not much significance to an archaeology-devouring Zionist ideology—the interest being in dead cities and a friendly sovereign[99]) of ancient "proto-Arab tribes" from which many *modern* Jordanian nationalists claim descent, the Bedouins of Jordan can transport the tourist into a different time, an ancient time, when Petra's monuments were built, presumably by similar-looking Bedouins. In the new age of mechanical reproducibility, as Walter Benjamin has shown, the authentic and the original no longer hold sway over the copy.[100] "Authentic" Petra, itself reduced to its most astounding architectural structure, namely, Pharaoh's Treasury or *Khaznat Fir'awn* (also called the Temple of Isis), was and is reproduced in Jordanian postage stamps, on Jordanian currency bills, and in tourist posters and tourist pamphlets, as the *image* of Jordan. It, along with other archaeological monuments, came to represent the nation's past tradition. As Benedict Anderson put it, "Monumental archaeology, increasingly linked to tourism, allowed the state to appear as the guardian of a generalized, but also local, Tradition."[101] Petra has indeed become the *logo* representing Jordan nationally and internationally. In addition to Jordan's official news agency, many Jordanian companies of all stripes adopted the name Petra. The use of Petra as a logo for the Jordanian nation-state, however, is not a postindependence nationalist invention but rather a colonial one. It was the British Mandatory authorities who transformed Petra into the national spectacle that its has become today. Postcolonial Jordan was simply continuing a *colonial*, not a national, tradition.[102]

As for the Bedouin, he or she is represented in full regalia as a metonym for Jordan by both the Ministry of Tourism and private tourism offices. Linda Layne reports that such representations offer the Bedouins as "the only people of Jordan."[103] She cites a number of Ministry of Tourism brochures with prominent pictorial representations of the Bedouins and Petra. Whereas there is a tendency to market the Bedouin, or rather her or his simulacrum, as the exotic part of Jordan, Layne exaggerates the representative abilities of the Bedouin as simulacrum. The Jordanian government is quite careful to offer the Bedouin simulacrum as the exotic representative of Jordanian culture insofar as she or he is juxtaposed to modern Jordanians and a modern Jordan. This is done on the ground insofar as Bedouin simulacra are presented at tourist locations such as Petra and Jerash, and in hotels, serving coffee, driving horses and camels, or acting as desert guides.[104] These Bedouin simulacra are offered to visiting tourists side by side with modern Jordanians who act as their multilingual modern guides, hotel managers, and staff, in addition to "real" Jordanians that tourists can see conducting their daily lives in the public places of Amman and other cities. In addition, tourist publications published by the Jordan Information Bureau in Washington,

D.C., which market Jordan to Americans, for example, are careful to show Jordan's modern sector, facilities, industry, streets, and hotels, as well as modern Jordanians of both sexes—scientists, architects, chefs, performers, computer operators, farmers, artists, and so on.[105] The magazine *Jordan* put out by the bureau was also available on all *ALIA, Royal Jordanian Airline* flights worldwide.

And this was not all. Radio and television songs and soap operas with Bedouin motifs jammed Jordan's airwaves after the 1970 Civil War. Although Jordan's first radio station had been established in the West Bank town of Ramallah in 1950, followed by the Amman radio station "Huna 'Amman" and the Jerusalem station, both established in 1959, early attempts to popularize Bedouin songs and motifs had not yielded positive results. Traditional Bedouin music genres such as the different Ahazij—Shruqi, Hjayni, and Hda' (as they are pronounced colloquially)—could not compete with the popular Egyptian, Iraqi, and Lebanese songs of the period, nor could some of their idiomatic expressions and dialect-specific words be understood by townspeople in Jordan, much less outside it. As a result, a new strategy was planned, wherein the music would be redistributed (by Lebanese composers such as Tawfiq al-Basha) and the words and dialects of the songs changed. This strategy proved more successful, albeit in only a limited sense, until the 1970s. By then, traditional Bedouin forms of singing were completely dropped in favor of an invented semi-Westernized musical genre with "understandable" accents and words that the urban population could understand and that could be exported outside to the rest of the Arab world. This new genre was sold to the urban and Bedouin population as *Bedouin* songs and music and was exported abroad accordingly. Moreover, the words of the songs were mostly sung in urban accents with a slight pronunciation variation (the *qaf* sound becoming a *ga* sound) and with the use of a few "Bedouin-dialect" words familiar to urbanites, which give the songs their "authentic Bedouin" flavor.[106] In the late 1950s and early 1960s, the radio station, which was headed at the time by Wasfi al-Tall (who was succeeded by Salah Abu Zayd), sought the help of the folk lyricist Rashid Zayd al-Kilani to rewrite the songs in an urbanese "Bedouin" dialect.[107] In 1964, the government established the first Information Ministry in the country's history, with the Department of Culture and Arts (Dai'rat al-Thaqafah wa al-Funun) set up in 1966 as one of the Ministry's departments. This department undertook the "study" of Jordanian culture and was to commission the writing and publication of many books on Jordanian culture as well as a cultural journal, *Afkar* (Thoughts).[108] In 1972, and in celebration of the country's fiftieth birthday, the department published a book of collected essays titled *Our Culture in Fifty Years*.[109] In 1968, Jordan established its first television station, thus giving not only songs but also soap operas, or *tamthiliyyat* and *musalsalat*, a new, more effective medium.

Soap opera productions such as *Wadha wa Ibn 'Ajlan* written by the Jordanian nationalist Ahmad 'Uwaydi al-'Abbadi, who is himself of Muslim Bedouin origins, and *Nimr al-'Adwan* written by Ruks Za'id al-'Uzayzi, of Jordanian Christian settled tribal origins, and produced for radio and television, were exported to the rest of the Arab world, launching the Jordanian soap opera genre. Such programs advertising Jordan's Bedouin identity were shown throughout the Arab world from Iraq to Morocco. The fact that Transjordanians of settled and Bedouin origins, Christian or Muslim, were active in promoting Jordan's Bedouin image attests to the inclusive project of Bedouinizing all Jordanians as a form of nationalizing them against the Palestinian national threat that was defeated on the battleground during the Civil War of 1970. The regime's military triumph in 1970 was now being buttressed by a peaceful strategy of consolidating Jordanian national identity.

In this sense, Jordan's living cultural past carried to the present by the Bedouins is being observed not only by foreign, mostly European and American, tourists, and by other Arabs, but also by modern Jordanians themselves. Although on the face of it Bedouin and modern Jordanians are living in a synchronic time and in a homologous national space, in reality they are not. The Bedouin is produced as a desert tent-dweller living far away from urban modernity, and as living in a *past* time, a *traditional* time, an *other* time, an *allochronic* time. Her or his geographic location, although nationalized, signifies the past history of the nation, which is contrasted with the urban location of modern Jordanians where the modern nation is always located. The evolutionary implication is that at some point *all those* who are today identified and who identify themselves as Jordanians must have lived like the Bedouins in their evolutionary childhood before they became modern urban adults. As such, the ability of the modern Jordanian and her or his European and Euro-American counterpart to *observe* the Bedouins and live in their time can take place "only if he outlives them, i.e., if he moves *through* the Time he may have shared with them" onto a level on which she or he finds modernity.[110] It is important to stress the Western colonial epistemology that the modern Jordanian is said to share with her or his European counterpart. As Johannes Fabian observes, "A discourse employing terms such as primitive, savage (but also tribal, traditional, Third World, or whatever euphemism is current) does not think, or observe, or critically study, the 'primitive'; it thinks, observes, studies *in terms* of the primitive. *Primitive* being essentially a temporal concept, is a category, not an object, of Western thought."[111] This use of time, as Fabian asserts, has the explicit purpose of distancing those who are observed from the time of the observer, a denial of coeval time.[112] In line with this epistemology, the modern Jordanian views her- or himself and presents that self to Europeans as constituted through a repudiation of tradition, a repudiation of the Bedouin self that is said to constitute her or his origin, while simultaneously reclaiming that tradition and that self as a *living* past! This double operation is the process through which national identification occurs in the context of modern Jordan. Modernity sublates tradition for the majority of Jordanians (wherein tradition is incorporated within and not replaced by modernity) in such a way that the traditional component can be projected onto the living Bedouin, who gives that projection physical manifestation and materiality. Europeans and modern Jordanians can appreciate the noble and primitive Bedouin as the proto-Jordanian (the builder of Petra?) and compare her or him to the modern Jordanian—the temporal distance between the two can be the measure of how much civilization modern Jordanians have achieved over their *living* ancestors. The fact that most Jordanians of Bedouin lineage have been settled by the state and now live in urban and rural centers, no longer inhabiting the nonurban "desert," is immaterial to this type of mythic representation, let alone the fact that much of what passes for Bedouin tradition is invented by the state.

Those Bedouins who still live in the desert and have a partial nomadic lifestyle can be and are packaged as tourist attractions. Those who stood in the way of "evolution," "progress," and "modernity," like the Bidul, of Petra were expropriated, resettled, and/or co-opted for modern tourist projects. The story of the Bidul is interesting in this context because of the nation-state's contradictory project of being modern-traditional, nomadic-settled, and Bedouin-Hadari.

It is unclear how long the Bidul Bedouins have lived in the Petra area. Whereas some accounts claim that they are newcomers to the area from the Sinai, documentary evidence mentions them as living in Petra for at least the last century. Their oral history asserts that Muslim Bedouins pursued their ancestors to Petra, where they took refuge. They were, however, converted to Islam—hence their name as the "exchangers" of religion from *baddala*, as in "to exchange." Others assert that the etymology of the name Bidul goes to their ancestor Badl, one of the sons of the Nabatean king Nabt, hence Bidul meaning the people of Badl. Since the mid-1960s, the government has tried to dislodge them from Petra, forcing them to farm outside the city within which they had farmed before. This was done after a new law was enacted with the recommendation of the Department of Antiquities (set up by the British during the Mandate) declaring Petra and other national monuments and ruins as national parks.

The Bidul, who used to live in the caves of Petra, had coexisted for the past century with visiting tourists, who saw them as part of the attraction, a sort of "living museum." More recently, the neighboring settled tribe of Layathnah, whose members reside in the neighboring town of Wadi Musa, has come to be much more integrated in Petra's tourist economy through its ownership of most of the horses used by tourists to reach Petra's ruins.[113] The Bidul were newcomers to the horse-operating ventures, although now they operate and own a large number of them. Many worked as tourist guides, rented out their caves, and sold archeological objects found in the caves, such as shards of Nabatean pots. They were even contracted by the Forum Petra Hotel to provide a meal of *mansaf* to tourists in Petra's al-Dayr — a Nabatean tomb once used by Byzantine monks as a monastery—while their donkeys carry the wine and beer to the site.[114] In the early seventies, the government's campaign to evict the Bidul from Petra was met with fierce and armed resistance. Finally, in the early 1980s the government built a settlement for them near Petra, giving them until 1985 to move or face forceful eviction.[115] By 1985, the government's decision had forced their relocation to new homes. The Bidul, with no choice but to comply, resisted the government by claiming Petra as theirs and the Nabateans as their direct ancestors, but to no avail.[116] In doing that, they were differentiating themselves from modern Jordanian nationalists who claim Petra and the Nabateans for all Transjordanians. Currently and following their forced settlement, the Bidul are increasingly integrating within the national fold through education and the media. Some of their members have specialized in hotel management at Amman colleges in the hope that they can manage the Petra tourist economy, whose big capital investors are from outside Petra, and increasingly from outside Jordan altogether. The story of the Bidul demonstrates the Jordanian state's continuing juridical and coercive abilities to define and redefine Jordan's national as well as Bedouin identities.

Women Between the Public and Private Spheres

Whereas the Personal Status Law takes care of women as unequal inhabitants of the domestic sphere in their roles as wives, mothers, caretakers, housekeepers, and divorcees, regulating such activities through a certain reading of religious tradition, the rest of the law controls women's integration into public life, the life of civil society—that of national citizenship. The duality of women's positions in the law is paralleled by that of men's. Men also have a dual status, one as part of civil society wherein they are citizen-nationals who are nominally equal to other citizen-nationals, and the other as heads of households in the private sphere with unequal privileges and rights that are juridically accorded. The discrepancy here between men's and women's standings in the private and public spheres is not based on women's sudden entry into the public sphere as workers, voters, nationals, citizens, and so forth, as women were always part of the extra-home economy, especially in agriculture but also in trade and property ownership, long before the advent of modern nationalism to the Middle East. What is new since the Ottoman Tanzimat is the Western assignment of modernity to the realm of "civil society" and tradition to the "private sphere." Indeed, the invention of this dichotomy, as Jürgen Habermas has shown,[117] is predicated on these valorizations assigned to them. For, after all, the private and the public, the industrial city and the rural village, are modern conceptions dividing social space. In the Arab world, the sociospatial division of *Hadar* and *Badiyah* (settled and Bedouin populations) has existed for centuries; however, their new significations of modern versus traditional resulted from their integration into the nation-state's modern epistemology of space. What I demonstrate in the rest of this chapter, however, is that the division of this social space is commensurate with, even constituted by, a temporal schema without which these divisions lose much of their functional signification and importance in the formation of modern citizen-nationals.

The transformation of Shari'ah into coded law is a modern phenomenon. It was the Ottoman Tanzimat that ushered in the transformation of Shari'ah, originally "a general term designating good order," from "a repertoire of precedents, cases and general principles, along with a body of well-developed hermeneutical and paralogical techniques" into a modern code.[118] It was also the Ottoman Tanzimat that classified Shari'ah into different sections, previously unknown, such as "civil," "criminal," "commercial," and "family," which itself is considered a subsection of "civil." The first such transformation was the Ottoman civil code, better known as the *Majalla*, enacted in the 1870s as the first-ever codification of Shari'ah. As for what came to be known as family matters, the Ottomans enacted the Law of Family Rights in 1917, a law that remained on the books in Jordan until 1947 (Turkey replaced the law in 1927 by adopting and adapting the "secular" Swiss code in its place). In the intervening years, Egyptian jurists became innovative in the area of what came to be family law. In 1893, Muhammad Qadri Pasha, Egyptian justice minister at the time, published his *The Shari'ah Provisions on Personal Status*, a book containing 646 articles on marriage, divorce, inheritance, gifts, and so forth. He was the first to coin the term *personal status* as a reference to family matters.[119] More transformations of "personal status" followed suit in the 1920s. The eminent Egyptian jurist 'Abd al-Razzaq Ahmad al-Sanhuri became the architect of the civil code of a number of Arab countries and made contributions to the debate on personal status laws, seeking to make them applicable to Muslims and non-Muslims alike.[120] Whereas the Ottomans relied on a certain reading and privileging of the Hanafi school of Shari'ah interpretation, Sanhuri called for more eclecticism. These transformations of Shari'ah coincided with the rise of the nation-state in Turkey as well as in the formerly Ottoman provinces. Codifying the Shari'ah therefore aimed at facilitating the governance of the modern nation-state — the modality through which "we" were to become modern while remaining traditional at the same time. Sanhuri was explicit on this matter: "Our law should be strengthened to the greatest extent possible from the Shari'a sources. We should work to have our law agree with our old legal traditions rectified by viewing it not as a static creation but a growing and developing thing, connecting our country's [Egypt's] present with its past. That is the historical aspect."[121]

Laws were therefore devised to address the juridical status of women in a way that accorded with this traditionalized vision of "our old legal traditions." This of course is not unique to the Middle East or Islam but to nationalism in the colonial world more generally. In charting the histories of nationalist and feminist movements in the Third World, Kumari Jayawardena[122] shows how, upon visiting western European countries at the turn of the century, Asian nationalist leaders "were struck by the openness of a society that permitted some men and women to take part in easy social intercourse. . . . Faced with societies that were sufficiently developed and powerful to subjugate them, and with the need to modernize their own societies, many reformers of Asia seized on the apparent freedom of women in Western societies as the key to the advancement of the West."[123] Jayawardena identifies the objectives of the reformers as twofold: "to establish in their countries a system of stable, monogamous nuclear families with educated and employable women such as was associated with capitalist development and bourgeois ideology; and yet to ensure that women would retain a position of traditional subordination within the family."[124] Such figures in the Arab world include Qasim Amin and Muhammad Abduh, who, since the latter half of the nineteenth century, saw the status of women in the Arab world as one of the main reasons why the Arabs could no longer "keep up" with Europe. They devised new schemes to "modernize" Arab women without compromising "tradition." What this project in fact intended was the new invention of Arab women (following European nationalist examples) as custodians of tradition and managers of the nation's moral life and that of its future generations. Therefore, while women's inferior status was to be maintained in the home and reinscribed as a tradition-inspired status, women, as custodians of tradition and as managers of the nation's young generations, had to be equipped with modern education (literacy, scientific hygiene, home economy, scientific child-rearing, nutrition) to protect the national heritage (al-Turath). This call for a new kind of existence, that of national citizenship, was predicated on the cultivation of women and men, their assumed and enforced asymmetry in duties and rights notwithstanding, in preparation for building the future of the nation. To be effective, these new criteria had to be codified into law.

I should emphasize that Sanhuri was the architect of the civil code not only of Egypt, but of Iraq, Syria, and Libya, and he was the architect of the commercial code of Kuwait. Jordan's Family Law of 1947 and of 1951[125] as well as the 1976 Personal Status Law[126] were all inspired not only by the Ottoman reading of the Hanafi tradition manifest in the 1917 Ottoman Law of Family Rights but also by Sanhuri's contribution to the Egyptian code and later the Syrian and Iraqi codes—all three influenced Jordan's laws substantially.

Although the first Jordanian family law was not issued until 1947, the need to assert the government's and Amir 'Abdullah's view of what Shari'ah was, was in evidence since the inception of the state. The amir's desire to impose a certain modern juridical view of gender relations that was in line with his reading of Shari'ah led 'Abdullah to issue a decree soon after Transjordan became a state, prohibiting the "convention of kidnapping girls," a kind of elopement then prevailing among the Circassian "immigrant" communities as part of marriage rituals: "The obeyed decree [Al-Iradah al-Muta'ah] has been issued prohibiting the convention of kidnapping girls from their family homes that is practiced by some Circassian immigrants at the time of the marriage contract and that from now on the basis of the esteemed Islamic Shari'ah will be followed in marriage contracts."[127] This was, of course, part of the normalization of the population as one that adheres to the same conventions, as this is crucial for any project of nationalizing a people.

In the first Jordanian family law,[128] enacted after independence in 1947, replaced with a similar law in 1951, and updated in 1976, there is a discrepancy between the rights and duties of men and women not only toward the state but also toward each other as subjects of the state. Whereas these laws are clearly modeled on the Ottoman Law of Family Rights of 1917 even in its details, what J. N. D. Anderson notes about the 1951 law applies to all three: "it also incorporates a number of the more drastic Egyptian reforms of 1920 and 1929, together with a few amendments and even innovations of its own, while it also includes a few topics which fall outside the scope of either the Ottoman or Egyptian legislation."[129] In the section on marriage (al-Zawaj), or proposal of marriage (al-Khutbah), most of the injunctions designate the limitations of men's disproportionate rights in marriage and an elucidation of women's rights and duties toward their husbands. Whereas the marriage contract *ipso facto* confers on the husband numerous rights (and duties), women's rights will have to be spelled out in the marriage contract as terms and conditions that the husband would agree to (article 19)—a woman's right to stipulate that her husband shall not compel her to leave the town or city where the marriage contract was signed, that she have the right to divorce herself from him, and that he not take another wife beside her, all three rights are not automatically conferred on a wife upon marriage. If anything, signing a marriage contract without these stipulations suspends a woman's constitutional right of voluntary residency in the town or city where she had signed the contract and waives her right to end a marriage whose conclusion in the first place was carried out with her approval and agreement. In short, in signing a marriage contract without these listed protective clauses, a woman ceases to be a full citizen and is ushered into a different realm of juridical existence. Therefore, the condition of nominally equal citizenship applies to all men and all unmarried women who have nominally similar rights and duties in relation to the state. In this, marriage seems to be not only a social liaison sanctioned, witnessed, and supervised by the state, but also a contract that infringes on the citizenship of women, bifurcating their juridical status into, on the one hand, limited juridical citizenship within the public sphere and, on the other, unequal juridical residency in the private sphere or the home. The discourse that the state appeals to in order to put forth this gendered project of citizenship is the discourse of nationalism, especially that which relates to "national traditions and conventions." The law itself is self-conscious of this discrepancy in rights and duties, and it attempts to make available to women certain legal avenues to equalize their status through the stipulations of some conditions in the marriage contract, which ameliorate but do not do away with this inequality. This avenue has been made available to women since the 1917 Ottoman Law of Family Rights (article 38), and was present in all three Jordanian laws (article 19 of the 1947 Temporary Law of Family Rights, article 21 of the 1951 Law of Family Rights, and article 19 of the 1976 Personal Status Law).

One of the more important areas where the public and the private spheres intersect in the Family Rights Law and the Personal Status Law is a married woman's right to work outside the marital home. Whereas the 1947 and the 1951 laws stipulate a husband's right to no longer support his wife financially should she move out of the marital home or, in such cases when she owns the marital home, she prevents her husband from entering it,[130] the 1976 Personal Status Law expands these conditions to include a married woman leaving the marital home to seek wage labor without her husband's permission or approval.[131] In the draft law of the early 1980s, which never came into effect, it was stated that a husband's approval of his wife's working outside the home can be "implicit or explicit even if it is not registered in the marriage contract," thus giving women more freedom in pursuing wage labor.[132] It should be noted that a woman can always stipulate that she will work after marriage as a condition of the marriage contract at the time of signing, in which case her husband's future disapproval will have no legal standing. Whereas the 1976 law asserted a husband's right to withhold financial support of his working wife if she worked outside the home without his consent, thus limiting women's right to work in a time of relative national economic prosperity, the draft law of the early 1980s relaxed that stipulation in response to the deteriorating economy and the need for a second income.[133] In addition, by the 1980s many Jordanian women (excluding peasant women who had been working and continued to work in agriculture, in most cases without financial remuneration) had obtained high university degrees and began to enter the wage labor market in relatively large numbers.[134] This situation, wherein husbands' rights can infringe on the rights of wives in the public sphere as a result of a mutually signed contract regulating rights in the private sphere, demonstrates the porous nature of these spheres, showing them to be less than discrete and separate entities. As a consequence of this situation, there emerges a juridical discrepancy. On the one hand, the Jordanian constitution of 1952 stipulates that "work is the right of all citizens," on the other hand, the Personal Status Law grants men the juridical right to negate a married woman's constitutional right to work.[135]

Another example is the Passport Law, which is commensurate with the Personal Status Law as far as married women are concerned. It stipulates that a passport is granted to a wife and to underage children after the husband's approval.[136] This is in contradiction to the constitution, wherein article 9-2 states that "it is not permitted to prevent a Jordanian from living in a particular area nor can he be forced to reside in a particular area except in situations specified by the law." This infringement of public rights by private rights is indeed the stuff of which the status of all married men and women in Jordan is made. The state's ability to refashion the Personal Status Law in such a way as to make it commensurate with the constitution and other areas of law, including the civil code and labor laws, is indeed great. How far it will go in that direction in the near future remains, however, uncertain. The last attempt that was made was a 1990 new draft law sponsored by then Crown-Prince Hasan.[137] However, this draft law was also shelved in favor of a newer draft law that is yet to be presented to Parliament.

This dissonance between the rights of married men and women is characteristic not only of the private sphere and its ability to infringe on the public but also of the inherent discriminatory laws of the public sphere as well.[138] Whether in nationality laws, as we have seen in chapter 1, or in labor laws,[139] the law of retirement, the law of social security, penal laws,[140] and so on, women are systematically treated differently from men, being accorded fewer rights and privileges. Examples include the light sentences given to men (but not to women) who commit "honor" murders (or murders of "passion") to protect their honor when it was sullied by an errant woman relative (wife, daughter, sister, niece, aunt, cousin).[141] This penal law (Qanun al-'Uqubat) is quite similar to, and is in fact inspired by, the Napoleonic Code. Many such laws are still on the books in a number of European countries and in a number of states in the United States. Recent attempts made by Jordan's King 'Abdullah II to remove article 340 (which grants men committing crimes of honor extenuating circumstances reducing their sentences) from the penal code have led to confrontations with Islamists and other conservative members of Parliament. The government and women's groups have been able to mobilize a large popular following for the removal of the article with massive demonstrations led by members of the royal family. The article, as of this writing, remains on the books.[142]

Countries who adhere to these modernized versions of family laws and personal status laws inspired by the Shari'ah are not unique in their according women a dual status in the law. This is indeed characteristic of non-Muslim Western countries also. In *The Sexual Contract*,[143] Carole Pateman advances a new way of conceptualizing what contract theorists (Locke, Rousseau, Hobbes, et al.) call the original foundational social contract of Western societies. She shows that the social contract has another hidden part to it that existed before the setting of the social contract. Pateman calls this hidden part the *sexual contract*. It is in the precontractarian domain that the axioms of the sexual contract exist, and it is through the social contract that they are concealed under the universal category of the individual. Pateman argues that "women do not appear anywhere as parties to the original contract; that contract is one between men."[144] Unlike Shari'ah, in its codified and precodified forms, which never questioned women's rights to own property, Pateman asserts that, within the Western legal tradition, "classic theorists construct a patriarchal account of masculinity and femininity, of what it is to be men and women. Only masculine beings are endowed with the attributes and capacities necessary to enter into contracts, the most important of which is ownership of property in the person; only men, that is to say, are 'individuals.' "[145] For Pateman, sexual difference is the difference between freedom and subjection. Citing Rousseau, Pateman states that "the social contract enables individuals voluntarily to subject themselves to the state and civil law; freedom becomes obedience and, in exchange, protection is provided. On this reading, the actual contracts of everyday life also mirror the original contract, but now they involve an exchange of obedience for protection; they create what I shall call civil mastery and civil subordination."[146] Pateman proceeds to say that women in Western societies "are incorporated into a sphere that both is and is not in civil society. The private sphere is part of civil society but is separated from the 'civil' sphere. The antinomy private/public is another expression of natural/civil and women/men. The private, womanly sphere (natural) and the public, masculine sphere (civil) are opposed but gain their meaning from each other, and the meaning of civil freedom of public life is thrown into relief when counterposed to the natural subjection that characterizes the private realm . . . what it means to be an 'individual,' a maker of contracts and civilly free, is revealed by the subjection of women within the private sphere."[147]

According to Pateman, only men who create political life can take part in the original contract, "yet the political fiction speaks to women, too, through the language of the 'individual.' "[148] Pateman concludes that if women were merely excluded from civil life, like slaves, or wives when coverture held sway, the character of the problem would have been self-evident; "But women have been incorporated into a civil order in which their freedom is apparently guaranteed, a guarantee renewed with each retelling of the story of the social contract in the language of the 'individual.'"[149] Note how much of what Pateman describes in European countries and the United States has been adopted by Muslim countries in the process of modernizing Shari'ah, not to mention the wholesale importation of Western laws in many areas of law—commercial, labor, criminal, civil, penal, and so forth. In light of the Western precedent, it is important to stress that in the Jordanian 1952 constitution, no discrimination is made between men and women, as following article 6 "all Jordanians are equal before the law with no discrimination among them in rights or duties even if they differed in race, language or religion." Moreover, article 43 of the Civil Law states unequivocally that "every person who reached full majority age and enjoys all his mental capabilities and who is not imprisoned is fully eligible to exercise his civil rights," where full majority age is considered to be eighteen solar years. More recently, the Jordanian National Charter concluded by the state and civil society in 1991 (it was in fact signed by over 2,000 Jordanians spanning the social and political spectrum in civil society, and by representatives of the state) and ushering in Jordan's new and exceedingly limited liberalization experiment stipulated in article 8, "Jordanians, men and women, are equal before the law, with no discrimination among them in rights and duties even if they differ in race, language, or religion. They shall exercise their constitutional rights and abide by the supreme interest of the homeland, and the ethics of national action in such a way as to guarantee the guidance of Jordanian society's energies, to release its material and spiritual capabilities, for the purpose of achieving its goals of unity, progress, and the building of the future."[150] Note that the charter did not use the language of the ungendered individual to describe the equality of all Jordanians, as do the constitution and most laws, but for the first time in Jordan's history, it specified both genders as equal before the law. This is indeed a more explicit commitment on the part of the state and civil society. This new commitment to gender equality in the charter was brought about by the participation of four women who were part of the committee that wrote it.[151] However, the charter is not a juridical document but one that articulates the new commitments on the part of the popular discourse of national citizenship whose history and transformation will be discussed in later chapters.

Returning to the juridical as the site of negotiating gender relations in relation to the national and state projects, we find that this situation is equally prevalent in Western countries at the level that constitutes the juridical. In her book, *Toward a Feminist Theory of the State*,[152] Catharine MacKinnon asserts that the state (in the West) is "male" jurisprudentially, meaning that it adopts the standpoint of male power on the relation between law and society. This stance is especially vivid in constitutional adjudication, though legitimate to the degree it is neutral on the policy content of legislation. The foundation for its neutrality is the pervasive assumption that conditions that pertain among men on the basis of gender apply to women as well—that is, the assumption that sex inequality does not really exist in society. The [U.S.] Constitution . . . with its interpretations assumes that society, absent government intervention, is free and equal; that its laws, in general, reflect that; and that government need and should right only what government has previously wronged. This posture is structural to a constitution of abstinence: for example, "Congress shall make no law abridging the freedom of . . . speech." Those who have freedoms like equality, liberty, privacy, and speech socially keep them legally, free of governmental intrusion. No one who does not already have them socially is granted them legally.[153]

What happened in the West in the transformation from medieval to liberal law is that gender as a status category "was simply assumed out of legal existence, suppressed into a presumptively pre-constitutional social order through a constitutional structure designed not to reach it." MacKinnon asserts that the "Weberian monopoly on the means of legitimate coercion, thought to distinguish the state as an entity, actually describes the power of men over women in the home, in the bedroom, on the job, in the street, throughout social life. It is difficult, actually, to find a place it does not circumscribe and describe."[154] Mackinnon concludes that the "rule of law and the rule of men are one thing, indivisible, at once official and unofficial—officially circumscribed, unofficially not. State power, embodied in law, exists throughout society as male power at the same time as the power of men over women throughout society is organized as the power of the state."[155] Our discussion of Jordanian laws bears out much of what Mackinnon describes in her Western examples.

Women in Public

The prevailing discourse in Jordanian government circles for the first two decades of the state is interesting to note. The Amir 'Abdullah was quite conservative on gender issues. He believed that his reading of Shari'ah and his ideas about gender were consistent. In the first manifesto that he issued to the Syrian people (i.e., the people of greater Syria) upon his arrival in November 1920 in Ma'an, then the northernmost city of the Hijaz, en route to Amman to begin the liberation of Syria from the French, he states, "The colonialist has come to you to rob you of the Three Graces: faith, freedom, and masculinity [al-dhukuriyyah]. He came to enslave you so that you will no longer be free, the colonialist has come to you to take away from you your weapons so that you will no longer be males [dhukur], he came to frighten you with his strength and make you forget that God is lying in ambush for him [bil-mirsad] so that you will not be faithful."[156] For 'Abdullah, as it is for most male anticolonial nationalists, masculinity is a contingent identity: a man being colonized is tantamount to being raped, which is tantamount to being castrated, an act that transforms the masculine into the feminine, and men into women. In this discourse, being raped and being a woman lead to a condition of unfreedom. Freedom, therefore, is the condition of a stable masculinity and femininity. 'Abdullah's interest, however, was not only the stability of gender identities, but also questions of public morality attendant to them. To safeguard public morality, a law against prostitution was issued in the country as early as 1927.[157]

Whereas most Jordanian women did not work in the wage labor market in the first few years after the state was formed, with the expansion of education, especially for girls, many women entered the wage labor market as teachers and school administrators in girls' schools. This situation raised much concern about the status of women in the public sphere, not by the population as much as by the amir himself and some clerics in the country. In late 1939, the amir became very concerned about the country's "public traditions and ethics" as reported by the Jordanian press.[158] More articles followed explaining the "un-Islamic" nature of sufur (revealing the face or unveiling) and citing a recent declaration by an Egyptian cleric to that effect.[159] The amir, responding to his and others' rising concerns about women's appearance in public places, sent an official letter to his government calling attention to the appearance of Muslim women as relates to their tabarruj (self-adornment and makeup).[160] In his letter, 'Abdullah ordered the education minister to launch an inspection campaign in all girls schools inspecting the women teachers and ascertaining that they were competent to uphold their "religious and ethical responsibility."[161] Finally, 'Abdullah issued a royal decree prohibiting adornment and makeup on women. In his decree, 'Abdullah cited several verses from the Qur'an to back him up. The prime minister proceeded by sending a letter to the supreme judge of the country (Qadi al-Qudah) urging him to follow the amir's decree by issuing a manifesto containing instructions to Muslim women on their public appearance, especially teachers, as the amir showed much concern about them and what they were teaching Muslim Jordanian girls.[162] But even that was not enough. The amir insisted on his "desire" that Muslim women don the *mula'ah* (a black covering that wraps a woman's body but not her face) outside their homes. He wrote a letter to the prime minister expressing his outrage at what he witnessed a few days earlier—women "belonging" to major families in the country unveiled and adorned in public places, which contravenes religion and "human honor." He asked that a law be issued forcing all Muslim women in the country to wear *al-mula'ah* in public in accordance with "religion." In addition, he considered all women who are unveiled and adorned in public to be apostates. 'Abdullah also insisted in his letter that men's walking in public places without head coverings ("hasr al-Ra's") is "against the conventional virtues inherited by the nation [*al-ummah*]."[163] Note how 'Abdullah's understanding of religion and religious tradition leads him to impose the *mula'ah* on Jordanian Muslim women, a dress gear that was never part of their religious tradition or any other tradition. The *mula'ah*, which was usually worn by urban middle-class women in the Arabian Peninsula, Iraq, Egypt, and some Syrian cities, was not known in most Transjordanian villages nor in its Badiyah. As Jordan did not have major urban centers and most of its population centers were rural towns whose population had its own way of dressing, 'Abdullah's wishes were in fact to assimilate Jordanian Muslim women into another tradition—his. While women were chastised for not being proper custodians of national religious traditions, men, as an aside, were reminded that head covering is part of the national inheritance of "conventional virtues." No decrees, however, were ever issued to force men to cover their heads.

'Abdullah's shock at unveiled women was experienced much earlier than 1939. On one of his first trips outside of the Arabian Peninsula as a child, accompanying his father who had been exiled to Istanbul (*al-Asitanah*), the family had a stop-over in Egypt, where 'Abdullah marveled at seeing Egyptian Christian women unveiled.[164] As a result of all these decrees and official letters, the question of the *Hijab* (the Islamist dress code for women) began to be debated in the press.[165] Advice to women teachers on how to treat their girl students was also published.[166] Without any sense of irony about controlling women's presence in the public sphere, an article was published in *Al-Jazirah* chastising the "Jordanian girl" for doing nothing but "copying" love letters from books and "reading silly novels about love" when other Arab women were "voraciously reading" ["yaltahimna al-safahat"] good books and partaking in their countries' "renaissance" ["nahdah"]. The author calls on women to join the struggle of life. For it is with the "arms of both groups [young men and women] that the nation shall build its glorious monument [sarh]."[167] Other articles were directed at men. One such article entitled "Do You Want to Become a Man? Elements That Are Needed to Succeed in Life" listed the prerequisites for manhood.[168] Notable in this period is a certain anxiety about public manifestations of gendered appearance and behavior. Not only should such appearance and behavior be regulated by the state according to its nationalist criteria, but also, as with the attention paid to schools and schoolgirls, education and the media should cultivate this newly invented "national tradition." None of the amir's edicts or decrees about women veiling or not adorning themselves were ever published in the *Official Gazette*, which means that they never acquired the force of law, and it is unclear why this was so. Jordanian women continued to appear in public unveiled and adorned, the amir's shock and horror notwithstanding.

'Abdullah's conservative interpretation of Islam and his commitment to it were in evidence elsewhere. His government licensed the Muslim Brethren (al-Ikhwan al-Muslimun) in January 1945 as the first nongovernmental political group allowed legal existence in the country.[169] Soon after, in February 1945, in an interview that he gave to the editor of *Al-Jazirah*, the amir insisted that although there exists a debate in the Islamic world as to whether Muslim women should remain in the home or enter public life, he supported the former opinion, as women cannot mix with men unrelated to them and should not adorn themselves in public. Although they can leave their homes to run their errands, they should do so veiled.[170] In line with this type of thinking, a professor of Islamic studies and an 'Abdullah protégé, Shaykh al-Mukhtar Ahmad Mahmud al-Shanqiti, wrote a poem chastising and ridiculing the adorned and unveiled woman.[171] The importance of 'Abdullah's stance on women was demonstrated by its use (by him and by others) as the *mark* of his public religiosity. In fact, his stance on women continues to be cited to this day by Islamists and conservatives as the primary evidence of his religiosity.[172]

'Abdullah, however, seems to have wavered slightly in his opinion of women by November 1948. In a conversation with the Mufti of Jerusalem, he makes fun of the latter. John Bagot Glubb reports the story:

> "Is it wrong to look at a pretty woman?" next enquired His Majesty with assumed innocence.

The learned shaikhs pulled long faces, and replied solemnly: "A sin, Your Majesty, a sin."

The King gave me a sidelong glance with a wicked twinkle. "I don't see how you get that," said His Majesty. "The Holy Quran says—'if you see a woman, avert your gaze!' Now, obviously you cannot avert your gaze unless you have already begun looking!" . . .

The good shaikhs were somewhat taken aback by these views. The Mufti, however, who was not to be easily defeated, remarked that we must insist that all women be veiled, and then no problem of looking at them would arise, because they would be completely invisible. . . .

"That's all very well," answered His Majesty, winking at the company, "but nowadays, far from veiling, they go and bathe in the sea. What are we going to do about that, O Mufti?" . . .

But even the Mufti was a man. "Is that so?" he replied, also winking at the company. "What a pity I am no longer a young man!"[173]

In 1951, 'Abdullah reiterated his views of Muslim women, insisting that they should not mix with men in public spaces, and that they certainly are not allowed by religion to swim in the sea with men ("al-nuzul ila al-sahil ma' al-rijal")—a theme over which he seems to have obsessed. He added that it was against "Arab valor" ("al-muru'ah al-'Arabiyyah") for "a woman to disrobe even in front of her husband" ("an tatrah al-mar'ah dir'aha hatta 'inda zawjiha").[174] The latter view, which is more reminiscent of Saint Paul's injunctions about women, is quite foreign to Islam but not to 'Abdullah's understanding of it. These views were expressed only two weeks after 'Abdullah's son Prince Nayif (at the time, the designated successor) had signed the 1951 Family Rights Law.[175]

Women and Politics

In light of 'Abdullah's annexation of central Palestine and the arrival of hundreds of thousands of Palestinian refugees who had been recently expelled by the Zionist forces, the political situation changed significantly in the country. Palestinians brought with them half a century of experience in political organization and activism. Palestinian women, who had had political organizations since the early 1920s and who had participated in the Palestinian revolt in the 1930s, were to introduce a new genre of politics to the Jordanian political arena. Although the palace had set up a number of women's organizations in the mid-forties, such organizations remained limited in membership to the upper classes and limited in goals and vision. The first organization had been set up on December 25, 1944, and was called Jam'iyyat al-Tadamun al-Nisa'i al-Ijtima'iyyah (the Social Society of Women's Solidarity). It was headed by 'Abdullah's wife, Princess Misbah (the mother of Talal), and its goals were "caring for children and housing them, and taking care of other social matters with the aim of improving the [economic] level of poor people and improving their situations."[176] Another organization, Jam'iyyat al-Ittihad al-Nisa'i al-Urduni (the Society of the Jordanian Women's Union), was also headed by the princess. This society's goals were philanthropy, improving the social conditions of Jordanian women, improving women's educational level, and spreading "the health basis" of caring for children as well as offering financial assistance to poor women. This society, like the social society, was based in Amman and did not have other branches. It had 80 to 100 members.[177] The bourgeois composition of both groups was a reflection of the newly emergent merchant class, whose enrichment during World War II increased its say in politics and its influence over the palace. In fact, much of the attention to the appearance of working and bourgeois women in the public sphere in this period had resulted from the increasing fortunes of the Jordanian merchant class, leading to some tension between 'Abdullah and other traditionalizers on the one hand and a more modernizing merchant class on the other. Most merchants were of Syrian origins with some of Palestinian origins and still fewer native Transjordanians.[178]

In 1949, the two women's societies merged, forming the Hashemite Society of Jordanian Women, which was soon dissolved.[179] In light of the Arab-Israeli war of 1948 and the arrival of refugees, the Jordanian Red Crescent Society was founded by Palestinian women refugees who cooperated with the Hashemite Society of Jordanian Women to provide services to the refugees.[180] In 1951, the Law of the Ministry of Social Affairs was issued, founding the first such ministry in the country. The purpose of the ministry was to organize and supervise all voluntary activity, societies, and organizations in the country. Between 1951 and 1979, there were over 340 societies in the country (excluding the West Bank) engaging in a number of activities, and they were represented by the General Union of Philanthropic Societies. Of these, only twenty-two societies were women's societies, whose services included day care centers, nutrition centers, an orphanage, services to senior citizens, vocational training, literacy campaigns, a school for the mentally disabled, and programs offering financial assistance to poor families and to families of soldiers.[181] Note that these services are an extension of services rendered by women in the domestic "private" sphere. Therefore, women's presence in the public sphere is predicated on their performing domestic "private sphere" services. Thus, women's private status can be rendered public, while their presence in the public sphere is privatized, in that their domesticity can be expanded to engulf the public sphere as can their private status, which remains what it is in all spheres—that is, private. In addition to these societies, a number of women's clubs were founded that mostly cater to middle- and upper-class women. Foremost among them is the Club of Business and Professional Women (Nadi Sahibat al-A'mal wa al-Mihan), which was founded in 1984 and includes a legal office offering advice to women as well as a research center for women's studies.[182] It also began publishing a newsletter in May 1992.[183]

In addition to these societies and clubs, the two more important women's organizations set up in the country were al-Ittihad al-Nisa'i al-'Arabi (the Union of Arab Women),[184] which existed from 1954 to 1957 during the liberal parliamentary period that granted women the vote (although its resolutions including women's suffrage were overturned by the palace coup of 1957), and the Federation of Jordanian Women, which existed from 1974 to 1981 and was founded the year women were granted the vote by royal decree. Whereas women's suffrage was decreed in April of 1974, the federation was founded in November 1974 by a number of Jordanian women who elected the feminist pioneer Emily Bisharat as federation head in preparation for the 1975 United Nations Conference on Women in Mexico City. In 1981, the Ministry of Social Affairs illegally dissolved the federation in an attempt to control women's independent activity in the country.[185] Shortly before dissolving the federation, however, In'am al-Mufti, minister of social affairs and Jordan's first woman minister, who had harassed the federation for months, had set up a government-controlled National Union of Jordanian Women.[186] In the meantime, in April 1978, the government for the first time ever invited three women (In'am al-Mufti, Widad Bulus, and Na-'ilah al-Rashdan) to serve as members of the first National Consultative Council (which had a total of sixty members) set up by the government in April 1978 as a body representing society in the absence of Parliament and with the limited power of being consulted by the government.[187] This was the first time women participated in any official governing body since the state was founded in 1921. The second consultative council, set up in April 1980, included four women members (Widad Bulus, Na'ilah al-Rashdan, 'Adawiyyah al-'Alami, and Janette al-Mufti Dakhqan) and excluded former member In'am al-Mufti as she had been appointed minister of social affairs in December 1979.[188] The third consultative council was set up in April 1982 and included four women (Layla Sharaf, Hayfa' Malhas al-Bashir, Samyah Nadim al-Zaru, and 'Iddah al-Mutlaq) out of seventy-five members.[189] As for women's holding of leadership positions in political parties, this began only in the early 1970s when women became members of Wasfi al-Tall's and Mustafa Dudin's National Union, wherein women ran unsuccessfully for its leadership position. Still, the union's executive committee included three women, one of whom was Sa'diyyah al-Jabiri al-Tall, Wasfi al-Tall's Syrian widow. The union was soon dissolved.[190] These major activities in the seventies were indeed spurred by the international attention accorded women, which the Jordanian government could not ignore. In addition to suffrage and political appointments, the government set up the Department for Women's Affairs in February 1977 in response to the recommendations made at the United Nations conference in Mexico City and those made in April 1976 by the Human Resources Conference panel devoted to women.[191] It was with this background of state-sponsored expansion of the public roles of women as citizen-nationals that the Personal Status Law was passed in 1976, limiting slightly husbands' rights vis-à-vis their wives (in comparison to the 1951 Family Rights Law) and maintaining women's inferior status in the home. By the early 1980s, new projects were in the making to replace the 1976 Personal Status Law, which remains on the books to this very day.

It is significant that the women's movement of the mid-1950s received a large amount of support from the massive anti-imperialist Jordanian national movement, which fought for democratic rights, Arab unity, and an end to the colonial presence in the country. Political parties (both legal and illegal ones) on the left and in the center, as well as pro-government politicians, supported and pushed for women's suffrage and women's right to run for elections. In fact, many of the women who were members of the Ittihad were wives of politicians, such as Lam'ah al-Razzaz, wife of Munif al-Razzaz (one of the leaders of the Ba'th Party), and Faridah Shubaylat, wife of Farhan Shubaylat (Minister of Defense in 1955), and Faridah Ghanma, wife of Nqula Ghanma (appointed member of the senate). Moreover, in 1951, the political program of the illegal Communist Party, which was published in its newspaper *Al-Muqawamah al-Sha'biyyah* (Popular Resistance), called for the "struggle to liberate Jordanian women from reactionary chains, and to equate them with men in all political, economic, and social matters."[192] The Ittihad itself actually met with the deputy of the chief justice (Qadi al-Qudah) demanding an end to polygamy and that constraints be placed on

Muslim men's right of divorce.[193] As early as 1952, the Women's Awakening League (Rabitat al-Yaqazah al-Nisa'iyyah) organized demonstrations demanding suffrage, calling for an end to British colonial policies in the region, and mobilizing women to celebrate International Women's Day. Such activities were circumscribed by the military, whose head, John Bagot Glubb, ordered the league dissolved. The league continued to operate underground and finally began operating publicly after the 1967 Arab-Israeli war.[194] In 1970, the league changed its name to Jam'iyyat al-Nisa' al-'Arabiyyat (the Arab Women's Society).

After women signed many petitions and organized many demonstrations demanding women's suffrage, which resulted in a parliamentary vote granting women the vote, the council of ministers issued a decision on October 2, 1955, approving the parliamentary vote to grant educated women the right to vote but not to run for elections. In light of this development, women's groups launched a wide campaign demanding suffrage for all women and women's right to run for elections. Emily Bisharat (the head of the Ittihad) wrote an open letter in the daily *Filastin* under the title "We want our full rights."[195] The Ittihad met in a general meeting demanding women's full rights and calling on the government to grant voting rights to uneducated women and to allow all women the right to run for elections.[196] On March 8, 1956, the league organized a huge demonstration (over 800 women participated) in Jericho (West Bank) demanding equal rights, full suffrage for women, women's right to run for Parliament, and the cancellation of the Jordanian-British Treaty (which maintained Jordan under British tutelage).[197] Women's activism continued unabated after the expulsion of Glubb Pasha, the head of Jordan's army. Women demanded that they join the National Guard, and many volunteered.[198] The Ittihad sent a memorandum to the defense minister in this regard.[199] The government's repressive measures against the national movement, however, did not spare women. As already mentioned, in addition to dissolving women's groups, and attacking women's demonstrations that had both an anticolonial nationalist agenda and a gender-equality agenda, government forces did not hesitate to detain women, to dismiss them from jobs, even to shoot them, as they did Raja' Abu 'Ammashah in December 1955 as she set fire to the British flag at the British consulate in Jerusalem in protest against the Baghdad Pact.[200] With the defeat of the national movement in 1957, women's political activity, like the rest of the popular movement, came to a standstill.

With the rise of the Palestinian national movement in the sixties and the presence of most of its new elements in Jordan, the women's movement found a new source of support. Still, most of the movement's groups did not go beyond calling for women's equality, and they incorporated women in their groups in service capacities. Although some groups enlisted women in their guerrilla units, that was aimed at national not gender liberation, as the leadership and its political agenda remained in the hands of men.[201] Still, the Palestinian national movement gave the impetus to the women's movement by providing it with an arena for activism. With the final defeat of that movement in 1970 and 1971 leading to the expulsion of its forces from the country, women's activism was halted one more time, not to be revived again until 1974 with the royal decree granting women the vote.

Despite the dissolution of independent women's groups in the country, women were able to infiltrate many fortresses in civil society that had been until then closed to them. In 1960 women participated and were elected, for the first time, as representatives in labor and professional unions, such as the Union of Dentists. Many women followed suit in other unions. The major cases were the Union of Lawyers (since 1971), the Union of Pharmacists (since 1977), and the Union of Agriculture Engineers (since 1984), where women were elected to the boards.[202] In addition, women participated as members of a number of government councils, including the Council on Education (since 1969), the Health High Council (since 1977), the Capital City Council (since 1980), and the University of Jordan Board of Regents (since 1983).[203]

Although women obtained the right to vote in 1974, the first time they had a chance to exercise that vote was in 1984, as Parliament had been suspended since 1967 as a result of the Israeli occupation of the West Bank, which prevented those Jordanians living under Israeli occupation from participating in such a national exercise of rights. However, it was not until 1989 that women ran for Parliament in what is considered the freest elections Jordan had ever seen. Of 647 candidates countrywide, however, only twelve were women, and none of them won a seat. However, 48 percent of voters were women.[204] It was not until the 1993 elections that the first Jordanian woman, Tujan Faysal, a feminist activist of Chechen ethnic background, won the first and only parliamentary seat to be occupied by a woman in the country's history. Although Faysal won, the 1993 elections were a setback for women. Of 534 candidates countywide, only three were women.[205] In 1997, with the majority of the Islamist and leftist opposition boycotting the undemocratic elections, of 524 candidates running, seventeen were women, the largest number yet, both relatively and in absolute numbers.[206] While campaigning, one of the women candidates, Wisaf Ka'abnah, representing the Bedouins of central Jordan, escaped an assassination attempt on her life.

In addition, unknown gunmen shot at her campaign headquarters. In an interview, Ms. Ka'abnah described those who were committing these criminal acts as "a group that is intent to prevent women from participating in political life and who reject [women's] role in society. . . . I am a Bedouin . . . but [!] I am qualified and I hold a university law degree and I practice law." She added that her entering political life is intended to "break the chains that constrict Bedouin women who live in conservative communities wherein the man has the principal role."[207] Not only did none of the women get elected, Tujan Faysal, the only Jordanian woman to enter Parliament, lost her seat. She accused the government of election fraud.[208]

The juridical and political history of Jordanian women since the inception of the state is a reflection of nationalist ideology (whose constitutive elements include Arabism and Islam, as well as a specific Jordanianness). On the one hand, political ideology seems to have led to and informed the codification of women's status as inferior in the private sphere with minimal state intervention, and a steady expansion of women's presence in the public sphere as nominally equal citizen-nationals with state protection. On the other hand, juridical rights (foremost among which are constitutional rights and personal status laws) inform an ideology of legal equality and expansion of rights, which many feminists and their state backers adhere to, and an ideology of traditionalization calling for circumscribing women's rights and their presence in the public sphere and keeping the state out of the home, which secular and Islamist antifeminists and their state backers adhere to. The nationalist tension between the notions of women as custodians of tradition inhabiting the private sphere (i.e., as custodians and therefore guardians of the eternal time of the nation) and women as "modern" mothers intermittently crossing through the public sphere (who, because of their national duties, which include the (re)production of the nation's future generations, must be cultivated in the areas of literacy, hygiene, child-rearing, and nutrition, according to modern scientific criteria for the nation's future to be ensured) can be resolved only through a recourse to juridical codifications and definitions and by soliciting support from both women and men for the national project. The inherent juridical and ideological contradictions plaguing such formulations of the status of women and men in the national project, however, do not lead to stasis; rather, they produce a dynamism that mobilizes the incessant rewriting of nationalist ideals, even of the story of the nation itself, by the state as well as society. By claiming the mantle of the nation and its traditions, both feminists and their state supporters (who claim that gender discrimination is against Islam and Muslim traditions) and antifeminists and their state supporters, secular and religious alike (who claim the same national and religious tradition on their side) can make productive interventions whose ultimate hegemony (depending on who prevails) will produce the Jordanian citizen-national, as well as define not only what this Jordanian citizen-national looks like today but also how this citizen-national has always looked.

As in the case of Bedouins whose position in nationalist discourse straddles that discourse's temporal imperatives, women are similarly positioned within this discourse. At the 1994 signing of the Jordanian-Israeli Peace Accords, both sides presented young girls (whose grandfathers were killed during the 1967 War) who offered flower bouquets to each country's leader, inaugurating the future *fraternity* being established between the two peoples. Yitzhak Rabin, Israel's Ashkenazi Prime-Minister, was accompanied by a young Ashkenazi girl, Leah Yotan, with blondish hair and "gentile" European looks and dressed in European modern fashion, symbolizing Israel's oxymoronic gentile-European ideals and identifications,[209] and King Husayn was accompanied by a young Jordanian girl, Hiba Smadi, dressed in "traditional" tribal Jordanian clothes. What was interesting about the Jordanian girl was not so much that no Jordanian girl dresses like this anywhere in modern Jordan, but that no Jordanian girl has dressed like this ever. The fashion the Jordanian girl wore to the signing ceremony was that of an adult woman of tribal heritage, which today is worn by older women who did not succumb to the march of Western modernity and its fashion industry in the country—it was certainly not a dress for a prepubescent girl. However, those who dressed the girl were right on target. The nationalist vision that governed their choice of fashion was inspired by the pride taken by nationalist Jordanians in the preservation of Jordan's "traditional" Bedouinized past in the present, and that not only Jordanian women but also Jordanian girls, of tribal or nontribal heritage, shall be the custodians of that past, of that tradition, while men will live the future of the nation alongside them.

3 Cultural Syncretism or Colonial Mimic Men

Jordan's Bedouins and the Military Basis of National Identity

The military is the most important homosocial nationalist institution within the confines of the nation-state. Its very *raison d'être* is the defense of that nation-state. Its symbols and its ideology are so suffused with nationalism that they cannot be conceived without it. Its flag, its anthem, its holidays, its songs, and its sense of cohesion are all nationally defined. As an institution, it is dedicated to the production of a certain species of nationalized beings, nationalists of a different variety from those outside the military institution. Their national existence is predicated not only on a being that is nationally constituted but also on acting in defense of that being. This nationalist agency is defined by that defense of the nation, of its physical and imaginary frontiers. But the military as an institution produces a gendered set of nationalist agents—namely, those of the masculine variety. It is a violent institution by definition (a "repressive state apparatus," as Althusser calls it) and relies on conventional masculine attributes of physical strength, endurance, and stamina. Its self-definition banishes from its ranks physical frailty, weakness, and fragility as feminine attributes. Although the military can accommodate women within its ranks, it is only women who uphold its masculine attributes that can become members.

Masculine behavior in a colonial context is always racialized. Establishing a new model of nationalized masculinity in the colonies proved to be a more complicated endeavor than its European counterpart. In European nationalist discourses, as Chandra Talpade Mohanty argues, it was always European white masculinity that defined nationalist agency at home. In the colonies, it was that same white colonial masculinity, made normative through

European colonialism, that reigned supreme in dealing with the natives.[1] In the process of European colonization of the Third World, the intersection of racial and sexual discourses is symptomatic of imperial rule. The institutions of colonial rule, the military, the judiciary, and the administrative service, have always been overwhelmingly masculine. "White men in colonial service *embodied* rule by literally and symbolically representing the power of the Empire."[2]

This chapter will look at the military's productive role. Although the military is generally viewed as a repressive and a coercive institution, its productive role has not been adequately studied. Following Michel Foucault's important contribution in this regard, I will show how, in addition to being a repressive apparatus, the military is also a productive institution, producing national identity as well as central aspects of what becomes national culture itself. Its coercive capacities aside, the military is characterized by its disciplinary role. As Timothy Mitchell puts it, "a restrictive, exterior power gives way to an internal productive power." Echoing Foucault, Mitchell, who is examining the workings of modern technologies of power in general and in the colonial context of Egypt in particular, states, "Disciplines work within local domains and institutions, entering into particular social processes, breaking them down into separate functions, rearranging the parts, increasing their efficiency and precision, and reassembling them into more productive and powerful combinations. These powers produce the organized power of armies, schools, and factories, and other distinctive institutions of modern nation-states. They also produce, within such institutions, the modern individual, constructed as an isolated, disciplined, receptive, and industrious political subject."[3]

This chapter will also look at how white colonial masculinity is institutionalized in a colonized domain as an *ambivalent* model for nationalist agency, later conceived as "anticolonial." We will look at the figure of John Bagot Glubb, who was second in command of the Arab Legion, Transjordan's army, from 1930 until 1939, and its chief from 1939 until his deportation from Jordan on March 2, 1956. Glubb will be shown to usher in a specific figuration of a syncretic nationalist agency imbricated in the culture of Empire while dressed up as authentically national. His syncretic cross-dressing will be shown to be of a substantially different variety than the culturally appropriative cross-dressing of T. E. Lawrence, who himself played a founding role in the establishment of Transjordan.[4] The study will focus on Glubb's own numerous autobiographical writings in relation to the history of the Jordanian armed forces. Glubb's investment in a certain Bedouinization of what became Jordan will be shown to have played a crucial role in *identifying* the country nationally, literally of conjuring up national cultural borders and a national personality, which is always already gendered and always already imbricated in racialized and classed imperial notions of comportment and aesthetics. (Although Glubb's personality marked his entire project, he was not a one-man show. Glubb, like all colonial officers, was part of a chain of command that went back to London. He was an executor of imperial plans and policies, although he would always stamp them with his personal imprints. The British Empire had several such officers, not only in its Arab territories, but also in other areas of the Empire.)

Although Glubb's project began as a military project, wherein the stated goal was the integration of the Bedouins into the nation-state through its most illustrious institution, thereby ensuring that the new militarized Bedouin would no longer threaten the nation-state and its laws, this process spilled over beyond the perimeter of the military and into the national life of civilians. The result was the invention of a specifically Jordanian national cultural product, ranging from mannerisms and comportment to national dishes (produced by British Mandatory trade relations), national dress and music (emulating the examples of Glubb and British cultural forms, respectively)—which the recently released and eruptive exclusivist Jordanian nationalism identifies as part of its very essence (see chapter 5).[5] Since nationalism lives through rituals, practices, and performances, it is through them that the nation is constituted. As Althusser has explained, "the existence of the ideas of [a subject's] belief is material in that his ideas are his material actions inserted into material practices governed by the material ideological apparatus from which derive the ideas of that subject."[6] What one eats, what sports and music one plays, what one wears, how one speaks, and how one moves became all-important rituals suffused with specific significations. Introducing these rituals and giving content to their signification was a central part of Glubb's transformative policies. The creation of new national icons, ranging from a flag to military dress, became part of this process of nationalizing not only the Bedouins but also everyone living in Jordan.

It is argued often that the military apparatus of Transjordan preexisted its establishment as a nation-state in March 1921.[7] Such a claim relies on the existence of military outfits trained by the British in that area since 1920. However, it should be emphasized that administrative and government apparatuses had also existed in much of what became Transjordan prior to its nationalization in the form of a state by the British and the Hijazi Amir ʿAbdullah. After the Ottoman defeat at the conclusion of World War I, the area of what became Transjordan came under the rule of the newly established Syrian kingdom headed by King Faysal. This situation lasted only until the defeat of Faysal's forces by the French imperial forces at Maysalun on July 24, 1920, which resulted in his expulsion from the country altogether. According to the Sykes-Picot Agreement of 1916 between the British and the French colonial powers, the southern part of Syria lying east of Palestine and the Jordan River was to be under British rule. British presence in the area, however, was minimal if not altogether lacking (as the British had withdrawn from the area in December 1919, relinquishing it to Faysal's government), leading to the establishment of a number of regional governments in the area, with their own administrative apparatuses. This was done with the help of the British high commissioner for Palestine, Herbert Samuel, who convened a meeting of the notables of the area east of the Jordan in Salt on August 21, 1920, for that purpose and dispatched several British representatives to the area to "advise" the populations and governments on political, military, and administrative matters. These local regional governments existed from August 1920 until April 1921, when 'Abdullah and Winston Churchill concluded a deal giving birth to a Transjordanian state, with 'Abdullah as its ruling amir, who, in turn, answered to the British Mandatory authorities. These advisors and officers included among them Lieutenant Colonel Frederick G. Peake (then seconded to the Egyptian army as commander of its camel corps) and Captain Alec S. Kirkbride, who were to play very powerful roles in Transjordan in the coming decades. Peake was dispatched to reorganize the disorganized gendarmerie left after the fall of Faysal's Syrian kingdom.

Captain C. Dunbar Brunton (who was stationed in Salt but later moved to Amman as the British representative there) set up the military Reserve Force in the area following the fall of Faysal to prop up the gendarmerie. Soon, however, events overtook the British. 'Abdullah, son of the Sharif Husayn and brother of Faysal, marched toward Syria, declaring his purpose to be the restoration of the Sharifian throne. He neared Ma'an, the northernmost Hijazi city closest to Amman, accompanied by several hundred fighters. The British then invited him to a meeting with Churchill in Jerusalem, which resulted in his appointment as amir over the new state. 'Abdullah contributed 750 men to the Reserve Force of the country, which Peake had already expanded to 750 men; thus the combined force, excluding the police, totaled 1,500 men. The police and military forces were finally unified in October 1923 and named the Arab Legion.[8] Peake and the British Resident H. St. John Philby were responsible for the name change: Peake states that "when I suggested to him that the name of the New Force, that I was raising, should be changed from 'Reserve Force' to Arab Legion, Phibly agreed at once, and the strange thing is, that nobody noticed the change."[9] The Arabic name for the new force was actually the Arab Army, or al-Jaysh al-'Arabi, because many of its members were veterans of the anti-Ottoman Arab revolt fought by the Hijazi-organized Arab Army. Peake thought that al-Jaysh al-'Arabi was too ostentatious a name for such a small force and thus translated its name into English as the Arab Legion.[10]

The Arab Legion, headed by Peake, consisted of Brunton's Reserve Force, the gendarmerie, and 'Abdullah's troops, as well as some of Faysal's retreating troops who had remained in the area. The force was commanded and funded by the British while simultaneously being at 'Abdullah's service insofar as his interests coincided with those of the British. Soon, however, the Arab Legion was converted into a mere police force because of its poor showing in 1922 in battle against invading pro-Saudi Wahhabi raiders. The Wahhabis were defeated after the intervention of the British Royal Air Force, and the Arab Legion became mainly a police force involved in crime prevention, tax collection, and arresting offenders, as well as responsibilities over immigration and passport control, motor licensing, and traffic control. The Legion was helped in its efforts by the Royal Air Force (controlled solely by the British) who held the responsibility of defending the regime—a task that it was called upon to carry out on several occasions in the 1920s. On April 1, 1926, the British high commissioner for Palestine established the Trans-Jordan Frontier Force (TJFF) under the command of the Royal Air Force. The TJFF's main task was the military defense of Transjordan's borders against tribal raids, especially in the east and the south. It was also to help the Arab Legion when called upon. This force was mostly recruited from the Palestine gendarmerie and was deliberately staffed largely by non-Transjordanians.[11] By 1927, the number of men in the Arab Legion had been reduced from 1,472 men to 1,000, and the issuance of the Arab Legion Law had formalized the new arrangement whereby the Arab Legion was confined to police duties. 'Abdullah and his administrative staff of Arab nationalists did not look favorably on the establishment of the TJFF, as it constituted a threat to the power of the Transjordanian government, who had no authority over this force, and concentrated more power in the hands of the British. The 1928 agreement between the British and the Transjordanian government effectively regulated security arrangements. Article 10 stipulated that Britain "may maintain armed forces in Trans-Jordan, and may raise, organize and control in Trans-Jordan such armed forces . . . necessary for the defence of the country . . . [and that] His Highness the Amir agrees that he will not raise or maintain in Trans-Jordan or allow to be raised or maintained any military forces without the consent of His Britannic Majesty."[12] Other stipulations included that the Amir accept that certain parts of the country be placed under martial law (article 14).

It was through such legal mechanisms that the Mandatory-Hashemite state established its monopoly on the use of force and armed coercion. Still, however, the matter of the armed Bedouin tribes had to be resolved for such a monopoly to be effected. It was in this context that a British officer by the name of John Bagot Glubb was recruited from neighboring Iraq, where he had been engaged in "pacifying" the Bedouins of that other Mandatory-Hashemite state headed by King Faysal. Having acquired a regional reputation as the Bedouin expert par excellence, his services were in much need in Transjordan. On his arrival in Amman in 1930, Glubb set out to establish a new force within the Arab Legion. He called it the Desert Patrol or Quwwat al-Badiyah, and he recruited its members solely from among the Bedouins. The task for this new force was to guard the borders with the Saudis, who had recently occupied the Hashemite kingdom of the Hijaz and annexed it. (This role was later expanded to include guarding the British-owned Iraq Petroleum Company's pipeline, which passed through Transjordan.) In response to the anticolonial revolt raging in neighboring Palestine, the Desert Patrol was enlarged in 1936 to become the Desert Mechanized Force, acting as a mercenary army under British control. Its major contributions to British imperial policy in the region included subduing Palestinian rebels and their Transjordanian supporters within Transjordan in the late 1930s, intervening in Iraq against the nationalist anti-British coup leaders in 1941, and later the same year intervening in Syria against the Vichy French. The Desert Mechanized Force was to become the nucleus for the postindependence Jordanian Armed Forces. It was due to its new international character that in 1944 the Arab Legion was renamed the Jordanian Arab Army (al-Jaysh al-ʿArabi al-Urduni) to distinguish it from other Arab military forces.[13] As we shall see in the next chapter, it was to be named and renamed several times in the coming decades.

The Bedouin Choice

On arriving in Transjordan, Peake launched his policy of defending the villagers against Bedouin raids, and he rallied the support of his government's resources. His biographer insists that Peake, unlike other British administrators in the Arab East, did not possess "a streak of poetry and romance." Such a typical administrator "sympathizes in every way with the nomad's eleventh-century outlook and regards any interference with his old Arabian rights and customs as the worst form of vandalism. . . . This point of view, needless to say, is shared by the traveller who visits Arab lands and afterwards writes a book on his experiences. He is not in the country long enough to appreciate both sides of the case, and as his guides and caravans are supplied by the Beduin, he is led to see only the nomad point of view."[14] The attraction to the Bedouin is also motivated by the British sense that Bedouins embody primitivism and modernity simultaneously, a sort of evolutionary enigma. Sir Mark Sykes (of Sykes-Picot Agreement fame), sums this up: "The Beduin is, indeed, the strangest of all mankind. His material civilization is about on a par with that of a Bushman, yet his brain is as elaborately and subtly developed as that of any Englishman with a liberal education. There is no reasonable argument he cannot follow, no situation which he cannot immediately grasp, no man whom he cannot comprehend; yet there is no manual act he can perform."[15]

Peake would have none of it. Through his influence, the British forced 'Abdullah to accept the abolition of the semi-independent Tribal Administration Department (Niyabat al-'Asha'ir) headed by Sharif Shakir Bin Zayd in the summer of 1924, forcing the enactment of new laws to control the Bedouins as early as October 1924.[16] The positions of Tribal Administration representative and deputy representative had in fact been established since the first Transjordan ministerial administration was set up on April 4, 1921; the position of deputy (occupied by Ahmad Maryud) was abolished on February 1, 1923, and the position of representative (occupied by Shakir) was completely done away with on June 26, 1926, two years after the abolition of the Tribal Administration itself.[17] In this vein, Peake proudly insists that "had not the British stepped into Trans-Jordan and the French into Syria there is little doubt that both countries . . . would soon have reverted to tribal rule and poverty." To achieve this important task, Peake set to work: "My policy was to raise a Force from the sedentary, or village, Arabs, which would gradually be able to check the Beduin and allow an Arab Government to rule the country without fear of interference from tribal chiefs. . . . It would have been easy to establish British rule and control enforced by British troops, but it would have caused much trouble and expense. Besides which I was always convinced that the old days of direct British rule were passing, or indeed had passed. Nationalism imported from the West with modern mass education had come to stay and was a force with which one had to reckon."[18]

With the increase in Ibn Sa'ud's territorial gains, which by the later twenties had reached the southern and eastern borders of Transjordan, cross-border tribal raids acquired an international character. It was in this context that John Bagot Glubb was called on to control the Transjordanian tribes.[19] Peake remarks that this new policy "was excellent, and the officer selected to run it under my direction could not have been better chosen." Yet, Peake seemed uneasy about how the strategy of policing the tribes was being pursued:

> Unfortunately, however, this new desert force was brought into being after the regular Arab Legion had completed its task of establishing public security in the settled part of the country. Consequently we soon saw the British government providing money with which to subsidize the tribes—the old evil of the *surra* [a money-pouch given to the Bedouins by Lawrence to aid the British effort during the Arab Revolt against the Ottomans, which Lawrence had learned about from the Ottomans who themselves used it to pay the tribes to prevent the latter from attacking the pilgrimage caravans] under another name; giving them armed cars with machine-guns, wireless sets, forts and other adjuncts to militarism, which had been denied to the old Arab Legion, who had had to carry on its task without them. . . . gradually we saw the desert nomads being turned into soldiers with modern arms and transport, while the old Arab Legion formed from the dwellers in the towns and villages remained for the most part mere police.[20]

Peake felt that such a transformation was tolerable as long as the British remained in control of the country, but he worried about the outcome of this policy, "should, in the future, a growing demand for independence be met by the withdrawal of British officers then we shall have given the tribal shaykhs an arm with which they can once again dominate the settled people. . . . My policy was always to prevent power from getting into the hands of the tribal chiefs as the country could not prosper if this occurred."[21] Peake's policy was endorsed by T. E. Lawrence who was in Transjordan as an advisor for a few months. Jarvis reports that Lawrence "agreed entirely with Peake's point of view that the future of the small State depended upon the cultivator, who must be protected from his desert neighbour."[22]

As a result of Peake's policy, there were very few Bedouins in the Arab Legion, which included Palestinians, Transjordanian Circassians, Chechens, and Turcomens—settled by the Ottomans a few years (in some cases decades) earlier. Initially, Peake had also recruited hundreds of Sudanese and Egyptians. This had had an impact on Transjordan's population, who until then had refused to be recruited in the Legion, seeing it as a new oppressive tax-collecting force. However, as Jarvis reports, fear of being policed by "foreigners" led many among them to join the Legion. The Legion officers included Arab Iraqis and Syrians who were ex-Ottoman officers. Recruitment from among educated town and village Transjordanians was to take place later, although Peake had difficulty finding men who combined the intellectual and physical qualities he required: "in the East these two essential qualifications are seldom found in company because education in some mysterious fashion has a deteriorating effect on physique."[23]

This was not the only problem faced by Peake. His Legion officers, most of whom were Arab nationalists, who had retreated to Jordan to regroup, making common cause with 'Abdullah's intention to evict the French from Syria, were now undercutting his plans to establish control in Transjordan. The debacle ended in 1924 with his purging the Legion's officer corps and expelling the nationalists, a decision ultimately supported by 'Abdullah whose excessive pragmatism toward the British was infuriating the nationalists.[24]

By the time Glubb arrived in the country, "[m]ore than half the officers and men were not in fact [Trans-]Jordanians, but came from Iraq, Saudi Arabia or Syria."[25] By the late forties, however, the Desert Mechanized Force had established an international reputation as an effective British mercenary force. The mystique of the Bedouins, however, had still not disappeared. Peter Young, who joined the Arab Legion after the Palestine war, remarks, "The bedouin are the most delightful people to serve with and to meet in the ordinary way. They are not unlike the Highlanders in the days of the '15 and '45; with their tails up and with leaders they trust they will fight admirably for short periods. . . . At the worst the bedouin can be stupid, sullen and fit for nothing, but there are few of this type. At the best, they are cheerful, willing and hardy soldiers, ready to go anywhere and try anything."[26]

On arrival, Glubb established a working relationship with Alec Kirkbride, the British resident in the country, as well as with the Amir 'Abdullah. All three agreed on the new policy of recruiting the Bedouins to join the Arab Legion. James Lunt states that this was "a deliberate policy based on a shared philosophy of all three men. According to Kirkbride the Arab Legion was intended to be a purely professional force, not a national institution."[27]

Glubb's dislike for town Arabs stemmed mostly from racial as well as cultural considerations. He considered them racial hybrids compared with the racially pure and martial Bedouins and villagers. This, for him, accounted for his contention that "the townsmen are rarely martial."[28] Lunt, in his biography of Glubb, defends the latter's preference for Bedouins stating that Glubb's intention of recruiting Bedouins was only to keep politics out of the army. He quotes a letter that was sent to P. J. Vatikiotis in which Glubb says nothing about Bedouins being better fighters than Hadaris. In his rush to defend Glubb, Lunt misses the many occasions on which Glubb did mention the martial superiority of the Bedouins in his writings.[29] The official historian of the Jordanian Armed Forces had the following to say about this matter:

[T]he eventual pacification and the successful recruitment of the Bedouin of Transjordan into the ranks of the Legion was due solely to the personal efforts, leadership and diplomatic skills of Major (later General) J. B. Glubb. The dash, offensive spirit and élan displayed by the all-Bedouin Desert Mechanized Force in the subsequent campaigns in Iraq and in Syria in 1941, was a tribute to Glubb Pasha's prowess as a leader and commander of Bedouin troops. His later attempts to distinguish between Bedouin and non-Bedouin (*Hadari*) personnel were, however, less than successful. In the opinion of Arab officers they were quite unjustifiable and, like Lord Plumer's motives in grafting a TJFF on an unwilling Transjordan government, suspect. On the eve of the pullout of the British military presence from Jordan in 1956, five out of ten infantry regiments and two out of three armoured regiments were Bedouin. One can fully appreciate and sympathize with Glubb's genuine and sincere loyalty towards the Bedouin, who like the tribal Pathan [in India], has many manly and admirable qualities — including a delightful sense of humour. But, the cold hard fact remains, that the Turkish Army recruited Arabs from all over the empire and employed them in all theatres of war with considerable success.[30]

Glubb's policies in the Arab East were indeed not unique. They were part of a generalized British imperial policy of *divide et impera* practiced elsewhere within the Empire. As Syed Ali El-Edroos explains,

There is little doubt that Glubb Pasha and the British officers who served with the Arab Legion, like their compatriots who served in the Indian Army, overplayed their hand on the subject of the so-called "martial" and "non-martial" races. At the same time, they exaggerated the so-called professional reliability of the *Fellahin* and the *Hadari* when compared with the Bedouin. Glubb Pasha's attitude towards the educated *effendi* (officer) class is also hard to understand. Like his compatriots in the British Indian Army, he appeared most uncomfortable when called upon to serve alongside educated, critical, and not overly obsequious Indian (in his case Arab) officers. The outstanding officers of the Arab Revolt were all from the so-called *effendi* class and included Arab regulars such as Aziz Ali el-Masri, Jafar Pasha el Askari, Nuri as-Said and Maulud Mukhlis, and no one can question their professional competence or courage. The ingrained British antipathy towards the educated class of officers and officials and a preference for the simple, illiterate, and naive peasant, farmer or bedouin, reflects a weakness in the British character.[31]

Still, Glubb insisted that no discrimination in the Legion should take place. Ignoring the real power imbalance manifested most clearly in the dearth of high-ranking Arab officers in the Legion in favor of British colonial officers, he states: "In the Arab Legion, we tolerated no racial, religious, or class distinctions. The British officers were not a class apart. On any given occasion, the senior officer present commanded irrespective of race. British officers saluted Arab officers senior to them in rank. The division between British and Arab was not the only potential source of dissension in the army. In Jordan, itself, there were Arabs and Circassians, Christians and Muslims, townsmen, countrymen and tribesmen, and different tribes unfriendly to one another. Latterly, there were East and West Jordanians—or, as we used to say, Palestinians and Transjordanians."[32]

Discrimination or not, the goal of Glubb's policy to have an all-Bedouin army was reached successfully: "The first Desert Mechanized Regiment was the genesis of the Jordanian Army as it exists today and it is important to note that it was chiefly bedouin in composition. There were technicians and clerks who came from the settled areas but the officers and the rank and file were all tribesmen, still wearing the uniform of the Desert Patrol, their hair long and in many cases worn in ringlets as was the bedouin fashion.[33]

By incorporating the Bedouins into the repressive state apparatus par excellence, Glubb ensured that not only would their internecine and international raiding be stopped, but also their group loyalty would be transferred to the nation-state, guaranteeing that the Bedouins would protect that state against all threats, especially so due to their contempt for city-folk from which anti-state threats might arise. Also, due to their kinship ties across the new national borders and their tribal affiliation, the Bedouins were seen as a threat to the nation-state. Nationalizing them, therefore, through territorialization, was part of nation-building. In fact, in addition to the military, the British government also dabbled with economic incentives, through transforming the Bedouins into agriculturalists: "The objects of the encouragement of bedouin cultivation are briefly (a) to broaden the basis of their economy and to prevent the whole of their livelihood depending upon one somewhat fickle form of capital, and (b) to give them a fixed stake in immovable property in the country, which will be not only an economic insurance but also a social anchorage."[34] As is obvious from this policy, the centrality of bourgeois forms of property to the national project could not have been more emphasized by the British. This policy was being enacted as the rest of Transjordan's communal property, as we saw in chapter 1, was being transformed into private property.

Cultural Imperialism and Discipline

The importance of studying the Jordanian military stems from its disciplinary function in the Foucaultian sense. Foucault views disciplinary regimes as supplanting juridical ones, or at least infiltrating them. In the case of Jordan, we will see how the law and the military are actually instruments employed simultaneously as complementary strategies by the juridical disciplinary state. Following Nicos Poulantzas, "law organizes the conditions for physical repression, designating its modalities and structuring the devices by means of which it is exercised. In this sense, law is *the code of organized public violence.*"[35] The imbrication of the disciplinary operation in colonial models of rule is just as thorough as the juridical aspect of governmentalization. In this case, the figure of Glubb, as a metonym for Empire, will be examined, insofar as the imperial institution of disciplinarian rule was effected via the establishment of the Arab Legion. It is, after all, Glubb par excellence who personified Empire in Transjordan/Jordan for almost three decades.

On arrival in Iraq in October 1920, his first station in the Arab world, Glubb knew very little about Arabs. To rectify this situation, he embarked on studying what other Europeans had written about the Arabs, so that such works would mediate his first-hand experience with them: "The impression [of seeing the Arabs] left on my mind was profound, but would doubtless have worn off in a few months if fortune had not placed in my hands a number of books. . . . As I bought books and more books, and read and reread them, a new and fascinating world was opened to my eyes."[36] He was fascinated not only with the Arabs but more so with the European explorers and Orientalists who wrote about them. His ferocious appetite for European knowledge of the Arabs was always in evidence. He informs us, "I devoured the works of the explorers of Arabia—Burkhardt, Doughty, Blunt and Palgrave—and determined to imitate them."[37] In this Glubb was not unique. As Edward Said demonstrated, "the transition from a merely textual apprehension, formulation, or definition of the Orient to the putting of all this into practice in the Orient did take place, and . . . Orientalism had much to do with that."[38] Glubb's imitation of Orientalist explorers and colonial officers did not pass unnoticed by anticolonial Arab nationalists. Glubb, in fact, was seen as nothing less than part of the chain of colonial officers. The newspaper *al-Istiqlal* had this to say about him: "Mr. Glubb is a modern Leachman, but the difference is that while Leachman was loud and violent, Glubb is soft and gentle. Their ends are however the same. There is another difference too. Leachman served the English cause with English money while Glubb serves it with the money of Iraq."[39]

Glubb was actually following in the footsteps of Colonel Sir Robert Groves Sandeman, the architect of the policy of Humane Imperialism. Sandeman had an impressive career pacifying the tribes in Baluchistan (where he worked as chief commissioner) and Afghanistan in the late nineteenth century. Sandeman's strategy was parsimoniously truncated to three words: "sympathy, subsidies and tribal law." He died in 1892 on the Sind border of a short illness. His biography, published in 1895, was widely read among colonial officers.[40] While in Iraq, Glubb had read the biography and Sandeman's reports. In 1935, Glubb commented in his monthly reports on an article that appeared in the magazine *The Near East and India* on the 100th anniversary of Sandeman's birthday. Underscoring the similarities between Bedouin and Baluchi tribes, Glubb articulated his own tribal policy: "Indeed, I would have the following principles painted in golden letters on the wall of the office of every administrator of warlike tribes: (1) humanity and sympathy; (2) light taxation and lucrative employment; (3) subsidies to shaykhs; (4) stick to tribal law."[41]

Glubb also had other models to draw on. Although he had been the first recipient of the Lawrence Memorial Medal, conferred upon him in 1936 by the Royal Asian Society in London, Glubb was quite a different man from T. E. Lawrence.[42] Unlike the latter, with whom he is often compared, Glubb's political philosophy in relation to "Arabs" was less culturally appropriative, although just as ostentatiously exhibitionist. Glubb was more interested in Arabs inhabiting a social formation suffused with a culturally syncretic "modernity." A mature Arabophile with little time for uneducated Eurocentric statements of slight dismissal (although Eurocentrism pervaded all his evaluative faculties), Glubb was a cultural relativist with views not so unlike those of some contemporary Western social scientists.

In commenting about the relation between Arab culture and foreign civilizations, Glubb insists that he has "not advised [the Arabs] to imitate the English, but rather the reverse."[43] He was clear on the European meaning of modernism. Under the title, "The Conflict Between Tradition and Modernism in the Role of Muslim Armies," he wrote, "I cannot avoid the impression that when we use the word modernism, we are in fact visualizing the things that characterize ourselves. . . . In other words, modernism means 'like us' and our title seems to imply that Muslims should endeavour to become more like us and that this process will inevitably involve a conflict."[44] In Glubb's view, the "present preëminence enjoyed by the West lies principally in the material field: in mechanics, technology, manufacturing, and similar activities. Other nations, however, are anxious to adopt these things, with the result that modernization in this sense necessitates little if any conflict. . . . The West, on the other hand does not enjoy any generally admitted preëminence in morals; consequently attempts to introduce Western standards of morality into other countries is likely to provoke opposition. Western democracy . . . is also by no means universally accepted as the best method of conducting the affairs of every nation."[45]

Glubb characterized the rule of law in Western countries as producing a "mechanical" sort of government, which worked well for Europeans and was in tune with their "temperament." This, however, he felt, was quite loathsome to Arabs, as they "do greatly prefer to follow men and not machines."[46] He explained how juridical rule, in his view, is unacceptable to Arabs: "I believe that Arabs like to be ruled by men, not by laws or committees; but at the same time they are the most outspoken and democratic of races."[47] Lest his comment come to be interpreted as opposing colonial rule, Glubb, always a committed imperialist, explains that what he is opposing here is "cultural and not . . . direct political influence, such as European colonization or the mandate system."[48] He, in fact, continued to sing the praises of the nineteenth century British Empire until the end of his life.[49] Still, he opposed the extension of the liberal democratic model to the colonies and felt that the political party system is unsuited for non-European cultures. He even appreciated the dilemma with which anticolonial nationalists were faced: "By identifying 'modern' with the system of party politics now in vogue in the West, we compel other nations to forego their traditions of personal loyalties or to accept the stigma of being 'backward.' "[50] Unlike most Orientalists, whose writings were suffused with the theme of "Europe teaching the Orient the meaning of liberty,"[51] Glubb was careful to remind his compatriots, "Britain may well have introduced the Arabs to democracy—but not to freedom."[52] In fact, he was eager to demonstrate that the Arabs' individual freedom did not have to derive from political freedom: "In happy England we have come, for centuries past, to identify our personal liberties with the political independence of our country. Few people in Britain have realized to what an extent personal and national freedom may be divorced. . . . In Turkish days, the Arabs had no political existence, but as individuals they were as free as any men in the world. Their freedom admittedly owed nothing to Turkish generosity. It was due solely to the inability of the Government to control them."[53] In emphasizing this, Glubb is asserting that Arabs and specifically Bedouins need never be freed from colonial rule to achieve freedom, as the two are mutually inclusive.

This type of thinking, however, did not prevent Glubb from falling in the trap of evolutionary and modernizationist thinking. If cultural-relativist arguments did not work in favor of abetting dictatorship in the Arab world, he had no qualms using modernizationist language: "No word in human speech has aroused more enthusiasm or commanded more profound devotion than the word 'freedom.' But it is always risky to transfer the customs of one nation bodily to another, without regard to local conditions. In a country where the masses are entirely ignorant of the world at large, and where everybody (even the rulers) are lacking in experience, unexpected results may ensue from the application of what, in England, would be regarded as the most elementary human rights."[54]

One would think that Glubb is being a full-fledged modernizationist here, in the sense that democracy will be suitable in the future to the Arabs, once their rulers are more "experienced" and their masses less "ignorant." This is, however, only partly the case. For Glubb, these ignorant masses did not necessarily need Western education *tout court*. As we shall see later, Glubb had an entirely different pedagogical program designed for them. For him, if democracy should ever come to the Arabs, it will happen after a number of centuries have elapsed. In light of the mid-1950s anti-imperialist demonstrations against Jordan's joining the pro-Western Baghdad Pact, Glubb writes, "the Arabs had for centuries been accustomed to autocratic rule. Suddenly autocracy had vanished, and they had slid into anarchy and mob rule, scarcely even passing at the intermediate stage of democracy. For democracy needs generations—perhaps centuries—to build up."[55] For Glubb, this is as much based on historical tradition as on cultural ones. In this case, Glubb identifies Islam as the culprit: "But I was also of the opinion that Arabs in general were more at home with a government which had a personal ruler on its head. This was partly due to ancient if unconscious tradition and partly to the religion of Islam. No Muslim country had ever been successfully governed by elected parliaments, assemblies or committees. The principle followed had always been the appointment of one man for every responsible task."[56]

Glubb ridiculed Jordan's brief experience with a partial-parliamentary system in the 1950s as an "imitation-British democracy . . . a system strange to the traditions of the country."[57] He preferred a "traditional" dictatorship not only for Jordan but also for Iraq: "Indeed if Britain is open to any blame in her relations with Iraq, it is probably due to the fact the she used her influence to install a system of democracy and party politics in that country. But this was due to a mistaken philanthropy, not to wicked imperialism. I have not the slightest doubt in my own mind that different races, owing to their differing temperaments and to thousands of years of varying culture and tradition, need different systems of government. To think that any one form of government is the ideal for the whole human race is dangerous illusion."[58]

Evidently, Glubb's recommendations in the sphere of governance insisted on supporting local dictatorial rule, defined by him as "traditional." He insistently concludes that "there need be no conflict between traditionalism and modernism in Muslim countries if one-man rule or some other form of authoritarian constitution be retained. . . . If some such system of government, broadly based on local traditions, were adopted, no conflict need arise between traditional and modern military methods."[59] However, careful not to leave anything to contingency, Glubb has particular strategies up his sleeve that non-Western countries, choosing the route of party politics, can pursue to ensure that the army stay out of politics. Such strategies do not involve laws; rather, in line with his antipathy to colonial legal structures in the colonies, he advocates more disciplinarian measures: "Our immediate object can best be achieved not by formulating laws or rules prohibiting military interference but by *producing* a spirit opposed to such intervention [emphasis added]." This shall be done by the production of a new tradition, by "mak[ing] abstention from politics a *military tradition* [emphasis added]."[60] Glubb is not conscious of the oxymoronic notion that tradition can be produced by modernity, although he seems unconsciously aware that tradition *tout court* is indeed the outcome of modernity and does not precede it—a notion he had to rely on, albeit unconsciously, for the logic of his strategy to work.

A disciplinarian by trade, Glubb was better able to understand the imposition of European laws on the Arab world than most other colonial officials. He explains, "Not only . . . does the imposition of European law courts on the Arabs destroy the initiative of judges, but it has also imposed on the people a complete system of laws which they are often unable to understand."[61] He lamented the change in Bedouin behavior upon the introduction of these laws: The Bedouins who live "under a régime of physical violence . . . [have] qualities of simple truthfulness and frank open manners, qualities so attractive, yet which seem to be lost when violence is replaced by justice and law."[62] He is even able to discern class differences as correlates to levels of Westernization among Arabs: "The educated classes have often gained European law degrees, and are doubtless expert lawyers and judges. But they are thereby separated by a wide gulf from their fellow countrymen. Perhaps four fellaheen or bedouins out of five who come before a law court of this type are unable even to understand what the whole procedure is about."[63] In answering the question of "[w]hy . . . have laws so unsuited to the population been introduced?" Glubb states, "Owing, as it seems to me, to a failure to differentiate clearly between what is suitable and what is unsuitable when borrowing ideas from Europe. I would remind you once more of Mr. Gandhi's phrase: 'I should make use of indigenous institutions and serve them by curing them of their proved defects.'"[64] Examples of existing legal traditions in the Arab world are cited by Glubb:

[T]wo elaborate codes of law already exist in Arabia (without adding a third)—namely, the Sheria, or religious law, and Arab [Bedouin] customary law. Let us try, if we can, to take Mr. Gandhi's advice and make use of these, at the same time gradually curing them of their proved defects. If we introduce an entirely new and already-made set of laws, they will probably be entirely unsuitable, will certainly cause injustice for a long time owing to being imperfectly understood, and may well be rendered ineffective by the non-co-operation of the inhabitants. But even if these new laws were the best, I would sooner start with the indigenous institutions and approximate them gradually to the new form by a process of building up on existing foundations.[65]

Glubb is exasperated with the lack of attention to local conditions. Following one of his recommendations to hold improvised courts in the countryside, and to abandon formality to give the "inhabitants" access to the courts, he states, "I know of no case where this is done, either in Iraq, Syria, Palestine, or Transjordan. The reason is that all eyes are fixed on the European law courts. There is not enough adaptability, it seems to me, nor accommodation to local conditions."[66]

Glubb's antipathy to juridical rule blinded him to the fact that without such rule, he could not have authority over the Bedouins. Aside from creating Bedouin courts and an apparatus imposing and reviewing Bedouin laws in relation to the Bedouin population as early as 1924, the Mandatory-Hashemite state had also enacted the Law of Supervising the Bedouins in 1929, just before Glubb's arrival in the country. This law effectively put all power in relation to the Bedouin population in the hands of the head of the army, or his deputy (in this case Glubb), thus relegating all Transjordanian Bedouins to living under martial law. It is the law that authorized Glubb throughout his career, a fact that, like the asymmetry between his colonial authority and the colonized status of his subjects, he conveniently forgets.

Glubb's apparent antipathy to imposing things European on the Arab world, however, extended beyond legal codes, military arrangements, and political ideologies, encompassing everyday practices. His attentiveness and sensitivity to detail, as the following will demonstrate, was central to the success of his transformative and productive project.

Cultural Cross-dressing as Epistemology

Glubb was a voyeuristic aesthete with equal commitment to colorful exhibitionism, albeit an exhibitionism projected onto his Bedouin subjects *qua* spectacle. He was meticulous in his plans for the production of a new species of Bedouins, nay, a new species of Arabs, albeit a species that came to be known as Jordanian. He knew exactly what the new Arab soldier should look like, what he (and it was invariably a "he") should wear, how he should move, what he should know, what he should view as tradition and culture, what he should accept as suitable modernity, and above all whom he should consider a friend and whom he should regard as foe; and herein lies the essence of the new Arab soldier, not so much whom to fight and how to fight, but just as importantly whom and what to protect and how. In that, Glubb's project entailed molding the Bedouin's body and mind into something new. The new Bedouin came to possess a new epistemology. But equally important was his possession of a new body, which Glubb trained, fed, treated, educated, and dressed. This new military man was to become the icon and the symbol of the emergent Jordanian nation. His body was to become the national body.

Glubb was attentive to all the intricacies of the colonial cultural and institutional project in the Arab world. He vehemently opposed the creation of an officer class in Arab and Muslim armies because "it does not represent any division of social classes in civil life, but is merely an imitation of European institutions. And I have found no weakening of discipline to result from abandoning these restrictions. This is because Arabs are not 'class conscious.' Surely, to introduce these distinctions amongst them would be a mistake."[67] Explaining that this European military division is rooted in the European premodern past, Glubb's indignation leads him to conclude that the "irony lies in the fact that this system has been adopted by Muslim armies in recent years on the supposition that it is Western and therefore 'modern' and efficient. There are no Muslim traditions to justify such a division; in fact Muslim tradition is here much more 'democratic.' This example illustrates the anomalies which may arise from the slavish imitation of our methods by Muslim armies."[68] Note Glubb's consistency in being suspicious of unchecked mimicry. The "Gandhian" formula was to remain always his guiding principle.

The matter of military clothing was of paramount importance for Glubb: "This sometimes seems at first sight to be merely a superficial matter, but it does not, on mature consideration, prove to be so. A change of clothing signifies that the wearer has abandoned his sentimental attachment to the past. It is an open confession of faith; he seeks to be Europeanized."[69] Glubb describes how the soldiers were clothed under Peake: "The Staff officers of the Arab Legion wore at the time a blue patrol jacket, blue overalls and Wellingtons. The other officers had a single wide red stripe down their overalls, but the Pasha had a triple stripe. Thus clad, and with a high black lambskin cap and a stout malacca stick, he could be seen daily striding through the town of Amman to his office."[70] Glubb's description is precise and measured, leaving out no detail as insignificant. As Foucault has explained: "Discipline is a political anatomy of detail."[71] Sounding like a modern fashion-show host, Glubb proceeds to describe Bedouin clothing:

> From a practical point of view, Arab clothing seems to me much more suited to Arabia than is European clothing. Being largely white, voluminous, and loose, it is ideal for a hot, dry climate. The kerchief or

keffiya worn on the head gives excellent protection from the sun. Tight coats and trousers and hats are supremely unsuitable. Again, a change of clothing necessitates a change of life, because in tight European clothes it is impossible to sit on the ground. Chairs, tables, and beds become a necessity to people wearing European clothes. There is no great advantage in furniture, that I can see. A room well carpeted, with low diwans and cushions, is more comfortable than most European drawing rooms.[72]

Glubb clearly understands the implication for the production of new bodies through cultural cross-dressing. Cultural cross-dressing results in a "change of life," a new corporeal culture wherein the very movement of the body is transformed, as are one's domestic surroundings, how one sits, how one eats, and so forth. This is not simply a matter of aesthetic sensibility. Glubb's defense of local traditions at times makes him sound like an ardent nationalist fighting cultural imperialism:

In the military sphere the wearing of European clothes become even more ridiculous. The rank and file of the army are of poorer classes, who wear Arab clothing and live in homes without European furniture. When they become soldiers they are made to wear tight breeches in which they cannot sit down. People who all their lives go barefoot, or wear sandals are made to wear boots. Again Arab clothing, being loose and voluminous, if supplemented by an Arab sheepskin cloak, is ideal for sleeping out on the ground in any weather. Tight European clothes are very uncomfortable to sleep in and cannot be wrapped around the wearer like a cloak. As a result, Arab troops dressed in European clothes suffer considerably when they sleep out, and, moreover, have to carry blankets, waterproof sheets, tents, and all the paraphernalia necessitated by the unsuitability of their garments for campaigning.[73]

Glubb vividly describes his new clothing designs for the Bedouin Desert Patrol, which he created in the early 1930s: "The uniform was cut in the same manner as their ordinary dress, long robes reaching almost to the ground and long white sleeves, but the outer garment was khaki in colour. With a red sash, a red revolver lanyard, a belt and bandolier full of ammunition, and a silver dagger in the belt, the effect was impressive. Soon the tribesmen were complaining that the prettiest girls would accept none but our soldiers for their lovers."[74]

It would seem that not only were pay and shooting good incentives for the Bedouins to join the service but sexual appeal to women as well. An added benefit was the Bedouins becoming a tourist attraction: "They are certainly the most picturesque body of men in the Middle East, and when the tourists are on the Petra run during the winter the Beduin patrol are photographed from daybreak to dusk."[75] The Bedouins come to form part of the exhibition into which modern European epistemology has transformed the world. Like the great nineteenth-century world exhibitions that formed part of the European colonial project, the world itself, as Timothy Mitchell demonstrates, is turned into an exhibition. Mitchell states that "the exhibition appears not just to mimic the real world outside but to superimpose a framework of meaning over its innumerable races, territories and commodities."[76] He proceeds to explain that the "Orient refused to present itself like an exhibit, and so appeared orderless and without meaning. The colonising process was to introduce the kind of order now found lacking— the effect of structure that was to provide not only a new disciplinary power but also the novel ontology of representation."[77] It is thus that the Bedouin becomes a fetishized commodity. The way he is produced by Glubb and colonial policies renders him a spectacle "where the perceptible world is replaced by a set of images that are superior to that world yet at the same time impose themselves as *eminently* perceptible."[78] The Bedouin becomes an image of what he should be by the new specular economy of Empire. Following Marx's insight about fetishized commodities, the Bedouin as a fetishized commodity is transformed into an exchange value *tout court*.[79] His use value *is* his exchange value as far as the imperial project is concerned. Insofar as he will secure imperial interests with little risk for Empire (white British boys won't need to endanger themselves to secure imperial gains; the Bedouins will do that for them[80]), provide entertainment for visiting tourists, and be paraded as a product of British civilizing efforts, the Bedouin as fetishized commodity becomes central to the imperial project in Jordan, as he will become later for the national project.

Glubb's fascination with his clothing designs provided him with a constant exhibitionist impulse. In his autobiography, he still finds the time to redescribe the Desert Patrol uniforms and the lasting impact they had had: "We dressed our patrol in their own natural clothing: white cotton trousers and a long white 'nightgown' or thob. Above this was a long Khaki gown, a wide, red, woolen belt, a mass of ammunition belts and bandoliers, a revolver with a red lanyard and a silver dagger. *The headgear was a red-and-white-checkered headcloth, which has since then (and from us) become a kind of Arab nationalist symbol. Previously, only white headcloths had been worn in Trans-Jordan or Palestine* [emphasis added]."[81] The rest of the Arab Legion wore Khaki hattas. When in 1933 the Arab Legion replaced the headcloth with a pith helmet; an exception was made for the Desert Patrol.[82] The importance of the male headgear is not to be underestimated. As we will see in chapter 5, Jordanian palace and popular nationalisms were to adopt the red-and-white *shmagh* or *hatta* as defining of Jordanianness. The red-and-white hatta was to act as a marker, marking out "real" Transjordanians from Palestinian Jordanians, who in turn adopted the black-and-white hatta as nationally defining of their Palestinianness in the national context of Jordan. What is ironic is that prior to Glubb's innovation, which was introduced in 1931, most Transjordanians wore the white or the black-and-white hatta, as many older Jordanians still do today. As for the Palestinians, it was in the early 1930s that the peasants among them adopted the Bedouin white hatta, and later the black-and-white and the red-and-white hattas.[83] The arbitrary choice made by Glubb, however, was to define one of the most visible and provocative gendered symbols of Jordanian and Palestinian nationalisms in Jordan.

This type of clothing, however, was not worn all the time. When it came time for battle, as it did during the Syrian campaign in 1941, battlegear was issued:

> The men still wore the long khaki ankle-length dress, with a red cummerbund, a dagger and crossed and highly decorated bandoliers—the traditional uniform of the Desert Patrol. It was some while before we were issued with standard battledress and webbing equipment; and when they were first obliged to make the change from their tribal dress, the men found this European type of uniform irritatingly uncomfortable. They were used to wearing open sandals which meant that their feet were unusually wide. British army boots were often an agony to them. So with their daggers they cut off the toe caps and made holes in the sides to let in the air. They found it difficult to understand why this was frowned on. It took weeks to get them to turn out in this new kit with their equipment properly and neatly in place.[84]

One wonders about the disciplinary methods used during those weeks to secure Bedouin submission to the clothing routine. Musa Bakmirza Shirdan claims that many Bedouins insisted on wearing their Glubb-designed "zu-bun" under the Western pants which made them look "funny," and "wherein the soldier among them would look inflated in his lower half"—a practice that did not last very long.[85] Following the period from 1941 to 1943, the dress of all fighting units was changed to European clothing, as this was seen as more appropriate for battle conditions. This coincided with the transfor-mation of the Arab Legion from a police force into a full-fledged army. Moreover, the change of clothing was effected for economic reasons, as Glubb's elaborate (and Victorian) designs were quite costly. However, Bed-ouin military police units continued to wear Glubb's original designs, as they still do today, along with the rest of the Desert Patrol.[86]

Glubb's interest in identifying all that he was introducing as compatible with and complementary to Bedouin culture was paramount. This goal extended to his very person. Glubb believed strongly that even he himself was seen by the Bedouins as internal to their culture and way of life. He fancied himself a cultural passer. To illustrate the believability of his pass-ing, he recounts a story of how captured Vichy-French soldiers reacted to him during the Syrian campaign at Sukhna in the early 1940s: "As I scram-bled from my car, three French officers got out of an armoured scout car in front of me. I was wearing an Arab kerchief on my head. They looked at me in alarm. 'Je suis Englais, messieurs,' I said, but their distaste seemed by no means lessened by the information."[87] Indeed, even if the French-men had believed him, for them, his going native was no less a cause for horror.

His identification with Bedouin Arabs in general, and with Jordanians in particular, was consciously clear for Glubb. He reveled in his knowledge of Bedouin culture so much that he claimed to be a mediator between the Bedouins and city Arabs. For example, he speaks of his resentment of the Syrian (which, for him, include Palestinians) and Egyptian lawyers who were surrounding Ibn Sa'ud in the early thirties, because they attempted to advise him—and, according to Glubb, they knew nothing of Bedouin life: "More than once I found myself obliged to explain bedouin customs and expres-sions to them."[88] Unlike Glubb, Westernized city-Jordanians also shied away from anything Bedouin: "officials and ministers in Jordan almost took a pride in not understanding bedu language or the customs of the tribes (of whom eighty per cent of the population consisted)."[89] Glubb was careful to exclude King 'Abdullah from this criticism, pointing out that his early years in the Hijaz had given him an instinctive sympathy for the tribes. Moreover, Glubb asserts that as a member of the Ottoman Parliament before World War I,

'Abdullah had acquired a much more comprehensive grasp of world affairs than any of his ministers.[90] It is unclear why such worldly knowledge would be important at all for 'Abdullah to understand the Bedouins.

In his writings about himself and the Bedouins, Glubb is acting like a classic Orientalist. As Edward Said asserts: "The Orientalist can imitate the Orient without the opposite being true. What he says about the Orient is therefore to be understood as description obtained in a one-way exchange: as *they* spoke and behaved, *he* observed and wrote down. His power was to have existed amongst them as a native speaker, as it were, and also as a secret writer. And what he wrote was intended as useful knowledge, not for them, but for Europe and its various disseminative institutions."[91] Applying Said's reading of Edward W. Lane to Glubb, we reach the same conclusion as Said: "that ego, the first-person pronoun moving through Egyptian [in our case Bedouin] customs, rituals, festivals, infancy, adulthood, and burial rites, is in reality both an Oriental masquerade and an Orientalist device for capturing and conveying valuable, otherwise inaccessible information. As narrator, Lane [and also Glubb] is both exhibit and exhibitor, winning two confidences at once, displaying two appetites for experience: the Oriental one for engaging companionship (or so it seems) and the Western one for authoritative, useful knowledge."[92]

Glubb's identification with Bedouin Arabs, as the basis for Jordanianness, was ultimately ratified through a formal declaration before 'Abdullah when the latter demanded it in 1939: " 'You are English . . . and this is an Arab country, and an Arab army. Before you take over command, I want you to pledge me your word, that as long as you remain in my appointment, you will *act* always as if you had been born a Trans-Jordanian.' . . . 'Sir,' I answered, 'I give you my word of honour. From now onwards I *am* a Transjordanian, except under the conditions you mentioned [the condition of fighting breaking out between the British and Jordan], and which I pray God may never come' [emphases added]."[93] Note that 'Abdullah is aware that Transjordanianness is actually an "act" not a "being," whereas Glubb responds that this "act" constitutes for him a "being"—albeit one that is *consciously and conditionally* constitutive of his self. It is crucial to point out here that the importance of national identity, as one that is performatively (not ontologically) constituted, was central to Glubb's project of nationalizing the Bedouins through a certain set of practices imparted to them under the rubric of military training.[94] Also, it is important to note the slippage, in Glubb's writings, of Bedouins into Arabs and vice versa. In the context of Transjordan, Glubb's conflation of Bedouin, Arab, and Transjordanian as one and the same is not at all unconscious but a reflection of his projected goal of Bedouinizing the country as a basis for its new national identity.

This act of being was so successful an act of passing that even "The East-or Transjordanians regarded me as one of themselves—not as a British general. Many Palestinians were my friends, even if they did not regard me quite as one of themselves, as the Easterners did."[95] In fact, Transjordanians, according to Glubb, were shocked at anyone's suggestion that Glubb's passing was just that. Glubb tells a story affirming that for Transjordanians, he *was*—rather than passed as—one of them:[96] The family of a distinguished Arab politician took refuge at a police station during a visit to Petra in 1947.

> In the corse of the conversation one of them asked the police:
> "How do you like having a British officer to command you?"
> "How do you mean?" answered the police sergeant, puzzled.
> "Why, Glubb Pasha, of course," was the answer.
> "Glubb Pasha isn't a British officer, cried the men indignantly. "He is one of us."
> It was what I had promised King Abdulla.

Ghalib Halasa, Jordan's most illustrious novelist, counters this version of Bedouin attitudes toward Glubb. In his novella *Zunuj, Badu wa Fallahun*, Halasah depicts Glubb on one of his visits to a Bedouin household. "On being served coffee," writes Halasa, "Glubb complains, saying, 'It needs fire, boy! Your coffee is cold.' "

> He [Glubb] was acting under the naive impression that he was gaining the loyalty of those Bedouins by claiming to uphold their traditions and by his exaggerated care in adhering to them. He is fooled by the acclaim that remarks like the one he made about the coffee elicit. In his presence, the Bedouins would pretend to be extremely attached to these traditions. . . . He would speak in an accent with strange pronunciation. A smile was drawn on the faces of the [Bedouin] shaykhs, one that they would conceal by knitting their eye-brows. . . . The British officer began speaking quickly, thinking that [by doing so] he could hide his funny accent.[97]

Glubb had even been renamed by Iraqi Bedouins as Abu Hunayk, or Father of Little-Jaw, in reference to a World War I wound that he had received.[98] This name was to stick with him after his arrival in Transjordan, only to be changed again upon the birth of his son, who was named Faris by Amir 'Abdullah. Glubb's new title was Abu-Faris, or Father of Faris.[99] His most famous title, however, was that of Pasha. "Glubb Pasha" is the way he was addressed and referred to by his contemporaries, and it is how he continues to live in the memory of Jordanians as well as in their history books.[100]

Glubb even followed Arab "tradition" by meeting with refugees, tribesmen, orphans, the poor, the ignorant, and others to solve their problems, rather than relegating them to an impersonal bureaucratic procedure. In doing so, he felt that he was passing as an Arab ruler: "Under the traditional forms of Arab rule, every post of authority is occupied by one man . . . [who] is accessible to everybody without exception . . . [but the] imitation of Europe . . . by the Turks . . . then . . . by the mandatory powers, destroyed this system." To remedy this situation, which "deprived the poor and illiterate of the traditional forms of justice which they understood, I tried to make myself accessible after office hours to the poor and the ignorant."[101] He explains: "This procedure may sound chaotic to Europeans. Perhaps it was. But it was much more congenial to Arabs than cold regulations of government departments."[102] Glubb did not completely appropriate Bedouin lifestyle. He felt the need for marking himself as different in appearance as well as manner. As his biographer remarks,

> Glubb was probably one of the few genuine Arabists who did not consider it necessary to adopt Arab dress. Unlike T. E. Lawrence, who attended the Peace Conference in Paris wearing Arab robes, or Harold Ingrams in the Hadhramaut who wore the *Futa* of South Arabia, Glubb's uniform was patterned on that of the British army. He wore, of course, the red and white checkered headcloth of the Arab Legion, known as shamagh; or the red and blue forage cap, called sidara; but otherwise he wore a khaki tunic and trousers, always with a black Sam Browne belt and sword frog. He wore khaki serge in winter and khaki drill in summer. He was not very impressive in uniform until one noticed his five rows of medal ribbons and realized that he had no need to draw attention to himself by the cut of his tunic. Off duty he always wore English clothes.[103]

Glubb's syncretic dress code, which combined European and Arab "tradition," was similar to that of the non-Bedouin units of the Arab Legion. In that sense, he was the equivalent of a city or village Arab in appearance, and Bedouin-like in manner. Unlike T. E. Lawrence, who presented himself as spectacle, Glubb was not necessarily part of the military spectacle that the Bedouins constituted. He remained outside that spectacle, too busy directing it.

Aside from dress and manner, he also observed Muslim religious rites, such as the Ramadan fast: "I fasted with them for the complete month. I did not do this from directly religious motives, but on the principle which constrains an officer to limit his kit to the same weight as that of men under his command."[104] Ironically, on one occasion, Glubb ridiculed the alleged difficulty with which Muslims had to establish prayer time. He also hated Muslim feasts because they involved official ceremonies requiring Glubb and the soldiers to report to work.[105] Despite his understanding of Islam, however, Glubb assures his readers that he was never tempted to convert: "I had had some experience of Muslim saints and religious men, and had observed in them many of the qualities which we associated with Christian saints. I had never been tempted to become a Muslim—Christianity laid more emphasis on love—but I found it easy to cooperate with Muslims in our common capacity of God Fearers."[106]

One of his fellow officers remarked on how Glubb had been transformed inside the Orient into a sort of chameleon man: "You never knew what was going on with Glubb. His mind had begun to work like an Arab's. He was all subtleties. He had the kind of mind that could understand the illogic of the Arabs and anticipate it. He knew they would act from their emotions, and he knew what those emotions were. He dealt as an Arab with the King's palace, as a Bedouin with the tribes, as a British officer with London. No one except Glubb knew everything that was going on."[107]

Although Glubb understood national identity to be performatively produced, he conceived of Bedouin identity in strongly essentialist terms—one is born, and does not become, a Bedouin. Although the etymological root of Bedouin (or *Badawiyy/a* in the singular or *Badu* in the plural) in Arabic derives from *bada* as in "to reside in the *badiya*" meaning the desert, hence a Bedouin is an inhabitant of the desert who leads a nomadic lifestyle, Glubb has a stricter criterion for such a definition. This is how he defines a Bedouin:

> The first requisite is that the bedouin must be a nomad who breeds and keeps camels. Any non-nomad is automatically ruled out. But there are tens of thousands of nomadic tribesmen in Syria and Iraq who live in tents and are continually on the move, but who are not bedouins for they do not primarily breed camels, but sheep and donkeys. Having decided that a bedouin must be a nomadic breeder of

camels, however, we have not completed our definition; for he must also be able to trace his descent from certain recognized pure-bred bedouin tribes. *You and I could never become bedouins. A pure-bred Arab, an agriculturalist in Iraq or Transjordan, could never become a bedouin unless he could prove pure bedouin descent.* We find therefore that a bedouin, in the strictest sense, is a camel-breeding nomad of certain specified tribes [emphasis added].[108]

Although Glubb saw himself, and was seen by other Europeans, as a sort of father figure for the Bedouins, his real function was more maternal, since his reproductive project involved the creation of a new species of Arab—one that is endowed with ancient noble traditions that are combined with modern soldiering. His biographer (or hagiographer) states, "Most of the Arab officers liked and admired Cooke Pasha [a Glubb associate]. He was in their eyes much more 'the very image of a modern major-general' than Glubb Pasha, whom they regarded more as a father-figure."[109] Peter Young observes, "It was customary for a bedouin soldier, who felt 'wronged' or otherwise 'obliged,' to seek an interview with his commanding officer, or even with 'Abuna el-Kebir' [our old/great father]."[110]

At times, Glubb saw the Bedouins, as a result of their encounter with modernity, as sick patients: "A bedouin unit needs as much care on the part of an officer as a hospital full of patients needs from a doctor. . . . Every man must be studied separately."[111] Glubb spent his life doing just that. In this, he was following the footsteps of T. E. Lawrence, who had recommended such a course of action to Arabophiles:

The beginning and ending of the secret of handling Arabs, is unremitting study of them. Keep always on your guard; never say an unconsidered thing; watch yourself and your companions all the time; hear all that passes, search out what is going on beneath the surface, read their characters, discover their tastes and their weaknesses, and keep everything you find out to yourself. Bury yourself in Arab circles, have no interests and no ideas except the work in hand so that your brain shall be saturated with one thing only, and you realize your part deeply enough to avoid the little slips that would undo the work of weeks. Your success will be just proportioned to the amount of mental effort you devote to it.[112]

Gawain Bell, a British officer who served in the Legion, states approvingly, "We would all have done well had we too been able to follow these precepts and impress them on those British officers who joined us with no previous experience of work in the Arab world. Some, but by no means all, had an instinct for this sort of approach to the problem of making modern soldiers out of illiterate but proud tribesmen."[113] Glubb lamented the few openly racist British officers (dispatched from Britain to assist him) who referred to Arabs as "Wogs."[114]

Glubb's biographer insisted, "Bedouins had little thought for the future and often behaved like children, furiously angry at one moment, in tears the next."[115] Glubb was at times disconcerted that Bedouins saw him as a sort of surrogate father. He states that a "serious and apparently increasing nuisance in the desert is the fashion spreading amongst bedouin fathers of dying and appointing me solemnly as guardian of the child."[116] Glubb's wife was to take up this responsibility:

> Immediately after we were married in 1938, my wife had taken a great interest in the barefooted little boys. . . . She rescued many of these boys, and we took an empty house for them, looked after them and engaged a schoolmaster to teach them. . . . One or two eventually became officers in the Arab Legion, one even going to Sandhusrt. Others became N.C.O.s or soldiers. A lame boy who had suffered from polio was set up as a shopkeeper in Kerak. We enabled another cripple, whom my wife found begging, to open a shop in Amman. When we had several children of our own, my wife was obliged to give up this work, but we maintained affectionate relations with most of these boys when they were established in the world.[117]

In addition to their biological son, the Glubbs did in fact adopt three children.[118] Naomi, whom they adopted in 1944, was a Jordanian Bedouin girl.[119] In 1948 they adopted two Palestinian refugee children whom they named Mary and John.[120] As for the boys they took care of, unfortunately, Glubb was disappointed to learn of the ingratitude of one of them:

> It was at the end of 1955 that one of these boys was sitting with a group of civilians in Amman. They were discussing the riots and one of those present made a derogatory remark about me. The boy whom we had brought up agreed with the denunciation of me. Another man present, however protested . . . "You ought not to say anything against the Pa-sha," he said. "After all, you owe everything to him." . . . "I used to think that myself," our boy replied. "But now the whole matter has

been explained to me. I realize how they did not care for me at all—it was all clever politics. That was why they helped me. We don't want any foreigners in this country."[121]

Glubb's relationship to this boy is obviously invoking a parallel between Britain and Jordanians (if not the colonized) more generally. The boy's rejection of his loving caretaker, and his imputing to him less than honorable motives, are quite similar to how Jordanian nationalists were soon to reject British tutelage through massive anti-British opposition in the country, which was to lead soon to the expulsion of Glubb himself and the abrogation of the Anglo-Jordanian treaty. Comparing the situation in 1978 to that in 1916, Glubb later commented in a different context: "Nowadays, in1978, the memory of the benefits conferred by British rule on backward countries has been largely forgotten. . . . The poor and primitive countries have so far advanced that they are now in a position to govern themselves. When the children are grown up, they rarely remember with gratitude the old nurse who directed their infant footsteps. In 1916, however, these benefits were still generally appreciated."[122]

Glubb, in fact, had become very distressed by the changes wrought by the arrival of the Palestinian refugees after 1948 and the impact they were to have on the Jordanians: "The people dwelling east of the Jordan were my people. I had grown old amongst them, and my home was in their midst. . . . Gradually [after the arrival of the Palestinians], the Trans-Jordanians were partially submerged, and the rock of Jordan, with its wise moderation and its broadminded comprehension of East and West, disintegrated in the flood of hate."[123]

The arrival of the Palestinians had in fact exposed Glubb as a passer, which marked the beginning of his alienation from Jordanians. He laments this unforeseen outcome, which was to end in his ultimate expulsion from Jordan in 1956: "Perhaps my principal handicap was the fact that I was British. Before 1948, the Jordanians had forgotten this and I had become one of them."[124] His sadness was of course real as, for him, "Jordan has been my country, *almost* as much as Britain [emphasis added]."[125] His worry about his place in Arab history books led him to predict and lament that "Perhaps for generations to come, the history books in most Arab countries will teach that Glubb Pasha betrayed the Arabs and gave Lydda and Ramle to the Jews, in accordance with orders received from Mr. Bevin in London."[126]

His prediction came true.[127] This was all the more sad for Glubb as he had seen his role and that of the British as somewhat of a corrective for what had gone wrong the last time Europe had visited the Orient—that is, before the modern era of imperialism. Glubb was fascinated by that last instance, when the Europeans had been in the Orient as Crusaders. This fascination influenced his political thinking as well as his personal life, including his self-conception in relation to the Orient. References to the Crusaders abound in his books and articles, as well as in his private life. Politically, he saw the role Transjordan was to play in British policy as one similar to the one that "the first Transjordan," or "la terre d'outre Jourdain," had played in the Crusades.[128] He explains this parallel:

> Just as the Arab League is regarded by the Palestine Zionists today as a menace to their continued existence, so the nightmare of the crusaders of the twelfth century in Palestine was the union of Syria and Egypt. As long as these two Muslim states remained isolated, the Latin Kingdom of Jerusalem was able to survive. To prevent their union, the Crusaders established the principality of Outre-Jourdain, or TransJordan, with its capital at Kerak. . . . The last Crusader Prince of Kerak was Renault de Chatillion, an unscrupulous adventurer, but a man of immense courage and initiative. He was not contented passively to bar the way between Arabia and Egypt, but resolved to carry the war into the enemy's country. . . . When the Crusader kingdom collapsed at the battle of Hattin [sic], Renault was taken prisoner by Saladin. He was put to death for his raids on the Muslim pilgrims during a period of truce.[129]

The parallels between the British establishment of Transjordan and the Crusaders' establishment of Outre-Jourdain are quite obvious to Glubb and to his readers. The function of modern Jordan to the British and to the Americans and the Israelis remains the same as it was for the Crusaders. The fate of Renault might be an ominous allusion to the possible fate of the rulers of modern Jordan, a fate perhaps unconsciously postulated by Glubb.[130]

As for the impact of the Crusaders on his private life, it is illustrated by the following story: "In . . . 1939, five weeks after war was declared, a son was born to us in Jerusalem. We were advised to christen him David, because he was born in the city of King David. We decided to call him Godfrey, after Godfrey de Bouillon, the first Crusader King of Jerusalem. But when we brought him back to Amman, His highness declared that he must have an Arab name. He called him Faris, which means knight or cavalier, a name which accorded well enough with Godfrey de Boullion. . . . Arabs are very proud of parentage, and often call themselves fathers of their children. Henceforward I was known as the 'Father of Faris.'"[131]

His being referred to as Abu Faris notwithstanding, Glubb continued to refer to his son as Godfrey in all of his subsequent writings (although today his son writes under the name of Faris). According to Edward Gibbon, Godfrey de Bouillon was proclaimed by the Crusader army as "the first and most worthy of the champions of Christendom. His magnanimity accepted a trust as full of danger as of glory; but in a city where his Saviour had been crowned with thorns the devout pilgrim rejected the name and ensigns of royalty; and the founder of the kingdom of Jerusalem contented himself with the modest title of Defender and Baron of the Holy Sepulcher,"[132] a role Glubb seemed to identify with, and one he wanted his son to mimic. De Bouillon, however, ruled only for one year, Glubb for twenty-six. Unlike De Bouillion, Glubb did not seek necessarily to fight the Arabs, but rather to control them through teaching them in the way of Empire—a task, he felt, for which the military institution was best suited. As for Glubb's son, he appeared to have political differences with his father as an adult. He lived in Beirut in the early 1970s and became a "resistance poet" allied with the Palestinian guerrillas. As a child, Godfrey/Faris "was often found in his father's company wearing a specially made copy of the Arab Legion's uniform, complete with *shamagh*."[133]

Imperialism as Educator

Glubb is not an essentialist nationalist. He is eclectic in what he draws on for philosophical inspiration. He understands all to well what his role as a representative of Empire means, and he is keen to carry out his task to the best of his knowledge. Consequently, he is not a rejectionist of all things Western in an Arab context but rather is partial to careful selectivity, and a proponent of cultural syncretism. Lest his European readers take him to mean that Europe has nothing to teach the natives, he is quick to explain: "What, now, are the essential lessons which Eastern soldiers can learn from Europe? The first is detailed organization, method, and discipline. This is ensured by mental and moral training, and does not necessitate the introduction either of foreign social distinctions or of foreign dress. The second lesson they require is the use of scientific weapons—motor transport, machine-guns, artillery, wireless and aircraft. I believe that it is possible for

Arab troops to learn the lessons which Europe can teach in organization, discipline, and scientific weapons, without departing from their hereditary customs, manners and dress."[134]

Glubb is committed to interpreting the other as different without *necessarily* assigning a hierarchy to the notion of difference (although on many occasions he does). He explains that another nation that differs materially from "ourselves" might do so for two reasons: "It may be less civilized and educated than ourselves . . . due to [its] 'backwardness,' " or the differences "between us arise from differences between our national characters, traditions, climate, or other factors, as a result of which our customs or institutions will *never* be suitable for the other community. . . . It will certainly never be possible, or even desirable, for them to become just like us."[135] His commitment to a serious understanding of the Orient led him to perceive himself as a chameleon man passing across cultures while being inhabited by them. He asserts, "I strenuously opposed any idea that East was East and West was West and that the two could never agree. I had experienced in myself, as I thought, the feasibility of living simultaneously as an Arab among Arabs and as an Englishman amongst Europeans. Why should not the two work hand in hand? There were, of course, many differences in outlook and temperament. But differences do not necessarily mean rivalry; on the contrary, they can be a means of harmony, for one becomes the complement of the other."[136]

Ultimately, this course of selective Westernization is what Glubb set out to accomplish. Teaching the Bedouins how to mimic certain, but not all, things Western was central to his transformative project. As Homi Bhabha asserts, "colonial mimicry is the desire for a reformed, recognizable Other, as *a subject of a difference that is almost the same but not quite*. Which is to say, that the discourse of mimicry is constructed around an *ambivalence*; in order to be effective, mimicry must always produce its slippage, its excess, its difference."[137]

Glubb, who fancied himself a race genealogist, never shied away from racialist descriptions and generalizations. Unaware of the many occasions in which *Bedouins* slip into *Arabs* in his text, he insists on the variability of the origins of those calling themselves Arabs (views which were later elaborated in his lecture on "The Mixture of Races in the Eastern Arab Countries"[138]), with a particular racist venom against Egyptians—whom he calls "lethargical," "tending to obesity," and "expert at intrigue," although "in many ways attractive" and having a "sense of humour."[139] These descriptions coincided with the Suez Crisis, as the book in which they appear was published in 1957.

Racial and cultural explanations were also deployed by Glubb to account for the difference between ʿAbdullah's attitude toward Zionism and that of other Arabs. The "Western Arabs—the Egyptians, Palestinians and the Syrians—have that logical mentality which deals only in purely intellectual conceptions. Such people are incapable of compromise."[140] This, of course, is unlike the more practical Bedouins. Although ʿAbdullah and his family hail from the oldest city in Arabia, Mecca, Glubb assimilates them into Bedouin culture as the latter is defined by Glubb: "King Abdulla never could see eye to eye with the Egyptians. Perhaps their differences were not solely due to a clash of interests, but also to some organic difference in their mental make-up. For King Abdulla was a practical man, always ready to make a bargain or consider a compromise."[141]

Glubb proceeds to tell us how Jordan's prime minister, Tawfiq Pasha, who is from the Palestinian city of Acre, is like the rest of the Western Arabs and therefore unlike the practical ʿAbdullah. He concludes on the same page by stating, "There is no doubt therefore that this peculiarity existed in the mentality of the Levantine Arabs; a kind of 'justice though the heavens fall.' " In fact, one of the only possible explanations that Glubb could give for the outrageous claim made by Palestinians that he, as a representative of the Empire, does not work for the benefit of the Arabs, is a cultural one: "The Palestinian Arabs are extremely intelligent. But their subtlety makes them unwilling to accept the obvious. They tend instinctively to seek a complicated and involved explanation for every event. . . . The plot was obvious, and I had sacrificed tens of thousands of Arabs in order to further Britain's wicked intrigues."[142]

Such claims were lies and fabrications, as far as Glubb was concerned, and characteristic of the Arab: "the Levantine Arabs and Egyptians . . . held [the] opinion . . . that morale must be kept up by telling lies. . . . This unwillingness to say anything unpleasant seemed, indeed, to be deeply engrained in the Arab character."[143] This should be contrasted with the honesty of the British Empire:

In Britain, people believe that honesty is the best policy. . . . I have not found in the Middle East that truth can be relied upon to emerge. . . . Perhaps, in the West lies are more liable to exposure than in the Middle East, because people are more sophisticated and have more varied sources of information. But in the Middle East, the gullibility of the masses is unending. . . . The explanation of the unending credulity of Middle East crowds lies perhaps chiefly in their emotions. For Arab politics are more guided by passion than by reason. . . . I trust that Britain will never tell lies, because to do so is wrong and undermines the moral character of the liar. But I have not found that, in Middle Eastern politics, honesty is the best policy.[144]

Add European ideas like nationalism and communism to the Arab traits of dishonesty and lying and the situation becomes truly explosive and detrimental to Western interests: "Our second difficulty arose from the intense propaganda which was circulating, to the effect that the Western Powers were unscrupulous and deceitful. The East tends naturally to consider that politics are a competition in duplicity, but this normal opinion had been intensified by Communist and Nationalist propaganda."[145]

This aside, other explanations about the Palestinians' cunning intelligence can be found in biological hybridity: "This faculty for attributing Machiavellian motives to their rulers seemed to be a particular characteristic of the Palestinians. Every action one performed was analyzed with a view to discovering the tortuous motive which actuated one. I do not know whether this quality is to be attributed to the considerable amount of Greek blood which flowed in their veins and gave them this intellectual subtlety."[146]

Of course, Arabs could not have acquired such intelligence unless they had been genetically altered by a superior race. Glubb states, "This intellectual subtlety, which attributes to every action a tortuous ulterior motive, is not to be found among the original natives of central Arabia, whose minds seem to work openly and in a straightforward manner. Their tendency was to speak the truth and to accept what they were told at its face value."[147] Glubb also explains the racial hybridity of Jordanians: "The Jordanians were of mixed origins . . . [Alexander and the Greeks having settled the Northern part of Jordan] with the result that the people of northern Jordan retain their subtlety of intellect today. The remainder of Jordan, however, was largely peopled by central Arabians, whose minds were more frank and straightforward."[148] Not only can the intelligence or stupidity of Arabs be genetically based, but so can their lack of political stability. Glubb quotes a French officer explaining to Glubb the reason why Syria, after World War II, had been unstable with many coups, and why Jordan was stable: "He replied that the Syrians were too intelligent. 'A certain amount of stupidity is necessary to political stability,' he added. 'The British, for example, are famous for their stability!' There may well have been some foundation for his opinion, for historically, Syria and, even more, Lebanon and the 'Arabs' of Palestine have been heavily interbred with Greeks—a nation famous for acuteness of intellect but not for political stability."[149]

The Frenchman's likening the stupidity of the "Arabs" to the British not-withstanding, Glubb buys the argument. Explaining his race theory of Arabs and what propels them to disobedience of authority, Glubb states,

> Although, however, the "Arabs" are not by any means one race, it is possible to trace one or two characteristics, which most of them share, and which differentiate them from Europeans. . . . The Arabs in general are hot-headed, hasty and volatile. They are proud and touchy, ready to suspect an insult and hasty to avenge it. To hate their enemies is to them not only a natural emotion but a duty. Should any man claim to forgive an enemy, they find it difficult to believe in his sincerity and suspect a trap. *Politically, they tend, like the proverbial Irishman, to be against the government.* Of whatever form or *complexion* it may be, they are usually ready to change it, *though they may later on regret their action* and wish to return to their former state. It is easy to conquer any Arab country, but their *natural inclination to rebellion* makes it difficult and expensive for the invader to maintain his control. Their mutual jealousies, however, provide their rulers with the means of playing them off against one another, an art which they themselves consider to be of the very essence of politics. . . . But while their hot-bloodedness makes the Arabs good haters, it makes them also cordial friends. No race can be more pleasant or charming. They are delightful company, with a ready sense of humour. . . . In one quality, the Arabs lead the world — it is the virtue of hospitality, which some of them carry to a degree which becomes almost fantastic [all emphases added].[150]

The parallel with the "natural inclination" of the Irish and the Arabs to rebel leads one to conclude that Arabs, like the Irish, are sociopaths, albeit with the possibility of a conscience to mitigate their otherwise anarchic behavior ("though they may later on regret their action"). The mention of complexion here is not at all figurative, rather one that sees epidermal markers as justifying colonial rule, as is the case in the paragraph about maintaining such rule. The point is that Arabs do not resist invaders as anticolonial resistance; rather, it is part of their "natural inclination" to rebel against any form of government regardless of "complexion" or form. As for the Arabs' analysis of Western politics, Arab dishonesty combined with nationalism and communism are all that can account for the Arabs' skewed antipathy to the West, and certainly not the historical and actual policies of the West itself.

In one of his periodic reports during World War II, Glubb predicted, "Whatever may be the result of this war in other directions, one thing is certain—'coloured' races are no longer going to accept with resignation a racial status inferior to that of the white races."[151] Glubb became increasingly concerned with possible anti-British revolts in the colonies. He worried that if the British continued to insist on not properly understanding the Arabs, as previous conquerors had not, revolution might ensue: "With the Arabs in particular, it is vital to remember the existence of a capacity for passionate and heroic courage concealed beneath their everyday venality. The Byzantines made the mistake of forgetting this no less than the Turks and the British. All of a sudden appears a cause or a leader possessing the flaming quality which can inspire the exalted courage that lies hidden deep in the Arab character. Suddenly they throw away money in disgust or exaltation, and develop a courage which staggers, if it does not sweep away, their astonished opponents. This is, indeed, yet one more quality in which the Arabs resemble the British."[152]

The Arabs, for Glubb, it would seem, are an unchanging lot of people, who across the centuries, since Byzantium and the Ottomans to the British, have been governed by the same eternal and essential spirit. He confirms such views in the context of his desiring British and Arab troops to fight together in Europe as equals during World War II. He states "I believe the Arab tribesman to be first-class military material. . . . I am convinced that they are the same men who conquered half the world 1,300 years ago."[153] This eternal Arab, for Glubb, never changes; *he* lives outside history. The passage of time signals no change at all, except when the British interfere and introduce the Arab to history and time, from which the Arab benefits by reconnecting with his eternal sense of "honour." In fact, British enlightenment has also been able to end abominable practices. Indeed, the march of history and progress cannot be stopped: "The days of the 'true light of God' are doubtless numbered, and in the full glare of modern democracy and (doubtless) enlightenment, the little red-hot spoon [a sort of Bedouin polygraph test wherein a red-hot spoon is placed momentarily on the tongue of someone suspected of lying. If the tongue blisters, due to dryness resulting from nervousness, then the person is a liar, otherwise, due to the presence of saliva whose evaporation protects the skin, she or he is not] will soon vanish."[154]

Empire's emotional commitment to its subjects is all too easily forgotten, laments Glubb. He quotes a Palestinian's testimony to the virtues of Empire and then proceeds to mourn the British Empire's historical fate: "Direct British rule is disappearing. History will record that we sailed the seas, that we conquered, that we ruled. But will she remember also that we *loved*— and especially that we loved the poor?"[155]

Masculinity, Culture, and Women

Glubb's views of the Bedouins in particular and of Arabs in general were underlain by interrelated discourses on gender, race, and culture, especially when explicit comparisons with the West were made. His views reflect the dominant Orientalist feminization of the Oriental other as well as the supermasculinization of that other. Thus, the Arab seems to inhabit a hermaphroditic existence of femininity and supermasculinity, as does the West, which is characterized as masculine in relation to the feminine Arab, and feminine in contrast to the supermasculine Arab. The following will explore the points at which Arabs and Westerners are marked as masculine and feminine, to clarify the gendering discourse underlying these claims.

Describing a procession of Bedouin Arabs soon after his arrival in Iraq in 1920, Glubb expresses curious amazement at the feminine appearance of Bedouin men in contrast to European men: "before my eyes passed in review a complete pageant of that nomad life which had not changed in essentials since the days of Abraham, but which was soon to pass away. An almost unending procession of tanned men's faces, framed by long ringlets like those worn by the young ladies of the Victorian age."[156] The Victorian comparison was to crop up on other occasions decades later. In the context of the Palmyra battle during the Syrian military campaign in the early forties, Glubb describes an old Bedouin soldier, Za'al, who had gone up a hilltop and loaded his rifle and began shooting at the Vichy-French fighter-bombers flying up ahead. Glubb reports, "The old man [a veteran of the "Faysal-Lawrence war"] himself was warming to the work. His headgear had fallen off. His thin grey hair was done up in tight little plaits, like a Victorian landlady in curling pins. He was shouting now, calling the name of his sister, and fighting right and left as the huge winged monsters tore over his head."[157] Glubb's fascination with the long hair and plaits of the Bedouin was always in evidence. Describing the process by which tribesmen in the service were taught to read and write, he states: "Each evening the circle by the fire would be wrapt in a tense silence, *while bearded faces bent forward, their long hair hanging in plaits over their shoulders*, and horny hands laboriously traced the letters of the Arabic alphabet in their copy-books."[158] As a result of their long hair, Glubb's Desert Patrol Bedouins were dubbed "Glubb's Girls" by British officers in the Middle East.[159] Although most Bedouin men had long hair, many did not have hair long enough to be in plaits, and this varied with the tribe. Long hair was characteristic of Bani-Sakhr and the Huwaytat tribes, in addition to some Iraqi tribes but not all.

The Arab Legion had no regulations for its soldiers' hair-length or whether they could or could not have facial hair. According to Ma'n Abu Nuwwar (a Jordanian army officer and a former head of the army's spiritual guidance division, or "al-Tawjih al-Ma'nawi"), these were considered matters of personal choice.[160] Things, however, changed in the early forties. On the occasion of the Arab Legion's involvement in battle, the men were issued battle dress and were ordered to shave their heads. Most of the Bedouin soldiers refused as they valued their long hair. To convince them, a Circassian officer named Musa Bakmirza Shirdan intervened. According to his elitist and derisive account, he claims to have told the Bedouins a story about nutrition, alleging that Bedouins have frail and skinny bodies because much of what they eat is used up by their bodies for hair growth, and that were they to shave their heads, they would have more plump healthy bodies. The soldiers, allegedly, bought this anti-Samson story and were convinced and subjected themselves to the head-shaving procedure.[161] By the late forties, long hair had disappeared completely from the Jordanian army, as British standards for masculine soldiery prevailed.

Comparisons with English women of yesteryear by Glubb were made not only with Bedouin men but also with Bedouin women. Narrating an incident in which he was disciplining Transjordanian Bedouins by confiscating their cattle, Glubb describes the scene as follows: "But within a couple of days, we had collected two hundred and fifty camels [belonging to tribal members who were away on a raiding mission against Glubb's orders] without firing a shot, although we had to run the gauntlet of the tongues of some terrible old women, shriveled and bent old hags like mediæval witches."[162]

The Bedouins' inability to understand the ways gendered appearance works in the West led them to commit many a faux pas, and one such was witnessed by Glubb during his trip across the Syrian desert with his Bedouin companion. As a result of cold weather, "I was obliged to accept some warm gloves [from the Bedouin companion], then a magnificent pair of Black French boots with pointed toes and buttoning half-way up the calf. I was doubtful for which sex they were originally intended."[163]

Noting the feminine behavior of a Bedouin lad, Glubb cannot help but make comparisons between the wider spectrum of male gender performance among the Bedouins and its much narrower parallel in England: "Standing demurely a few yards away, I saw a slender youth of perhaps fifteen years old [ibn Hamdan], *with those refined, almost girlish, features which are sometimes to be seen amongst desert dwellers.*"[164] Two years later,

> I was sitting in one of our new desert forts in Trans-Jordan, when a tall, slender youth presented himself. "I am Nehhab, the son of Hamdan," he explained. . . . "I want to be with you." I thought him at first too young to be enlisted, but two months later I gave way. After a year's service, he became my orderly. His whole manner breathed gentleness. His beardless face was frank and open, with delicate features. He spoke softly and with a gentle kindness."[165]
>
> With this quiet and mild disposition, he combined absence of fear in battle and a clear brain which enabled him at all times to grasp the essentials of a situation. Arab courage and hardihood are to some extent appreciated in Europe. Their code of chivalry has not passed completely unnoticed by travellers and historians. *But this streak of gentleness, which here and there runs through the Arab character*, has rarely been remarked by Western writers.[166]

Glubb chides his compatriots for their much more rigid criteria of gender performance and is confident that Nehhab would have led a miserable life had he been an English lad:

> In England a boy so gentle as Nehhab would have been tormented and mocked. We seem at times to think much of toughness, and to mistake loudness and bad manners for courage. Amongst the bedouins, who lived in a world of violence, bloodshed and war, gentleness was not mistaken for cowardice. Intimacy with Arab tribesmen enabled me to visualize more clearly the age of chivalry in Europe. . . . I have seen among the Arabs depths of hatred, reckless bloodshed and lust of plunder of which our lukewarm natures seem no longer capable. I have seen deeds of generosity worthy of fairy-tales and acts of treachery of extraordinary baseness. Unscrupulous men of violence, and others so gentle that they could scarcely have lived in modern England . . . The Arabs, like all other races, are neither all saints nor all sinners. But the contrasts between them are more striking and dramatic than those which are outwardly perceptible between the inhabitants of Western Europe.[167]

Note how Glubb depicts the Arabs as living in a different time and as reflecting the childhood of Europe ("the age of chivalry in Europe"). Although, on the one hand, the Arabs' feminine gentleness can no longer be found in modern supermasculine Europeans, on the other hand, the violent acts of the supermasculine Arabs are acts "of which our lukewarm natures seem no longer capable." These extreme hermaphroditic characteristics of the Arabs, their being simultaneously "unscrupulous men of violence" and yet "so gentle" prevent them from living, or even existing, in "modern England." The emphasis here is, of course, on *moderation* and a lack of passion characteristic of England as a different space, and of modernity as a different time. Note how the modern gender criteria of Britain and the British, who are characterized as both feminine, in the sense of the civilized being too refined and feminine to appreciate excessive masculine violence, and masculine, wherein Europeans are too rational and thus masculine to appreciate homosocial gentleness characteristic of Arabs and of European childhood ("the age of chivalry"), are based on interrelated discourses of gender, race, development, modernization, and culture. It is the site of European urban modernity, and the different space and time that the Arabs inhabit, that can explain these gender variations. Although, on other occasions, Glubb attempts to locate such differences in geography, climate, and temperament, here there is no room for such explanations. Europeans used to be like the Arabs but not any more; the differences are more related to an immanent temporal schema ending with the telos of modernity, not some material considerations. In fact, Glubb's encounter with the Bedouins is, for him, a journey through time: "My intimacy with the bedouins seemed to take me back in time. Knowing them well, I felt that I could feel with the ancient Britons, with Arthur or King Alfred or perhaps with the American Red Indians."[168]

In this narrative, modernity proves to endow Europeans with phallic technology that the Bedouins still lack. In describing the southern terrain of Transjordan, Glubb states: "it was as though we were, indeed, in a new world. . . . The whole place had a silent and virgin feeling about it, as though it were the mountains of the moon. The clean white sand seemed never to have been trodden by the foot of man. This was, of course, not the case, for the tribes periodically passed this way, but it was quite possible that this valley had not been visited by man for two or three years. Nor is it likely that it had ever been seen by a European, and it is absolutely certain that it had never before been crossed by wheels."[169]

Here, what is of paramount importance is that it must be a European armed with European technology ("wheels") who is capable of violating the virgin land, which is not quite so virginal except to Europeans, as no other defloration is really a defloration—for "the tribes" who have been there before are not real men with the deflowering phallus of Western technology. What a European has not seen, for Glubb, looks not like another part of the planet that "he" had not seen before, but like a part of a different world, indeed a different planet.

Glubb is also interested in contrasting gender relations among Bedouins with those in England, especially with regards to men's views of women: "Their attitude toward women reveals a number of contradictions. . . . On the one hand, free and romantic courtship remains the ideal, and there are still remnants of the old custom under which widows and divorced women had their own tents and themselves received suitors. Bedouin poetry and legend are full of tales of romantic love worthy of Arthur and the Round Table. Simultaneously, however, there are constant traces of the feeling that women are servants and inferior to man."[170]

Although the age of chivalry is no longer part of the European present, it remains part of Glubb himself, so much so that the Bedouins end up being less chivalrous than he. When in Iraq in the 1920s, a party of gypsies camped by Glubb and his Iraqi Bedouin workers labor camp: "the gypsy girls danced before the workmen. Some of the latter had no hesitation in kissing and indulging in physical familiarities with the girls, who were doubt-less accustomed to such treatment and, indeed, earned their living by it." Such behavior was horrifying to Glubb: "But my innocent and chivalrous attitude to women filled me with disgust at such conduct. I collected all my labourers and made them all remove their *agals*, the little circles of rope by which they kept their kerchiefs on their heads. The *agal* was the mark of manhood—women did not wear it. I then had all their *agals* burned. My gesture was intended to express my opinion th[at] they were not men. The labourers, who saw no harm in their handling the gypsy girls, were mystified by my action and merely thought me a little mad."[171]

Glubb's disappointment in the men stems from his projective fantasy of them as "chivalrous" by tradition. The fact that they failed to live up to his fantasy of who they should be filled him with horror. For "[h]is Orient is not the Orient as it is, but the Orient as it has been Orientalized."[172] As Said notes in *Orientalism*, "the Orient is thus Orientalized, a process that not only marks the Orient as the province of the Orientalist but also forces the uninitiated Western reader to accept Orientalist codifications . . . as the true Orient. Truth, in short, becomes a function of learned judgment, not of the material itself, which in time seems to owe even its existence to the Orien-talist.[173]

Despite all the cultural differences between Europeans and Bedouin Arabs, Glubb asserts that "[w]hen we have studied all the history, the folk-lore and the religious precepts of the Arabs, we find to our surprise that, inside the bedouin tent, the relations of man and wife are more like those of Mr. and Mrs. Smith of Tooting than we had visualized."[174] It is noteworthy that the only occasion that Glubb shows any interest in Arab women is during the 1948 War:

> Glubb: "I really cannot rattle through Jerusalem in a huge armoured car with the vizors closed, while the streets are full of women wandering about unconcerned. . . . "
> The young soldier [who was "very young. A new moustache was just beginning to pencil his upper lip"] surveyed with distaste two remarkably pretty girls in brightly coloured summer frocks, and with high heels, who walked past arm in arm. . . . "It does not matter much if the Jews kill a few girls," he remarked, "but [referring to Glubb] an army is no good without its general."[175]

Note the difference in opinion about the Palestinian "girls" between the young Jordanian Bedouin soldier and Glubb. Of course, the young man's opinion is attributed to him by Glubb, who shares his alleged distaste but not the idea that "girls" are dispensable compared to colonial army generals. The military as the institution with which the Bedouin was to affiliate has indeed succeeded. This was just another instance in which the project of shifting the male Bedouin's filiative loyalties to his tribe and clan to an affiliative loyalty with his military comrades showed much success.[176] This was the first step for the subsequent affiliation of the Bedouin with the nation.

In his autobiography, Glubb speaks of his personal sexual history and how completely asexual he had always been, marrying at the late age of forty-one only because he wanted a family. His Protestant anti-sex attitude is so pronounced that he is appalled at ideas of divorce, or of women's liberation from parental authority. He states, "I have devoted a great deal of time to the study of the rise and fall of past civilizations, and was intensely interested to discover that most national periods of decadence have been marked by increasing ease of divorce and sexual laxity." Tragic examples include the Roman Empire.[177] He also writes glowingly and homoerotically of his father, emphasizing the latter's "virility"[178] and crediting him with imparting to him his sexual mores.[179] Such mores led him to assert, "I have not the slightest

doubt that young girls do need protection. They constitute the greatest trea-
sures of our race and it is on them that the whole future of our people
depends, for it is mothers who form the characters of their children."[180]
Glubb held these views until the last days of his life, reflecting his increasing
concern that the British race was in jeopardy.

Transforming the Bedouins

With the advent of the British, the lifestyle of all the population (Bedouins, villagers, and city dwellers) was to undergo immense changes. Glubb,
as usual, fully absorbed in his Bedouin obsession, commented that before
British authority was established, "the Governments concerned had not yet
attempted to bring the desert under control, and the bedouins still migrated,
raided and fought unmolested."[181] This situation was to be radically transformed, so much so that the desert that Glubb crossed in 1924 from Baghdad
to Amman, with its attendant risks of heat, water shortage, and Bedouin
raids, was no more: "Ten years later the Iraq Petroleum Company's pipeline
passed this way, a pumping station had been built in this waste, and English
ladies were taking their tea out for a picnic in these stony valleys. That ten
years [1924 to 1934] was to see the passing of an era."[182]

In describing the territories east of the Jordan river before the arrival of
'Abdullah, Glubb explains how this "wild and unwanted [by whom?] territory east of the Jordan was out of hand and without a government. Negotiations were opened, and the Amir Abdulla was persuaded to accept the
sovereignty of the unwanted territory. Trans-Jordan was born." Glubb elab-
orates:

> The task facing His Highness was by no means a simple one. Trans-
> Jordan was four-fifths desert, inhabited by nomadic bedouins who had
> not been subjected to any government for many centuries, if, indeed,
> they had been so subjected even by the first Muslim Empire in the
> eighth and ninth centuries. In the cultivated area society was almost
> entirely tribally organized, under paramount shaiks rarely powerful
> enough to maintain order but always able and often willing to destroy
> it. In the extreme north the villagers had been accustomed for a gen-
> eration or more to the efficient control of the Ottoman Government.
> Throughout the remainder of the country the Turks had been in oc-
> cupation for only a few years, and almost the whole population rec-

ollected perfectly the great days before the Turks came. . . . The task
was, therefore, to create rather than to take over the Government. . . .
One of the first problems to be faced was obviously the organization
of armed forces to commence the task of establishing public security
and bringing the independent tribes to order.[183]

Whereas Peake recruited only from rural and urban areas having an overall boycott of Bedouins as potential recruits, Glubb was to transform military
recruitment and ultimately the military identity of the Arab Legion. This
was to also form the very national identity being fashioned in Transjordan.
However, the process of recruitment of Bedouins was not done easily. Godfrey Lias, a chronicler of the Arab Legion, states that "the ice which had
constrained the nomad mind for 1,000 years is just beginning to crack. Local
Beduins, as well as those from other parts of Arabia, have begun to enlist in
the ice-breaker, Desert Patrol, and the next leap forward is about to start."[184]
Actually, several disciplinarian strategies had to be enacted to effect the desired result—the transformation of Bedouin culture and lifestyle, in short,
the de-Bedouinization of the Bedouins as a precursor to the Bedouinization
of Jordanian national identity. Glubb cites some of the difficulties he faced
in 1931 upon launching his new project for the Bedouins: "But enlist as
soldiers they would not. The idea that the Government was their bitterest
enemy was too deeply *engrained in their minds* to admit such a *novel* idea."[185]
In fact, the idea was not really novel as the Huwaytat and the other tribes
had been subject, albeit intermittently, to governmental rule and they simply
did not like the oppressive policies of governments. Their enmity for governments was not "engrained in their minds" but based on historical and
present experience. Although Glubb recruited at first Iraqi and Hijazi Bedouins, slowly Transjordan's Bedouins were joining.[186] This was for a number
of reasons. On the one hand, the ending of Bedouin raiding as an activity
made the military the only sanctioned place for warfare that the Bedouins
could engage in. On the other hand, the deteriorating economic situation
of the Bedouins, with the drought and ensuing famine from 1932 to 1933,
drove more of them into the Arab Legion where they could earn a living.
In addition, Glubb paid many tribal shaykhs money to control the raiding
and earn their favor.[187] The Legion's incorporation of the Bedouins was so
successful that soon civilian firms began to employ them as watchmen. The
British-owned Iraq Petroleum Company financed the expansion of the Desert Patrol by seventy men, almost double its original size, so that the new
recruits could be used to protect its stores and camps along the pipeline that

crosses into Transjordan.[188] Only a couple of years earlier, the Bedouins had been feared as the main threat to the safety of the pipeline.[189] In the meantime, since Glubb still had to rely on non-Transjordanian Bedouins, the Desert Patrol was exempted from recruiting citizens exclusively, thus waiving the condition that had been asserted by the Travel-Documents law of 1927 (the precursor law to the 1928 Nationality Law). At one point, Transjordanian Bedouins protested the recruitment of Saudi/Hijazi Bedouins into the Arab Legion. Although as George Dragnich explains, "it would be hasty to conclude that the former were developing a national awareness—other evidence does not support that conclusion for this time frame, and they may have only wanted other members of their tribe to be enlisted."[190]

For all his ostensible dislike of European laws, Glubb would not have been able to carry out his task without relying on them. In addition to the military having authority over its Bedouin recruits, the law was marshaled to increase the power of the military over the civilian Bedouin population. As mentioned earlier, in 1936 the Law of Tribal Courts bestowed on the head of the Arab Legion (who at the time was Peake, with Glubb replacing him in 1939) not only the duty to execute the rulings of the tribal courts but also the complete authority of a *mutasarrif*, or governor, over the Bedouins throughout the country.[191] As the following clarifies, Glubb was aware of the productive quality of laws, of their ability not only to repress, restrict, constrain, or simply erase certain practices, but as importantly to produce new identities, new classifications, a new taxonomy by which the population was to be segmented in relation to the law. In a statement presaging Foucault's conclusion about the modern prison's role in producing criminals, Glubb states, "In the past everybody raided, and raiding was a custom not a crime. From now onwards, we developed in a mild way a criminal class."[192] Glubb happily explains how raiding was ended in Transjordan without "violence," in contrast to neighboring Arab countries, and how credit should go to the Desert Patrol men who "by their wisdom, their devotion to the cause in which they were engaged and their brotherly love for one another, so impressed the tribes by their example that they gave to tens of thousands of wild nomads a vision of a new kind of life."[193]

Glubb insisted on following the Gandhian formula of which he was so fond, namely, that "we should start with local institutions and then modify them as is found necessary to suit *modern* conditions. This was the system we adopted with the nomadic tribes which had never been administered by a Government."[194] Despite Glubb's reticence to transform Bedouins into "moderns" due to his understanding that *modern* meant *like us*, he still proceeded in that direction, hoping that sublating existing laws rather than simply replacing them would eschew that pitfall. We shall see how such a course of action achieved no such thing. The Christian patriarch that he fancied himself to be, Glubb describes the transformation of the Bedouins — from nomads into settled soldiers and farmers, from illiterates into literates, and from people beyond the reach of European state laws to ones subjected to and produced (subjectified) by them — under the heading "Labour of Love."[195] He concludes that the "limits of cultivation in Trans-Jordan have been extended, the standard of cultivation has been improved, tribesmen have been digging new wells, building storehouse, enclosing gardens. Why? Because, for the last few years, they have acquired confidence in the permanence of law and order. . . . If a breakdown of public security were to take place, this constructive work by tribesmen would cease."[196] Indeed, the Bedouins understood the logic of capital, bourgeois property, and the laws protecting both so well that limits had to be placed on their enterprising attempts. According to Glubb, "The usual [Bedouin] tactics were to go some fifteen miles out into the desert, plough up about fifty acres and sow it with barley. The idea was that if a man owned a village on the edge of the desert and a microscopic piece of cultivation fifteen miles out, he automatically owned all the desert in between. This hasty rush to stake out claims to land far out of the desert naturally produces some sharp disputes between rival stakers of claims."[197]

To alleviate the optimism of this Bedouin view of capitalist relations, Glubb suggested that the "only solution would appear [to be] to limit the cultivation in the desert to a strip lying along the east of the Hejaz railway and to forbid the staking of claims in isolated valleys far out in the desert." He is, however, conscious of the irony of the situation: "the necessity for preventing Bedouins in Transjordan from cultivating is amusing in view of the fact that it is generally considered necessary to adopt every possible means to compel then to cultivate. A second irony is the high state of public security in the desert which has emboldened all and sundry to race to stake out land claims in an area where formerly only raiders armed to the teeth could travel."[198]

Glubb's task was successfully accomplished through a strategic juridico-disciplinary dyad. He explains how Bedouin life-style was transfigured in tune with British imperial policy. Due to government penalties, "raiding was no longer worthwhile, and soon ceased."

This we were able to do only because the Desert Patrol was in itself entirely composed of bedouins, including men of all the tribes concerned in these feuds. These men felt no scruples in this degree of efficiency by the high moral standard which we had inculcated in our own men. Their numbers were so few and the desire of the tribesman to enlist was so great, that we were able to pick and test each man individually. We spent much time in explaining to every individual man exactly what we were trying to do, how the age of raiding was past, and how much better it was for the tribes to learn to accommodate themselves voluntarily to the conditions of the modern world. Every soldier had ocular proof of the benevolent intentions of the Government, when he saw new medical clinics and hospitals opened, the sick and the old receiving free treatment, and the children admitted to school. Finally, the penalties we inflicted were not vicious or ruinous, so that the tribal soldier did not hesitate to arrest his own fellow tribesmen. He knew that they would meet not only with justice but with mercy, and just enough of a penalty to deter them from repeating the offence. . . . The men of the Desert Patrol were the most ardent missionaries of reform. They acted with all their power to put an end to raiding by their own fellow tribesmen, because they believed the latter to be mistaken and deluded, and they longed to convert them to the gospel of the new age.[199]

The result of this process of selective modernization was civilizing the "wild" Bedouins, thus rendering them of much value for British imperial policy in the area. The transformation was dramatic:

These men who never committed crimes and never even accosted women, were not graduates of Eton and Oxford. Many were half-wild tribesmen who, a few years ago, would have thought little of cutting the throat of an enemy. But they were filled with an immense pride in the race from which they sprung, in the Arab Army to which they belonged, and in the martial traditions of their ancestors. Leaving for the first time their remote mountain villages or wandering desert tribes, they found themselves suddenly the cynosure of every eye, and the comrades of the soldiers of strange nations of some of whom they had never heard. They were not the men to disgrace their ancestors and their companions before foreigners.[200]

This transformation of the Bedouins through a new juridico-disciplinary regime was accomplished not only through overall generalized policies but through individual attention to whomever Glubb encountered. He, the self-designated father, was going to teach each and every one of them a lesson. He narrates an incident in which a Bedouin of the Khushman tribe, assigned guard duty, failed to carry out the task: "Perhaps I was tired with long nights and days in the desert. . . . I lost my temper, and walking up to the man, I struck his sneering face with my fist. I then went back to my car and drove away."[201] On hearing of this injury, the brother of the accosted man confronted Glubb.

> "Did you strike my brother?" he screamed.
>   I was standing alone and unarmed on a flat piece of desert. Near by my driver, also alarmed, sat in the car. I saw for an instant a dark bearded face, with wild matted hair hanging over the eyes."Yes I hit your brother," I said, "and I'll teach you a lesson too."[202]

As punishment, Glubb confiscated the camel herds of the Khushman. Other tribal leaders intervened on their behalf, pleading with Glubb for forgiveness. Having a big heart, Glubb relented telling the delegation "to tell the Khushman not to be naughty again, and gave them back the camels."[203] A similar punishment was meted out to the Huwaytat tribe for also being "naughty."[204]

Another dimension of "caring" for the Bedouins was the creation of the Desert Medical Unit in 1937. It consisted of one doctor, four nurses, and a driver. This unit would roam the desert providing free medical care to the Bedouin population at the "mobile clinics" installed outside the posts of the Desert Patrol. These clinics treated 10,000 patients in 1937, 15,000 in 1938, and 22,000 in 1939. Patients were treated for a variety of ailments, including eye diseases, malaria, syphilis, and bilharzia (or schistosomiasis).[205] This was not the first effort to provide medical care to the army. Peake had already enlisted the services of a British missionary physician, Dr. Charlotte Purnell, to oversee the army's medical care as early as 1923. Indeed, the Jordanian physician Hanna al-Qusus wrote a number of articles in 1924 in *Al-Sharq al-'Arabi* (the precursor to *Al-Jaridah al-Rasmiyyah*) to raise the soldiers' consciousness on matters of health and hygiene.[206]

Education, Surveillance, and the Production of Bedouin Culture

Glubb's commitment to a certain version of tribal Bedouin culture led him, through the different arms of the state at his disposal, to completely redefine what is Bedouin and what is not, adopting new ways of thinking and acting and recoding them as traditional, while simultaneously banishing whatever he considered harmful to the interests the new Arab was to protect and recoding them as foreign. He was able to do that not only as the head of the Arab Legion since 1939, but also with his juridical authority as mutassarif, or governor of all Bedouins, a status bestowed on him by the Tribal Courts Law of 1936. Glubb's ingenuity lies in his putting in motion a whole cultural production that came to de-Bedouinize Jordan's Bedouins while redefining all that he introduced as "Bedouin." This was carried out through a Bedouinization policy that all Jordanians, Bedouins or not, were to undergo, wherein the entire country, with its different populations, was Bedouinized at the same moment that the Bedouins themselves were being properly (de)Bedouinized à la Glubb through a selective process of mimicry.

Glubb's initial contradictory project of segregating Bedouins from non-Bedouins was instrumental in achieving his goal of rendering them the core of Transjordan's new identity. The integration of the Bedouins into the state structure, the process by which they were and are still disciplined, had to be done with an absence of contamination from city and village Arabs. Only Glubb could be the Bedouins' window to the outside world. Disciplining the Bedouins of course required repressing them not only through killing them, beating them, expelling them, imprisoning them, confiscating their property, and exiling them, but also through educating them (in the way of Empire), providing for them (financially), protecting them, even "loving" them. As Althusser has explained, "There is no such thing as a purely repressive apparatus. . . . For example, the Army and the Police also function by ideology both to ensure their own cohesion and reproduction, and in the 'values' they propound externally."[207] Although one of Glubb's first colonial activities was a bombing raid on Iraqi Bedouins, killing, according to him, "[o]nly one old woman,"[208] he was later to follow more peaceful means: "The basis of our desert control was not force but persuasion and love. In the office of every desert fort, a notice was fixed on the wall: 'Example is stronger than precept, so guide the people by your noble deeds.' I visited all the desert posts at frequent intervals and spoke to them of our duty to the people. These were rough men, brought up to raiding and robbery, but they were simple. I have often seen the tears run down their faces as I spoke to them of our duty to the nation."[209]

A new nationalist pedagogy was born. The concept of the nation was so strong that even rough men were driven to tears. The use of persuasion as the preferred method was so successful that Glubb summarizes it as follows: "I had arrived alone in Jordan, and had succeeded in ending desert raiding (and even stealing) without firing a shot or sending a man to prison. The tribes, previously the bitterest enemies of the government, had become its most loyal adherents."[210] James Lunt, Glubb's biographer and a former officer of the Arab Legion, recaps how the "persuasion" strategy had led to the establishment of state authority: "If 1931 had been the year of persuasion, 1932 was the year for showing the flag throughout the Transjordan desert. 1933 was the year of consolidation when the forts were built."[211]

Glubb's stress on education and his personal enjoyment of it are important in this regard.[212] He explains that "[e]ver since I had been commander of the desert area before 1939, I had taken an interest in teaching boys."[213] This task was carried institutionally through the introduction of homosocial military schools: "Within a few years, we built up an Army Education Branch, which eventually provided for several thousand children. . . . all the boys joined the Arab Legion on discharge from school—not compulsorily but voluntarily. . . . All officer cadets in 1955 came from Arab Legion schools likewise."[214]

The school system became instrumental in the production of the British-imagined "Transjordanian." It is in those schools, or what Althusser calls the ideological state apparatus, that a gendered Transjordanian nationalist agency was first conceived. The responsibility of the military school system was to teach the boys a new ideology, nay a new epistemology, through which they were to apprehend their identity as well as the function it was to have: "The need for the production of Arab officers cadets, apprentice tradesmen and future NCO's from Arab Legion schools was to become more pressing as time went on. The government schools were saturated with politics, and many school-teachers were Communists. In Arab Legion schools, every effort was made to teach the boys a straightforward open creed—*service to king and country, duty, sacrifice and religion* [emphasis added].[215]

Glubb reduces this formulaic creed to its bare essentials. In the "military preface" to 'Abdullah's memoirs, written for the benefit of the troops in a special edition released to them, he says, "All that we soldiers have to do is to do our duty to *God, the King and the nation* [emphasis added]."[216] In a slight but crucial variation of the British original, this parsimonious truncation of the creed into a proper hierarchy was to guide the definition of Jordanian nationalist agency to this very day. In accordance with nationalism, the creed was to be rearranged as such: "God, Homeland, King" or "Allah, al-Watan, al-Malik." Glubb's gradual project was one of transforming the Bedouins' loyalty from tribal to military and finally to nationalist loyalty. The final stage was to come to fruition long after Glubb had left Jordan. As for military loyalty, it manifested itself strongly during the first international intervention it was to carry out against Iraqi anti-British nationalists in 1941. Glubb states that the Bedouins of the Arab Legion abetted the British in their policy "from a feeling of military loyalty. Having served with us when things were easy, they were too honorable to desert when things went wrong."[217]

Glubb dismissed nonmilitary education as inappropriate for the Arabs. He always denigrated it as causing instability and mayhem. He affirms that "[i]n the Arab countries, where education is so new and so rare, intellectual pride is a common and unattractive quality of the young secondary school graduate. It is a form of snobbery which never inspires loyalty in fighting men."[218] This statement was made by Glubb in response to Jordanian nationalists' complaints against him that he did not promote educated men to be officers and in fact had a number of illiterates reach that status.[219] In this light, it is instructive to note his terror at these arrogant young graduates who thought they could actually become equal to him rather than obey his British majestic self. He explains, "In the Arab countries, where knowledge is still a novelty, it commands even more reverence than in Europe. . . . Indeed, in the Arab countries, shepherds may more likely possess it [knowledge] than university graduates. For knowledge is still rare in the Middle East, and its possession is therefore liable to give rise to intellectual pride, whereas, in the pursuit of wisdom, no quality is more necessary than humility."[220]

The result of the introduction of political intrigue in the country by educated men was nothing less than the retardation of Jordan's development, including in the realm of education. Glubb here waxes modernizationist: "There was still so much to be done in Trans-Jordan. With the universal concentration on Politics alone, there was no longer any time to give to the activities of the years of construction, the schools for the illiterate, the medical clinics for the poor, the importation of tractor ploughs, the education of the nomads in agriculture. There were still those children who were backward, those Roman masonry cisterns choked with earth—so much building up to be done."[221]

In fact, nonmilitary education, according to Glubb, had destroyed the once noble Bedouin personality. He laments such loss while identifying the educational system as the culprit: "In the early days bedouins rarely lied. Their faces were frank and open. In their commercial transactions or their relations with the older generations of merchants, receipts were never asked nor given. All parties trusted one another. Then we began to teach them to write, and they gradually learned to lie and deceive. What is there at fault in a system of education which, while teaching men to read and write, seems simultaneously to introduce them to forgery and deceit?"[222]

Glubb's schools were designed to impart a special kind of education. According to the British government, these schools followed "a special curriculum designed to suit the needs of the Beduin."[223] Glubb concurred, asserting that for Bedouin men "suitability may be defined as an education which will not destroy their traditional moral background, and which will on the material side fit the pupils for the type of life which they will lead."[224]

In addition to education, surveillance was of the essence. This had started before Glubb's arrival in the country. Whereas the Arab Legion had established a criminal investigation branch as early as 1926 and a passport office in 1927, by 1928 the British boasted that the Legion's new fingerprint bureau was "proving of considerable benefit."[225] In addition, several laws were enacted in 1927 to enhance the state's control of the population. Such laws included the Prison Law, the Trailing of Persons and Search of Premises Law, the Crime Prevention Law, the Exile and Deportation Law, and the Extradition Law. As discipline is a regime of detail, Glubb in turn pursued a meticulous surveillance strategy, amassing intricate details about every angle of a soldier's life. James Lunt states,

> Memories of these days recall to mind the Confidential Report system in use in the Arab Legion. These had to be compiled on every officer and soldier and comprised a five or six page booklet which listed every known military virtue and failing. On every page were columns marked Excellent, Good, Fair, Bad and Nil. The reporting officer was required to put an X against such abstruse questions as "Give the extent of this man's belief in God," or even more difficult to answer, the extent of a man's interest in sex. In the case of the latter it was hard to know in which column the X should best be written, an "Excellent" signifying either too great an indulgence or monastic abstinence. One never knew."[226]

These surveillance reports were crucial to a soldier's chances of promotion, a procedure almost fully controlled by Glubb. In fact, Dragnich explains that the educational efforts on the part of the Legion "were conceived as more than a remedial step until a better educated generation could take over. The need was partly administrative: files and records had to be kept at the desert forts."[227] This is how another British officer of the Legion describes it: "Promotion examinations were a great feature of life in the Arab Legion and occupied quite a lot of one's time. . . . The promotion examinations for

junior N.C.O.'s were organized by brigade headquarters, and for senior
N.C.O.'s and officers by Division. Successful candidates were promoted if
they were recommended by their commanding officers, and if their annual
confidential reports held at Qiada [Army headquarters], were deemed sat-
isfactory. This elaborate system was no doubt intended to check the nepotism, which is a feature of Arab life."[228]

The reports themselves are described by Young, who seemed less confused than Lunt as to their evaluative system, especially as regards sexual
activity:

> Annual confidential reports were written for every officer, N.C.O. and
> man, and were secret. Officers were not required to initial their reports,
> but even so Arab C.O.s whether because they are too kind-hearted, or
> because they are afraid that their remarks will come to light and be
> held against them, are extremely reluctant to describe the failings of
> their followers. For this reason a five- or six-page document, in both
> languages, was devised, which listed every known military virtue and
> defect. At the top of each page were written: Excellent, Good, Fair,
> Bad, and Nil. All the C.O. had to do was to put an X in the appropriate
> column. If you thought that a man's belief in the Value of prayer was
> Nil you merely put an X in the space provided. It was made perfectly
> clear by elaborate notes that if a man was notoriously keen on sexual
> offences the X was not meant to go under Excellent."[229]

Part of the training of the Bedouins was introducing them to European
sports—team loyalty being ostensibly a complementary feature of strengthening tribal and national loyalty (Althusser had identified the role of sports,
which is part of the cultural apparatus, as central to imparting chauvinism
and nationalism[230]). To achieve this task, one of Glubb's associates, Sam
Cooke (known as Cooke Pasha), translated the British Army's Manual *Games
and Sports in the Army* into Arabic. Lunt remarks, "If by this he had intended
to teach Jordanians cricket, or to discourage the bedouins from cheating
when taking part in a tug-of-war, he was to be disappointed. When two
bedouin teams were pulling against each other it was necessary to surround
the arena with barbed wire to discourage spectators from joining in."[231] Still,
some British officers began training the Bedouins in sports. Some of the
problems they encountered were reported by Peter Young:

> James Watson, who had long held the British Army record for putting
> the weight, was very keen on all kinds of athletics, and had built up a

strong [9th] regimental team. The star turn was Hassan Atallah, known as "Abu Sibil," "Father of the Pipe." Unfortunately, his fame has spread to 7 Regiment's team, and when they saw a lean and bearded bedouin loping along with a pipe in his mouth they ran up to him and cried, "Are you Abu Sibil?" He replied that he was, whereupon they threw him to the ground and ran over his prostrate body! This horrible story was related to me afterwards by the outraged members of our team, anxious to explain why they only got second place. 7 Regiment were first.[232]

Sports activity in which the Arab Legion participated included cross-country running.[233] One British officer, John Adair, a cultural cross-dresser who was renamed Sweilem, "took our athletics team in hand, and they won the brigade sports. . . . Of these the most important was the winning of the Lash Cup. This is a great silver trophy presented annually to the Regiment whose rifle team gets the highest score in the Legion. Our team had won it in Watson's day, but had lost it in 1953."[234]

One sporting activity that disturbed the sensibility of the Bedouins is described by Gawain Bell, another British officer:

Every morning we began with forty minutes' physical training. This was an activity which the Bedu found difficult to appreciate. They were hard fit men in any case, their lives had been spent in open air, they were used to active existence; why then was it necessary to subject them to the absurdities of jumping up and down, bending and twisting their arms around? There were two exercises in particular of which they found the propriety doubtful to say the least. Press-ups they were prepared to do under some protest and with a good deal of embarrassment. Was it necessary, with all its apparently male associations, to do something quite so crude? As for the companion exercise that involved lying on one's back and making circular movements with one's legs in the air, no: this was an utterly unseemly activity for men. We abandoned it. But when it came to things like going through an assault course which called for the sort of muscles and the agility we had hoped to develop through these PT parades, they were all enthusiasm.[235]

Clearly, sports here not only are intended to foster a team spirit commensurate with nationalism but also act as masculinizing rituals. Insofar as

British corporeal movements conflicted with Bedouin gender epistemology, they were resisted, insofar as they did not, they were assimilated into the Bedouin's own masculine rituals. In the context of the military, all masculinizing rituals are always already nationalist rituals. The function of sports in the military, therefore, is to couple masculinity and a militarized sense of nationality, of nationalizing masculinity itself. This new nationalized masculinity becomes the model for the nation.

The Arab Legion also introduced European musical instruments and European music to its soldiers through setting up musical bands. In 1921, the first Massed Bands were formed consisting of eighteen musicians, ten from Egypt and eight from Syria. It was led by the Egyptian Muhammad Khatir.[236] Peake tells the story of the genesis of the Massed Bands:

> The government decided that His Highness should leave his capital with all possible pomp and glory. I was therefore asked to line the streets with the Reserve Force and to allow the band, the instruments for which had arrived about fourteen days before, to march in front of the Amir's car. At the last moment the big drum fell off the lorry bringing the band back to Amman and was crushed under the wheels. It was therefore necessary to hire the town crier, who had a drum. The procession started after the usual delays, when suddenly the band burst into activity, emitting an incredible amount of tuneless noise. . . . Then came the final guard of honour, on the right of which I saw with trepidation the two buglers sounded, not the usual Royal Salute, but "Come to the cook-house doors." The culprits explained later that it was all they knew. Abdullah, who had been a soldier, undoubtedly recognized the call but, after his experiences with the band, was probably beyond caring what happened and so said "good-bye" to me politely. On his return things were better. I had asked the bandmaster of the Palestine police Band to come over for a day or two, and he had impressed upon the Arab Legion Band that noise was not all that was required, the audience had a right to expect some tune.[237]

The bands' repertoire had expanded measurably, including the tune to Transjordan's princely (later royal) anthem "'Asha al-Amir" or "Long live the Prince," which was later updated to "'Asha al-Malik" or "Long live the young king," following the self-appointment of 'Abdullah as king upon independence in 1946. The anthem's lyrics were written by the Syrio-Palestinian 'Abd al-Mun'im al-Rifa'i, with the music composed by the Lebanese

'Abd al-Qadir al Tannir.[238] By the mid thirties, the bands had become such a big hit in Transjordan that they were invited to play at private parties and celebrations. The demand became so high that the government was compelled to issue a statute listing the fees to be paid to the Massed Bands for being contracted out for private events.[239] In September 1940, for example, the bands, along with the Amir 'Abdullah, were invited to play at the inauguration of the new building housing the Circassian Charity Association in Amman.[240] Moreover, on the occasion of King Husayn's coronation in 1953, the Massed Bands were also a major hit. Lieutenant Colonel Peter Young reports how that "evening . . . the Massed Bands beat their retreat in [the new king's] honour on the parade ground in Zerqa Camp and gave us a fine selection of 'British' martial music, including 'Les Huguenots' and the slow march from 'Scipio.' "[241] There were actually three bands in the Arab Legion: the blue, the red, and the green. "In winter they wear khaki battle-dress, and in the summer white service dress. They can be distinguished one from the other by the colour of their lanyards, epaulettes and pipes. All musicians wear a lyre badge on the right arm above the elbow."[242]

The most important musical instruments to be introduced to the Legion were the bagpipes.[243] This was done in 1929 by the order of the Amir 'Abdullah himself. Six members of the bands were selected and sent to Jerusalem, where a British Mandatory Bagpipe Band existed. A British officer named Patterson who was fluent in Arabic took on the training of the six musicians for two years, after which the musicians returned to Transjordan to form the first Bagpipe Band in the country. They would march in front of the amir on his way to the mosque on Fridays.[244] It is also said that the Black Watch trained the Legionnaires to play them.[245] The bagpipes have remained to this very day the most distinguishing hallmark of the Massed Bands of the Jordanian Armed Forces [al-Jawqat al-Musiqiyyah]. The bands, in fact, had made so much progress that in 1955 they went on a tour of Britain. Glubb proudly describes this achievement as one of the last over which he was to preside: "People who imagined Arabs to be wild desert camel riders were surprised to see the massed bands beating retreat on the Horse Guard's Parade, or the Arab Legion pipes and drums marching down Princes Street, Edinburgh. It was our swan song—within eight months the Arab Legion had ceased to exist."[246]

It would seem that for Glubb, playing Western musical instruments and Western music has transformed the Bedouin Arabs from "wild desert camel riders" into modern men. The success of this civilizing mission has actually borne much fruit. Today, the Massed Bands of the Jordanian Armed Forces have acquired an international reputation. They perform worldwide and are the recipients of a number of international awards and prizes. Their music and their bagpipes are nationalist icons, which, as Theodor Adorno stresses, "appear . . . as a representative of the nation, and everywhere confirm . . . the nationalist principle."[247]

Other activities including use of the camp latrine proved equally problematic. As Gawain Bell reports, "Camp hygiene was a constant headache. The Bedu just hated using the latrine. Being extremely modest in these things they wanted privacy, the privacy of a fold in the ground or the shelter of a bush. Once we had moved from the wide spaces of the desert where all three regiments did all their initial training, first to Jericho in the Jordan valley, and then to the hutted camps along the coast of Palestine south of Gaza, this became a real problem involving constant and at times self-defeating disciplinary action."[248]

Other problems included diet. Bedouins had to deal now with British Army rations, which included food items to which they were not used:

> The Bedu had come to accept and indeed to like bully beef, but for fresh meat we could no longer buy sheep once we had moved away from Azraq. We had therefore to rely on British Army supplies, which meant accepting frozen mutton from Australia and New Zealand. There was no knowing whether it had been slaughtered in accordance with Muslim practice, but this was not the real worry to the men, which was whether it was sheep at all. It might, they suggested, be dog. There was that little tail on the carcass that looked more than suspiciously like a dog's tail. And then the head was missing from the carcass. Why? A lot of the men refused to eat it until we took a party of Squadron Commanders and NCOs to the RASC cold stores in Jerusalem to examine the carcasses in detail, to talk to the British officer in charge who, with Indian and other non-Christian units to serve, had a wide and sympathetic experience of these problems. He reassured us. The regimental *Imam* added his own conviction that the meat was genuinely sheep and nothing sinister, and finally all was well.[249]

Still, rations-related problems remained. One such case was reported by Young: "Eid Hweimel, who was really a very passable N.C.O., got it into his head that the ration meat was not properly killed as an orthodox Moslem was entitled to expect. He therefore refused to eat his rations, and lived on his pay—that is to say on what remained after his relations had visited him. This I only discovered because I noticed that his face had become covered in blemishes. He steadfastly refused to eat the rations and, as I was equally determined not to support him from the canteen fund, we reached an impasse. Fortunately, he was dispatched to the Cadet School and his apparently insoluble problem went with him."[250]

Between the military rations and the opening up of Transjordan to the world economy through British colonialism, the way Transjordanian Bedouins ate was to change substantially. Glubb states that "the effects of the opening up of the country to trade" on the inhabitants included their "learn[ing] to drink tea," as they were formerly coffee-drinkers.[251] The types of meat and grains used in cooking also changed. Camel meat, once the hallmark of Bedouin food, has but completely disappeared from their menu. Although drought and raiding had reduced the size of the Bedouin flocks, the colonial state's sedentarization campaigns transforming the Bedouins from nomadic camel herders into agriculturalists were the major factor. The introduction of guns and military hunting obliterated in turn the ostrich and gazelle population of the country—the meat of both animals had been part of the Bedouin diet.[252] As for burghul (cracked wheat) and farikah (roasted green wheat) which were used in most dishes, by villagers and urbanites alike (Bedouins mostly used bread as their main accompaniment to meat), they were to be substituted with white rice, which, because of its high price, was used by the Bedouins and the peasants previously only on festive occasions. Colonial trade relations had made the once expensive rice more affordable and available, thus competing with local grains.[253] This has been such an important transformation that mansaf,[254] which came to be coded by the architects of Jordan's "Bedouin" identity as the Bedouin dish *par excellence*, and which the Bedouins used to cook with meat (lamb or camel), meat broth, and bread *only* (what is also known as *tharid*), is now mostly made with white rice.[255] It is said that merchants introduced rice to the Balqa' region in 1925. An invitation was extended to many people in Ghawr Nimrayn to come and eat rice-based mansaf, "and people saw how rice is cooked and is incorporated in the mansaf and immediately copied this method."[256] The transition was in fact gradual. At first, mansaf would be made with burghul and covered with a thin layer of rice on top. Slowly, rice became more fully incorporated replacing burghul completely. In addition, the main contemporary characteristic of mansaf is *jamid*, or *laban jamid*, sour dried yogurt made from goat milk, which is used as a sauce (*sharab*) over the meat and rice (or burghul or farikah), and which most Bedouins did not use in cooking mansaf before their sedentarization by the nation-state. Only village folks used jamid with mansaf, whereas most Bedouins used meat broth or Samn Baladi (ghee) instead.[257] Although jamid was made by Bedouins and eaten dry during bad years as a last resort when no other food was available, it was never used as the base of any type of sauce, and never in association with mansaf. [258] Today, the new white-rice mansaf with jamid is ironically considered "traditionally" Bedouin as well as being Jordan's exclusive "national dish"—although the peasants and Bedouins of southern Palestine and Syria also ate (and eat) it.[259] These claims are made not only by lay Jordanian nationalists but even by Jordanian and foreign social scientists. In a study of Jordan's Bedouins, some such social scientists go so far as to claim that the fact that Bedouins would "*often* [emphasis added] eat . . . balls of dried yoghurt called *jamid*," constitutes evidence that they used it in cooking mansaf![260] After describing the jamid mansaf, which they identify as Bedouin, the authors tell us in a matter-of-fact way that "mansaf has become the national dish of Jordan."[261] Moreover, they ahistorically inform us that among Bedouins, "Tea is the most common household beverage."[262]

The change in the Jordanian population's habits of consumption was registered by Glubb himself. Responding to Eliahu Epstein, who claimed that the economic situation of the Trans-Jordanian tribes was worsening,[263] Glubb retorts by asserting that it "is true that their economy has changed a good deal since the Armistice [at the end of World War I]. They have acquired a taste for many luxuries formerly unknown to them, and they live in greater physical comfort. . . . Their desire to buy imported luxuries and manufactured articles has caused them to spend more freely."[264]

Through the disciplinary mechanisms of surveillance and education, Glubb's policies not only *repressed* and erased much in the Bedouins' way of life that conflicted with imperial interests but also *produced* much that was new and combined it with what was "inoffensive" and "beneficial" in their "tradition" in a new amalgam of what was packaged as *real* Bedouin culture. The new Bedouin culture in fact sublated much of pre-imperial Bedouin culture foreclosing certain venues while opening a myriad others, erasing practices while preserving and transforming others. Even Jordan's own flag was designed by the British. Sir Mark Sykes had been the one who designed the flag under which the Arab Army under Faysal and Lawrence marched on Damascus during World War I, which later became the basis for Jordan's flag.[265] Just like the new uniforms that the Bedouin members of the Desert Patrol wore, the new culture of the Bedouins looked on the surface to be of Bedouin make, but on closer scrutiny, neither its color nor its texture, much less its style and cloth material, resembled anything that the Bedouins would call theirs before the colonial encounter. In fact, many of them were at first ashamed of being seen in them. Those who were sent by Glubb as missionaries to recruit others "were ashamed of being seen in uniform. The metal badges in their ageyls, or headbands, were especially unpopular, and the men often took them off before entering an encampment, and always when going on leave. In those days the badge seemed to the desert Beduin to be a mark of servitude—the mark of the beast which was how they regarded the Government. They think differently today."[266] As Edward Said remarks, "since one cannot ontologically obliterate the Orient . . . one does have the means to capture it, treat it, describe it, improve it, radically alter it."[267] Indeed, for the Bedouin produced by Glubb is but a faint simulacrum of an original that does not exist. Glubb's Bedouin is nothing less than a catachresis designating a wrong referent,[268] a spectacle to himself and others, albeit one that is nationally constitutive. "The spectacle's externality with respect to the acting subject is demonstrated by the fact that the individual's own gestures are no longer his own, but rather those of someone else who represents them to him."[269] Glubb's white colonial masculinity masquerading as "Bedouinism" becomes the occasion of a double mimesis,[270] wherein the Bedouin of the Desert Patrol is supposed to imitate Glubb's white colonial masculinity's imitation of a phantasmatic "Bedouin." The image of what a Bedouin should be is, actually, Glubb's social fetish. If we approximate Freud's psychoanalytic finding, that the fetish is a substitute for a loss,[271] to this situation, Glubb's Bedouin becomes a substitute for the "real" Bedouin whom he had read about in Orientalist books and could not find in real life. Glubb's realization that the real Bedouin is not the same one he had read about, causes him a sense of loss that he overcomes by substituting a simulacrum of the Bedouin for the real one. Thus, he was able to avert the crisis of false representation on which his entire epistemology of the Orient had been based. The Glubb-created Bedouin is the fetish with which Glubb cathected throughout his entire life.

By the time Transjordan obtained its independence in 1946, declaring itself as the Hashemite Kingdom of Jordan, the lives of its inhabitants had been radically altered: "Where formerly nomadic tribes had terrorized the villages, a modern State had been built up—a State which had gained the respect of the world."[272] Glubb recaps Jordan's history, extolling its achievements: "In 1921, the Amir Abdulla had arrived in a wild tribal land, never before regularly administered. He was without a government, without an army, without police or any of the attributes of a modern State. On this day

[May 1946], twenty five years later, he was proclaimed king of a loyal, happy, proud and contented country. A simple people, united behind the throne, had stood like a rock while rebellion followed rebellion in Palestine, Syria, Iraq and Saudi Arabia."[273]

For Glubb, Jordan was truly exceptional in the Middle East, as far as its openness to the West. Thanks to "her" acceptance of British help, "[u]nder the King's wise guidance, she developed a broad and statesmanlike attitude to the world, a genial welcome to foreigners and a stalwart common sense, qualities so often conspicuous by their absence in the narrow and embittered politics of the Middle East today."[274] Other "unwise" Arab leaders "reacted by refusing the help [from Europe]—and remaining backward and chaotic."[275] Glubb, of course, personified that "British help" of which he was so proud. In fact, thanks to Glubb's efforts, Jordan's Bedouins had been successfully transformed from "wild" albeit "noble" "primitives," into modern soldiers. His biographer summarizes Glubb's outstanding achievements in the following words: "Glubb had succeeded in preserving the bedouins' traditions while at the same time turning them into modern soldiers. . . . But the credit was not his alone; he would have been the first to acknowledge the support he received from his Arab deputy, Abdul Qadir Pasha al Jundi [of Libyan origin], Norman Lash, Ronnie Broadhurst, Gawain Bell and many other Arab and British officers."[276]

Proof of Bedouin loyalty to their surrogate father became evident to Glubb in his last days in Jordan. After learning of the expulsion orders issued by King Husayn, Glubb reports how his Arab officers bid him farewell tearfully and how one of them drew out his revolver to avenge him.[277] According to him, one or two units of the Arab Legion had contemplated action to redress him against the king, but in "every case it was the British officers who prevented incidents."[278] In fact, Glubb owed his very life to a Bedouin who had saved him from drowning in 1920 in the Diyala River in Iraq.[279] As he is departing Amman, he cites how a former Jordanian prime minister had told him once that he had been "a founder member of this kingdom." He summarizes his history in relation to Jordan, likening it to a child that he reared: "I had first seen Amman in 1924. . . . Then it was a little village. Now it is a city of a quarter of a million inhabitants. For twenty-six years I had watched the country grow up. From a handful of policemen, I had seen the Arab Legion grow to an army of 23,000 men and a National Guard of 30,000. When reservists were called out, they could put nearly 60,000 men in the field. . . . Now, in a few hours, twenty-six years of work had been destroyed."[280]

On the departing plane flying over Amman, Glubb states, "Fascinated, I watched the Arab coast fade into the blue mist. . . . I turned away and laughed."[281] Glubb's laughter was not so much cynical as it was a conclusive acknowledgment of his surviving legacy. His twenty-six years in Jordan, a country that he never visited again (he died in 1986), had been a success. The next thirty years of his life were spent writing books and lecturing about Jordan and the Arabs. Disraeli's dictum "The East is a Career" still rings true. Glubb had indeed left an indelible mark on every aspect of life in Jordan. His policies channeled through the institution of the army were central to the production of a Jordanian national identity that pervades every aspect of Jordanian life today and will for many years to come. But not only did Glubb's army produce the Bedouins as national subjects who were juridically defined within the framework of the nation-state, the army produced them as holders of a specific national culture that itself was also produced by the army. As Timothy Mitchell notes, the modern army appears "to consist on the one hand of individual soldiers and on the other of the machine they inhabited . . . this apparatus has no independent existence. It is an effect produced by the organized distribution of men, the coordination of their movement, the partitioning of space, and the hierarchical ordering of units, all of which are particular practices. . . . But the order and precision of such processes created the effect of an apparatus apart from the men themselves, whose structure orders, contains and controls them."[282] This juridical-military dyad introduced by British colonialism was both a repressive and a productive success. Today's Jordanian national identity and Jordanian national culture are living testament to that achievement.

4 Nationalizing the Military

Colonial Legacy as National Heritage

As we saw in the last chapter, the colonial concept of modernization that was deployed in Transjordan by the British Mandatory authorities and by Glubb Pasha was racially and imperially inflected. By virtue of their interrelated racial and colonial status, the colonized had no agency. This colonial modernization aimed at producing the colonized as obedient subjects who can be employed to serve imperial aims. In Jordan, as in many colonized countries, this situation produced two different yet related kinds of anticolonial nationalisms.

One type, that which rallied around a non-Hashemite Arab nationalism, sought to achieve technological modernization in the European sense, while adopting a certain selection of "traditions" and religion for use in the private sphere. As discussed in chapter 2, the new subjects of the nation had newly defined gender roles that permeated their national identity and their citizenship. These roles were inspired by Western juridical and political practice, which had become ideologically hegemonic within this strand of nationalism. As far as the public sphere was concerned, symbols of these traditions, including religious traditions but not necessarily faith, were deployed in the public sphere. These nationalists saw Jordan as part of a divided Arab world with which it should and would be ultimately unified, be that in a confederal or unionist form. For these nationalists, the army was seen as a central institution to unify the nation. Its role was to integrate a varied citizenry within the framework of national defense, the supreme duty of a nationalist. For these nationalists, Jordanian Arab national identity was constituted in opposition to colonialism, which constituted its *other*.

Another kind of anticolonial nationalism was also deployed in the country, and it was spearheaded by the Amir 'Abdullah. The amir's Arab nationalism was mainly anti-Ottoman and unionist. A unified Arab world would be ruled under the banner of the Hashemites. Internationally, this nationalism was friendly to the West and collaborated with Western powers in driving out the Ottomans and in setting up the new states in the region. It also saw Western powers as its natural allies against myriad enemies. This type of nationalism was the ruling one in Jordan until the early 1950s. The role of the Arab Revolt, which was led by the Hashemites against the Ottomans, and in alliance with Britain, has been a constant symbol of Hashemite Arab nationalism. Its use for regime legitimation remains constant after seven decades, especially in confronting those who accuse the regime of a lack of Arab nationalism. Commemorating the revolt is an annual regime ritual that remains strong to this day. This Hashemite Arab nationalism portrayed the West as a friend and ally against Israel, communism, internal subversion, and other undefined enemies that might threaten national security. Its alliance with the West was always justified rhetorically as being primarily beneficial to the nation. The king's palace nationalism constituted itself originally as anti-Ottoman. Absent the Ottoman threat, however, it was to reformulate itself in opposition to an internal *other*, represented by "subversives" and followers of "foreign" ideologies.

This nationalism shares with colonial modernizationists their view of Jordanian national culture, tradition, religion, and gender relations, in that it does not aim at replicating European norms completely but more syncretically. It participated in the creation of a colonially based national culture that it now claims to defend as the *true* national culture. Issues of religious faith were deployed in the public sphere as part of a legitimating ideology. Muslims with different folk practices (e.g., the Bedouins and the Circassians) were duly Islamicized according to state dicta, supported by a team of religious shaykhs and religious government departments and official rhetoric. The army was seen both as unifying its adherents and as dividing them from its opponents, who had to be cast out. By the late 1950s, this nationalism itself was transformed into a more particularist and exclusivist Jordanian nationalism unifying Bedouins and Hadaris, Arabs and Circassians, but excluding Palestinian Jordanian citizens. The new exclusivist nationalism continued with the same philosophy that 'Abdullah's Arab nationalism had espoused in relation to questions of tradition, modernization, and national culture more generally.

These two kinds of nationalisms are not peculiar to Arab countries. We see similar trends in Africa and the rest of Asia, where new postcolonial elites espouse pro-Western nationalisms, and where popular nationalisms insist on an anti-Westernism as definitional of their anticolonial ideologies. In this chapter, I discuss the history of both nationalisms in the context of the Jordanian army, and their clash in the 1950s. I present a thorough history of that clash based on new material, including the memoirs of army officers who played central roles during the period. The subsequent emergence of the new particularist nationalism and its clash with Palestinian Jordanians is also discussed, as it constituted a turning point for the consolidation of the new particularist nationalism. At the end of the chapter, I analyze the gendered strategies used by the state to mobilize soldiers and the role of religion in the legitimation of state power and the delegitimation of the opposition. I also discuss the impact of the changing role of women in society on the military's policy toward women. The military's gendered strategies combined with the new military policy on women are shown to be part of the nation-state's project of nationalizing a certain brand of masculinity and femininity, which it then identifies as "national tradition."

Anticolonial Nationalism and the Army

The defeat that befell the Arab armies in the Palestine War in 1948 devastated morale among army officers as well as the rank and file, especially in the Jordanian Arab Army. Although British officers (who had joined the Jordanian army in the last few years and who led it during the 1948 war) tried to exhaust the Jordanian officers with excessive training exercises to prevent them from having the time to join or form political groupings, the level of despair among many of the recently trained Jordanian officers had to find a political outlet. Whereas, as we saw in the last chapter, the military's disciplinarian role was hegemonic in its production of soldiers as juridical national subjects with specific national cultural practices, as Timothy Mitchell stresses, we should not overstate the "coherence of these technologies. . . . Disciplines can break down, counteract one another, or overreach. They offer spaces for manoeuver and resistance, and can be turned to counterhegemonic purposes. Anti-colonial movements have often derived their organizational forms from the military and their methods of discipline and indoctrination from schooling."[1]

In the case of Jordan, disciplinary strategies indeed overreached themselves and began to break down. The first signs of their overreach were felt among officers who had been trained at British army barracks in Palestine in the early to mid forties in places such as Sarafand. These officers began to publish a weekly magazine in the summer of 1948, which they called *al-Qunbulah* or "The Bomb," to express their resistance to the prevailing order.[2] According to Shahir Abu-Shahut, one of the magazine's founders, all artillery officers partook in editing the weekly, which was issued handwritten. Contributors included the future head of the army and close regime confidant Habis al-Majali.[3] The magazine was distributed to other army units, where it was received with much excitement. *Al-Qunbulah*'s editors were also able to build bridges with civilian nationalists Kamal Nasir and Hisham Nashashibi, who began publishing the magazine *Al-Jil al-Jadid*, or the "New Generation," in Ramallah on the West Bank. A working relationship ensued between the two magazines, which won them much popular following. Soon, however, *Al-Qunbulah*'s editors received an oral warning from Glubb Pasha conveyed through Muhammad Ma'aytah (a Karaki and future Free Officer) commanding them to put a stop to this "childish behavior." They obliged by stopping publication of the magazine and by destroying all published issues.[4]

A Jordanian officer, 'Abdullah al-Tall, who was at the time the military commander of Arab East Jerusalem, would come and lecture to artillery officers about the importance of the Palestinian struggle and the imperatives of liberating Palestine from Israel's occupation. He would also share with the officers the opinions of the country's political leadership, as he was privy to the armistice talks with the Israelis in his capacity as one of the king's negotiators and go-betweens. In his account of that period, Abu-Shahut insists, however, that 'Abdullah al-Tall never recruited anyone for any secret or open organization, contrary to subsequent accusations leveled against him by the government.[5]

The story of 'Abdullah al-Tall is important to note here, as he came to constitute in the minds of Jordan's rulers the first military threat to the regime. His importance also stems from his espousal of an Arab nationalism that defined itself in opposition to British colonialism, thus countering the state's and 'Abdullah's brand of British-friendly Arab nationalism. Al-Tall was born in 1918 in the northern city of Irbid, the center of northern opposition to 'Abdullah's emirate project in the early 1920s. He enlisted in the Arab Legion in 1942 and rose quickly within its ranks, becoming a major in 1948. Within a few months, he was noticed by King 'Abdullah, who took a liking to him and promoted him to the rank of colonel.[6] Al-Tall was the hero of the battle of Jerusalem, after which stories of his heroism became commonplace in the Jordanian press. He became a confidant of the king, serving later as his emissary during Jordanian-Israeli negotiations after the 1948 war.

He commanded the 6th Battalion during the war, but he was dismissed from his command by Glubb because of his vociferous political views and was appointed military ruler of the city of Jerusalem in September 1948. Glubb later dismissed him from the army, entirely against King ʿAbdullah's wishes. The king, bypassing Glubb, appointed him the civilian governor of the city in March 1949, a position he held until his resignation (or dismissal) in June 1949.

Al-Tall speaks of a concerted campaign by the Jordanian army's British officers against him (due to his public expression of anti-British views), which led the Jordanian authorities to decide on his dismissal and transfer to the Washington or London embassy as Jordan's military attaché there. He cites an Israeli newspaper report (in *HaMashkif*) as early as April 27, 1949, stating that he was viewed by the British and Jordanian authorities as inimical to Jordanian-Israeli *rapprochement*, which is why they decided to transfer him to Washington.[7] When he saw the newspaper report and heard the palace rumors about his impending dismissal, al-Tall submitted his resignation on June 7, 1949, retiring to his native city of Irbid. He left the country in October 1949 not to return for 16 years.[8]

In Jerusalem, al-Tall made alliances with Palestinian nationalists who opposed ʿAbdullah's control of central Palestine and those Palestinians who supported the Mufti and the Husayni family, whose archenemy was King ʿAbdullah. Moreover, he also befriended Palestinian Baʿthists and other Arab nationalists. Al-Tall also sought alliances with Transjordanian Arab nationalists including the Group of Free Youth (Jamaʿat al-Shabab al-Ah-rar), in existence since the mid forties. He also sought the support of King ʿAbdullah's son, Amir Talal, rumored to oppose his father's policies toward the British, the Israelis, and the Palestinians.[9] Moreover, as early as December 1948, al-Tall began making individual contacts with Jordanian army officers to recruit them to stage an anti-government (but not anti-regime) coup d'état.[10] He names only two of these officers, ʿAli Abu-Nuwwar and Mahmud al-Musa (who at the time of the writing of his book were already in exile); he refrains from naming others to protect them from government retaliation.[11] Al-Tall also sought contacts with neighboring Arab governments, especially with the Syrian coup leader Husni al-Zaʿim. In his talks with al-Zaʿim, al-Tall asked that in the event ʿAbdullah is deposed, al-Zaʿim would send him into exile in the eastern desert around the Syrian town of Dayr al-Zur without harming him physically.[12] Al-Tall also met in April 1949 with the Amir Talal and devised a plan wherein the government would be changed, Glubb and his coterie of British officers would be arrested, and

Talal himself would take over the management of the kingdom. The amir was assured that no physical harm would befall his father or any member of the royal family.[13] It is important to note, contrary to subsequent government claims, that al-Tall was opposed to the British presence in the country as well as to King 'Abdullah's support of that presence, but not to Hashemite royal rule in Jordan per se. His Arab nationalism did not necessarily lead him to espouse republican ideas. In fact, republicanism never became part of the anticolonial nationalism of any group in the army, before him or after him.

Glubb had become increasingly uncomfortable with al-Tall's reported activities. Based on intelligence information he obtained, Glubb submitted in June 1949 a report to King 'Abdullah detailing al-Tall's preparation for a coup. It was based on this report that the government reasserted the necessity to distance al-Tall from the political theater of the country by dispatching him to Washington or London. No legal proceedings were filed against al-Tall, however, as no material evidence existed to support Glubb's claims. Finally, after al-Tall consulted with the Egyptian authorities, the Amir Talal, and members of the Free Youth Group and the "Free Officers," it was recommended that he leave to Egypt and resume his national struggle from there.[14] Following al-Tall's departure, Glubb created a new military surveillance outfit charged with spying on Jordanian officers. Soon, this outfit grew to include all army departments and answered directly to the Department of Military Intelligence. 'Ali Abu-Nuwwar mentions the establishment of a second intelligence office called Da'irat al-Mabahith, operated by a number of Jordanian officers loyal to Glubb.[15]

In addition to having alliances with local anticolonial nationalist leaders, al-Tall also met with the famed Jordanian nationalist Subhi Abu-Ghanimah, who had been Jordan's most vocal voice against British rule for decades and had been living in exile in Syria at the time.[16] While in exile in Cairo, al-Tall published his memoirs in 1950 in Egyptian newspapers, accompanied by photostatic copies of secret documents and letters that he had carried between King 'Abdullah and the Israelis during the armistice talks, detailing the king's dealings with the Israelis in a manner considered treasonous by the prevailing Arab consensus at the time.[17] Al-Tall's story, however, did not end with his self-imposed exile. He was later accused of conspiracy in the assassination of King 'Abdullah in 1951 (although no material evidence existed against him) and was sentenced to death in absentia.[18] Glubb Pasha, his archenemy, testified against him in court.[19] Al-Tall denied the charges completely.[20]

'Abdullah al-Tall did not seem to play any lasting role in the formation of nationalist groups in the Jordanian army. He did not recruit many people in the army and made few contacts outside civilian nationalist circles. He also was not to play any future role in the nationalist politics of the country, in the military or otherwise, as evidenced by his absence during the 1954 to 1957 nationalist agitation in society and the military.[21] His, however, remains the first recorded defection by a Jordanian military man. His emergence was a reflection of how the political realm outside the military establishment was infiltrating the military. This was the result of the increasing enrollment of settled Jordanians in the army. These were less susceptible than the Bedouins to Glubb's ideological influence by virtue of having come from Jordanian towns with politically active public spheres. This, coupled with the increase of anticolonial nationalist sentiment in the country since the Palestinian revolt of 1936 to 1939, which many Transjordanians actively supported, and the continuing events through the 1947 to 1948 Palestinian exodus and the defeat of the Arab armies, created an unprecedented situation in the army that Glubb could not contain. In fact, during the Palestinian uprising, many Transjordanian volunteers joined the Palestinian guerrillas. To stem the nationalist tide, the government opted to open the Arab Legion for volunteers (mostly of settled origins). Later, the Amir 'Abdullah prevented Transjordanians from traveling to Palestine altogether (see chapter 5).[22]

A more politically aware kind of Arab nationalism began making inroads throughout Arab societies in the aftermath of the Palestine defeat. Prominent among those calling for Arab unity at the time was the Ba'th party. A number of Jordanian officers were attracted to the Ba'th's nationalist ideology and decided to join it in 1950. The first were Shahir Abu Shahut and Mahmud Ma'aytah. Soon, however, these two officers began recruiting other officers to their cause. These included Dafi Jam'ani, Mundhir 'Innab, 'Azmi Mihyar, Salim al-Tall, Fawzi Abu-Nuwwar, and 'Abd al-Qadir Shuman.[23] When the civilian leadership of the party was informed of these activities, it rejected them vehemently—as the large-scale incorporation of military personnel, they feared, could lead to a deviation from the party's principles and goals—and asked that they be discontinued. Abu-Shahut and Ma'aytah opted, as a result, to have their military group independent of the party, and they named it al-Tanzim al-Sirri Lil-Dubbat al-Urduniyyin (the Secret Organization of Jordanian Officers), with its professed slogan being "the liberation of the Jordanian army [sic] from the influence of British officers, and the establishment of military unity with Syria."[24] Soon, many more officers joined the organization. Abu-Shahut, Ma'aytah, and Dafi al-Jam'ani were nominated as the collective leadership of the group whose name was modified to al-Tanzim al-Sirri Lil-Dubbat al-Wataniyyin fi al-Jaysh al-Urduni, (the Secret Organization of Nationalist Officers in the Jordanian Army), with Abu-Shahut, later the same year, being nominated as its leader.[25] In 1950, the organization's members were mostly artillery officers. By 1951, membership expanded to include officers in engineering, armor, mechanics, and infantry.[26]

Following the coup d'état in 1952 by the Egyptian Free Officers, whose leaders were initially on good terms with the Ikhwan al-Muslimin (Muslim Brothers), a meeting was arranged in Jordan between the Jordanian officers' organization and the leader of the Jordanian Ikhwan, Muhammad 'Abd al-Rahman Khalifah, to arrange through him a meeting with the Egyptian officers. Khalifah agreed to arrange the meeting on condition that they join his movement. Committed to a secular brand of nationalism, the officers refused and the proposed meeting with the Egyptians never materialized. Still, the impact of the Egyptian Free Officers was far reaching. Soon the Secret Organization renamed itself Harakat al-Dubbat al-Urduniyyin al-Ahrar (the Movement of Free Jordanian Officers) and embarked on establishing a founding committee that included representatives from all the branches of the army who were elected by the movement's cadres.[27] The committee issued internal bylaws for the movement, which continued to be led by Abu-Shahut. They decided to contact some of the higher-ranking Jordanian officers for the purpose of inviting them to be advisors and honorary members of the movement. These included Habis al-Majali, Muhammad al-Ma'ayta, 'Ali al-Hiyari, Radi al-Hindawi, Mahmud al-Rusan, and 'Ali Abu-Nuwwar, all of whom were to play important roles in the coming few years.[28]

Following the death of King 'Abdullah, the government and Glubb were consulting about the possibility of preventing the Amir Talal from acceding to the throne. The amir was in Switzerland at the time, receiving treatment at a mental institution. Rumors in Amman had it that the government and Glubb were preventing him from coming back and that reports about his health problems were British fabrications. In the army, a British-educated officer, 'Ali Abu-Nuwwar (born to a Jordanian Circassian mother and a Jordanian Arab father[29]), called on the Free Officers informing them of a plan to bring prince Talal back to Jordan and place him on the throne by force. Abu-Nuwwar asked for the Free Officers' military support once the operation began.[30] Abu-Nuwwar had dispatched the Palestinian Jordanian doctor 'Awni Hannun (who was in the Jordanian army) to Switzerland to check on the amir and bring him back. Hannun, however, was not allowed to see the amir, as the British authorities had given strict instructions to the hospital that no one was to see him. The amir did ultimately return to Jordan and acceded to his throne without military intervention. Hannun, on returning to Amman from Switzerland, was shocked to find that Glubb had already dismissed him from the army on the grounds that he incited discord between Jordanian and British officers and that he urged Jordanian officers to quit the army and join the Egyptian Fida'iyyin fighting the British at Suez. No evidence was presented to support either claim. Still, the matter was not over. King Talal himself intervened on Hannun's behalf but was turned down by Glubb after a noisy argument between the two.[31] According to some reports, Talal, who had served briefly in the Arab Legion in 1943, hated Glubb and argued with him constantly.[32] For example, such reports abound in the unverifiable memoirs of King Talal, which were said to have been communicated to one Subhi Tuqan from Talal's exile in Turkey.[33] Glubb reports one hostile interaction between himself and Talal as early as 1939,[34] but otherwise he sings the praises of the king and laments his mental condition.[35]

Later, when the government was preparing to put a vote before Parliament to depose King Talal because of mental incapacity, many in the army thought that this was another plot against Talal. They sought a meeting with the king to arrange for a response to the alleged plot. The meeting was to be arranged by the king's aide-de-camp 'Abd al-'Aziz 'Asfur, who was a Free Officer himself. 'Asfur, however, confirmed the king's mental condition, which shocked the officers, who strongly believed that the king had been set up.[36]

By the time the brief reign of Talal had ended, anticolonial nationalist officers in the Jordanian army were already a force to be reckoned with. Although committed to the monarchy, they were equally committed to ending the colonial presence in the country. Whereas they had disagreed with 'Abdullah, they agreed with Talal. After the latter's deposition, the officers decided to wait until succession took place to decide the next step.

King Husayn and the Nationalist Officers

A unified front was suddenly to emerge in the country, one consisting of nationalist officers, nationalist politicians, and the young and increasingly nationalistic king, all of whom were to stand up to Glubb and to British military influence. As this section will clarify, King Husayn's shuttling between his grandfather's Hashemite Arab nationalism and the new Nasirist Arab nationalism sweeping the country was to define the outcome of the coming clash.

As was the case for 'Abdullah al-Tall, the fate of any officer who was discovered to be harboring political views inimical to British military control in the country was banishment by Glubb to one of Jordan's embassies abroad. Prominent among those who faced such a fate was 'Ali Abu-Nuwwar, who is originally from the northern city of Salt. Abu-Nuwwar was one of four Jordanian officers who had returned at the end of 1950 from Britain after graduating from a British military academy, where they studied for one year. The other three were Mahmud al-Rusan, 'Ali al-Hiyari, and Sadiq al-Shar'.[37] Abu-Nuwwar was exiled to the Paris embassy by Glubb during Talal's reign, on suspicion of conspiracy against the British.[38] Glubb also accused Abu-Nuwwar of contacts with a foreign government (namely Syria), which Abu-Nuwwar denied, and of conspiring against the British presence in the country, which he did not. Glubb further accused him of preparing a coup, and then he decided to dismiss him from the army. A number of ministers intervened on Abu-Nuwwar's behalf but to no avail. He was finally exiled to the Paris embassy as a military attaché.[39] Mahmud al-Rusan, in turn, was exiled to the Washington embassy.

With the deposition of Talal, the entire nationalist movement in Jordan, both civilian and military, received a major blow to its anticolonial plans. It seemed that the British, and their archrepresentative Glubb, were there to stay. Talal, however, was not the first or the last Jordanian king to espouse part of the anticolonial nationalist agenda. The young King Husayn was to flirt with the nationalist anticolonial project from his first days on the throne and for some years to come.

When Husayn reached the legal age (18 lunar years) to assume his responsibilities as king, he was called back from London where he was attending Sandhurst military academy. On his way back to Jordan, Husayn stopped in Paris where he met Abu-Nuwwar, who shared with the king his nationalist anti-British ideas. According to Abu-Nuwwar, the young king was very attentive. A few months later, in August 1953, King Husayn invited Abu-Nuwwar to London to attend a party honoring the king. The king was accompanied by a number of Jordanian officers.[40]

When Abu-Nuwwar arrived in London, he met with Shahir Abu-Shahut, who was also in London at the time attending military school. In an attempt to recruit his friend, Abu-Shahut told Abu-Nuwwar about the Free Officers and their goal of "Arabizing" the Jordanian army. Abu-Nuwwar in turn informed Husayn of the existence of the group, in order to enlist the king's support. The young king was impressed and asked to meet with some of the officers including Abu-Shahut, whom he met later at the party. The two agreed to meet soon in Amman.[41] The meeting, however, was not to take place for more than two years.

At the party, Abu-Nuwwar condemned the British presence in Jordan, drawing applause and support from the Jordanian officers. The king was impressed and sought to strategize with Abu-Nuwwar about what was to be done. It was decided that the king would order the return of Abu-Nuwwar and Mahmud al-Rusan to their posts in the army back in Jordan. From the late summer of 1953 to the end of 1955, the king tried to do just that, but to no avail, as Glubb rejected his requests to transfer the two officers back. In the meantime, however, the young king continued his contacts with Abu-Nuwwar, visiting him in Paris and later sending him as his envoy to Egypt to consult with 'Abd al-Nasir. He also called him to Amman in 1954 for consultations.[42] Finally, in November 1955, the king made up his mind and issued a decision to transfer Abu-Nuwwar back to Jordan against Glubb's insistent rejection.[43] On his arrival, Abu-Nuwwar had an audience with Glubb, who refused to give him a military job and threatened to "shorten his life" if he attempted to foment discord in the country.[44] As a result, Abu-Nuwwar was appointed a senior aide-de-camp to the king.

In the meantime, Abu-Shahut and the Free Officers made contacts with Syrian and Egyptian nationalist military elements. The Syrians suggested that the Jordanian Free Officers undertake a campaign of blowing up British air force jets as well as a campaign of assassinating British officers. The Jordanians were shocked at these suggestions and insisted that they were a group of anticolonial nationalists and not a band of thugs.[45]

Abu-Shahut himself was to undergo a fate similar to that which befell al-Tall and Abu-Nuwwar before him. In 1954, he sat for a promotion exam and was told by the examining officer that he passed with flying colors. However, when the formal results were announced, Glubb informed him that he had failed. Incensed, Abu-Shahut resigned from the army, only to be invited later by Glubb for a tête-à-tête. Glubb confirmed to him that he had failed him in the exam because of his political involvement, as intelligence reports stated that Abu-Shahut had been critical of the government when he was studying in London. Glubb's strategy was to co-opt Abu-Shahut by appointing him as his military aide-de-camp. Abu-Shahut, relieved that Glubb did not know of the Free Officers or of their contacts with the king, accepted the position. He met with his colleagues, who agreed that they should be more circumspect as Glubb had eyes everywhere—something Habis al-Majali, one of the Free Officers at the meeting, stressed strongly.[46]

Abu-Nuwwar's arrival in Jordan coincided with the country's rising opposition to the British and U.S. attempts to include Jordan in an anti-Soviet pact dubbed the Baghdad Pact, which included Iraq and Turkey as members. British Chief of Staff General Gerald Templer visited Jordan on a mission to sell the pact to Jordan's rulers. The king and his ministers, especially Hazza' al-Majali, supported the venture,[47] while the anticolonial nationalist tide in the country vehemently opposed it. Within the officer corps, the nationalist officers opposed the pact, whereas officers more loyal to Glubb supported it. For example, the Circassian officer Musa 'Adil Bakmirza Shirdan was one of those who supported the pact, condemning all opposition to it as "communist" and pro-Soviet.[48] Abu-Nuwwar wavered at first and then came out against it.[49] The Free Officers insisted that the enemies of Jordan were the *British and Israel,* and not the USSR.[50]

As a result of the massive demonstrations against the Baghdad Pact and the British, the army was deployed in the streets of Jordan's cities and began to shoot at civilians. Tens of demonstrators were killed.[51] Still, the nationalist tide did not ebb. Police were hit by stones, as were British army officers. The crowds burned army Land Rovers. Many Hadari and some Bedouin soldiers deserted the army and joined the crowds.[52] The demonstrations took place all over the West Bank and the East Bank. East Bank cities and towns from Amman and Zarqa' to Irbid, Salt, 'Ajlun, Ramtha, and even the village of 'Anjara were full of demonstrators. People in Ramtha, on the border with Syria, were said to have moved the border demarcations and raised the Syrian flag. They also stoned the minister of defense. 'Ali al-Hiyari, a Free Officer, was sent to Ramtha and rectified the situation by forcing every household to fly the Jordanian flag.[53] Around the same time, the Free Officers issued pamphlets condemning British army officers as well as Arab collaborators.[54]

One of the British officers in Zarqa', Lieutenant Colonel Patrick Lloyd, was killed by a mob while his entire army regiment (composed of Hadari soldiers) stood by watching without firing a shot.[55] Peter Young, a British officer in the Army, states, "It is easy to condemn his soldiers for not opening fire in his defence, and I feel that bedouin soldiers would have used their rifles. For the haderi soldiers the strain was becoming so great. The mob were their kith and kin, and at least to that extent the soldiers sympathised with the rioters."[56] Zarqa' police refused to enforce the curfew and would release violators arrested by the army.[57] In fact, the stress became so high that some Bedouin soldiers (of Syrian tribal origins) deserted their army regiment.[58] To regain control of Zarqa', military aircraft flew over the town for reconnaissance, terrifying the populace.[59] According to Young, the "bedouin as ever were solidly behind anything that the Pasha approved. In 9 Regiment this was so much the case that it was hardly necessary to lecture the men and tell them what the [Baghdad] Pact was for."[60] Still, Young is forced to acknowledge that some among them, even in his own Bedouin Regiment 9, "had not cared for operating in Zerqa. It was too near home."[61] Young rationalizes their reluctance: "Every battalion in every army has in its ranks a few of those aptly described by the Americans as 'weak sisters.' I reckoned there were not many left in 9, and that Saoud [Rashdan, a loyal Bedouin officer from the central Saudi Arabian Mutayr tribe] and I had a pretty good idea who they were. In fact, in February 1956, the Regiment was better than it ever had been. . . . Most of the duds had gone."[62]

Abu-Nuwwar arrived in Amman in the middle of this upheaval. According to Abu-Shahut's account, Abu-Nuwwar met with him immediately after his arrival and arranged for a meeting with the king, who had not yet met with the Free Officers since the London meeting two years earlier. Abu-Shahut told the king of his new position as Glubb's aide-de-camp and informed him that Glubb was going to submit to him a long list of twenty or more nationalist officers to be dismissed from the army. Abu-Shahut warned the king that Glubb was going to represent the officers as enemies of the throne itself. Husayn insisted, "I would kick the throne with my foot if it were going to prevent me from serving my people and my country and my good brothers. Worry not, for I shall protect you from this injustice."[63] Abu-Shahut was thrilled with the nationalist king. The king decided that Abu-Nuwwar and two more Free Officers, Mazin al-'Ajluni and Mundhir 'Innab, be appointed as his aides-de-camp. As a result, the king came to be identified more openly with the anticolonial struggle that had overtaken Jordan in the last few years.[64] As for the matter of the dismissal of the officers, according to the king, the night before Glubb's dismissal "I was presented with a list of officers about to be dismissed. Their only fault was that they were nationalists and ambitious. How could they be anything else? . . . I refused to sign the document. I threw the list on the table in my office and told the Prime Minister: 'Tell Glubb Pasha I refuse to sign this.'"[65]

For his part, Abu-Nuwwar does not mention the meeting with Abu-Shahut. He claims that in light of the Baghdad Pact debacle and its resolution in favor of the anticolonial nationalists—with the king finally resolving to be on the nationalist side—King Husayn approached him and reopened the discussion about an army revolt against British control. At the same time, according to Abu-Nuwwar, pro-British and pro-Iraqi government elements in Jordan began recruiting among army officers for the removal of the nationalist king and for establishing a government that would be unified with Iraq under the rule of the Hashemite Iraqi throne. Nothing came of the plan. By February 1956, the army had gone back to the barracks and the situation calmed down. However, anti-British rage among the nationalist officers had intensified as a result of the clashes that Glubb had precipitated between the army and civilians. It was around the same time that flyers bearing the signature of the Free Officers circulated in Amman.[66]

The emergence of the Free Officers was reflective of the changing features of the Jordanian Arab Army itself. Whereas in 1948, the army had 300 officers, in 1956 it had 1,500, and a number of them were graduates of the newly built cadet school.[67] They were for the most part young officers under the age of twenty-four, and they had junior military ranks ranging from first lieutenant to second lieutenant. Few of them led military units. Moreover, a number of them were sent to British military schools for training.[68] A number of Palestinians had also joined the army and served in the newly formed air force, engineering, artillery, signals, and administrative services.

A training center for the army was established in 1950, and in 1951 a formally organized cadet school to train subalterns (Murashshahin) was opened. The training center included a school for boys, which recruited from Bedouin and other tribal groups. Boys (as young as ten years) would spend seven years in the school before they were inducted into the army. The school was known as the education wing of the training center.[69] The center also included a training wing, which in turn included schools and sections for tactics, small weapons, provost marshal, administration, military justice, basic training—boot camp lasting 16 weeks—and a police training college. The center was commanded by a British officer, with an Arab officer as second-in-command. Cadre officers on the staff were all of Hadari origins, as were all the instructors. A number of British officers instructed drill and physical training. The school for boys was staffed mostly by recently arrived Palestinians. The training center was controlled by the general headquarters of the army in Amman through its newly established education branch.[70] By 1953, knowledge of English became required of officers. According to P. J. Vatikiotis, a historian of the Arab Legion, all officers until 1956 came from either the school for boys or they were regular noncommissioned officers (NCOs). Members of both groups would be selected to go to cadet school. By 1953, at least two Arab officers would be sent to Britain to attend Camberely or Sandhurst. As other Army branches expanded (artillery, engineers, and armor), more Arab officers would be sent to Britain for training in their respective areas.[71]

In view of this expansion, Glubb opted to ensure the separation between the Bedouins and the Hadaris within the army. In the meantime, he continued to recruit Bedouins from within and without Jordan, as a large number of Bedouins were of Syrian, Iraqi, Hijazi, and even Nejdi origins, the latter having been at odds with the Saudi regime.[72] Vatikiotis claims that in "some of the infantry and armoured car regiments over half the men came from tribes *outside* Jordan, that is, Iraq, Saudi Arabia, and Syria. To this extent, these recruits constituted an essentially mercenary group that would have been difficult to interest in political movements aimed against the regime short of lucrative material promises."[73] Jordanian Bedouins mainly came from the Huwaytat and the Bani Sakhrs, although members of northern tribes such as Bani Khalid and Ahl al-Jabal (mainly from the Syrian Druze Mount) also joined. Later, after 1948, Palestinian Bedouins from the Beersheba region in the Naqab desert also joined.[74] Not all Bedouins were loyal to Glubb. In fact, a number of Bedouin officers, like Salamah 'Atiq, were part of, or sympathized with, the Free Officers movement, although the majority were indeed loyal to Glubb and to their British commanders.

The three infantry brigades of the Jordanian Arab Army comprised ten regiments: five Bedouin and five Hadari. The armored brigade was almost entirely Bedouin. The entire army comprised eighteen regiments, of which seven were exclusively Bedouin, not counting the camelry of the Desert Patrol and the Reconnaissance Squadron, which were also exclusively Bedouin.[75] Although the army had only 6,000 men in 1948, it came to have between 17,000 and 20,000 men in 1953 and close to 25,000 men in 1956.[76] In addition, there were 30,000 men in the newly constituted National Guard, which recruited from rural areas, especially West Bank border villages.[77]

As a result of this sudden and immense expansion in the army, new needs and trends emerged. Glubb's hostility to educated Arabs persisted and manifested itself in his refusal to promote the young educated officers in favor of the existing officers (many of whom were not necessarily of Transjordanian origins) and Bedouin officers with little, if any, education. This led to much resentment by the young cadres, who were not only refused promotions (as in the case of Abu-Shahut, for example) but were even dismissed from the army when news of their political views became known to Glubb. These young officers, as a result, were influenced both by the raging societal upheaval surrounding them and by their own direct experience in the army, including with Glubb himself.

The first sign that military opposition was forming manifested itself through a number of pamphlets that were distributed to army units in 1952, signed by the Free Officers. The pamphlets were directed against Glubb, who claims that they were prepared by an officer in the Supply and Transport Corps who had been dismissed "for financial dishonesty" and was then residing in Beirut. Glubb claims that he obtained information about the officer through the Lebanese police and then sent him a warning, which he appeared to heed, as no more pamphlets appeared for a while.[78] When the pamphlets appeared again in 1955 and 1956 with the same signature, Glubb attributed them to the Egyptian authorities, as according to him, they included Egyptian military terms that were not in use by the Jordanian army.[79] He continued to deny the possibility that such a group as the Free Officers was real, even after his dismissal. His opinion, however, was not shared by another British officer, Peter Young. Young claims to have known of the Young Officer's Movement since the summer of 1954. In his estimation, it recruited more "among the intelligentsia—the artillery and the engineers."[80]

Clash of the Titans: Glubb Pasha and the Uneasy King

Contrary to most historical accounts of the period, the nationalist officers were not a unified group. Whereas most historians lump the Free Officers with other nationalist officers, such as Abu-Nuwwar and al-Hiyari, it is clear from memoirs written by officers in both camps that this was not the case. The memoirs, as we shall see, reveal much less unity of purpose and much more divergent interests, not to mention personal antagonisms between officers of both camps (especially Abu-Shahut and Abu-Nuwwar, and within the same camp especially between Abu-Nuwwar and al-Hiyari), than was thought before.[81] For now, however, the nationalist officers had a similar agenda: the expulsion of Glubb and Arabizing the army.

The resentment of the army officers was shared by the young nationalist king. In a meeting on April 9, 1955, with his cabinet, which included Glubb, the king outlined his demand for reforms in the army and the promotion of Arab officers who graduated from British military schools as opposed to uneducated officers (who were mostly Bedouin) with seniority. He also called for the establishment of an air force.[82] Reflecting his nationalist ideology, the king, in a speech he delivered on May 25, 1955, on Independence and

Army Day, identified the army as "the heart that pulsates within the home-land's being." He also identified army soldiers as "the grandchildren of the Conquering Arabs [al-'Arab al-Fatihin]" in reference to early Muslim con-quests.[83] King Husayn speaks in his autobiography of the period of wanting to involve the people of Jordan in running its affairs, including the army, a goal that contradicted Glubb's plans. The king affirms that despite Glubb's "love for Jordan and his loyalty to my country, [he] was essentially an out-sider, and his attitude did not fit at all into the picture I visualized. . . . Consequently, to be blunt about it, he was serving as my commander-in-chief yet could not relinquish his loyalty to Britain."[84] The king articulated his position as follows:

> Throughout the Army this led to a fantastic situation in which the British dominated our military affairs to a great degree. Around me I saw junior Arab officers who would obviously never become leaders. Some of them were men lacking in ability and force, men prepared to bow to Whitehall's commands (transmitted by senior British offi-cers), men who had no spark, men without initiative and who could be trusted not to cause any problems. These were "officer material." . . . Those with nationalist aspirations, who hoped for a Jordanian Arab Legion, never had an opportunity for promotion, and when they did they were assigned to unimportant positions with no promise of ad-vancement. It was bitterly frustrating to young men. Time after time I demanded that the British should prepare more Jordanian officers and train them for the higher echelons of the armed forces. Time after time my requests were ignored. The highest active post a man could hold was regimental commander.[85]

After months of "patient negotiations," the British agreed to submit a plan for the Arabization of the military "in due course."[86] In Glubb's own projec-tions at the time (1955), he foresaw that Arab officers would not be qualified enough to take over from British officers before 1965 (later modified to 1961):

> [A]lthough we unwillingly decided that, for the present, the British officers were necessary to ensure efficiency, we prepared extremely detailed plans for their replacement. As a result of my personal inter-vention, we secured two entries a year at the British Staff College, Camberley. Calculating in considerable detail the ages of all officers,

their qualifications and the output of the Staff College, we produced a plan according to which the last British officer would leave in 1965. The senior Jordanian officer, who would assume command as a lieutenant-general, would then be forty-five years old. . . . This plan was submitted to the King, who accepted it and proclaimed himself satisfied. Later on we produced a modified plan for a period of six years for the take-over. This proposal would have entailed a considerable drop in efficiency, as it would not have been possible in that time to produce officers qualified for all the posts which would be vacant. . . . The King accepted our proposals without comment or criticism. Had he or the government asked for a shorter period, we should have revised the scheme in any way they desired, while pointing out the possible dangers.[87]

King Husayn reports the story differently. Told that an Arabization plan was underway, he perceived a "victory." "Imagine the excitement when I told my Cabinet. All that remained was to discover what 'in due course' meant. But my elation was short-lived when I was gravely informed that the Royal Engineers would have an Arab Commander by 1985!"[88]

For the nationalist king and the nationalist officers, the army had to be nationalized hand in hand with the nationalization of the state and society more generally. The army was of particular importance, in that, as King Husayn stresses, it stood for the defense of the nation as well as for Jordani-anness itself: "we had to give our own men a chance, especially in a country like Jordan where the Army is not only an instrument for defense against foreign incursions but is part of everything Jordanian. To Jordanians, with their martial history, it is and has always been an honor and a privilege to be a soldier. No man in the Arab world held this higher than did the troops of the Arab Legion. But for the officers it was very different, for they saw in a profession to which they were devoted no hope of rightful progress."[89] Note, how the king's nationalist views (like those of other Jordanian nationalists) are in tandem with Glubb's Orientalist views of Jordanians as Bedouins, and that Bedouins, unlike other Arabs, have a uniquely admirable "martial history," the latter being part of Glubb's (and subsequently successive Jordanian governments) de-Bedouinization and re-Bedouinization campaigns in the country (as we saw in chapter 3).

The king's problems with Glubb were all coded in the language of national self-determination and nationalist defense. Like the army officers, the king argued with Glubb over the necessity of having not only a defensive strategy (exemplified by the formation of the National Guard) but also an offensive one. The king wanted Jordan to have the ability to retaliate against the routine Israeli cross-border attacks and massacres targeting Jordanian border villages and towns. In this regard, the king states, "I argued that every time such an outrage occurred we should select a target on the other side and do the same to them. It would soon have stopped the Israelis. As it was, we accepted these outrages meekly. . . . Our soldiers were ridiculed, a great gulf grew between the Army and the people. . . . In vain I pointed all this out to Glubb. To all my pleas he advised cautious patience."[90] Glubb also advocated a strategy of withdrawal to the East Bank, effectively allowing Israeli occupation of the West Bank, a solution that outraged the king. "I argued with Glubb on this principle of defense. There were other arguments when I learned that we were short of ammunition. I realized that he had some justification for his theory. But this was not a matter of theory; this was the margin that separates the honor and the shame of a nation."[91] Recognizing that Glubb took his orders from Whitehall,[92] the king asserted that "though it was not Glubb's fault, his very presence in our country was without doubt an important factor in the trouble. We were in the hands of foreigners."[93] Glubb's lectures to officers about abandoning the West Bank in case of attack angered Husayn "extremely."[94] As a result of all these problems, "I was determined to build up strong, well-balanced armed forces, including an Air-Force, and since this was not possible with Glubb, our self-respect demanded that we fight our battles alone."[95]

The king also stressed that there were also "personal problems":

Glubb, who was now only a month away from sixty, had been with us so long, it was hard to imagine what life in Jordan without him might have been. He had been part of the Arab World since 1920, when, at twenty-three, he served in Iraq. He first came to Transjordan (as it then was) in 1930 to command the Desert Force and had been in command of al-Jeish al-Arabi—to give the Legion its Arabic name—since 1939. . . . His cherubic face beneath its silver hair and his brisk figure jumping in and out of his Land Rover were as much a part of the landscape as the great Mosque of Amman. Politicians held sway and slid into oblivion. Ambassadors came and departed. But Glubb went on forever—efficient, energetic, good-mannered, unchanging. But one thing had changed. The times.[96]

Note how Glubb's Orientalist images of a noble and unchanging Orient (discussed in chapter 3) are now used by the nationalist king against Glubb himself. The nationalist discourse of which the king was a product did not question the epistemological underpinnings of Orientalism and the colonial discourse of modernity; it simply sought to complement them by assuming (contra both) its own agency. The problem with Glubb was not his colonial modernist project as such, but rather his failure at taking it to its logical conclusion by accepting the agency of the colonized as a response to colonialism. He also had become static, dragging a modernizing Jordan (which "modernized" thanks to Glubb and his colonial government's efforts) down with him. The king's use of Glubb's own imagery against Glubb himself, whether conscious or not, is indeed ingenious. Note his following statement:

> Twenty-six years is more than a third of man's allotted span, and in this period General Glubb had been largely isolated from the outside world. To be quite frank, it was my impression that he smacked too much of the Victorian era. He said that I was young and impetuous, while maintaining that he himself was older and more cautious. That is true. But Jordan is a young and impetuous country, and we were, and still are, in more hurry than Glubb was to achieve our national aims. And because of this very vitality, the last thing I wanted was a cautious army. Although a fine soldier, Glubb at fifty-nine was old-fashioned in many ways.[97]

Husayn's description of Glubb as a Victorian is fully in line with the king's nationalist and modernist commitments. Identifying Glubb as "old-fashioned" was certainly an indictment of Glubb's commitment to Arab "traditions" (with which the king and the nationalists concurred), at the expense of modernization (with which they did not). For the king and for the nationalists, as we will see, tradition and modernity combined in a way that was quite different from what Glubb had envisioned.

As for the king's continuing frustrations with Glubb, he had discussed matters with the British Foreign Office as early as 1955, when he informed British officials of his disagreement with Glubb, but nothing changed. Although, the king does not specifically mention meetings with nationalist officers, their influence on him was becoming more apparent. He states, "Although I felt Glubb must go, I had not yet fixed the exact time. Then two events occurred."[98] These were the matter of the list of officers that Glubb wanted dismissed, and the matter of the separation of the police force from army leadership (i.e., from Glubb's control), as the two were under the same administration. The king attempted to disentangle the two in a meeting with the prime minister two days before Glubb's dismissal, but the prime minister warned of serious repercussions. Glubb's submission of the list of officers slated for dismissal on the last day of February was construed as the straw that broke the camel's back. The king, as already mentioned, refused to approve the order: "I remained obdurate, for what really made me angry was the realization that even my own ministers, however loyal, felt helpless to act within their rights."[99] Appalled, the king described Glubb's powers frankly: "Glubb operated from a position of such strength our political leaders tended to turn to him or to the British Embassy before making the slightest decisions."[100] That same day, the prime minister responded to the king, informing him that the separation of the police from the army was not possible at that time. The king was livid: "That night, I decided Glubb Pasha would have to go immediately. I have told General Glubb since then that the last thing I desired was to hurt his feelings, nor was it a pleasant task to dismiss a man who had served our country so faithfully for twenty-six years. . . . Though I knew that General Glubb would be upset at the brusqueness and suddenness with which this painful episode took place, it had to be done the way I did it."[101]

On the morning of March 1, 1956, the twenty-one-year-old King Husayn drove up to the prime minister's office in military uniform, "preceded and followed by Land Rovers containing my escort of armed soldiers." He told an aide, "This is one of the most important days of my life. I don't know what its end will be, but one can only live once and only with honor."[102] Husayn had written the dismissal order on a piece of paper that he presented to the prime minister (the king denies Glubb's later allegations that he threw the paper on the prime minister's desk). "Those few lines ordered the immediate dismissal of Glubb Pasha. . . . 'These are my wishes,' I told him. 'I want them executed at once.' . . . I then told the members of the Cabinet: 'I believe what I am doing is for the good of the country.'"[103]

The Prime Minister met with Glubb at two in the afternoon and gave him two hours to leave the country. Glubb, outraged, responded: "No, sir! . . . I cannot! I have lived in this country for twenty-six years. Almost all my worldly possessions are here, to say nothing of my wife and children."[104] An agreement was reached. Glubb and his family would leave at seven o'clock the next morning.

The king was harassed all night with unexpected visits from the British ambassador cautioning and then threatening him in an attempt to convince him to reverse his decision. According to Abu-Nuwwar, Glubb, who was confined to his house all night, attempted to leave his home at five the next morning to contact the British ambassador and loyalist army officers but was prevented from doing so by a nationalist Bedouin officer, who had initially been recruited by Glubb himself.[105] Meanwhile, the king remained steadfast. He points out that "though he was dismissed, [Glubb] was dismissed with full honors. He was driven to the airport in my own royal car. My Defense Minister represented the Cabinet and my Chief of Diwan represented me. They both bade him good-by [sic]."[106] Before boarding the plane, Glubb was presented with a portrait of King Husayn in a silver frame. The King wrote on it, "With our acknowledgment of the good services and untiring exertions and with our best wishes for His Excellency General Glubb Pasha. 1/3/1956. Husain Tellal."[107]

Glubb claims that the king dismissed him because of a misunderstanding and the intrigues of nationalist officers and politicians:

> [A]nother immediate irritant had been an article which appeared in an English periodical . . . [implying] . . . that I was the real ruler of the country, while the king had little power. This of course was what the intriguers had been telling the King. He was incensed at seeing the same idea reproduced in an English newspaper. . . . The King had been enthusiastically determined to enter the Baghdad Pact, and had thereby incurred the hostility of Egypt and of the Jordan extremists. The policy had failed. It was pointed out to him that he could regain his popularity with these extremely vocal enemies at one stroke. To perform some act of defiance towards Britain and to dismiss me would immediately re-establish his popularity with the noisy politicians at home, and would quieten the active hostility of Egypt. At the same time, however, the King's mind and imagination had been genuinely fired up by Arab nationalism.[108]

In Glubb's estimation, King Husayn "was the originator of the order [of dismissal]. Ali Abu Nuwar and two other young A.D.C.s, were the King's advisers. Three other young officers, friends of the A.D.C.s were also aware of what was afoot. The names of all six officers were known to us as being intriguers. But they were friends of the king."[109] Although the king concurred with part of Glubb's analysis, he insisted that dismissing the latter was the ultimate act of saving Jordan from national annihilation: "Let it not be thought that I dismissed an old and trusted friend in a fit of emotional pique. Glubb Pasha is a great man and knows as well as I that this is far from the truth. . . . It was a surgical operation which had to be done brutally. I knew I was right; indeed, I would say that if Glubb had been in command of the

Army a year longer, it would have been the end of Jordan. The country would have been carved up among the other Arab states seeking aggrandizement."[110] The British and Glubb, who were seen by 'Abdullah as instrumental in creating Transjordan and in unifying much of its disparate Bedouin population, came to be seen by King Husayn as the main reasons why the country would no longer exist.

On March 3, 1956, the Jordanian government issued a manifesto explaining the reasons for the dismissal of Glubb, which included the disaffection felt by Jordanian officers, disagreement on military strategy, the inaccurate information that he transmitted to the king, and "Glubb's role in the 1948 defeat."[111] The order that dismissed Glubb also dismissed two British officers and three Jordanian officers. The king took pains to communicate to the British government that "[w]ith regards to British officers serving in the Arab Legion, kindly note that Jordan will honour her obligations towards them according to their contracts and to the [Anglo-Jordanian] treaty."[112]

The king's decision to dismiss Glubb from his job did not signal a change in British-Jordanian relations. The king (and Glubb) took pains to stress that dismissing Glubb was an internal Jordanian affair, as Glubb was officially a Jordanian government employee. He assured the British that the dismissal of Glubb "had no bearing on my admiration of his country."[113] He wrote a long letter to Britain's prime minister, Anthony Eden, explaining that the disagreement with Glubb was of a personal nature and that it did not affect existing relations with Britain.[114]

This aside, Glubb's dismissal became a national day of celebration to be commemorated every year with speeches by the king and other government and army officials. After Glubb had been dismissed, a number of songs were composed for army soldiers, extolling the nationalist king for rendering "the hearts restful after the expulsion of Glubb."[115]

"Arabizing" the Jordanian Arab Army

The goal of nationalizing the Jordanian Arab Army, long sought by nationalists in society and in the army itself, was finally going to be realized. Immediately prior to Glubb's dismissal, the army was busy with training programs and reorganization following the Baghdad Pact events. As a result, many of the Free Officers who were on the Founding Committee were unable to meet. Abu-Shahut states that on a visit to Zarqa', he was told by a fellow Free Officer that a number of colleagues had recently met with the king and with Abu-Nuwwar, who informed them that the "operation" that would Arabize the army was imminent. Abu-Nuwwar, on his part, reports that the king asked him in the last week of February if the "[Free] Officers" were ready to take over the army. The king received an affirmative answer.[116] On the last day of February, the king met again with Abu-Nuwwar and reviewed the plans of Arabizing the army.[117] On the same day, Abu-Shahut (who was hospitalized in an army hospital in the West Bank for a strong case of influenza) was informed of the impending dismissal and of the new appointments in the army, including his own.[118] Major General Radi 'Innab (who held only police functions before his new promotion) took over the army from Glubb. 'Ali Abu-Nuwwar was promoted (from major to major general) and appointed second-in-command, and soon after, on May 24, 1956, he replaced 'Innab as head of the army. Massive purges, courts martial, desertions, transfers, and new promotions and appointments followed to effect the Arabization of the army.[119] Most of the sixty-four British officers were retired or dismissed, with the few remaining lacking any command functions.[120] Karim Uhan, of Maryamite army fame (he was one of the leaders of a small group of armed Christians composed of Palestinians and Transjordanians, organized by the state),[121] was transferred as military attaché to London. The British, however, by virtue of the Anglo-Jordanian Treaty, still had an army garrison in 'Aqaba, an armored car regiment stationed at Ma'an, a number of ordnance depots, and Royal Air Force bases at Amman and Mafraq.[122]

Peter Young claims (as does Glubb) that some Bedouin officers were prepared to restore Glubb by force but were stopped from doing so by the British commanding officers.[123] Still, by the end of May 1956, over 1,000 Bedouins left the army, including a hundred each from the two armored car regiments and the First Infantry Regiment. Young reports that they "have been told that there is no difference between haderi and bedu. This they may not believe. Many of their senior officers . . . have been sent to the National Guard [composed of Hadaris from both Banks], which, however unfairly, is despised by the bedouin. It is no wonder that they are trickling away."[124] In reorganizing the army, Abu-Nuwwar reports that, when he addressed Bedouin soldiers and officers, he stressed the new leadership's appreciation for their courage and sacrifices, clarifying to them the importance of educating their children in schools at the army's expense to qualify for army careers. Abu-Nuwwar frankly told the Bedouin regiments, which were being integrated, that there is a promotion ceiling to uneducated officers. As a result, many Bedouin senior officers were either retired or reappointed to noncommand positions. Abu-Nuwwar acknowledges that this led to some unfairness to many officers who were bypassed for promotions despite their seniority privileges, as they did not have the proper qualifications that a "modern" army required.[125]

The new nationalized army had little use for the British colonial notion of "tradition." Like nationalists everywhere, they were committed to a modernization project that redefined tradition, and not to a Glubb-like traditionalization project that defined modernization. On May 26, 1956, Jordan's defense minister, Muhammad 'Ali al-'Ajluni, issued a decision abolishing the red-and-white shmagh/hatta of the army, which he said was not practical and was "not a military head-dress."[126] The soldiers will now wear khaki berets. Peter Young defends the "military-appropriate" shmagh. Appalled by the decision, he states that the "imagination boggles at the thought of the bedouin in those hideous and unromantic pancakes." He proceeds to state that the "present régime in Jordan welcomes change for its own sake, and in twenty years time little will be remembered of the uniforms we knew."[127] His prediction was only partly true. Although most of the armed forces in Jordan today do not uphold the erstwhile uniforms, the Bedouin security forces (Quwwat al-Badiyah) that continue to exist in the Jordanian armed forces today continue to uphold Glubb's "traditional" clothing designs. As for the *shmagh*, it was to infiltrate society at large as a symbol of Jordanianness (see chapter 5).

The new nationalist leadership saw the army as an instrument of national unification. Upon assuming office, the nationalists embarked on achieving just that. The Arabized leadership integrated the National Guard into the army, which was going to achieve the integration of East Bankers and West Bankers as well as Hadari and Bedouin soldiers. This brought the total number of men in the army to 55,000.[128] The long-sought-after separation of the police and the army was also effected in July 1956. Bahjat Tabbarah (of Lebanese origin and Turkish trained) was appointed head of police. On his part, 'Ali Abu-Nuwwar, reorganized the entire army in the summer of 1956. He abolished division headquarters under which infantry brigade groups had been organized and reorganized them into separate brigade group headquarters. P. J. Vatikiotis states that, presumably, "independent Brigade headquarters afforded the new Chief of Staff the opportunity of dealings with each Brigade commander without the intermediary of a division headquarters."[129] Also, to avoid the fraudulence that accompanied the previous elections (in 1952 and 1954) in which the army was involved, by virtue of its members' votes, it was decided, in a joint meeting between the officers and the king, that army soldiers no longer be accorded voting privileges. A law was drawn up to that effect (see chapter 2). 'Ali Abu-Nuwwar, who was late to the meeting, seemed unhappy with that decision.[130] As a result, army soldiers did not participate in the October 1956 elections, which brought to parliamentary power (for the first time in Jordan's legislative history) a wide spectrum of Jordan's nationalist opposition.

The Arabization campaign did not go unopposed. Several disaffected elements in the army began to make trouble. An assassination attempt on the life of Mahmud al-Ma'aytah, a Free Officer, was made by Majid al-Rusan, but it did not succeed. Other conspiracies began to unfold. One such conspiracy aimed to topple the king and the Free Officers. It is alleged to have been an alliance between East Bank Transjordanian nationalists and Bedouins. The Hadari officers involved hailed from northern Jordan (especially Irbid), whereas the Bedouin officers were mostly from the East Bank (especially members of the Bani Sakhr). Members of the conspiracy included Mahmud al-Rusan (Majid's brother), Radi al-'Abdullah, Muhammad Ahmad Salim, Salih al-Shar', 'Abdullah Mjalli, Sulayman Rutaymah, and many others. It was alleged that the conspirators were plotting with Nuri al-Sa'id, Iraq's strongman and the British Empire's most loyal subject in the Arab East.[131] Regionalism was also a motive, as the Irbidis involved felt that the army was being controlled by Saltis.[132] This attested to the incomplete unification and nationalization of the country under one supreme national identity. One of the conspirators, 'Abdullah al-'Ayid Mayyas, confessed and details were revealed at the trial. Others followed suit. A court martial took place and all the conspirators were indicted and sentenced to prison terms. They were all expelled from the army. 'Ali Abu-Nuwwar intervened on their behalf with the king, who issued an amnesty in their favor.[133] Around the same time, Jordan's long-time politician and prime minister of many terms, Tawfiq Abu al-Huda (of Palestinian origin), who was also Britain's main man in the country, committed suicide by hanging himself.

Whereas 'Abdullah al-Tall's nationalism in the late 1940s centered on ridding the country of the British, the anticolonial nationalism of the Free Officers was more complex. Although, like al-Tall before them, they were committed to the monarch and to ending British control, increasingly they began to articulate a social agenda, one of democratization of society and the state. These were ideas already elaborated by the civilian opposition, which have by now infiltrated the army.

This situation manifested itself in the left–right split among nationalist officers themselves. The Free Officers were increasingly becoming disaffected by 'Ali Abu-Nuwwar, who was never effectively a member of their group. His new appointments and transfers were all done without any consultation with them. Many of them felt that he was trying to co-opt officers to be loyal to him personally and not to the Free Officers as a group.[134] Many among the Free Officers were resentful, as many were being bypassed for important appointments by officers of lesser ranks including Abu-Nuwwar himself, who before his recent promotion was a junior officer in comparison with a few of them. The founding committee of the Free Officers met, and after a heated debate it was decided that they meet with Abu-Nuwwar and offer him the position of head of the Free-Officer's group, so that they would be able to work more closely with him, thus avoiding divisions. Abu-Nuwwar rejected the offer, stating that the main goal of the group was the Arabization of the army, which was underway, so there was nothing left for their group to do. The Free Officers insisted that their goals also included democratizing the country as well as military unity with Syria and Egypt. Abu-Nuwwar assured them that he would pursue their goals on their behalf and that it was time that they rested.[135] By late 1956, the Free Officers were becoming very uncomfortable with Abu-Nuwwar's personal style and his marginalization of their group. They began meeting regularly with members of the newly formed nationalist cabinet (following the October 1956 elections), who were also disaffected with Abu-Nuwwar's arrogance in dealing with them. They explained to the ministers that they did not approve of Abu-Nuwwar's actions and that he was not one of them. These meetings continued until the palace coup in 1957.[136]

The Palace Coup: The End of an Era

The dismissal of Glubb by King Husayn, although reflective of the king's nationalism and his rivalry with Glubb, was also a political maneuver aimed at silencing the opposition while maintaining the traditional influence that Britain had on the country, as Glubb, contrary to many of his detractors, was not the only conduit for that influence, although he was a central one. His removal did indeed neutralize domestic opponents of government policy as well as criticism from Arab nationalist circles abroad. This aside, the British annual subsidy continued and relations between the two countries did not seem to suffer much. The British foreign office and the war office announced respectively the continuation of the economic aid and the seconding of British officers to the Jordanian army.[137]

On the first anniversary of the expulsion of Glubb and the Arabization of the army, the king spoke of his happiness that a year had passed since "the liberation and Arabization" of the army whose leadership, responsibilities, and commitments were "Arabized as we and the Arab nation desired it to be."[138] The new nationalist prime minister, Sulayman al-Nabulsi, stated in a speech commemorating the event, "this army which [Glubb] had wanted to render loyal to himself and to his country, to execute his will, to obey his orders, smiting with his sword this army, the army of the people, the army of Palestine, the army of a liberated Arab nationalism, the army of the one Arab nation, is celebrating today the day of its Arabization, the day of its salvation, the day of its victory, the day of the expulsion of the tyrant. . . . Glubb was removed, and this Arab army became Arab in flesh and blood, Arab in thought and spirit, Arab in its hopes and ambitions."[139]

Al-Nabulsi's confidence and expectations for the army, however, were not justified by the events unfolding in the country. The general situation did not bode well for anticolonial nationalists in the country or for anti-British Arab governments, including Saudi Arabia, Syria, and Egypt. The leaders of the three countries made offers to King Husayn to replace the British subsidy. The king welcomed the offer of aid without connecting it to the British subsidy or the Anglo-Jordanian Treaty. He later declared that he would welcome Arab aid provided it had no "ulterior motive."[140] The situation soon changed, following the 1956 tripartite invasion of Egypt and the new elections in Jordan. In light of these events, Jordan's new nationalist Parliament, through its foreign relations committee, recommended in November 1956 the termination of the Anglo-Jordanian Treaty.[141] A new Arab Solidarity Agreement was signed in January between Jordan, Egypt, Syria, and Saudi Arabia. It stipulated aid to Jordan and informally terminated the Anglo-Jordanian Treaty. A formal termination finally came in March 1957 after negotiations with the British that lasted more than one month. British forces still stationed in the country would be withdrawn within six months (the British force in Aqaba numbered 1,500 men), and the Jordanian government pledged to compensate the British for the evacuated facilities and matériel.[142]

Following the expulsion of Glubb and the rise of the anticolonial Jordanian Arab nationalist tide in the country, the king's men were increasingly nervous about their situation. Whereas the king's nationalism shared the nationalist officers' desire to oust Glubb from the army, his nationalism was not anti-Western, let alone republican, in the way Nasirism was. For the king's men, the increasing popularity of Nasirist and Ba'thist Arab nationalism in the neighboring Arab countries, combined with its local popular support, signaled the end of their power, if not the end of the monarchy. The British invasion of Egypt in 1956 left little room for them and for the king to appeal to the British as friends of the Arabs. This situation, however, was to change quickly and drastically. The entry of the United States on the scene as a supporter of 'Abd al-Nasir's efforts against the tripartite invasion was seen as a welcome maneuver. Events in Jordan in the coming months, if not the coming decades, were to be altered in accordance with these developments. The rise of the influence of the United States stands out in this regard, as does its impact on elites throughout the recently decolonized and the still colonized countries in Asia and Africa. Elites in these countries, who had a Western-friendly nationalism, could simultaneously condemn European colonial powers while befriending the United States, which did not yet have a colonial record in these continents (the Philippines and Korea excepted).

As the Jordanian government was still looking to end the treaty in January, the Americans declared their new formula for the cold war on January 5, 1957. It was called the Eisenhower Doctrine. The Saudis, increasingly nervous about the rising tide of Arab nationalism and its increasing republicanism, immediately endorsed the doctrine. In Jordan, reaction was mixed. Whereas nationalists preached neutrality, the king welcomed the doctrine and U.S. aid if the latter was offered "without political strings." The government protested the king's positive reaction. Incensed at what he perceived as their communist leanings, the king sent a now infamous letter to the government in which he condemned communism, warning the nationalist prime minister to be on guard against this "new kind of imperialism."[143] The letter, coming on the eve of treaty negotiations with the British and the announcement of the Eisenhower Doctrine, signaled the increasing gulf separating the king from his cabinet as well as from nationalists in the army and in society.[144]

Earlier, when the October 1956 elections were approaching, members of the king's coterie were already advising him to suspend the constitution and to cancel the elections, as they expressed concern over 'Abd al-Nasir's recent nationalization of the Suez Canal. Prominent among those advocating such solutions were old 'Abdullah associates Bahjat al-Talhuni, current chief of the Royal Diwan, and Bahjat Tabbarah (who was present with 'Abdullah at the Jerusalem talks with Churchill in 1921 leading to the foundation of Transjordan, and who had been recently appointed as head of public security, or police). When the king sought the advice of Abu-

Nuwwar, the latter cautioned against such measures and advised the king to proceed with the elections.[145]

Soon, more rumors began circulating in the country that a coup d'état was being planned against the recently formed nationalist government of Sulayman al-Nabulsi and the popularly elected Parliament as well as against the Free Officers. It was alleged that Bedouin units in the army would spearhead the coup.[146] Moreover, the involvement of major regime personalities was being reported, especially that of Husayn's uncle (Queen Zayn's brother) the Sharif Nasir Bin Jamil, who arrived from Iraq a few years earlier. Rumors had it that the sharif and a number of officers were distributing money and weapons to Bedouin tribes and to the Muslim Brotherhood. The king himself reports that he had become increasingly worried after he received a report from "an army officer from Beirut on a special mission . . . who must remain nameless" informing him that he was "very worried about the way our army officers are behaving in Beirut and Damascus . . . spending fortunes in the night clubs—money they couldn't possibly earn. They always seem to be with Russians or the Egyptian clique."[147] Upon more investigation, the king claims to have learned that a number of nationalist politicians and Abu-Nuwwar, who is identified as having been "once a close friend of mine," were "traitors" dealing with the Soviets and the Egyptians. The king reports that his chief of Diwan, Bahjat al-Talhuni, informed him that they brought over $300,000 into the country from their foreign masters to bribe Jordanians in preparation for their alleged coup.[148]

The king's alienation from the Free Officers was complete. He began making plans to replace them. Muhammad al-Maʿaytah (brother of the Free Officer Mahmud), an army officer who until recently served as military attaché in Syria, was called back to the country by Bahjat al-Talhuni and appointed senior aide-de-camp to the king. Maʿayta is said to have been contacted by the king who proposed to him that he take over the army as soon as he (the king) removes Abu-Nuwwar from his position, and that Maʿayta would then liquidate the Free Officers by retiring them, exiling them as military attachés outside the country, or dismissing them from the army altogether.

On hearing of this, the Free Officers met and discussed their options. They decided to approach the king and ask that the anti-nationalist conspirators be arrested. The list of conspirators included Bahjat Tabbarah, the Sharif Nasir, Samir al-Rifaʿi (former prime minister for many terms and a ʿAbdullah and Glubb confidant), Sadiq al-Sharʿ (army officer), Radi al-ʿAbdullah (future head of Jordanian intelligence—Mukhabarat), and

Talab Fahd. The list was submitted to Abu-Nuwwar and 'Ali al-Hiyari, who were not present at the meeting. The committee then went to Zarqa' to meet with the rest of the senior officers about the plan. There, officers shared with each other the direct threats communicated to different officers by al-Rifa'i, Tabbarah, and the sharif, who did not mince words in informing them that their "days are numbered."[149] Abu-Nuwwar submitted the list to the nationalist prime minister and then met with king. The king informed Abu-Nuwwar that he had information that Abu-Nuwwar and other officers were scheming to assassinate him, allegations that Abu-Nuwwar denied categorically, claiming that this was false information propagated by the anti-nationalist conspirators and requesting that they all be dismissed from their jobs—the request was also submitted by the cabinet on April 7, 1957. The cabinet order included at least twenty-two officials to be retired.[150] The king refused to dismiss his uncle (who was a senior advisor) or al-Talhuni (who was chief of the Royal Diwan), but he relented on dismissing Tabbarah from his position as head of police, replacing him with Muhammad al-Ma'ayta. The storm seemed to have been weathered, or so thought the Free Officers.[151]

Meanwhile, it was decided that the Free Officers would schedule routine military maneuvers to flex their muscles against the anti-nationalist conspirators. The maneuver, which involved the first armored regiment (led by Nadhir Rashid), was coded "Hashim," a tribute to the royal family and the nationalist king. It took place on April 8 and 9, 1957, and was supposed to take a census of cars coming in and out of Amman in preparation for a contingency plan to move troops from the East Bank to the West Bank in case of an Israeli invasion.[152] The old regime men, including Bahjat al-Talhuni, Bahjat Tabbarah, and the Sharif Nasir, used the maneuver to warn the king of an impending coup against him. Glubb, in his book, concocts an incredible propagandistic conspiracy theory involving the Soviets, Egypt, and the Free Officers, wherein the army maneuvers are said to have had the aim of forcing the king to abdicate and to declare a republic.[153] Abu-Nuwwar, in his memoirs, which were written after his rehabilitation, claims that these were routine maneuvers, although they involved certain troop movements of which he was not informed, implying that others (a veiled reference to 'Ali al-Hiyari, who, according to Abu-Nuwwar, was al-Nabulsi's choice to replace the difficult Abu-Nuwwar as head of the army[154]), and not he, may have been preparing for a coup.[155] He met with the king and assured him that no coup was in the making and ordered the cancellation of the Hashim maneuvers. The young king, torn between his recent nationalist allies and his trusted family and old regime friends and allies, began to waver. The United States, with its Eisenhower Doctrine in full gear, was also becoming nervous about nationalist rule in Jordan.[156] In light of all this, the king chose his long-time advisors against the nationalists. Following the cancellation of the Hashim maneuvers, he states, "The time for action had come."[157] According to the king, his uncle, the Sharif Nasir, and other family members told him that "everything seems to be lost and the rumors and reports indicate that you are alone. Are you going to stand and fight or should we all pack our bags?" Responding to them, the king proudly stated, "I am going to stand and fight, whatever the consequences."[158]

Soon after, on April 10, and after the failure of the prime minister to provide the king with an explanation of why the maneuvers were ordered — a situation that was compounded by the cabinet's new order of April 9 dismissing trusted regime friends, including Bahjat al-Talhuni — the king dismissed the nationalist cabinet of Sulayman al-Nabulsi, calling for a new one. Al-Nabulsi duly resigned. Public pressure was mounting with opposition rallies and meetings calling for al-Nabulsi's restoration. The king did not waver. He appointed Dr. Husayn Fakhri al-Khalidi (a Palestinian) as the new prime minister, but he resigned after twenty-four hours. The Hashim maneuvers seem to have backfired. Instead of weakening the anti-nationalists, they strengthened them.

Amidst public protests, the situation was becoming more complicated. The king was still attempting to appoint a new prime minister. He finally chose regime confidant Sa'id al-Mufti (a Circassian) to head the government. Army officers were concerned that unless a nationalist prime minister is chosen (they advised the king to choose the more "moderate" 'Abd al-Halim al-Nimr), the country would be engulfed in demonstrations and chaos. If that were to occur, they were not prepared to shoot at civilians. They were supported in their decision by the new chief of public security, Muhammad Ma'aytah.[159] In light of this situation, rumors were spread that the king was assassinated, eliciting a battle in Zarqa' in a regiment headed by Abu-Nuwwar's cousin Ma'n Abu-Nuwwar. The battle raged between Bedouin soldiers and those loyal to 'Ali Abu-Nuwwar. Moreover, armed Muslim Brotherhood members joined the fight on the side of the Bedouin troops against the "Communists."[160] Two soldiers were killed and twenty-five injured. Other Bedouin units (whose members were Bedouins from neighboring countries) also mutinied against the nationalist officers, especially in the first armored brigade.[161] On hearing of the situation, the king sent for

'Ali Abu-Nuwwar and both went to Zarqa'. The king, in army uniform, showed himself to the soldiers as alive and well, putting an end to the fighting.[162] The soldiers were chanting death to Abu-Nuwwar, who was rushed back to Amman. The king's intervention became a mythologized event describing his courage and bravery. He addressed the soldiers, thanking them for their "noble patriotic feelings and for rallying around the throne."[163]

'Abbas Murad, a historian of the Jordanian army, claims that the palace spread the rumors in the army to rouse loyal troops. He relied, for example, on Glubb's account that the king's brother, prince Muhammad, and a cousin visited a Bedouin regiment in Zarqa' on April 13, prior to the alleged coup, warning them of the impending "coup" against the palace. The troops went into the streets of Zarqa' burning cars and chanting "long live the king."[164]

That same night, the king submitted to Abu-Nuwwar a list of officers in the army to be dismissed. He refused, as he did not think that they were to blame. The king gave it to 'Ali al-Hiyari, who, according to Abu-Nuwwar, duly issued the dismissal orders. Abu-Nuwwar felt that the king's action of bypassing him meant that he no longer held his job. Abu-Nuwwar is said to have collapsed crying and asked the king to save him. The king decided not to kill him for "[i]f I had put him to death, his name might have been much more revered than it is today."[165] He decided to let him go. Abu-Nuwwar met the king on April 14 and asked for a two-week vacation, which he planned to spend in Rome.[166] He left to Syria on his way to Beirut to board a plane to Rome. When he arrived in Syria, he was told that a number of Free Officers had fled to Syria the night before, including Nadhir Rashid. On April 15, Radio Amman reported that Abu-Nuwwar had in fact fled to Syria after having led a failed coup against the king. Abu-Nuwwar called the palace to speak to the king but was unable to get through. On his part, the king dispatched Muhammad al-Ma'aytah to Damascus, promising that the Radio Amman broadcast would not be repeated and asked for Abu-Nuwwar's resignation for the sake of "national necessity and the preservation of army unity."[167] 'Ali al-Hiyari was appointed new head of the army.

On April 15, the king successfully asked Dr. Khalidi to form a government. This time, he succeeded. It included members of the deposed nationalist cabinet, including Sulayman al-Nabulsi himself. The remaining Free Officers, including Abu-Shahut, were shocked, as they were not informed of any of the events that had transpired, and they had to deal with the new facts of fleeing army officers and those arrested and accused of conspiracy. They discussed their options, following the events precipitated by the palace coup, including fleeing to Syria before they fell victims to the expected persecution. They opted to remain in the country and in their jobs as if nothing had happened.

On April 16, 'Ali-al-Hiyari informed the officers of his appointment as a replacement for Abu-Nuwwar and asked for their support. The officers gave it to him, as they did not know why Abu-Nuwwar had left to Syria in the first place. The king met with army officers on the evening of April 16 to check on the army. That same day, a Bedouin army officer, 'Akkash al-Zabn, who commanded army tanks, and a group of 200 Bedouin shaykhs went to the royal palace to pledge allegiance to the king.[168] The *New York Times* reported that a Saudi airplane brought gold to Amman to be distributed as a reward to loyal troops and Bedouin shaykhs.[169] The next day, 'Ali al-Hiyari informed the Free Officers that there were orders to rid the army of them and that certain politicians and officers, including Sadiq al-Shar' and Habis al-Majali, were urging the king to do so. On April 18, the Free Officers were invited to a meeting where they were informed by an officer, Radi al-Hindawi, that the king had ordered an investigation and that they were from that moment under house arrest. The officers present included Abu-Shahut, Mahmud al-Ma'ayta, Nayif al-Hadid, Ma'n Abu-Nuwwar, Dafi Jam'ani, Ahmad Za'rur, Ja'far al-Shami, Turki al-Hindawi, and Tawfiq al-Hiyari. On April 19, 'Ali al-Hiyari left for Syria for talks about Syrian troops posted at the border with Jordan and opted to remain there, essentially defecting. He proclaimed at a press conference that a great plot was launched against Jordan by palace officials and "foreign military attachés"—in reference to the United States.[170]

Habis al-Majali, a friend of King 'Abdullah, was appointed new head of the army. On April 22, a military court was set up and the Free Officers remaining in the country were all accused of conspiracy. Twenty-two people in total were accused of the plot. The court found five officers innocent, including chief of police Muhammad Ma'ayta, Nayif al-Hadid, and Ma'n Abu-Nuwwar. The remaining fifteen officers, including Abu-Shahut, Hindawi, Jam'ani, and Shami, faced prison terms ranging from ten to fifteen years. As for those who defected, including 'Ali Abu-Nuwwar, 'Ali al-Hiyari, and Nadhir Rashid, they were sentenced in absentia to fifteen years. 'Ali Abu-Nuwwar, in a press conference he held in Syria, denied all the accusations and stated that "the alleged plot was planned and designed by the American embassy in Jordan and by collaborators with colonialism in order to reach their goals."[171] A Free Officers' pamphlet, which circulated later in August 1957, accused "supporters of the Baghdad Pact and palace men" of the plot and stressed that "there was no plot against the throne."[172] The trials effectively ended a chapter in Jordan's anticolonial nationalist movement.[173] The purges of the army proceeded in earnest, restoring the status quo ante, which had prevailed under Lieutenant General Glubb Pasha. Bedouin officers who were dismissed by Abu-Nuwwar were reinstated, and the predominantly Palestinian Fourth Infantry Brigade was split, with many of its officers dismissed.[174]

On April 23, U.S. Secretary of State Dulles spoke of the U.S. government's "great confidence in and regard for King Hussein," offering assistance "to the extent that he [Husayn] thinks that it can be helpful."[175] On April 24, al-Khalidi's cabinet resigned in the midst of massive public protests against the palace coup. The king appointed Ibrahim Hashim (of Palestinian origin, and one of 'Abdullah's confidants) to head the new government and declared martial law later that night.[176] Curfews were imposed in Amman and other cities, politicians were arrested, Parliament dismissed, parties banned, and unions and associations dissolved. Five newspapers were closed down, and the constitution was suspended. A thorough purge of the civil service was in full gear, and a number of politicians fled the country in fear of persecution.[177] Moreover, the long-sought-after separation between the police and the army was revoked placing the security forces under army command, as was the case under Glubb.[178] They were to be separated again in 1958 after the crackdown on the opposition was successfully completed.[179]

The king, for his part, informed the Americans earlier on the night of April 24 of his planned martial law and asked for their help in case of foreign intervention. The White House immediately expressed its support with a public commitment to "the independence and integrity of Jordan," which it deemed "vital" to the United States. The U.S. Sixth Fleet was on its way to Lebanon's shores, technically at the request of Lebanese president Kamil Sham'un, while U.S. military planners considered airlifting troops to Mafraq and Amman. This, however, proved unnecessary, as the king informed them that same night, "I think we can handle the situation ourselves."[180] In May, the United States provided Jordan with $10 million worth of arms and military equipment, and this was followed in June by the signing of an agreement for economic and technical cooperation with Jordan.[181]

The five-year history of an ascendant unionist Arab nationalism in Jordan came to an end. Following the palace coup, the new regime strongly resembled that which existed under King 'Abdullah and Glubb Pasha. The same men who helped 'Abdullah and Glubb run the country were back in power helping 'Abdullah's grandson remain on the same course. Like similar regimes in Africa and Asia that could not openly support European colonial powers, the Jordanian regime's Western-friendly nationalism found in the United States a sponsor.

Army resistance to colonial discipline manifested after the Palestine War was crushed. Although the Free Officers' nationalism reflected that of society, it also reflected the internal dynamics of the military as a colonial institution. Colonial repressive and productive techniques had elicited nationalist resistance. The Arab identity that the officers and society assumed in opposition to colonialism was, however, reformulated by the state. Although the regime, and the state more generally, did not question the country's Arab identity, they questioned its supremacy over a more local Jordanian Bedouin identity that was linked to the monarchy. It was by reasserting this identity whose *other* was not colonialism but internal subversives that the state and the regime were able to reequilibrate. As we will see, the regime's triumph inaugurated a new exclusivist Jordanian national identity.

Palace Repression and the Forgiving King

Jordanian anticolonial nationalists saw themselves as part of a general Arab anticolonial nationalist movement and believed that Jordan could not survive outside of a future federation among Arab states. The palace espoused a different kind of Arab nationalism, one inspired by the anti-Turkish revolt during World War I, spearheaded by the Hashemites. Therefore, both parties spoke the language of Arab nationalism, although each accused the other of being an agent for foreign powers. For the anticolonial nationalists, palace men and their allies were collaborators with British and U.S. imperialism, whereas for the palace, the anticolonial nationalists were instruments of ʿAbd al-Nasir's hegemonic plans and Soviet communism, which King Husayn had called a "new kind of imperialism."[182] For King Husayn, "Nasser's Arab nationalism was taking the place of pure Arab nationalism,"[183] and those who supported ʿAbd al-Nasir's version in Jordan constituted, for him, a national threat to the homeland. He called on "ostracizing the party which almost blew away [our] independence and destroyed [our] being."[184]

Following the palace coup, which rid the country of internal threats to the prevailing order, the situation in the Arab world was changing so rapidly that the king and his triumphant advisors were becoming more worried about external threats. The unification of Egypt and Syria in what became known as the United Arab Republic was declared on February 1, 1958, to the consternation of the anti-ʿAbd al-Nasir rulers in Amman. The regime opted for an immediate federal union with Hashemite Iraq (one that had been long sought by Iraqi strongman Nuri al-Saʿid) dubbed the Arab Federation (al-Ittihad al-ʿArabi) and signed on February 14, 1958.[185] According to the bylaws of the federation, the Jordanian Arab Army was to be united with its Iraqi counterpart. The unified armies were to be called the Arab Army, although each would keep its separate identity in its respective state.[186] On March 29, 1958, the two countries issued a federal constitution called the Constitution of the Arab Federation.[187] The federal constitution was open to other Arab countries wishing to join. King Faysal of Iraq (Husayn's cousin) was appointed the president of the federation, and during his absence, King Husayn would be the president.[188] The Arab Federation, which was more of a confederation, had a short life. The Iraqi revolution in July 1958 (led by Iraqi army officers) violently eliminated the royal family (and the visiting Jordanian prime minister, Ibrahim Hashim, who had declared martial law the year before in the country) and declared a republic. The rulers of Jordan panicked. The king asked for immediate British and U.S. help to maintain his throne. Four thousand British troops landed in Jordan while U.S. soldiers landed in Beirut. U.S. planes also helped transport oil to Jordan, after it was surrounded on all sides by enemies (the rapprochement with the Saudis, the Hashemites' historic enemies, who had been allied with ʿAbd al-Nasir against the Baghdad Pact, had not yet fully taken place). The British soldiers remained in the country until November 2, 1958. They left only after the Americans pledged to support the throne and to provide the country with $40 to $50 million as an annual subsidy, replacing the British subsidy.[189]

In the meantime, pamphlets began circulating in the Jordanian army calling on soldiers to "become part of the people to save the homeland from unjust rule and to stand up in the face of attempts to render the army a group of guards to the traitors and the corrupt [al-khawanah wa al-maʾjurin] and an instrument to beat the people and to repress patriotic sentiments [al-shuʿur al-watani] in the country." The pamphlet revealed that there were "more than 250 officers, who constitute the best military and nationalist personnel, under arrest."[190]

On July 16, the Jordanian authorities uncovered an alleged coup attempt led by retired officer Mahmud al-Rusan. The coup was supposed to have taken place on the same day as the Iraqi coup, July 14, later postponed to July 17.[191] Al-Rusan, a Camberley-educated Jordanian officer from Irbid, had been exiled by Glubb to the Washington embassy between 1953 and 1956. When he returned to Jordan in 1956, he was accused of the "Irbidi" coup against the Saltis and, after receiving amnesty, was forcibly retired from the army.[192] A major new purge of the army was conducted and arrests of recently retired senior and serving junior officers followed.[193] This time, the arrests included friends of the palace (such as Radi al-'Abdullah, whose brother was accused of conspiring with the coup leaders). The entire army structure was reorganized immediately. Al-Rusan was sentenced to ten years' imprisonment.[194]

Another alleged coup attempt was discovered in March 1959 upon King Husayn's return from a trip to the United States and Taiwan. This time the alleged coup leader was Sadiq al-Shar' along with sixteen others, including civilians. Al-Shar', a Jordanian officer from Irbid,[195] was alleged to have been plotting his coup since the resignation of Abu-Nuwwar. He and two others were sentenced to death, a sentence that was later commuted.[196] Finally, the government claimed to have uncovered another coup attempt in August 1960, this time allegedly led by Musa Nasir, who was immediately arrested. Although the army was increasingly emptied of nationalist elements, there still remained officers who sympathized with the nationalist cause. In November 1962, three Jordanian air force pilots defected to Egypt with their planes and revealed Jordan's military involvement in Yemen on the side of the Imam. More officers defected to Syria in 1966.[197]

Regional divisions in Jordan were unraveling among Transjordanian-regime allies. The king sought to remedy the situation by asserting a unified Jordanian identity. In a radio-delivered speech he gave on April 15, 1961, the king spoke of his conversations with soldiers, asserting that among them "was the Bedouin and the Hadari, those who came from the west of the country and its east, from its north and its south, and those among them who were Muslims or Christians, Arabs or Circassians," all of whom asserted to the king that "we are all in our armed forces, the soldiers of this country, and the servants of this nation, and our value stems from our giving it our souls, blood, and spirit altogether, as sacrifices to it and to its future."[198] Through the accession of the youthful government of Wasfi al-Tall to power in 1962, the king sought to satisfy northerners with positions of power to counter the southerners' control of the army, as Habis al-Majali, head of the army, is a Karaki from the south. The king was also ensuring that no regionally based coup would take place in the army, such as the Irbidi one that was staged against Abu-Nuwwar. Soon, al-Tall's government set up an office it called the military secretariat (da'irat al-sikritaryat al-'askariyyah), which limited the power of the army chief. It also ordered the retirement of a number of army officers who were allies of al-Majali. When al-Tall's government resigned the following year, al-Majali undertook the retirement of northern officers and returned his allies to army service.[199]

In the wake of the palace coup against the nationalists, a number of assassination plans were also uncovered by the regime. For example, a number of officers were arrested and accused of attempting to assassinate the king's notorious uncle, the Sharif Nasir. The king himself speaks of being the target of such attempts, once in 1961 with acid, and once in Tangiers, in Morocco, in August 1962.[200] Even police officers were the target of the purges. Two of them were accused of another attempt on the life of the Sharif Nasir. The one assassination attempt that did succeed was the one targeting prime minister Hazza' al-Majali (of Baghdad Pact fame). Al-Majali was killed on August 29, 1960, when a big explosion destroyed the building housing his office and the prime ministry. A number of others were also killed in the explosion. Sixteen people were arrested, among them a number of army and police officers. Hisham 'Abd al-Fattah Bakhit al-Dabbas, an officer in army engineering, was sentenced to death by a firing squad. This time, the sentence was carried out.[201]

The situation calmed down briefly, only to be roused again by the victory of the Ba'th party in both Syria and Iraq in 1963, leading to talk of unity between these two countries and Egypt. The Arab nationalist tide was reinvigorated in Jordan, which saw massive popular demonstrations for the first time since the imposition of martial law. The regime reacted swiftly, with mass arrests of civilians and military personnel, especially police officers and officers in the National Guard for refusing to shoot at demonstrators. On March 21, 1963, a long list of officers was issued announcing their forced retirement; it included many regime supporters, leading to much resentment on the part of many in the army. The situation became so grave that the king himself met with senior officers, promising them that a committee would be set up to look into the cases of the forcibly retired officers. It was revealed then that less than five out of 2,000 officers had a clean Mukhabarat (secret police) record.[202]

After the 1958 Iraqi revolution, the income of army soldiers and officers was increased as part of the government's strategy to ensure army loyalty, a measure that would continue to be used through the present.[203] In February, 1962, on the occasion of the birth of the king's second child and first son, prince 'Abdullah (whom the king designated immediately as his successor to the throne), the king offered amnesty to the imprisoned officers (including Abu-Shahut and others who had been in jail since 1957, and Sadiq al-Shar' and his alleged group of co-conspirators).[204] Soon after the assumption of the Ba'th to power in Syria and Iraq, all the released officers were rounded up again.[205] They were imprisoned for a year and were finally released in 1964 after staging a hunger strike.[206]

In the meantime, following the first Arab League summit in 1963, King Husayn met with over 100 nationalist officers (who had been purged over the last few years) at the palace. He chastised them for having worked against the regime and told them that their future is linked to their loyalty to the regime.[207] Wasfi al-Tall, who was prime minister at the time, feared that the newly declared Palestine Liberation Organization (PLO) and its leader Ahmad Shuqayri might obtain the support of Jordan's exiled military personnel. In April 1965, his government enacted a law of general amnesty to preempt the PLO.[208] Pursuant to the law, the king ordered all jails emptied of political prisoners. Two thousand were released.[209] He also issued an amnesty to all fugitives living in exile, including the three pilots who had defected to Egypt. The amnesty included 'Abdullah al-Tall, 'Ali al-Hiyari, and the Free Officers living in Syria and Egypt. 'Ali Abu-Nuwwar was pardoned by the king after the 1964 Arab summit.[210] This was part of a new policy that sought to co-opt enemies of the regime. Spearheading the co-optation campaign was Muhammad Rasul al-Kilani, who had been a low-level officer when he interrogated the Free Officers back in 1957 following the palace coup. He also came to prominence in 1959 during the interrogation and torture of Sadiq al-Shar'. He was later sent to the United States for Central Intelligence Agency (CIA) training. On returning to Jordan, al-Kilani, on the CIA's recommendation, was appointed head of the General Directorate of Intelligence (al-Mukhabarat al-'Ammah).[211]

Al-Kilani was instrumental in the co-optation process, as many ex-officers were offered jobs as intelligence agents. Eighty percent of ex-officers were given jobs in the police or the Mukhabarat.[212] Others were given more prominent political appointments. Few were returned to army service. 'Abdullah al-Tall, for example, was granted amnesty by King Husayn, whereupon he returned with his family to Jordan in 1965 after sixteen years of exile.[213] He was received at the airport by none other than Muhammad Rasul al-Kilani, head of the Mukhabarat, who was representing King Husayn. After he left the airport and before proceeding to his family home in Irbid, 'Abdullah stopped by his cousin's, Wasfi al-Tall's, home to greet him.[214] Al-Tall was quickly rehabilitated through his seeking forgiveness from the throne.[215] He also sent a letter to King Husayn in June 1966, condemning the PLO's Ahmad Shuqayri for his attacks on the late King 'Abdullah.[216] Two years after his arrival in the country and in the context of increasing propaganda attacks on King Husayn by the Egyptian government, al-Tall made further amends with the king by sending a letter to Jamal ʿAbd al-Nasir in January 1967, chastising him for using his memoirs against the Jordanian regime and for defaming the late King ʿAbdullah, "whose positions [on the Palestine question] . . . were shown to be far-sighted leading to the preservation of Jerusalem."[217] In his memoirs, al-Tall had called King ʿAbdullah a traitor.[218] Al-Tall's new-found love for the late king, however, did not stop there. In August 1967, he wrote a forward to Taysir Zibyan's book about King ʿAbdullah, in which he exonerated the king of all wrongdoing during the former's 1948 to 1949 negotiations with the Israelis—adopting the official Jordanian line on these events. He further added, "I consider that justice, fairness, and national duty dictate to the Arab nation that King ʿAbdullah be considered a nationalist hero. If erecting statues in order to immortalize heroes was part of our religion and traditions, it would have been imperative that a statue of King ʿAbdullah be erected in every capital of every Arab country."[219]

Al-Tall worked briefly as a governor in the Ministry of Interior (November 1970 to January 1971) and was then appointed by the king as a member of the senate (Majlis al-Aʿyan), a position he occupied until his death in 1972. He also became a prominent member of the General Islamic Conference.[220] As for other former opponents of the regime, ʿAli Abu-Nuwwar, ʿAli al-Hiyari, and Radi al-Hindawi were all appointed ambassadors. Abu-Nuwwar later became the king's special envoy. Ahmad Khasawnah and Mahmud al-Rusan were nominated to and became members of Parliament, although al-Rusan's membership was dropped after his support of the Palestinians in the 1970 Civil War and his escape to Syria.[221] Nadhir Rashid was appointed a high-ranking intelligence officer and allegedly received 18,000 Jordanian dinars as compensation.[222] He recently (spring 1998) served as Jordanian minister of the interior. Sadiq al-Sharʿ was appointed head of the passport department, then a governor of the Northern Governorate, and he was later appointed cabinet minister twice.[223] Those who remained outside the regime's co-optation efforts were few. Prominent among those was Shahir Abu-Shahut.

The new honeymoon lasted for one year. After the Israeli raid (and massacre) of the Jordanian West Bank village of Samuʿ in November 1966, massive demonstrations erupted throughout the country, leading to a new civilian–army confrontation in which a number of civilians were killed, especially in the West Bank city of Nablus. This was the period when army confrontations with the newly formed Palestinian guerrillas became commonplace (see chapter 5). Concomitant with these events, a fresh campaign of arrests of a new crop of nationalist army officers was launched. Tens of officers were arrested.[224] New pamphlets appeared in army units signed by the Revolutionary Committee of Free Jordanian Officers, calling for the overthrow of the monarchy and the declaration of a republic in both banks, and renaming the country Palestine.[225] It would seem that Jordanian officers of Palestinian origin who supported the Palestinian guerrillas were responsible. This was the first and last open call to overthrow the king by nationalist officers. On the eve of the 1967 June War, a large number of Jordanian army officers lay in jail.

Palestinians and the Military

Even before the annexation of central Palestine to Jordan, it was decided that Palestinians be involved in the defense of their country. In January 1950, the government issued the Law of the National Guard, inaugurating the foundation of a new military force in the country.[226] The National Guard was Glubb's idea. Immediately, after sending a memorandum to the government on June 25 proposing to set up the force, Glubb began recruiting for the National Guard.[227] A few months later, he was able to "persuade the government to prepare a Bill making National Guard Training compulsory for every *male* Jordanian of military age [emphasis added]."[228] He felt that it was necessary to set it up for two reasons:

> Firstly, it was obvious that we could neither rely on the other Arab governments if Israel should attack, nor could we long resist an enemy about seven times as strong as ourselves. . . . Obviously, we must get more troops. The men were available, and anxious to enlist, but we had no money or equipment for them. . . . Secondly, the other Arab countries had never recognized the union of Palestine and Trans-Jordan [which interestingly enough was not to be made completely official for at least four more months]. Some did not hesitate to sow dissension between West Bank and East Bank. One of the major points they used to stir up resentment was that the Jordan government did not trust the Palestinians. The Arab Legion was depicted as a purely East Bank army. The Communists went farther. They labeled the Arab Legion — "The Anglo-Hashemite Army of Occupation in Palestine."[229]

He added that the Palestinians "could not be half-citizens. We must make them feel trusted, and the first sign of trust was to arm them."[230] King Husayn himself asserted that the purpose of the National Guard was to "defend the border in order to allow the better trained and equipped army, in the event of [Israeli] aggression, to direct its strikes at specific targets."[231]

The National Guard was to be an unpaid army. Its first recruits, who were from frontier villages, were armed and trained to resist Israeli raids. Whereas, by law, serving was compulsory, "for lack of money, we could only arm, clothe, feed and equip a very much smaller number. It seemed, therefore, unnecessary and inadvisable to use compulsion—there were always more volunteers than we could train."[232] Most of the volunteers came from the West Bank frontier villages. Initially, opposition to the National Guard was ubiquitous. It was opposed by the Jordanian government because it feared that the National Guardsmen would use their weapons against the Jordanian regime and/or for crime, while West Bank Palestinian notables opposed it because they were not yet reconciled to the "unification" project still being finalized.[233]

The National Guard, as Avi Plascov remarks, "was neither equipped, trained nor designed to carry out its assigned tasks. With twenty bullets, a few rifles, little training and hardly any co-ordination or transport, very little could be done in the face of an attack. This was because the regime feared mobile troops of this type."[234] He affirms that the National Guard's "real task, in fact, was to control border infiltration [into Israel] by its members' own brothers."[235] Public pressure forced the government to expand recruitment and training and to stipulate that National Guardsmen would be used for army purposes in certain periods, at which time they would have to abide by Arab Legion regulations. Plascov states that this was a preliminary step toward the integration of the two forces, which was not to take place until May 1956 in the wake of Glubb's dismissal.[236]

Popular pressure increased further after continuing Israeli raids culminated in the Israeli massacre of sixty-six civilians including children in the West Bank town of Qibya in October 1953. Demonstrators and newspaper columnists blamed the civilian and military authorities and demanded better arming and training and larger recruitment of the Palestinian refugees. Few had any remaining respect for the National Guard, which was viewed by many as the protector of Israel from Palestinian infiltrators.[237] In addition, Arab governments were increasingly insisting that the National Guard be placed under joint Arab direction and leadership (an Egyptian officer was suggested as its possible commander), as opposed to the Arab Legion led by

Glubb and other British officers, and they pledged to support the force financially, something the British government had refused to undertake until
1955. Realizing the dangers of such an eventuality, the king did not object
to the ultimate integration of the Guard with the Arab Legion, which took
place in May 1956, two months after the expulsion of Glubb.[238] Moreover,
integrating the two forces was part of the process of Jordanizing the Palestinians, which the National Guard failed to do, as it consisted mostly of
Palestinian villagers.[239] Vatikiotis insists that the integration of the two forces
had been part of Glubb's plan all along. The act of integration merged "an
essentially élite regular force of beduin, tribesmen and Transjordanian peasants with a territorial frontier force wholly consisting of settled Palestinian
agricultural peasants and a few townsmen."[240] Still, the actual merging took
place under army commander ʿAli Abu-Nuwwar and under the direction of
Defense Minister Muhammad ʿAli al-ʿAjluni.[241] The National Guard was
finally abolished in 1966 in light of the November 13 Israeli raid on the
West Bank village of Samuʿ (which killed fifteen Jordanian soldiers and three
civilians and wounded fifty-four people), and it was replaced with compulsory national military service (al-Khidmah al-Wataniyyah al-Ijbariyyah), applying to "all Jordanians" between the ages of eighteen and forty.[242]

In the meantime, the Jordanian Arab Army remained mostly Transjordanian in composition and exclusively Transjordanian in leadership. Although many Palestinians joined the military, especially in its technical services divisions (signals and engineers in particular), their military ranks
remained low on the hierarchy. Vatikiotis states that Palestinians "soon came
to man almost exclusively the [Arab] Legion's maintenance workshops, for
example."[243] He adds that "until 1956 General Glubb believed that he could
maintain the Legion as a *corps d'élite* and resisted the inevitable influx into
the technical branches of personnel that had perforce of needed skills to be
recruited from among Palestinians."[244] Also, by expanding the political establishment to include a large number of Palestinians, King Husayn is said
to have minimized "the infiltration of disruptive ideas held by the discon-
tented and alienated among them into the army officer corps, particularly
now that the *Jeish* [Army] comprises so many more administrative and technical personnel who are Palestinians."[245] Vatikiotis concludes, "the monarch
has been careful to retain the traditional tribal element as the preponderant
one in the operational ground force units, namely, infantry and armoured
car regiments. In doing this, the monarch has managed to continue to identify himself with the traditional forces in the Legion, while at the same time
he had led the process of a viable integration of the various elements in the

country that is so essential to political stability."[246] Palestinians recruited in the army were from among those refugees who did not have previous experience in war. They were heavily scrutinized to ascertain that they had not had any political involvement.[247]

Threatening the Nation's Masculinity and Religious "Tradition"

As discussed in previous chapters, the nation-state undertakes the nationalization of masculinity according to a traditionalized view that it identifies as "traditional" and "national." The masculinity of soldiers is of particular interest to the nation-state. As a male homosocial institution predicated on a specific identity and a specific set of practices, the military's *raison d'être* is the assertion of that nationalized masculinity (as identity and practices) as the *only* possible masculinity within the modality of the nation-state. Conventional masculine values of strength, victory, and loyalty are opposed to a sexist convention defining femininity as weakness, defeat, and treachery. The military institution was able to co-opt existing conventions of gender norms and endow them with nationalist signification.[248] As we saw in the last chapter, certain gendered practices, especially those of the Bedouins, were repressed while new ones were produced. We will see how these strategies affected the constitution of the new exclusivist Jordanian national identity and its *internal* others.

Following the defeat of the Jordanian army in the 1967 June War and the loss of the West Bank to the invading Israeli forces, rumors were rampant among the populace that the Jordanian army handed the West Bank to the Israelis and retreated to the East Bank, which they defended diligently. The accusations were leveled by Palestinians who felt that the Jordanian army did not *really* consider the West Bank Jordanian territory and therefore saw it as expendable, something that did not apply to Transjordan proper.[249] Sa'id al-Tall, a former minister and brother of the late prime minister Wasfi al-Tall, rebuts many of the arguments questioning the Jordanian army's commitment to defend the West Bank and the army's military abilities, and he labels such arguments as *Iqlimiyyah* or anti-Jordanian "regionalist chauvinism."[250]

In 1968, the Jordanian army and the increasingly powerful Palestinian guerrillas stationed in the country were able to erase part of the 1967 defeat through a partial victory over invading Israeli forces at al-Karamah, a small

village on the East Bank (see chapter 5 for details). Al-Karamah, which led
to the unprecedented popularity of the guerrillas, however, also signaled the
beginning of the countdown to the 1970 Civil War between the army and
the guerrillas. During and after the civil war, 5,000 members of the Jordanian army defected to the guerrillas' side. The army's triumph in the war,
however, inaugurated an important step toward a new national demarcation
in the country. Transjordanians of Hadari (Arab and Circassian), and Bedouin backgrounds were now united in a Transjordanian East Bank national
identity against Palestinian Jordanians, who, as we will see in the next chapter, were increasingly perceived as a grave national threat to the identity of
Jordan. The civil war, in fact, solidified and intensified the formation of a
stable Jordanian national identity, which, unlike its Arab nationalist prede-
cessors, was *not directed at colonialism but at the Palestinians.* This process
was augmented by a shift in the regime's powerful constituencies in civil
society. Whereas since the 1940s, the regime's societal support (outside of
the tribes and the military) came from the pro-regime Palestinian- and
Syrian-dominated merchant class, by the late 1960s, the Transjordanian-
dominated state bureaucracy (mostly staffed by settled Transjordanians)
was ascendant, especially following the civil war, when its power was solidified, curtailing the power of the once powerful merchant class.[251]

Another dimension to these new developments was an explicit gendered
ideology of mobilization used in the army against the guerrillas. For example, the Jordanian army saw al-Karamah as an important event in restoring
the masculinity of its soldiers "lost" in the 1967 War. Its efforts after that war
were directed, according the department of spiritual guidance (Mudiriyyat
al-Tawjih al-Ma'nawi) of the Jordanian Armed Forces toward the restoration
of its dignity and the "taking of women's dresses [fasatin al-Nisa'] off its
body."[252] Identifying military defeat as a defeat of masculinity, not maleness,
and its transformation into femininity, symbolized by the image of the soldiers dressed in drag, became one of the dominant themes in mobilizing
soldiers for battle. Moreover, feminizing the enemy became a correlate strategy for mobilizing the army. King Husayn himself participated in this discourse after one of the confrontations between the army and guerrillas in
1968. In a speech he delivered after one such confrontation in November,
he stated that these guerrillas were not serving the Palestinian cause and
were in fact paid agents against it. He added that "they don the attire of
manhood when manhood is innocent of [being implicated in] them."[253]
This was not new for the king, as he had identified the nationalist threat of
the 1950s as "conspiracies directed at [this country's] Arabism, at its manhood, its sovereignty, and its dignity."[254]

The Jordanian military began to mobilize its soldiers against the guerrillas' national "threat" by portraying it as a threat to the soldiers' masculinity. The guerrillas, who were portrayed as godless communists, were also portrayed as castrated men whose femininity was going to be imposed on a nation of manly men as a paradigm to be emulated. In the military newspaper *Al-Aqsa* (in reference to al-Aqsa Mosque in Jerusalem), a story was printed portraying an "elegant" young guerrilla attempting to proselytize a Jordanian soldier by speaking to him about nationalism or "wataniyyah."

THE SOLDIER PRAYING: Praise belongs to God the Lord of all Being,
   the All-Merciful, the All-Compassionate. . . . [255]
THE YOUNG MAN INTERRUPTED HIM: Didn't you hear that Marx said . . .
THE SOLDIER RAISED HIS VOICE: It is You whom we worship and it is
   You whom we implore for help.
THE YOUNG MAN SAID: As for Engels, he said . . .
THE SOLDIER CHANTED HIS [QUR'ANIC] RECITATION: Say, I take
   refuge with the Lord of men . . . [256]
THE YOUNG MAN SAID: What do you care about this kind of talk? Religion is the opium of the masses.
THE SOLDIER RAISED HIS VOICE IN PRAYER: . . . from the evil of the
   slinking whisperer.
THE YOUNG MAN SAID: It is [political] reaction which has . . .

The soldier continues his prayers and then turns and threatens the young man that he will use force. "The young man got up, dusted off his tight pants, lifting his long bangs off his foppish forehead and withdrew shaking his posterior as he vanished delicately and coquettishly." As for the soldier, he "remained sitting and lifted his arms to Heaven and said . . . Lord, render al-Husayn [the king] and his soldiers victorious, . . . the soldiers of Muhammad, over Zionism and the atheist and Godless Zionists."[257] Note that not only is the guerrilla feminized according to Western perceptions of what it means to wear "tight" pants, and to strut around "shaking his posterior," but also according to a purely Western criterion that until recently contradicted Arab Bedouin notions of masculinity. Whereas, as we saw in the last chapter, Bedouin soldiers until the 1940s had long hair, which many among them wore in plaits, the Westernization of the Bedouin soldiers' notions of masculinity and femininity had been thorough. Long hair is now coded according to modern Western criteria as "feminine," and it is then passed on as an "authentic" Arab Bedouin judgment that is part of Bedouin "heritage" and "traditional" Bedouin notions of masculinity. Furthermore, consonant with prevailing Western notions at the time about communists and subversives, army propaganda spoke of how guerrillas "grew their hair and beards and assumed the names of revolutionaries, which they took as models, like Castro, Che Guevara, and others."[258] Male and female "comrades" were said to be living in the style of "collective kibbutzes," thus portraying the guerrillas as both communist and as emulating the Zionist enemy in one stroke.[259]

Other accusations included explicit references to the male guerrillas' engaging in sexual relations with other male guerrillas, *liwat*,[260] in addition to sexual relations with guerrilla women outside the sanctity of marriage. Leftist guerrilla men (fida'iyyin), of the Democratic Front for the Liberation of Palestine (DFLP) especially, were accused of paying nocturnal visits to guerrilla women (fida'iyyat) in their tents (in training camps) for sexual purposes, which allegedly outraged the Bedouin soldiers.[261] In fact, similar accusations were made against enemies of the regime back in the 1950s. In his propagandistic book against the nationalist opposition in Jordan, Musa 'Adil Bakmirza Shirdan accused 'Ali Abu-Nuwwar and Sulayman al-Nabulsi of being alcoholic womanizers: al-Nabulsi is portrayed as a chaser of Egyptian dancers[262] and Abu-Nuwwar as simply "woman-hungry."[263] Shirdan is further horrified by al-Nabulsi for beginning one of his public political speeches by addressing his audience "women citizens and men citizens" (*ayyuha al-muwatinat wa al-muwatinun*), changing the "traditional" hierarchy of "men citizens and women citizens."[264] Moreover, Shirdan accuses Fu'ad al-Halabi, the general secretary of the Syrian republican palace, and other Syrian Arab nationalists, of being homosexuals who are attracted to handsome Russian and Lebanese men.[265]

Between the military propaganda and actual offenses committed by the guerrillas themselves, the soldiers internalized the gender dichotomy between themselves and their enemy. However, the gender identity attributed to the guerrillas and to army soldiers by Jordanian army propaganda was not always stable. On the one hand, the guerrillas, as we saw, were feminized as being not "real" men, and on the other, the Jordanian army's allowing the guerrillas' "femininity" to exist unchallenged feminized the Jordanian army soldiers themselves. This sense of being "feminized" manifested itself when the guerrillas were seen to be roaming the country and challenging the authority of the Jordanian state and its military. This was not only implicit but manifested itself explicitly upon an inspection conducted by King Husayn of an army tank regiment in early September 1970. The regiment was determined to enter Amman to attack the guerrillas. When the king arrived, he spotted, from a distance, an unseemly object hanging from a radio antenna. It was a woman's brassiere. The Bedouin troops who hung it were said to be communicating to the king that they would not stand by "like women" while the guerrillas ruled the streets.[266] Note how, concomitant with army notions of male soldiers in drag, it is women's clothing for men, or simply drag, that constitutes the clearest mark of femininity for these soldiers. In addition, the soldiers were questioning the king's masculinity, if not his maleness, as he permitted this guerrilla penetration to take place. When he asked about the brassiere, the king was told that "it was because their king was a woman who was afraid to take action against their country's enemies."[267] The king spent three hours with the soldiers trying to convince them to turn back, which they reluctantly did.[268]

On the issue of religion, the government campaign against the guerrillas continued to identify them as "atheists" and as "the forces of darkness."[269] The army newspaper *Al-Aqsa* lamented the loss of al-Aqsa Mosque because of those atheists who "have sold their conscience to the devil."[270] Habis al-Majali, the army chief, congratulated his victorious army by saluting, "your faith in your creed and in your transcendental Message [of Islam] which you carry and which remains and shall remain planted in your souls challenging all the campaigns of hatred and atheism which seek to put it in doubt."[271] In fact, the army leadership distributed 60,000 copies of the Qur'an to soldiers before the fighting began in September 1970.[272] Plans were under way to distribute the bible to Christian soldiers.[273] This religious campaign of de-legitimation was more believable as the more radical elements of the Palestinian guerrillas committed certain irreligious acts horrifying many people. One such reported act was the hoisting of red flags and Lenin's portraits from the minaret of an Amman mosque on the occasion of Lenin's birthday. This drew the ire of many Transjordanians and Palestinian Jordanians alike.[274]

The use of religion during the civil war was not in fact new. As we saw in the last chapter, Glubb was very interested in the level of religiosity of soldiers. In fact, he had set up a Da'irat al-Ifta' al-Dini (the department of religious counseling) in the army, consisting of a number of Muslim clergymen led by Shaykh 'Abdullah al-'Izb. The clergy would undertake delivering religious sermons to army units. These sermons were to include mention of the Hashemite heritage of 'Abdullah, which links him to the progeny of the Prophet Muhammad himself. Glubb used the shaykhs as informants for his infamous reports on the soldiers. This was quite known to the soldiers, who dubbed one of the shaykhs (Shaykh Dawud) as Dawud the Guard (Dawud al-Natur).[275] Moreover, palace and army propaganda against the nationalists in the 1950s also identified them as atheists and communists. King Husayn himself articulated these positions. In the context of increased attacks on his regime after the palace coup, the king stressed that "we shall remain on the same course . . . until the Arabs become clear on who are the pretenders of heroism and who are the parties of trickery and atheism, [who are also] the partisans of defeat and of deceiving the people."[276] Moreover, the new educational system, whether through army schools or civilian government schools, served to centralize religion and religious traditions among the population in accordance with the views of state-appointed shaykhs. Folk religious traditions among the Bedouins and Circassians, and to a lesser extent among villagers and urbanites, that did not follow state-sanctioned notions of Islamic practice were slowly eliminated. For example, whereas the Circassians had been partially Islamicized by the Ottomans (who ensured that all their males were circumcised by 1878 and that their secular Circassian names were changed to Turkish names), on the eve of their immigration to what became Transjordan, many Circassians arrived in the country carrying with them salted pork and their traditional alcoholic drink *bakhsima* (made of fermented barley).[277] Salted pork fell out of use due to unavailability and local peer pressure, but *bakhsima* remains available, albeit among the few. Attacks on Circassian traditions also came from within the community. Religious members began attacking Circassian customs including wedding celebrations, dancing, and of course alcohol.[278] The predominance of Syrian merchants among the Amman elite added Damascene "religious" traditions and practices, namely in terms of the veiling of urban women. Circassian women of Amman, like most Arab women of nonurban backgrounds, duly followed the Damascene example by veiling, a practice unknown among them before.[279] Similar transformations occurred in the Bedouin communities whose Islam was considered "lacking" in practice and belief and was slowly replaced with state Islam.

To make the Hashemite link to the Prophet more direct, the palace decided as early as 1954, during the heyday of massive secular opposition to government domestic and international policies, to add the article *al*, or *the*, to the name of King Husayn rendering it al-Husayn.[280] In 1969, on the eve of the civil war, the *al* was added to the name of the crown prince in *Al-Jaridah al-Rasmiyyah* (the country's official gazette). However, he continued to be referred to as Prince Hasan by the nongovernment press, until 1986 when a similar *al* was added to his name rendering it al-Hasan in all newspaper, radio, and television coverage.[281] Al-Husayn and al-Hasan are actually the names of the grandsons of the Prophet Muhammad, sons of his daughter

Fatimah and his cousin 'Ali Bin Abi-Talib, the two being the first (al-Hasan) and second (al-Husayn) Imams of Shi'ah Islam and important figures in Sunni Islam. By adding the *al* to their names, the Sunni king and his brother have surrounded themselves with a halo of religious legitimacy and with a direct line to the Prophet, bypassing tens of generations in between. Moreover, in 1981, the government set up a new military university called Mu'tah. The university was built south of Amman near the site of the Battle of Mu'tah that took place during the time of the Prophet Muhammad, further linking religion and the army.[282] This strategy continues to be espoused by the department of spiritual guidance in the army today. One of its more recent books for soldiers considers religion as central to any sense of national belonging.[283]

Outside the military domain, the government established in 1981 Mu'assassat Al al-Bayt (the Family of the Prophet Foundation), also known as the Royal Academy for Islamic Civilization Research, further linking Islam and the Hashemites in an academic setting. The king and the crown prince as well as government officials would also include references to the Qur'an in their speeches, if not outright Qur'anic verses. This went side by side with the king's and the government's sponsorship of mosque construction throughout the country. Television also would show the king attending Friday payers at local mosques and attending as well as hosting Ramadan breakfast banquets during the holy month.[284] One the more ostentatious achievements in this regard was the early 1980s construction of the King 'Abdullah Mosque in the 'Abdali neighborhood of Amman (itself named after 'Abdullah) with its overarching blue dome dominating the Amman skyline.

The Military and the New Jordan

Following the upheaval of the civil war, the Jordanian army was able to recuperate as a unified force with an unwavering commitment to defending the monarchy, a commitment that prevailed even under the nationalist officers in the mid 1950s, government propaganda notwithstanding.

The government launched a major campaign of army recruitment after the civil war that targeted Transjordanians and excluded Palestinian Jordanians. This included all branches of the military. For example, in 1972, the Cadet School had twenty Palestinians out of 273 candidates. Moreover, Palestinians in the army were retired early along with nationalist Transjordanian officers.[285]

As a result of the new confidence the army acquired after its civil war victory, tribalist Bedouin chauvinism increased within its ranks (as the different tribes were jockeying for power positions), leading to few internal skirmishes between members of different tribes as soon as October 1971 in the First Regiment, leading the chief of staff and the king to intervene. The king had attempted to resolve similar matters earlier when he had appointed members of most Jordanian tribes in the military government set up during the civil war.[286] Moreover, in 1973, members of the royal family, including the king's brother and designated successor Prince Hasan and his uncle the Sharif Nasir, sought to encourage a group of chauvinist officers to apply pressure on the king to refuse adamantly the return of the Fida'iyyin to Jordan, which was under discussion at the time. The king, in fact, began involving high-ranking army officers in palace politics as he began to pay frequent regular visits to army units and to spend a portion of his working day in army headquarters.[287] As we saw in chapter 2, this is the period when the palace convened a series of tribal conferences, aiming to unify the country's tribes, which culminated in *Mahdar al-Qasr*, a document of palace–tribal understanding on the role of the tribes in the country.

Army presence in people's lives and in national culture skyrocketed after the early 1970s. The culture the army invented for its members was now overflowing into society, generating concomitant cultural productions by other state institutions, especially the state-controlled media. In fact, ever since the campaign against the guerrillas began, Jordanian television began airing special programs about the army. The army's department of spiritual guidance, in cooperation with Jordanian television, produced sixteen special programs about the Jordanian Arab Army in 1970 alone. There was also a daily radio program especially directed to soldiers.[288] Moreover, army songs had been playing since 1970 on Jordanian television with background pictures of excited soldiers surrounding King Husayn, who was seen in military garb, at some times aboard a tank, at others pointing a gun as if in a military drill, with the soldiers embracing him and kissing him. The army musical bands were also shown on television, regularly playing their bagpipes. This also led to the formation of a state-sponsored civilian bagpipe band (set up by Jordan television) performing for television viewers regularly, thus exporting military culture to society at large. This television campaign continues through the present.

The regime felt secure with the post-civil war army, as it had been emptied of all nationalist elements through defection to the Palestinian resistance or through forced resignations. Unexpectedly, however, in October 1972, the government uncovered a plot by Jordanian army officer Rafi' al-Hindawi, who allegedly colluded with six people, all civilians. Al-Hindawi was allegedly planning to murder the king and his brother, Prince Hasan, after which he would receive diplomatic support from Palestinian guerrilla groups and Libya's Mu'ammar al-Qadhdhafi. The government panicked upon its discovery of the plot and launched a witch-hunt in the army that resulted in the arrest of 500 officers, all of whom were subsequently released for lack of evidence. This resulted in many complaints leveled against the government by the army.[289] The al-Hindawi coup attempt came a few months after the regime's amnesty for all Jordanian civilians and military personnel who had left Jordan during and after the civil war fearing government persecution, allowing them to return to the country without repercussions. This was in line with the U.S.-inspired policies that the regime had followed since the 1962 amnesty. More amnesties followed, one of which included that of al-Hindawi himself.[290] Few internal upheavals occurred in the army after that. The government felt so strong that it reinstituted compulsory national military service in 1976 for men over eighteen years of age.[291]

As women's issues entered the civilian public sphere, they did so also in the military and the police. An important development that took place in the wake of the civil war was the establishment of a women's police force, al-Shurtah al-Nisa'iyyah, in December 1971. As women were increasingly entering the urban public sector through employment and education, the police force was going to provide for them more choices of employment and careers. The public security directorate also set up a school to train future policewomen. At first, the role of women was limited to prison and rehabilitation centers' inspectors. In 1972, only six women joined, a number that increased to seventy-two by 1975.[292] Moreover, policewomen set up their own handball team in 1975.[293] This upward trend has continued through the present. Women's duties expanded rapidly, including technical positions in the Criminal Investigation Administration, public relations, the Administration of Residency and Foreigners Affairs, as well as in the security apparatus in airports and aboard Jordanian airline flights. The most visible aspect of policewomen, however, was in their role as traffic officers in the streets of Jordanian cities, especially in Amman.[294] Then, by the mid 1980s, policewomen were seen less and less in this role as they more frequently filled administrative positions,[295] but more recently (by the summer of 2000), female traffic officers have again become conspicuous in Amman's streets.

As far as the military was concerned, women began joining the army in 1962 in technical capacities, mostly as nurses and midwives. Later, as education spread, women joined the army as physicians, computer scientists, and technicians, and also as social workers, librarians, and secretaries. Women also became teachers in army schools.[296] Most women who join the army are well educated and have military ranks, although none of them has ever joined or been allowed to join fighting units.

Moreover, some of 'Abdullah's early Westernizing projects were pursued in the army in the same spirit. This was especially true in the area of the Massed Bands founded under Peake. The 1950s had already seen an expansion of the Massed Bands. In 1951, King 'Abdullah ordered the establishment of a Musical Band associated directly with the Royal Palace (al-Qusur al-Malakiyyah). It was called the Hashemite Band and was subsequently attached to the Hashemite regiment. Three more bands were also formed soon after.[297] Also in the early 1950s, Muhammad Sidqi, an officer in the Jordanian Arab Army, was sent to Britain for four years for musical training, while four more officers were dispatched to a music college in Pakistan.[298] The expansion continued throughout the 1960s.[299] In 1966, a music conservatory was established in the army, led by Jamal 'Abd al-Karim 'Atiyyah, who had also studied in Britain. The conservatory trained not only Jordanian members of the bands but also members of neighboring Arab countries, including Saudi Arabia, Kuwait, Lebanon, Yemen, Qatar, Bahrain, Oman, Syria, and the United Arab Emirates. In fact, through the seconding of officers, the Jordanian Musical Massed Bands played a central role in the training of the Massed Bands of Arab Gulf countries.[300]

The Massed Bands' participation in international concerts earned them a great reputation. Ever since their first performance in Britain in 1955, they performed throughout the Arab and Islamic worlds,[301] and the in the Western world.[302] In 1981, on the occasion of the establishment of an army symphony orchestra, twenty-three musicians were dispatched to Austria on a scholarship, where they studied from three to seven years. They were joined soon after by fifty-four more musicians. By the late 1980s, all of them returned to staff the first *army* symphony orchestra in the entire Arab world. The orchestra performs classical and "international" music. It has given concerts in Austria and Jordan. The orchestra also began to train students in Jordan.[303]

The Bands used to wear a yellow hatta (or kufiyyah); this was subsequently changed into Glubb's red and white shmagh, which they continue to wear today, except that some of the bands wear helmets. As for the orchestra, its members wear Western clothes with no Jordanian cultural markers.[304]

Although the first bagpipes were introduced to the Massed Bands in the period from 1929 to 1931, it was done on a small scale. In the early 1950s, bagpipes were imported into the army's bands in large numbers, making them the hallmark of the Jordanian Massed Bands. In 1981, following the establishment of the symphony orchestra, piano and string instruments were introduced. In 1994, the bands claimed that they anticipated the introduction of "Eastern string instruments like the 'Ud and the Qanun soon."[305] This is yet to happen. The bagpipes, however, remain the quintessential instruments distinguishing the Massed Bands. Their importance to Jordan's international image was further confirmed during the internationally televised funeral of King Husayn in February 1999.

Colonial or National Legacy?

Ever since its inception, the Arab Legion, played an important role in imparting to its members, and through them to the rest of society, the rules of the game of the nation-state. The military was a central vehicle for the advancement of a new culture that is nationally defined and governed by the laws of the nation-state. From music to clothes to food to the very "tribalist" culture that Jordanian national culture came to represent, the Jordanian army was a central instrument in its formation. This army served both to unify and to divide the people, commensurate with different strategies used by those who controlled it. Peake set out to exclude the Bedouins from the military during the first decade of the state, serving to exacerbate existing divisions between the Bedouins and the Hadaris. Glubb sought to exclude the Hadaris from the army and to unify the various Bedouin tribes inside the country and Bedouins from outside it by integrating them into a military *corps d'élite* with specific Glubb-designed cultural attributes identified as "Bedouin." Glubb then attempted to make this culture the basis of Jordanian nationality.

When nationalist officers took over the army, they sought to modernize it by ridding it of Glubb's "traditions," which they did not recognize as Glubb's but fell into Glubb's trap by identifying them as Bedouin. Anticolonial nationalists are clearly not immune to colonial epistemology. As Timothy Mitchell put it, "in abandoning the image of colonial power as simply a coercive central authority, one should also question the traditional figure of resistance as a subject who stands outside this power and refuses its demands. Colonial subjects in their modes of resistance are formed *within* the organisational terrain of the colonial state, rather than some wholly exterior social space."[306] Since the anticolonial nationalist officers were committed modernizers, there was no place in their schema for "Bedouin" traditions. Having a colonial epistemology that denigrated the Bedouins (Glubb's idiosyncratic and unique colonial views notwithstanding), they sought to nationalize the Bedouins by integrating their separate units into the rest of the army. Being nationalists, they sought to unify the army with the National Guard for the purpose of nationalizing Transjordanians and Palestinians into a nationally representative army. Another attempt at integration was tried by the king himself, when compulsory national military service was reinstituted in 1976. This, however, did not result in a thorough integration of Palestinian Jordanians in the officer corps of the army, but it did help to integrate settled Transjordanians with the Bedouins.

Following the palace coup, old Glubb patterns were replicated in the army, stressing its Bedouin character as its most "traditional." These were further extolled by the king and the army leadership in preparation for the civil war confrontation. These trends have continued also in society through the present, as we saw in chapter 2. Throughout the 1970s, senior army officers remained mostly of Bedouin origins, especially in armor. Circassians also remained prominent in the military, although by the 1970s and 1980s, they began to occupy mostly advisory positions or were placed in the special forces (al-Quwwat al-Khassah).[307]

Change was occurring in the army. Army personnel are much better educated today, and conscription has transformed the composition of the younger officer corps. Whereas older officers remain Bedouin, the younger officers are urbanites. Although older Palestinian officers continue to be in the army, they are never allowed to command strike units at the battalion level or above.[308] According to Jureidini and McLaurin, numbers aside, "Key positions at senior levels—more important than numbers of personnel—have been and continue to be held by bedouin of specific tribes . . . such as the Bani Sakhr, the Huwaytat, the Sirhan and the Shammar,"[309] the same tribes that Glubb had courted since 1930. The 1976 conscription was mandated by the need for manpower as the expanding economy was attracting potential recruits, and by the "changing nature of warfare," which came to require more technical know-how. By the mid 1970s and beyond, however, the value system of the army was changing. Although King Husayn's "religious legitimacy is still accepted . . . [it] is less germane to the concerns of army personnel, even of the bedouin."[310] Also, the 1976 conscription coincided with the normalization of the Bedouins in the realm of national citizenship through the cancellation of tribal laws.

Indeed, legitimacy was no longer sought through a Bedouin identity but rather by a nationalist Transjordanian one. By the time of the civil war—

that is, fifty years after the state was founded, and twenty years after its expansion and the incorporation of the Palestinians—the political, juridical,
and military strategies employed by the state succeeded in rendering the
new national identity as the main unifying identity for those whose Transjordanian geographical origins can be traced back to the founding of the
state.

With the increasing professionalization of the army, however, it began to
lose its exclusively tribalist character. As Jureidini and McLaurin conclude,
King Husayn's "political legitimacy is accepted increasingly [in the military]
for East Bank interests—the safeguarding of the interests of historical Transjordan and the Transjordanians. Economic issues are more important to
tribesmen, including those in the army, while the role of the Hashemite
kingdom is of less importance."[311] These trends increased with the onset of
the 1980s and the 1990s. In 1980, for example, the king granted reserved
seats at Jordan's universities (which are much sought after by ordinary students who cannot get in because of limited seats) and full scholarships to
the children of army officers and servicemen whose fathers served for more
than ten years in the Jordanian armed forces.[312] Moreover, the economic
role of the military became more important with the establishment of dis-
count, customs-exempt military stores and commissaries for the exclusive
use of military personnel. Indeed, as in the 1930s, the military's economic
role is primary in maintaining the loyalty of its members.

The integration of all Bedouin and settled Transjordanians into one national identity led many Jordanian nationalists to feel unburdened by the
Palestinian West Bank element after the 1988 disengagement. They turned
their attention to East Bank Palestinians as the main threat to their recently
asserted identity. In fact, and as we will see in the next chapter, Palestinian
Jordanians came to constitute the *other* against whom Jordanian national
identity would define itself.

Concomitant with the many changes and developments in the country's
political life, the very name of the army underwent corresponding transformations. Whereas, as already mentioned *al-Jaysh al-'Arabi* or the Arab Army
(known in English as the Arab Legion) was renamed in 1944 the Jordanian
Arab Army;[313] the name of its head, the Chief of the Jordanian Arab Army,
was changed in 1947 to the chief of general staff of the Jordanian Arab Army,
or Ra'is Arkan Harb al-Jaysh al-'Arabi al-Urduni.[314] Following the palace
coup and the dissolution of the union with Iraq, the head of the army experienced another name change: he was now to be called general commander of the armed forces.[315] During the short-lived union with Iraq, the
Jordanian Arab Army merged with its Iraqi counterpart, and the two com-

bined armies were called the Arab Army, while each retained its independent name locally.[316] The Jordanian Arab Army itself was renamed in 1964 the Jordanian armed forces,[317] only to be renamed again in 1966 the Arab Army.[318] On the eve of the civil war, it was renamed again the Jordanian armed forces,[319] a name that it has retained through the present.

Although the first change in 1944 was justified by the Amir 'Abdullah as necessary to distinguish the Jordanian Arab Army from neighboring armies, especially as it came to play an international role in conflicts, except for the change under the union with Iraq, no justifications were provided for changing the name of the military on other occasions. Perhaps the most perplexing of all is the change of 1966 to Arab Army, as the Jordanian armed forces would be a logical change since it came to refer to all military branches in the country including the air force, the navy, and the National Guard. The 1966 change was done in the regional context of Jordan's increased isolation, with the Egyptians intensifying their campaign in the summer against King Husayn as a "reactionary." Moreover, it preceded the November signing of a defense treaty between Syria and Egypt and the November 13 Israeli raid and massacre at Samu' and the ensuing call for compulsory national military service. Within this context, it remains unclear why such a change was made.

By the mid 1980s, many events and figures were being rehabilitated by the new particularist Jordanian nationalism, including Glubb Pasha himself. After Glubb's dismissal, the king made a point to make amends with him. They met a number of times "including one evening when, with genuine pleasure, we had a long talk at a reception in London." They also corresponded and sent each other cards. The king admired Glubb's lack of bitterness after his dismissal despite how "hurt" he was "at what happened": "Another man, less wise, would have become so emotionally aroused that he might have damaged the work he had undertaken for so long and all the success he had brought about. Glubb Pasha acted with restraint and dignity in a great crisis of his life. . . . I hope he will return to visit us one day. He will always be most welcome."[320]

Glubb never did. After he died in 1986 at the age of 88, King Husayn eulogized him at a memorial service held in Westminster Abbey on April 17, 1986. The king spoke on his own behalf and on behalf of the people of Jordan:

Rarely has a man left such a profound imprint upon a people as has General Glubb, better known in Jordan as Glubb Pasha, in recognition of the singularly meritorious services which he rendered devotedly, and with the greatest integrity and fullest dedication, in the service of my country. . . . Sir John Bagot Glubb became so immersed in the innermost lives and concerns of my people, the humble and the exalted alike, that I wondered, often times and without any reflection, on his ultimate love and loyalty to his own mother country, where his life and heart dwelt and identified after so many years of service and association with Jordan. . . . He contributed immeasurably to the enhancement of the disciplined, martial, and professional traditions of the Jordanian Arab Army in its early formative years. . . . His memory will live in our hearts.[321]

The king was not alone in his praise of Glubb. Shahir Abu-Shahut, who as a Free Officer fought against Glubb's presence in the country and served as his aide-de-camp, also admired the colonial general. Abu-Shahut, like the king, admired Glubb's ability to praise Jordan after his dismissal without showing resentment, but unlike the king, he did not forget his colonial role in the history of Jordan.[322] Following the king's example, Jordanian newspapers eulogized Glubb lavishly. Like the king, they forgot his history as a colonial official, not to mention the reasons for which the king had expelled him in the first place.

Glubb's legacy has outlived him in ways he never anticipated. The Jordanian armed forces, as we saw in this chapter, continued to fulfill their prescribed domestic role of defining the new Jordanian national identity, but they also continued to fulfill their international role, as practiced under Glubb. Aside from the 1970s training of the militaries of a number of Gulf countries, the Jordanian armed forces played a central role alongside the shah's army in quelling the Omani Zufar revolution in the early and mid 1970s.[323] Today, the Jordanian armed forces are a privileged sector of Jordanian society. They live in exclusive suburbs, in villas built for them by the government. They shop at special military stores with low, controlled prices, which are exempted from customs and taxes. They have the best health care system in the country. They are highly paid compared to the rest of the population, and their children have reserved seats in Jordan's most prestigious universities, which they attend at government expense (this, however, contrasts sharply with the situation of many older army retirees, who live in poverty relying on relatively low pensions). Their central role in defining the national boundaries of Jordanianness continues afoot. Commensurate with Glubb's assiduous efforts, his colonial legacy has been effectively transformed into national culture.

5   The Nation as an Elastic Entity

The Expansion and Contraction of Jordan

In this chapter, I discuss the geographic and demographic expansion and contraction of Jordan and their impact on the development of a Jordanian national identity and national culture. I demonstrate how the arrival of the Palestinian population to what came to be known as the East Bank, as well as the addition of central Palestine to the kingdom, served to consolidate the already developing political unity of the people of Transjordan, and how through the years, the presence of the Palestinians in the country was crucial to the emergence of a specific configuration of Jordanian national identity and national culture that became increasingly exclusivist of large sections of the Jordanian citizenry with every passing decade. The Palestinians, who came to be identified as "other" by the Jordanian regime and its allies, were instrumental in helping the formation of a Jordanian national self opposed to that other, wherein, for the new exclusivist nationalists, citizenship and nationality were no longer to be conflated as one. Although, initially, 'Abdullah and Glubb never thought that the Palestinians could serve such a purpose, nor did any state agency at the time, it became clear to 'Abdullah and Glubb as well as to most state agencies (especially the military, the judicial system, and the bureaucracy) that they could marshal their resources to foster such an identification, which would help dispel the threat that the Palestinians brought with them—namely, that of a non-Hashemite Arab nationalism. Although ideas of Arab nationalism, as we saw in chapter 1, had already permeated the Jordanian national movement long before the arrival of the Palestinians, the Jordanian state feared that the Palestinians, through their sheer numbers and their level of despair, could tip the balance against Hashemite hegemony. The Jordanian state, however, was ambivalent about this new project. Whereas the discourse of Jordanian nationalism was the more readily available weapon at its disposal to ward off enemies of the Hashemite monarchy, be they Transjordanian or Palestinian, wherein the regime identified itself with the Transjordanian population so much that opposition to it came to be identified as opposition to Jordan and Jordanianness, the Jordanian regime feared an exclusivist Jordanian nationalism, which, like the one it encountered in nativist form in the 1920s, would exclude the Hashemites themselves from Jordanian identity on the same basis that it would exclude the Palestinians. We will see in the course of post-1948 history how the Jordanian state's ambivalence manifested itself and on what occasions it opted to resolve its ambivalence in favor of partiality. Moreover, this chapter shows how state policies unleashed a Jordanian nationalist momentum with its own nationalist discourse that the state itself could no longer control, and which, it feared, would engulf it at the end by redefining it according to its own dicta.

Although 'Abdullah's expansionist ideology was constitutive of his entire political thought and strategy since before 1921, including the tactic of accepting the formation of a state that came to be known as Transjordan as a basis for such expansion (schemes to rule over and unify Syria, Palestine, Iraq, and Transjordan continued to be pursued by 'Abdullah until his death in 1951[1]), the concrete geographic and demographic expansion of Transjordan was not to take place until 1948. At that moment, the installation of the European-Jewish settler colony on the geographic and demographic majority of Palestine led the way for 'Abdullah's annexation of the remaining central-eastern part of that territory to Jordan (renamed upon independence in 1946). Like his previous attempts to impose his expansionist will on Syria, his bid for Palestine had always faced intense opposition from a large Palestinian nationalist bloc (not to mention the ambivalent support from Zionist colonial settlers), which by 1948 was no longer able to muster political or military power against 'Abdullah's takeover. Although such resistance was ubiquitous and continuous, 'Abdullah and his local Palestinian allies were able to co-opt or coerce a large number of powerful Palestinians to the cause of annexation, inaugurated at the Jericho Conference in December 1948. This process of geographic and demographic expansion had a major impact on Jordan in all areas of political, economic, and social life, the effects of which served to redefine and reconstitute Jordan in ways that became ineradicable. The difficulty encountered by the surging Jordanian nationalist exclusivism, which was cemented in 1970, is precisely in its inability to disentangle a pre-1948 mythologized vision of a pure and purified Jordan from an equally mythologized vision of a post-1948 contaminated Jordan. The success of more recent attempts (since the late 1980s) to recreate a nationalized Jordanian historical memory whose purpose is to return contemporary Jordan to a mythical idealized view of a pre-Palestinians Jordan for the purpose of reestablishing a post-Palestinians Jordan remains to be seen. What is visible, however, to all who live in Jordan today, is the impossibility of such complete disentanglement, much less such purification.

The Project of the Unification Decision (or Mashru' Qarar al-Wihdah) was the way the Jordanian government titled the annexation proposal. The opening statement of the government's declaration, inaugurating parliamentary debates on the question, asserted that its and Parliament's decision was based, inter alia, on the "reality [waqi'] of both banks (of Jordan), the Eastern and the Western, its nationalist, natural and geographic unity ["wihdatiha al-qawmiyyah, wa al-tabi'iyyah, wa al-jughrafiyyah"], and the necessities of their common interests."[2] The parliamentary decision called for the "complete unity between Jordan's eastern and western banks, and their consolidation into one state which is the Hashemite Jordanian Kingdom" or al-Mamlakah al-Urduniyyah al-Hashimiyyah (wrongly translated into English as the Hashemite Kingdom of Jordan).[3] 'Abdullah's Speech from the Throne (Khitab al-'Arsh), which inaugurated the parliamentary session that voted for "unity," stressed that this "is the first time in the history of the constitutional life of Jordan that the people's council [Parliament], which grouped both banks (of Jordan), emanates from the will of one people, one homeland and one hope. And that this is a blessed step which the two banks have embarked upon and which the people, who are the concerned party, has set to achieve, aiming to strengthen its nationalist unity, its patriotic pride [wihdatihi al-qawmiyyah wa 'izzatihi al-wataniyyah] and its common interests." 'Abdullah analogizes the new expanded Jordan to "a bird whose wings are its East and its West, and who has a natural right to have its people and relatives come together."[4] Whereas the bird's wings correspond concretely to the East and West Banks, the bird's body representing Jordan has no concrete geographic correspondence. It is unlikely that the Jordan River is its concrete representation, as a river in this metaphoric concept is not even abstractly considered a country. Jordan, as a country, is abstracted here into a concept with no geographic correspondence. Jordan, in fact, as a malleable entity that expands and contracts, exceeds its geographic reality of East and West Banks, which are mere wings that help it fly. As an abstracted concept then, Jordan is immaterial; it is beyond geography and physicality. In line with such metaphors, in its response to His Majesty's Speech from the Throne, the senate described the East Bank as the "sister" of the West Bank and described 'Abdullah as an "experienced captain of a ship . . . ploughing a way for his ship in the middle of raging storms of whims and inclinations."[5] Whereas this biological metaphor—wherein Jordan is a mother whose daughters are the two banks—like the bird metaphor, renders Jordan, the mother, abstract, incorporeal, and immaterial, the ship metaphor endows the project of annexation, as a means of transportation, with a *body* (that of the ship) traveling through a sea of moods and psyches seeking a safe port. It is unity that constitutes this teleological safe port of Abdullah's annexation project: "the unification of the West Bank with its sister the East Bank . . . in one kingdom shaded by [or under the protection of] the Hashemite crown."[6]

'Abdullah asserts that the unity of both banks is "a nationalist and factual reality." Its nationalist reality is attested to through "the entanglements of [people's] origins and branches and the coalescence of vital interests and the unity of pain and hopes." Its factual reality is attested to by "the establishment of strong unionist links between both banks since 1922. . . . Those important and notable links included unity of currency [in reference to Transjordan's use of the Palestinian pound as its official currency], common defense, utilization of ports, reinforcement of border security, and facilitation of custom and travel barriers, [all] based on the unity of interests and cultural and legislative exchange which have rendered each of the two banks an excellent center especially for the other."[7] The discourse permitting this union, like the one used to found Transjordan itself back in 1921, is Arab nationalism. 'Abdullah stresses that "when Great Britain surrendered its mandate over Palestine, which has been excised from the mother country [al-watan al-umm] and the storms of the Arab-Zionist dispute raged, it became imperative to assert the rights of the Arabs and to stand up to aggression through a general Arab cooperation . . . and, in our opinion, there is no security to any Arab people except in its real unity and in the coming together of its scattered parts wherever this is possible and reflective of the general will and is not a breach of any covenant or agreement."[8] 'Abdullah views the parliamentary elections in both banks preceding their "unification" as "evidence of a sense of self" that the people of both banks have.[9] His speech further stipulated plans to unify the laws of both banks. He concluded by saluting and congratulating members of Parliament and stressing that "you have marched with me in past years and I shall march with you in forthcoming years under your constitutional responsibility and with my paternal guidance, wishing the best for the homeland."[10] Jordan's Parliament "voted" for unity based on "the right of self-determination, the reality of (Jordan's) two banks, the Eastern and the Western, its nationalist, natural and geographic unity, and the necessities of their common interests and vital domain."[11] Whereas the senate likened the Jordanian kingdom to the *mother* of both banks, 'Abdullah is clear on his role as *father* to all whom this kingdom encompasses. His "paternal guidance" was much appreciated by the Lower House's "Response to the Speech from the Throne." In it, those pretending to speak for Parliament "praise . . . Your Majesty's paternal affection ['Atf] toward the [Palestinian] refugees and your work to save them from their despair."[12] (Certainly, such metaphors are not specific to Jordanian nationalism, as they are rampant in all European nationalisms where the idea of the nation as a motherland, or fatherland, depending on the context, and its leaders/founders as fathers—note the use of the term *Founding Fathers* in the U.S. context—was first instituted.[13]) Whereas Arab nationalism is the discourse deployed to "unify" Jordan and Palestine, it is Transjordanian nationalism, not Arab nationalism, that must define the new "unified" and expanded entity. We will see soon how this was not an unintended outcome of the absorption of a stateless territory and people by an existing state, but rather an intended policy of Jordanization and de-Palestinization.

Expanding the Nation: The Road to Annexation

The background to annexation was a full-fledged campaign launched by the Jordanian government to establish itself as the representative of the aggrieved Palestinians.[14] Contingency plans for such a campaign had in fact been in preparation since the United Nations voted to partition Palestine. Whereas the members of the Peel Commission on Palestine were the first to recommend the annexation of the "Arab" parts of Palestine to Transjordan as early as 1937, which led 'Abdullah to submit a proposal to the British government calling for the establishment of "a unified Arab kingdom composed of Palestine and Transjordan under royal Arab rule,"[15] practical plans to achieve this goal were put in place following the UN partition plan.[16] King 'Abdullah was very clear on his right to represent the Palestinians soon after his army entered Palestine on May 15, 1948. He states with no equivocation that "the Arab Higher Committee no longer represents the Arabs of Palestine."[17] This situation became more complicated after the establishment of the General Palestine Government (Hukumat 'Umum Filastin) in

September 1948, which was supported by the Arab League, and especially Egypt. To counter the authority of the new Palestine government, 'Abdullah convened a conference in Amman on October 1, 1948, (which he dubbed the Nationalist Conference on Palestine, or Mu'tamar Filastin al-Qawmi), the same day the Palestine government had called for a conference in Gaza, to which he "invited" 500 Palestinian community leaders and notables.[18] To ensure that the Palestinians attended the Amman conference and not the one convened in Gaza, a number of repressive measures were taken by the government (it should be noted that at the time all the parts of central Palestine that were under Jordanian army control were being run under the 1935 defense law), including preventing delegates from going to Gaza and forcing them to go to Amman instead (many parts of central Palestine were still at the time under Iraqi and Egyptian army control).[19] The conference delegates issued a number of resolutions stating that they "confer upon His Majesty full and absolute authority to speak in the name of the Arabs of Palestine and that he negotiate in their stead and that he resolve their problem in the way he deems fit. He is our representative [wakil] in all matters pertaining to the future of Palestine." Furthermore, the delegates decided to send a telegram to the Arab Higher Committee informing it that the delegates are "removing from it the trust of the Arabs of Palestine, for it does not represent them and it does not have the right to speak in their name or to represent their opinions."[20] As 'Isam Sakhnini points out, the Amman conference was 'Abdullah's first step to exact an authorization for himself from the Palestinians to represent their cause, while simultaneously denying the legitimacy of the General Palestine Government, thus rendering him the sole representative and caretaker of Palestine and the Palestinians. On October 5, 'Abdullah called formally for the dissolution of the Palestine government. A month later, on November 15, 1948, and upon 'Abdullah's visit to Jerusalem, he was proclaimed by the Coptic bishop as the King of Jerusalem.[21]

The Jericho Conference

Whereas the Amman Conference took preliminary steps to ensure 'Abdullah's free hand in dealing with central Palestine and the Palestinians, the Jericho Conference, which he convened on December 1, 1948, strengthened his grip and his resolve to annex the area. As mentioned, central Palestine had already been emptied of anti-Hashemite opposition and resistance through a number of repressive measures undertaken by the Jordanian army, and with a swift and wide-ranging campaign to destroy the Army of Sacred Struggle (which during the war used to answer to the Mufti of Jerusalem, Haj Amin al-Husayni), thus eliminating any organized resistance to 'Abdullah's plans. Concomitant with these repressive measures were a series of appointments of 'Abdullah's allies as provincial governors and municipal mayors throughout central Palestine, in addition to the deportation of many members of the anti-'Abdullah Palestinian Arab Party, and the imposition of strict surveillance on those members who remained (especially in the big towns of Jerusalem, Bethlehem, Ramallah, and Nablus).[22] In addition, the king ordered 'Abdullah al-Tall, military governor of Jerusalem and one of 'Abdullah's chief negotiators, to sign an armistice agreement with the Israelis, which he did on November 30, 1948, the day before the Jericho Conference convened. It was with this as background that over 1,000 Palestinian delegates, most of them refugees from the war, were transported in military vehicles by the Jordanian army to Jericho to attend 'Abdullah's conference.[23] 'Arif al-'Arif reports that many state employees were also brought to attend the conference, while those who refused were dismissed from their jobs or were forced to resign.[24] 'Abdullah al-Tall reports how the Jordanian government met with Shaykh Muhammad 'Ali al-Ja'bari, Hebron's mayor, and a protégé of 'Abdullah, before the conference and informed him of its plans for the conference and its projected goals. The government along with 'Abdullah, according to al-Tall, provided al-Ja'bari with the declarations that the conference was supposed to issue with a consensus vote at its conclusion.[25] Al-Tall adds that the largest delegation attending the conference came from Hebron, where al-Ja'bari coaxed many "who do not mind spending a vacation of a day or two at the government's expense! Had travel costs been at the expense of the delegations themselves, only a few people would have come to Jericho."[26] At the conference, al-Ja'bari was elected president of the conference. The mayors of Jerusalem and Nablus (the latter was under the control of the Iraqi army) along with many Palestinian notables refused to attend the conference despite all of 'Abdullah's measures.

The conference resolutions called for a "Palestinian-Jordanian unity" and affirmed that the only way the Arab nation would be able to confront the dangers it faced was through complete national unity: "we must begin by unifying Palestine with Transjordan as a prelude to real Arab unity." The conference also declared that it "elects [yubayi'] His Majesty King 'Abdullah as king of all Palestine and it salutes Him and His brave army and the Arab armies who have fought and are fighting in defense of Palestine." At the conclusion of the conference, its delegates headed to the king's palace in Shunah, in the Jordan Valley, where they informed him of their resolutions, including his election as king of Palestine.[27] Some accounts add that one of the resolutions called on the Jordanian government to "change its name so that it becomes the Hashemite Arab Kingdom in addition to removing all borders between Palestine and Transjordan."[28] This, however, would have brought more condemnation from other Arabs and Palestinians. Twelve days later, Jordan's twenty-member Parliament, which had no constitutional authority whatsoever over the executive branch, issued a declaration supporting unification and the government's positive response to the Jericho conference.[29] The Arab League and its member states, including the Palestine government, in turn declared their open hostility to the conference and to 'Abdullah's annexation plans. Soon after, however, all member states established diplomatic relations with the kingdom, implicitly recognizing its expansion—although not a single Arab state has ever recognized it officially. The United States and Britain also declared their recognition of 'Abdullah's annexation, except for Jerusalem.[30]

The renaming of central Palestine as the West Bank did not take place officially until a year following the Jericho Conference, and before juridical unification, when the government issued an ordinance stipulating that "sheep and cattle are allowed to be exported to the West Bank of the Hashemite Jordanian Kingdom."[31] The government term used prior to this ordinance was "the western territory," or "the western territories" or "Palestine."[32] Later, the word *Palestine* itself was to be erased and replaced by *West Bank*. In a postal ordinance issued on March 1, 1950, the third article specified that "the word 'Palestine' is hereby abolished as a reference to the West Bank of the Hashemite Jordanian Kingdom wherever it appears in the ordinances and decisions and instructions that are listed in the first article of this ordinance."[33] John Bagot Glubb commented in this regard that "the names Palestine and Trans-Jordan, used in the past, were no longer entirely suitable."[34] Moreover, in 1953, the government issued a new law, which it termed "the law unifying the laws of both banks of the Hashemite Jordanian Kingdom," which transformed the expanded country into a juridical unity.[35]

In preparation for "unification," other measures were undertaken by the government. A new cabinet was formed in May 1949, which included three Palestinian ministers, one of whom, the Nablusite Ruhi 'Abd al-Hadi, served as foreign minister—an important choice especially with regard to the Arab states and their expected reaction to 'Abdullah's annexation (a fourth Palestinian became temporarily minister of refugees, a ministry that was later abolished).[36] After the war ended, the military government set up by the Jordanians on entering Palestine in May 1948 was dissolved and replaced by an administrative government in March 1949.[37] The government appointed former military officers to top civilian positions of ruling central Palestine: ʿUmar Matar, a Transjordanian who served as general military governor of Palestine during the war period, was appointed administrative governor of the territories, a position that answered to the Jordanian interior ministry. The position of administrative governor was abolished by royal edict on January 16,1950, in preparation for annexation.[38] After that date, the administration of central Palestine was to be directly linked to the interior ministry.[39]

As mentioned in chapter 1, the Palestinians were nationalized through an amendment to the Law of Nationality in December 1949. Prior to that, however, and as a preliminary step on the way to nationalization, the Jordanian government had enacted in February 1949 an amendment to the passport law, wherein "any Palestinian Arab holding Palestinian nationality can obtain a Jordanian passport according to the Passport Law number 5 for the Year 1942."[40] In July 1949, a law was enacted rendering the Jordanian dinar the only currency in the country.[41] It should be noted that the Jordanian dinar was being invented during this period to replace the Palestinian pound that had been the official Transjordanian currency since 1927.[42] Soon after, the Jordanian consulate in Jerusalem was closed down, as Jerusalem, by then, was under the jurisdiction of the interior ministry.[43] Moreover, all customs and tariffs between Palestine and Jordan were abolished in December 1949.[44] By the end of 1949, all steps, administrative and legal, were taken to unify central Palestine, now renamed the West Bank, with Jordan. This process was so thorough that the Jordanian prime minister declared early in 1950 that "on the occasion of the lifting of barriers between the East and the West Banks of the Hashemite Jordanian Kingdom, there is no longer a reason to consider the country [al-bilad] located in the West Bank a foreign country . . . the two countries located in said two Banks are considered one unity [wihdah wahidah]."[45] It was with this as background that the postal ordinance (mentioned previously) of March 1, 1950, abolished the word *Palestine* and replaced it with *the West Bank*.

There remained one crucial step to be taken to seal the upcoming juridical unification—namely, parliamentary elections. The preparation for this step had begun on December 13, 1949, when the Jordanian Parliament was dissolved by royal decree to take effect on January 1, 1950. It was further decreed that new elections would be held that would include Palestinians.

To achieve this, the electoral law was amended so that "twenty representatives elected on behalf of the western territory administered by the government of the Hashemite Jordanian Kingdom are added to the representatives whose numbers and districts are specified in the seventeenth and eighteenth articles of the Electoral Law of Parliament."[46] April 11, 1950, was the date set for the new elections.

The debate over the elections in what has become the West Bank was intense. Factions ranged from those completely opposed to the elections (especially the Palestine government and the Arab Higher Committee), who saw participation in the elections as an admission that Palestine had been lost forever to the Zionist colonial settlement, to those who saw holding the elections as a *fait accompli* and urged people to participate so that they can at least have a voice in running their own lives, to those who were completely in support of "unification" [members of ʿAbdullah's new bureaucracy, remnants of the Defense Party (Hizb al-Difaʿ), and remnants of the British Mandatory apparatus]. The Communist Party, which had supported the UN Partition Plan in 1947, opposed ʿAbdullah's elections and called for the establishment of a Palestinian state in accordance with UN resolutions.[47]

The government interfered in the elections, supporting and opposing candidates according to its loyalty criteria. It also used army votes, as members of the army were allowed to vote at the time, to ensure that government candidates won. Glubb Pasha tells of how he provided his soldiers with lists of candidates with marks next to government candidates, although he claims that "[n]o pressure would be used to make them vote for the government's candidates."[48] This is aside from the unfair seat distribution, as East Bank voters numbered 129,000 and West Bank voters numbered 175,000 but each Bank had twenty seats in Parliament. In addition, much gerrymandering was undertaken to ensure a loyal Parliament.[49] A new cabinet was set up the day after the elections that included five Palestinian ministers.

On March 24, both chambers of Parliament met to begin deliberations on the annexation (or "unification") of central Palestine. A number of Palestinian and Jordanian members of Parliament (MPs) walked out in protest, as many had asked that the constitution be changed before deliberations began on the question of "unification." After some mediation, the MPs returned and one of them proposed that deliberations on unification be postponed. The matter (of postponement) was put to a vote and lost, thanks to the vote of the upper chamber senators (Aʿyan), who were in their entirety (as they remain today) appointed by the king. The postponement vote that lost was considered by the government a vote *for* unification, as the matter of unification itself was never put to a vote! At the end of the parliamentary session, Tawfiq Abu al-Huda, former prime minister (of many terms) and ʿAbdullah's right-hand man, who was elected speaker of Parliament, issued the parliamentary "decision" of unification as a decision approved by a parliament that represents both Banks.[50] Soon the British government recognized the new expanded Jordan (except for Jerusalem, which, according to the UN Partition Plan, was supposed to be under UN rule), as did the Israelis, although less unequivocally. On being prodded by the Palestine government in Gaza, the Arab League, which had remained largely silent about all the preparatory steps taken by the Jordanian government to annex central Palestine, issued a decision opposing the annexation and called for the dismissal of Jordan from league membership.[51] The Jordanian government reacted by asserting that it had reached the conclusion that "the matter of unification is a done deal with no room for discussion."[52]

On Friday, July 20, 1951, after touring the West Bank, ʿAbdullah, accompanied by his young grandson Husayn, headed to al-Aqsa mosque to perform their prayers. The mosque was full, with 1,000 worshipers attending prayers. The service was being broadcast live on radio. On entering the mosque, ʿAbdullah was shot dead by a young Palestinian, Mustafa ʿAshshu, who was shot and killed immediately afterwards by ʿAbdullah's guards. Army soldiers on guard outside rushed into the mosque, shooting indiscriminately and killing, in the process, twenty people and wounding 100 more. The Hashemite regiment guards then ran amok in Jerusalem, firing at people, destroying windows, looting property, and beating people with their rifle butts and fists.[53] Hundreds were detained and questioned. Two days later, some of the worshipers at the mosque were still not allowed to go home.

Rumors of the Old City being turned over by the army to Israel as punishment for the Palestinians were rife. Cars with Palestinian license plates were stoned in Salt. At some refugee camps, however, there was public rejoicing. At a camp near the Philadelphia Hotel in downtown Amman, angry Transjordanians attacked and killed three Palestinian refugees and wounded others.[54]

Ten people were accused of plotting the assassination with ʿAshshu and were presented to a military court, headed by three Transjordanian officers.[55] The prosecuting lawyer was the Palestinian Walid Salah, who also served as the court's judicial advisor. Four of the ten were acquitted and the remaining six were sentenced to death. Two of the six were Transjordanians who had fled to Egypt. One of them was ʿAbdullah al-Tall, former military governor of Jerusalem, who had recently defected to Cairo, while the other was Musa

Ahmad Ayyubi, originally from Salt. They were sentenced to death in absentia. The four Palestinians in custody were speedily executed by hanging on the recommendation of the British ambassador Sir Alec Seath Kirkbride.[56]

The New Jordan

The Arab-Israeli War of 1948, along with the Zionist expulsion of close to a million Palestinians from their homeland, led to hundreds of thousands of refugees' flooding those parts of Palestine not yet conquered by Jewish forces as well as neighboring Arab countries. Almost 360,000 refugees entered central Palestine (soon to be renamed the West Bank) and 110,000 refugees entered Jordan proper (soon to be renamed the East Bank). At the time, the population of central Palestine was 425,000 people, and Jordan's population was 375,000.[57] As a result, the total population of the East Bank rose to 485,000 while that of the West Bank rose to 785,000 people, making the total population of the new expanded Jordan 1,270,000 people. Therefore, Jordan was transformed demographically overnight from a country of 375,000 people to one of over a million, a rise of almost 300 percent. As a result, the proportion of the newcomer Palestinians in the 1951 to 1952 period was 64.57 percent of the total population of Jordan (which includes all the West Bank Palestinians as well as all registered Palestinian refugees in the East Bank). If we include the Palestinians who were living in Jordan before 1948, the proportion rises at least to 68.81 percent. As for the East Bank, the proportion of newcomer Palestinians to the total population was 19.77 percent, which rises to 29.31 percent if the pre-1948 Palestinians living in Jordan are included. This proportion increases further to 34.42 percent if we count Palestinian refugees registered in the East Bank, pre-1948 Palestinians living in Jordan, and West Bank Palestinians who moved to the East Bank between 1948 and 1952. Thus, around the time of "unification," Palestinians constituted one third of the population of the East Bank alone. In 1961, that proportion rose to 43 percent, and it further increased to 47.1 percent on the eve of the 1967 War. Moreover, the proportion of the total Palestinian population to the whole population of the East and West Banks had risen to 70.35 percent on the eve of the 1967 War.[58]

After the 1967 War, due to the new wave of refugees expelled by the conquering Israelis, the proportion of Palestinians living in the East Bank increased to approximately 60 percent (although estimates are inaccurate for this period).[59] The population increased substantially again after the Gulf War in the early 1990s, when the return of 200,000 to 300,000 Palestinian Jordanians who lived in Kuwait and the rest of the Gulf raised the proportion of Palestinians—the majority of whom live in Amman and neighboring cities—in the East Bank even further.

Indeed, this immense and sudden demographic expansion had a major impact on all aspects of life in the new Jordan. It is important to stress here the urban nature of much of that expansion in the East Bank, as the majority of the Palestinian population who took refuge there resided in the cities. Amman had already seen much expansion during World War II, when its population increased to 30,000 in 1943. It rose again to 70,000 in 1948, then to 120,000 in 1952, and still further to 246,475 in 1961.[60]

In addition, there existed a number of socioeconomic differences between the incoming Palestinian population and the indigenous Transjordanian population. Palestinians were more urban, more educated, and more experienced in political participation, and they had more exposure to the mass media (newspapers and radio). The Palestinians were also used to better medical care and higher health standards as well as lower child mortality rates.[61] Palestinian merchants brought with them their capital as educated Palestinians brought with them their expertise and skills. Palestinian workers also brought with them their organizational expertise and political experience. These differences placed new economic, social, and political demands on the Jordanian state, and on Jordan's pre-war population more generally.

On the social level, these visible markers of difference created more tension. There was a general perception among the Transjordanian urban population that the Palestinian upper and middle classes, expelled from their cities to relatively less developed small towns in Jordan, were engaging in a nation-class narrative of superiority over Transjordanians. Such a discourse was clearly offensive, especially to those in the Transjordanian upper and middle classes who had an education comparable to that of the Palestinians, although they were smaller in number. Jordanian Christians, disproportionately educated thanks to missionary schools, especially took offense and felt endangered by Palestinian competition. The Palestinian elite, however, lacked political power that would allow it to institutionalize this discourse against the Transjordanians, as its political power had always derived from the Hashemite regime, whose antipathy to Palestinian nationalism (and sympathy to a Transjordanian nationalism of its own making) was always in evidence. Moreover, the Palestinian working classes and former peasants, who were living in refugee camps, did not partake in this discourse of superiority, as they lacked any real material superiority over indigenous Transjordanians. On the contrary, their economic lot came to infuriate rich landowning Jordanians, including Circassians, on some of whose lands the refugee camps were set up by the government. At the time, the land had very little value. As the 1970s (the decade of land speculation) encroached and the land appreciated measurably, many of these Transjordanians expressed horror at these squatters, whom they wanted to evict. Thus, nation and class were intertwined in the discourse of both Palestinian and Transjordanian chauvinists at different periods since 1948.

Palestinians and the West Bank

Despite early Palestinian opposition to annexation, most Palestinians came to accept their new status as a *fait accompli* that they did not wish to challenge. Whereas Palestinian Jordanians were politically active in the anticolonial struggle of the 1950s, which centered on Jordan's relationship to Britain on the one hand and to Jamal 'Abd al-Nasir's Egypt on the other, they did so in conjunction with Transjordanians who spearheaded and led the nationalist mobilization efforts. If anything, the popular discontent of the mid 1950s manifested itself in demonstrations, which mostly took place on the East Bank where the opposition was based (although many occurred on the West Bank also). Moreover, imaginary and real threats that the regime claimed to have faced from the military centered exclusively on Transjordanian figures, as, with very few exceptions, there never were highranking Palestinian officers in the army.

This does not mean that Palestinians were completely satisfied with their new situation as Jordanian citizens. Palestinian demands that the Jordanian government treat the West Bank like the East Bank as far as development policies were concerned were being voiced from the start.[62] In 1950, Palestinian merchants, for example, claimed that they were discriminated against in the issuance of import licenses, "a complaint that seems quite reasonable given that two-thirds of the import licenses were given to East Bank residents."[63] The Jordanian government, in fact, did channel most development funds into the East Bank, expanding its transportation systems (including railways), as well as developing its agriculture and industry. Jamil Hilal states that the Jordanian government, faced with an economically more advanced West Bank, "followed a specific economic policy based on encouraging investment and the development of some industries only in the East Bank,

hoping in the meantime to weaken the productive base of the West Bank.
... This regionalist/chauvinist (iqlimiyyah) policy manifested itself toward
the West Bank through specific practical procedures, the most important of
which was the concentration of large industrial projects in the East Bank of
Jordan and the placement of obstacles and difficulties in the way of the
employment of Palestinian capital in productive projects in the West Bank
of Jordan."[64]

This situation led to the migration of many West Bank Palestinians to the
East Bank, where the bulk of work was, and to the Gulf Arab states.[65] Plascov
remarks that the "development of the East Bank was carried out mainly by
Palestinians, who, having little option, put their knowledge, skill, and talents
at the disposal of the regime. Amman, the kingdom's backward capital, was
to become a flourishing town thus shifting the center of economic gravity."[66]
The only sector that was developed at all in the West Bank was tourism. One
Palestinian explained it this way: "Since they could not transfer Jerusalem
... the only thing they allowed was the development of the tourist industry."[67] As Yazid Sayigh asserts, however, it is unclear if government discrimination was directed at Palestinians generally or at the West Bank more
specifically.[68]

Competing Representatives: The PLO and Jordan

The Jordanian government had opposed any Palestinian body claiming
to represent Palestinians, such as the General Palestine Government set
up in Gaza in 1949, or the Higher Palestine Organization (al-Hay'ah al-
Filastiniyyah al-'Ulya), based in Cairo and Damascus, which was presided
over by Haj Amin al-Husayni. However, it decided to support the Arab decision to establish the Palestine Liberation Organization in 1964, albeit hes-
itantly,[69] especially so since the PLO did not claim at the time to be the sole
representative of the Palestinian people and made no claims of sovereignty
over the West Bank. Its position, therefore, did not challenge the existing
Jordanian claims to both.[70] In fact, the PLO's Palestinian Nationalist Charter
stressed that "this organization does not exercise any regional sovereignty
over the West Bank in [sic] the Hashemite Jordanian Kingdom or the Gaza
Strip or the Himmah area."[71] Moreover, PLO head Ahmad Shuqayri, in a
press conference in Cairo, declared that the new Palestinian organization
will cooperate with the Jordanian government and that this cooperation will
have "a special character because the majority of the Palestinian people live

in Jordan as does Palestinian land [exist therein]."[72] Responding positively to these assurances, in his letter designating his new prime minister, Wasfi al-Tall, King Husayn wrote that one of the "central" points of the new government's policies toward the Palestinian cause should be "the support of the Palestine Liberation Organization and close cooperation with it in Jordan, the Arab World, and all international fora. This position is surely based on our faith that as long as our brothers, Palestine's children, in Jordan and outside it, choose the Organization as a way to mobilize and organize the efforts of Palestine's children, we shall stand by the Organization, support it, agree with it, and back up its efforts until Palestine's children and the Arab nation reinstate Arab rights in Palestine."[73] In a speech that he gave in April, the king stressed his belief that the new Palestinian organization "will not at any moment harm the unity of our one Jordanian family . . . rather, on the contrary, it will strengthen and deepen this unity and double its abilities to grow and take off."[74]

The situation began to change rapidly as the PLO began to make demands on Jordan that the Jordanian government felt competed with its own interests as a representative of the Palestinians. Such demands included calling on Jordan to institute compulsory military service and fortifying frontier villages. In an attempt to echo the Jordanian position that the Palestinians and Jordanians are one people, Shuqayri declared in an Amman press conference his choice of Transjordanians such as Najib Rushaydat for membership in the PLO's executive committee and 'Ali al-Hiyari (former head of Jordan's army) as general director of the PLO's military division. Moreover, he added that Jordan is "the homeland of the [Palestine Liberation] Organization and Jordan's people are its people." He also reminded his audience that the "East Bank" had been "torn" from Palestine in 1919 and that "the return of the East Bank to the motherland, in mind and conscience, and in spirit and body, is a basic step on the road of the return of the stolen homeland."[75]

However, with the deterioration of relations between the PLO and Jordan within a short period after these declarations, especially regarding the PLO demand that Jordan institute compulsory military service, Jordan's response changed. In a speech he delivered at the royal palace, King Husayn insisted that "we shall not discriminate between the eastern Jordanian and the western Jordanian and no one will be able to tear this unity asunder and take the brother away from his brother and take the soldier away from his unit . . . and much of what we have recently heard and continue to hear . . . is only meant to break apart the one structure, and to tear apart the one entity, which is what we shall not permit under any circumstances."[76] In a famous letter that King Husayn wrote to Egyptian President Jamal ʿAbd al-Nasir, the king insisted that "the argument that Mr. Shuqayri uses in his vituperations is that Jordan obfuscates the work of the Organization and does not permit it freedom of activity . . . wherein freedom of activity, in his understanding of it, and as it has been clearly revealed, aims to tear the Palestinian-Jordanian citizen west of the River Jordan from his brother the Palestinian-Jordanian citizen to its east, and to stir up hidden rancor [hazazat] and dormant discord [fitnah], and to break up the people's and the army's unity."[77] The Jordanian government countered by insisting that Jordan was a country where "human and nationalist melting" or "al-Insihar al-Bashari al-Qawmi"[78] takes place. Finally, King Husayn did not mince words when he declared in a speech he delivered in the northern city of ʿAjlun in June 1966 that "the [Palestinian] cause ceased to have a Palestinian character the moment the Arab armies entered the land of Palestine . . . and we in this country have a solid belief that the unity of both banks is a unity blessed by God and supported by the people and that it constitutes a vanguard nucleus for the larger [Arab] unity." He proceeded threateningly to declare that "we shall cut off every hand that extends itself in harm to this unity, to this one struggling country, and we shall gouge out every eye that looks askance at us, and we shall not be lax or tolerant, not even a fingertip, from this moment on."[79] These words were addressed not only to Shuqayri's PLO but also to the Palestinian guerrilla movement that was outside PLO authority. Between 1965 and 1967, the guerrilla movement, spearheaded by Yasir ʿArafat's Fath, the reverse acronym for the Palestinian Movement of Liberation (Harakat al-Tahrir al-Filastiniyyah), was already launching a number of attacks on Israel from Jordanian territory. The Jordanian government sought to prevent such attacks by force. In fact, Fath's first "martyr" was killed by the Jordanian military rather than the Israeli enemy. The rest of the movement was continually pursued by the Jordanian military aiming to curb its activities. This led to more mutual recriminations between the PLO and Jordan, on the one hand, and between Fath and the Movement of Arab Nationalists [the precursor to George Habash's Popular Front for the Liberation of Palestine (PFLP)].[80]

It was with this as background that the Israelis attacked the West Bank village of Samuʿ on November 13, 1966. The Israeli raid was followed by massive demonstrations in the West Bank against the government's ineptitude in protecting the population. It was in this context that the Jordanian government opted to institute compulsory military service, as mentioned earlier, to satisfy popular demands. This was the first time since annexation that demonstrations against the government were limited to the West Bank exclusively. This situation prevailed only seven months before the outbreak of the June 1967 War, which resulted in Israel's occupation of the entire West Bank in June 1967.

The occupation of the West Bank led to a massive exodus of tens of thousands of Palestinians from the occupied territories to the East Bank, thus further increasing the proportion of Palestinians in that part of the country to around 60 percent of the total East Bank population.[81] The "setback" (al-Naksah) of 1967 led to the emergence of a new era, one wherein Palestinians were beginning to take matters into their own hands. Although most Palestinian guerrilla groups had been forming since the late 1950s, many were consolidating themselves and improving their organization following the 1967 War. The Fida'iyyin (Sacrificers) were coming of age through larger mobilization of the Palestinian refugee population, especially in Jordan. Prominent among these groups was Fath.

Despite their increased presence in the lives of Palestinians, the guerrillas had not yet distinguished themselves in any major battles, until the famous Battle of al-Karamah in March 1968. Al-Karamah, a small Jordanian town (on the East Bank) in the Jordan valley, and the site of a Palestinian refugee camp where many guerrillas were stationed, became the target of a major Israeli operation. Through coordination with Jordan's army, the guerrillas and the Jordanian army were able to force the Israelis to withdraw after inflicting heavy damages on them. The Israelis, however, were not defeated. On the contrary, before withdrawing they had leveled the town of al-Karamah and inflicted heavy damages on the guerrillas and on the army. What was different this time, however, was that the Israeli military, successful as it might have been in its operation, could not escape unscathed (as it had during the 1967 War and on many other occasions). For the first time in its history, it received heavy damages in personnel and *matériel*.

Depending on whose account one reads, both the Jordanian army and the guerrillas minimized the role of the other in the operation and claimed victory for themselves.[82] Still, al-Karamah (which also means "dignity") became the rallying cry of the Palestinian masses, who were thirsty for any kind of victory over their always victorious enemy. In the wake of this victory, thousands of Palestinians in Jordan volunteered to join the guerrillas.[83] For the Jordanian military, al-Karamah also became one the most important victorious occasions in its recent history, one that it would commemorate every year henceforward. The disproportionate public attention given to the

Palestinian guerrillas infuriated many in the Jordanian military who had, in fact, been the more effective party (on account of their weaponry and numbers) in forcing the Israelis to withdraw. Still, the popularity of the Fida'iyyin guerrillas had reached such international levels that King Husayn himself declared in an interview on British radio and television on May 4,1968, that "there will come a day when we all shall become Fida'iyyin in that part of the world."[84]

As a turning point for the guerrillas, however, al-Karamah signaled the beginning of the most serious challenge the Jordanian state and regime were to face since their inception in 1921. This was a challenge not only to the Jordanian state's authority and sovereignty, or to the throne itself, but also to the state's claim to represent Palestinian Jordanians, and in some cases, a challenge to the very Jordanianness of parts of Jordan itself (and sometimes all of it), not to mention the Jordanianness of its Palestinian-Jordanian citizens.

Toward Civil War

The popularity of the guerrillas was such a serious challenge to the Jordanian state and regime that a whole campaign was unleashed by the military and political leadership of the country against the guerrillas. This campaign included military confrontations with the guerrillas, who were accused of "provocations," leading to what came to be known as Black September.[85] Serious guerrilla misconduct, in a number of instances initiated by Jordanian agents who had infiltrated the guerrillas, came to be seen as a *casus belli* by the regime.[86] An internal propaganda campaign was in full swing in the military: the guerrillas were accused of a battery of crimes ranging from atheism and recklessness to outright collaboration with the Zionist enemy. Moreover, the tribal leadership was mobilized through tribal conventions throughout much of 1970, preparing them for the upcoming confrontation.[87]

It is unclear how many Palestinians were in the Jordanian army in 1970. Some accounts claim that the army was 60 percent Palestinian.[88] King Husayn himself asserted that the majority of his army consisted of Palestinians.[89] These figures, however, seem exaggerated. More accurate calculations are provided by Yazid Sayigh, who assesses the percentage of Palestinian soldiers in the Jordanian military as close to 45 percent in the mid sixties (at the time when two thirds of the population of the country was Palestinian), with the percentage of Palestinians in some infantry units in 1968 not exceeding 15 percent to 20 percent,[90] and even this decreased measurably after the civil war. Sayigh puts the percentage of Palestinians in the military at fewer than 25 percent in the mid 1980s.[91]

One of the major complaints of the Jordanian government was its claim that the basic contradiction between the guerrillas and the Jordanian state was the presence of the former in the cities. However, this is belied by the fact that the government's enmity to the guerrillas predates their entry into the cities. For example, after the February 1968 Israeli "retaliatory" raid on Jordan killing forty-six civilians and ten soldiers, King Husayn asserted that the "Jordanian authorities will strike with an iron fist all elements who, through their actions, provide Israel with a pretext to apply pressure on Jordan," adding that "those persons who expose Jordan to enemy attacks will be prevented from crossing Jordanian territory after today."[92] At the time, there existed no guerrilla presence in any of Jordan's cities; rather, they were all concentrated on the border with Israel and the Israeli-occupied West Bank. This, of course, does not underestimate the increased level of threat to the Jordanian regime and state that the guerrillas constituted, but it reveals the Jordanian state's and regime's perception of such a threat at a much earlier moment, even before al-Karamah, when the Jordanian government was vehemently opposed to a separate Palestinian army. The exclusive rights that the Jordanian state arrogated to itself in representing its Palestinian-Jordanian citizens and its Palestinian-Jordanian territory could not be sustained much longer in the presence of such a rival power. The fact that the guerrillas were divided among several groups under several leaderships (mainly Fath and PFLP) and that these leaderships were not always in control of their rank and file's activities in the cities (e.g., brandishing weapons, collecting "donations" from shop-owners, and in some cases, harassing people, which alienated many), gave the Jordanian government a golden opportunity to attack the guerrillas ideologically as well as militarily. This was made easier by the Palestinian nationalism of the guerrillas, who ignored Transjordanians in their mobilization campaigns and gave credence to regime claims (borne out by PFLP slogans, for example) that the guerrillas wanted to turn Jordan into a Palestinian state.[93]

The Jordanian government renewed its call for mandatory military conscription in January 1968 with a new law increasing the period of mandatory military service from ninety days to two years,[94] an injunction engineered to prevent the likelihood of Jordan's youth joining the guerrillas. It decided to cancel military service in July 1970, however, as this policy failed to yield

positive results and as the military training of the entire population (Palestinians and Transjordanians) might prove fatal to the regime itself.[95] However, the government opted for a different military alternative that would
implicitly select only Transjordanians for such service—namely, the setting
up of the voluntary al-Jaysh al-Sha'bi (the Popular Army). The idea of a
popular resistance (composed of civilian militias in Jordanian East Bank and
West Bank cities and villages) first appeared after the Arabization of Jordan's
army under nationalist rule in November 1956 for the purpose of fighting
back Israeli military attacks. It was never put into effect, however, due to the
1957 palace coup.[96] The regime was to revive it, however, following its first
crisis with the guerrillas in February 1968, and Prime Minister Bahjat al-
Talhuni expressed the government's plan to set up such a force on February
20.[97] It should be noted that the situation in 1968 was substantially different
from that in 1956: in 1968, such a force could not be formed in the Israeli-
occupied West Bank, so it would be limited to the East Bank only. Moreover,
although the popularity of the guerrillas following the battle of al-Karamah
increased exponentially among Palestinian-Jordanian and Transjordanian
youth,[98] the Jordanian civilian population (irrespective of geographic origins)
was becoming increasingly dissatisfied with guerrilla arrogance and harassment, exaggerated by government propaganda, and the government was certain that only Transjordanians would join the force, a logical conclusion that
was to be justified by subsequent events. The force did not materialize until
mid August 1969, when the government began to organize it, to train it, to
arm it, and to prepare it for a possible confrontation with the guerrillas. An
ordinance calling for the organization of the popular army was issued on
January 2, 1970, replacing the 1956 ordinance and renaming the popular
resistance the Popular Army.[99] The force consisted mainly of Jordanian army
officers who undertook the training of mostly rural Jordanian volunteers
(mainly peasants). The importance of this force was further alluded to in
February 1970, when a government communiqué banned possession of
weapons by citizens except those in "popular resistance organizations."[100]
Moreover, on February 11, the commander of the popular resistance declared that by January 1970, more than 45,000 Jordanians had been trained
as part of the popular resistance, and that they were armed and prepared
and deployed throughout all of Jordan's cities and towns. The king himself
confirmed the government's policy of viewing the popular army as a division
of the Jordanian armed forces when he instructed Khalil 'Abd al-Dayim,
second in command of Jordan's army, to supervise all "our fighting units . . .
added to which our popular army which is supervised and directed by

me personally."[101] Units of the popular army were organized at the town level and were given the task of defending the towns during the civil war in September.

The Jordanian government's mobilization campaign extended beyond the enlistment of Jordanians in the Popular Army. It included explicit statements criticizing and condemning the Fida'iyyin, rumormongering, press campaigns (especially in the military press), and the convening of tribal conferences attended by tribal chiefs, who would be incited by government representatives.[102]

The mobilization of the Bedouin tribes was one of the more important elements in the government strategy, as the monarchy had always relied on their support in society and on their members in the military. This was carried out with the help of high-ranking army and police officers as well as high-ranking intelligence officers (Mukhabarat) who themselves hailed from Bedouin tribes. The government also enlisted the help of retired officers, and tribal chiefs and high-ranking government administrators of Bedouin origins. This campaign was coupled with financial donations, taken from the military budget and made to the tribes for the purpose of arming tribal members.

The first convention was held on February 20, 1970, in Umm Rummanah, north of Amman, where 200 tribal Bedouin chiefs and notables met. They pressed the king "to strike with an iron fist those who defy Jordanian law," all the while assuring him of their "total support for the application of the laws of the state." The king responded on February 23 by announcing the promotion of fifty security (Mukhabarat) officers, of mostly Bedouin backgrounds.[103] Other conferences followed before and after the June crisis unfolded, when the most important military confrontation (with the exception of the coming civil war) took place between the regime and the guerrillas. One such conference was convened in Sahab (a city whose population consists mostly of mid- to late-nineteenth century Egyptian Bedouin settlers) a few kilometers southeast of Amman, near the Wihdat refugee camp. It is said that more than 1,000 delegates attended. According to one tribal chief at this conference, the delegates demanded that the government put a stop to "subversive activities," that it support only "honest" Fida'i activities, and that the Fida'iyyin organizations put a stop to "bad behavior."[104] Another conference was held in the small town of Suwaylih, near Amman, on August 21, which issued a communiqué, distributed widely in the country, calling for a general tribal conference.[105] The communiqué stressed the unity of the two Banks, and it criticized the Fida'iyyin for deviating from their important task of liberating Palestine through subverting public order in Jordan. In addition, the communiqué praised the Jordanian armed forces and praised soldiery: "As our Jordanian people believes with all its pride and might ['Izzah] that soldiery is the most honorable service in the most honorable arena, it believes categorically that our Armed Jordanian Forces are the fence of the homeland and its protector, it [the homeland] is the pupil of their [the Armed Forces'] eyes, and the reason for their pride, and that it is always in the vanguard of their struggle, the title of their authenticity, the repository of their hopes and the guarantor of their desires. . . . Our Jordanian people affirms its denunciation and contempt of all statements and actions that attempt in any way to undermine the reputation of our family, our army, and our régime."[106]

After the king's motorcade was attacked on June 9, 1970, Bedouin units shelled two refugee camps in Amman. As 'Adnan Abu 'Awdah states, the "army reaction was both revealing and alarming. The choice of two refugee camps as the target of the army's anger implied that the army looked on all Palestinians as an extension of the fedayeen and vice versa."[107] According to Abu 'Awdah, the king attempted to defuse the issue.[108] In the middle of the summer of 1970, crown-prince Hasan, Husayn's brother and designated successor, paid a visit to the southern city of Tafilah, where he met with tribal leaders and attempted to rouse them against the presence of Fida'iyyin physicians who practiced in their city, and calling on them to evict the Fida'iyyin altogether from Tafilah. One tribal chief responded angrily, telling the crown prince, "when you evict them from Amman, we will evict them from here."[109] Another conference was held in the south of the country in Ma'an on September 4, 1970, less than two weeks before the monarchy's final onslaught on the Fida'iyyin. It was presided over by Parliament member Faysal Bin Jazi, of the southern Bedouin Huwaytat tribe. At the conference, it was decided that the Fida'iyyin must be evicted from the entire south of the country. Following most of these conferences, Bedouin forces would attack the offices of the guerrillas' organizations and of individual Palestinians.[110] It should be noted, however, that the events in the south of the country remain unclear and contested. Mahjub 'Umar, for example, shows a much more ambivalent stance taken by tribal chiefs toward the monarchy during its preparation for a showdown with the guerrillas.[111]

The two-week fighting that began in mid September killed thousands and destroyed large sections of Jordanian cities, especially the capital Amman, in the process. Although the government and King Husayn insisted that the death toll was somewhere between 1,500 and 2,000,[112] the guerrillas and foreign journalists reported that it was much higher, between 7,000 and 20,000 people, some of whom were said to have been buried in mass graves by the Jordanian army.[113]

In the few days preceding the civil war and in the days during which it was fought, 5,000 Palestinian and Transjordanian members of the Jordanian armed forces deserted their posts and joined the resistance.[114] Jordanian Military Chief of Staff, Mashhur Hadithah al-Jazi (of the southern Huwaytat tribe) resigned his position and was subsequently placed under house arrest by the government because of his perceived sympathies for the guerrillas.[115] One Jordanian officer, Bahjat al-Muhaysin, from the southern town of Tafilah, was convicted by a military court for disobeying orders by refusing to fire on the city of Irbid during the civil war.[116] Furthermore, the government-appointed military governor, the Palestinian Muhammad Dawud (who was asked by the government to form his military government on September 16 as a prelude to launching the government's military campaign against the guerrillas), resigned and requested asylum in Libya after being disowned by his daughter Muna on September 19, 1970, on Voice of the Palestinian Revolution radio station broadcasting from Baghdad.[117]

After the defeat of the guerrilla forces in 1970, their remaining power in the country continued to erode until they were routed to the northern towns of Jerash and ʿAjlun. There, they were finally assaulted by the Jordanian army, which forced all remaining guerrilla units outside the country. To erase the memory of the civil war and the competing but now defeated Palestinian political presence, the Jordanian government destroyed the Tomb of the Unknown Martyr on May 31, 1971, which had been erected by the PLO in Amman (in Jabal al-Ashrafiyyah) on October 21, 1970, after the September 1970 massacres.[118] As an act of final revenge on the part of the Palestinians, Prime Minister Wasfi al-Tall, who had coengineered Black September and who was in office during the final assault in the summer of 1971, was gunned down in Cairo on November 28, 1971, by a new Palestinian guerrilla group calling itself Black September.[119]

The triumph of the Jordanian army over the guerrillas forced the PLO to review its record in Jordan, and it admitted to a number of mistakes that helped precipitate the clash.[120] On the other hand, the Jordanian government as well as politicians and individuals, with few exceptions, continue to insist that the government had no other option but to act militarily.[121]

A New Nationalist Era

In the wake of the civil war, the new civilian government of Wasfi al-Tall embarked on massive purges of the government's bureaucracy and military, ridding them of any guerrilla supporters. This effectively meant that large numbers of Palestinian officers and bureaucrats, and a number of Transjordanians, were dismissed from their jobs. This was concomitant with al-Tall's war on the newspapers and the massive arrests that the government launched against "subversives."[122] Many newspapers were closed down (such as 'Amman al-Masa', Al-Sabah, and Al-Difa') and had their licenses withdrawn and their Palestinian editors dismissed (including 'Arafat Hijazi, Ibrahim al-Shanti, and 'Abd al-Hafiz Muhammad).[123] Al-Tall started a new newspaper in 1971, called Al-Ra'y, or The Opinion, which remains to this day Jordan's largest daily.

Within two months of the final liquidation of the Palestinian guerrillas in the country, the Jordanian monarch, on the advice of his prime minister, Wasfi al-Tall, embarked on a new national project, which he called the National Union, or al-Ittihad al-Watani. Husayn declared, from his Basman Palace, the formation of the union on September 7 amid much media fanfare. It was going to be the only legal political organization in the country, as all parties remained banned. He addressed the "one Jordanian family," asserting that after the preceding year and as a result of its difficult events, there arose "the need for the establishment of a general organization [tanzim] which includes all the people, men and women, wherein [this organization will] organize the energies and potential of society and will direct it toward specified and clear goals."[124] The king insisted that the National Union was not a political party at all; rather, he conceived of it as "a general framework which organizes life and human beings in our beloved country, it is an immense crucible which melts all our energies, with all the differences and varieties [of these energies], in order to make of its outcome the Jordanian miracle which will open for us the road to victory." This union, the king asserted, will help Jordanians achieve the goals of "al-Huriyyah, al-Wihdah, wa al-Hayat al-Afdal," or "liberty, unity, and the better life," which Wasfi al-Tall had used as his slogan when he first became prime minister in 1962. The king offered the press and the people of Jordan the union's charter, which, he asserted, was the outcome of numerous discussions with the "representatives" of the people. The charter, in line with what we discussed in chapter 2, had separate sections for women and for Bedouins.[125] In fact, the National Union, which was conceived by Wasfi al-Tall, had another important purpose—namely, the formation of a popular base of support for the regime. Still, its declared purpose was to unify the citizenry into one national identity that had been torn asunder by the civil war.

Al-Tall was the son of the famed Jordanian intellectual and poet Mustafa Wahbah al-Tall, who back in the 1920s had coined the anti-Hashemite and anticolonial nativist slogan "Jordan for the Jordanians." Wasfi was born in 1919 in Iraqi Kurdistan (his mother was an Iraqi Kurd), where he spent the first five years of his life. When he arrived in Transjordan in 1924, he spoke only Kurdish.[126] Before becoming prime minister, Wasfi Al-Tall was always interested in the new emergent class of intellectuals who lacked traditional powerful backgrounds, whether military, tribal, or even bourgeois. He conceived of the National Union as a forum for many in this class to assert themselves. He even foresaw himself as presiding over the Union after his term as prime minister ended.[127]

The first National Union Conference took place on November 25, 1971, in Amman. The king invited 2,400 "representatives" of the people to attend. He took the opportunity to affirm to the people of Jordan, whom he addressed as "my brothers and sisters in the two beloved banks," that "the Union is your Union. It is for every one of you and of every one of you."[128] Wasfi al-Tall, the Union's architect, did not live long to pursue his project. He was killed three days later. Still, the king pursued the project and on December 9, 1971, appointed a Temporary Higher Executive Committee for the National Union.[129] The National Union included a large number of Transjordanians, some of whom were former leftists, such as Ibrahim Habashnah, who used to be close to the communists and had been active in the national movement of the 1950s, but who more recently had experienced a *volte face*. It also included a number of Palestinian Jordanians who had stood by the regime during its confrontation with the guerrillas. Such figures as ʿAdnan Abu ʿAwdah, a West Banker, formerly an operative of the Mukhabarat who later served in the king's military government set up a week before the Black September massacres (he later occupied several ministerial and ambassadorial positions, as well as the position of advisor to both King Husayn and King ʿAbdullah II), and Mustafa Dudin, formerly part of the national movement of the 1950s and later a collaborator in the 1970s and1980s with the Israeli occupation authorities in their Village Leagues scheme in the West Bank,[130] were, at the time, ministers in al-Tall's post-liquidation government. Dudin (who was minister of social affairs) was appointed secretary-general of the union, and Abu ʿAwdah (who was information minister) was appointed a member of the executive committee and, later, secretary general of the union.[131]

The union became very active, especially in the northern part of the East Bank, from which al-Tall himself originally hailed.[132] Hani Hurani explores the class politics of the National Union, charting the rise to power of what he terms the "bureaucratic bourgeoisie," mainly consisting of Transjordanians, alongside the military-tribal alliance that the regime had depended on in its most recent crisis, and the erosion of the power of the merchant bourgeoisie (of mostly Syrian and Palestinian origins), which, until the 1970 to 1971 crisis, represented the most important pole of societal support for the monarchy. The union's executive committee consisted of thirty-six members, six of whom were current ministers. It also included three women, one of whom was Sa'diyyah al-Jabiri al-Tall, Wasfi's Syrian widow.[133] The committee also included Wasfi's brother Sa'id.[134] The union used the mass circulation newspaper *Al-Ra'y* as its mouthpiece. Despite all the attention surrounding the union, interest in it began to wane slowly after al-Tall's assassination, leading the government to finally dissolve it in February 1976.[135] However, this was not caused by the government's disinterest in redefining the country's national identity (the express goal of the National Union), but rather the government found a new framework for that redefinition, namely, the United Arab Kingdom.

The United Arab Kingdom (al-Mamlakah al-'Arabiyyah al-Muttahidah) was proposed by the king in March 1972 in response to the increasing threat that the PLO came to constitute to Jordanian claims in international fora. It was slated to include a federated Jordan comprising two autonomous provinces, the West Bank and the East Bank, each with its own governor, parliament, and government, which would deal with all matters except foreign affairs, the military, and the unity of the kingdom. These matters would be controlled by the central government. The capital of the United Arab Kingdom was going to be Amman. Arab reaction to the king's plan was swift. Syria and Egypt broke off relations and the PLO accused the king of liquidating the Palestinian cause by proposing autonomy rather than independence for the Palestinians.[136] The project for the United Kingdom went nowhere as the vociferous Palestinian opposition to it continued unabated. The project was quietly withdrawn as the king and the Jordanian government no longer made references to it.[137]

The PLO continued to pursue its recent claim of being the sole representative of the Palestinian people—a claim that began to be firmly asserted after the guerrilla groups took over its leadership. Such declarations were being made at the Palestine National Council (PNC) meetings as well as to the press and in PLO publications. The Jordanian government refused such statements vehemently. The Jordanian Parliament responded by affirming that "every claim and pretense of representing the Palestinian people is a conspiracy based on killing national unity and inciting division and separation among the sons of the one homeland." The Parliament proceeded to "declare that the Hashemite Jordanian Kingdom, with its two banks, includes one people within one state represented by His Majesty the Exalted King and legitimate state authorities."[138]

Jordanian and PLO jockeying for position on the issue of representation continued unabated. In 1973, the PLO was recognized by the nonaligned nations at the fourth summit of the movement in Algiers as "a legitimate representative of the Palestinian people," and in November it was recognized by the Arab League in a secret resolution as the "sole representative of the Palestinian people," about which Jordan expressed its reservations. Jordan's King Husayn, taking advantage of the increasing hostility between Syria and Egypt, met with Anwar Sadat in Alexandria in July 1974, and the two issued a joint declaration stating that the "PLO is the legitimate representative of the Palestinian people except for those resident in the Hashemite Jordanian Kingdom," which ostensibly includes the West Bank. Arab and PLO anger followed, forcing Sadat to retreat from the declaration at the meeting of the foreign ministers of Syria, Egypt, and the PLO in Cairo in September. Finally, the situation came to a close with the open Arab League decision issued at the Seventh Arab League Summit, held in Rabat in October 1974, recognizing the PLO as the sole legitimate representative of the Palestinian people wherever they are, which was soon followed by international recognition of the PLO as the sole legitimate representative of the Palestinian people by the United Nations' General Assembly. In response, King Husayn declared at the Arab Summit that, based on this recognition of the PLO, Jordan had been rendered practically exempt from all political responsibility toward the Palestinian cause, for this responsibility has been demanded by the PLO for itself. Following these developments, the king reorganized the Jordanian cabinet, whereby Palestinian representation was reduced.[139] In a speech he gave after his return from the Arab Summit, however, the king asserted that the Jordanians, whether "Muhajirin or Ansar," are "one tribe and one family."[140] He was referring to Palestinians and Transjordanians, respectively, with terms from Muslim history (the Muhajirin consisted of the Prophet Muhammad and the early Muslims who immigrated to the town of Yathrib, whereas the Ansar are the indigenous Yathribis—the Aws and

Khazraj tribes—who received and supported them; the two communities established the first Islamic state). He continued to use the "Muhajirin and Ansar" analogy for the rest of his life.

Clothes, Accents, and Football: Asserting Post–Civil War Jordanianness

Simultaneously with these political events at the level of the state, other developments were taking place in society. As we saw in chapter 2, the palace was rearranging its relations with the country's Bedouin tribes through a number of meetings and conferences. Moreover, the increasingly popular Jordanian television (founded in 1968) was airing many programs on the military as well as a number of soap operas about Jordanian "Bedouin life." Similar programs were also aired on the radio. As already discussed, a large number of songs were being aired on radio and television, exalting Jordan, Amman, the army, and King Husayn, in addition to the new genre of Bedouin songs which were becoming popular even outside Jordan. It was none other than Wasfi al-Tall, in his capacity as director of Jordanian radio broadcasting in 1959, who began forming music groups to collect folk songs from their "original sources." These groups, with the help of the lyricist Rashid Zayd al-Kilani and the composer Tawfiq al-Nimri (a Transjordanian Christian from the northern town of Husn), recast these songs and launched the Jordanian "folk" song on the radio.[141]

The search was proceeding for new popular symbols of the new Jordanianness. On the official level, the government was setting up a number of clubs fostering the celebration of "Jordanian national culture." One such club, named Nadi Ihia' al-Turath al-Sha'bi al-Urduni (the Revival of Jordanian Folk Culture Club), was headed by none other than Wasfi's wife, Sa'diyyah. The club organized its first show of Jordanian folk fashion (al-Azia' al-Sha'biyyah al-Urduniyyah) in the summer of 1971, representing both banks.[142] On the societal level, for example, Transjordanian urban male youth began to assert their Jordanianness sartorially. They started to wear the red-and-white *shmagh* or *hatta* (which, as we saw in chapter 3, was originally coined as exclusively Jordanian by Glubb Pasha) as a winter scarf around their necks as an assertion of national pride. Palestinian Jordanians followed suit by wearing the black-and-white *hatta* as a scarf; those among them seeking assimilation wore the red-and-white *hatta*. The urban youth's donning of the red-and-white *hatta* was, in fact, following in King Husayn's footsteps, as he had begun to wear it as a head-gear much more frequently after 1970, especially when he addressed tribal leaders or the military, or when on trips to the Arab states of the Gulf.[143] Moreover, the king's picture wearing the *shmagh* appeared on Jordanian currency bills and on Jordanian postage stamps.

Clothing items, however, were not enough to assert national loyalty. There emerged a whole new corpus of markers to assert it more strongly. One of the most important developments of this period was the battle of the accents, or what came to be defined as a Jordanian accent and a Palestinian accent. An example is the letter *qaf* in classical Arabic. Whereas most urban Palestinians pronounce the *qaf* as a glottal stop in colloquial speech (so *qalb*, meaning heart, is pronounced *alb*), as opposed to rural Palestinians, who, depending on their region, pronounce the *qaf* as it is, or as *kaf*, or as *ga* (*qalb*, *kalb*, or *galb*), and Palestinian Bedouins, who pronounce the *qaf* as a *ga*, most Jordanian men after 1970, regardless of urban, rural, or Bedouin backgrounds, began to pronounce the *qaf* as *ga*. Jordanian accents also varied from north to south, and between the rural population and the Bedouins not to mention educated town Jordanians, who from the 1920s through the 1960s studied in Palestinian and Syrian schools in Palestinian and Syrian cities and acquired urban accents. Also, most Palestinian and Syrian Jordanians whose families had been in the country since the 1920s or earlier also spoke with an urban accent. Moreover, for many Jordanian villagers, not all words with *qaf* are pronounced with a *ga* sound: many are in fact pronounced with a *kaf* sound.[144]

This situation changed drastically after the civil war. The Jordanian and Palestinian accents were redefined rigidly as national markers. They also acquired a gendered attribute. After 1970, most urban Jordanian men began pronouncing all *qafs* as *ga*, asserting this as "masculine" and as "Jordanian," whereas Jordanian urban women retained their glottal stop as a "feminine" characteristic. Many young Palestinian-Jordanian urban men, feeling feminized by the new accent configuration, began using the *ga* instead of the glottal stop as an assertion of masculinity, especially when in the company of men (particularly if these men were Transjordanian).[145] What is interesting about this new situation was that most Transjordanians and Palestinian Jordanians believed that these indeed were essential and rigid accents that were national markers, when in fact, a large number of Palestinian refugees living in Jordan's refugee camps, and who hailed from rural backgrounds in the south, have always pronounced the *qaf* as *ga* and not as glottal stop. The difference between the two pronunciations, for these Palestinian refugees, remains one between an urban accent (madani) and a rural accent (fallahi). Increasingly, many Transjordanian nationalist feminist women are questioning the gender criterion of the accents and are beginning to use the *ga* to assert the equal-access nature of this new Jordanian nationalist marker.

The age criterion of this development is also noteworthy. As the accent became nationalized and gendered, urban Palestinian and Transjordanian prepubescent boys who use the glottal stop transform their pronunciation on reaching puberty in line with the *ga* pronunciation as another way of affirming their newly acquired masculinity. Most urban Transjordanians continue to speak with an urban accent and continue to use urban idioms with the slight change of their *ga* pronunciation. Transjordanians hailing from nonurban backgrounds, however, also have local idioms and expressions in addition to the *ga* pronunciation that urban Transjordanians do not use, as they retain their urban expressions. Moreover, there was and is no gender distinction between men and women in those sectors of Palestinian or Transjordanian society who spoke with a *ga* before the ideological co-optation of the *ga* by exclusivist nationalists. The gendering began with the process of nationalization.

It is important to note the vantage point of these judgments of accents as masculine or feminine. Whereas the *ga* pronunciation was being identified as tribal and Bedouin by both Transjordanians and urban Palestinian Jordanians, it was a Bedouin vantage point that was used in identifying the urban accent as feminine, a judgment that is in line with predominant Bedouin views of city folk, which denigrate and feminize them. This shows that the state's efforts to Bedouinize Jordanians were increasingly successful wherein the varied population had internalized the state-imposed nationalist definitions. Whereas the *hattas and shmaghs*, as sartorial gendered symbols, serve to identify the men who wear them visibly, the transformation of non-gendered, location-based accents (urban, rural, or desert Bedouin) into gendered national accents (Palestinian or Jordanian) became the universal *audible* marker of national identities in Jordan.

Anthropologically speaking, an interesting exercise to do in Jordan would be to locate the slips in everyone's accents, be they *assimilated* Palestinian-Jordanian men or nationalist Transjordanian *urban* men and women, especially when their *ga* slips into a glottal stop, as the new national mask becomes more difficult to wear all the time, because its artificiality is too recent and has yet to be completely naturalized. The nationalized *hatta/shmagh*, along with the nationalized accent, thus became corporeal and verbal performances that guarantee national identity. Affirming both pub-

licly became part of the daily rituals of staging Transjordanianness and Palestinianness.

Another aspect of further polarization in the Jordanian population was
the new reference to Palestinian Jordanians as Baljikiyyah, or, in line with
colloquial Jordanian/Palestinian Arabic, Baljikiyyih, meaning Belgians. It is
unclear what the origin of this anti-Palestinian epithet is, although a number
of stories circulate. The most credible states that the Palestinian guerrillas
wore Belgian-made military boots and fatigues, which distinguished them
from the U.S.-equipped Jordanian army. Other stories include that during
the 1970 civil war, many Transjordanians suggested that they get rid of the
Palestinians by shipping them to Belgium (a far-away country), or that there
was supposed to be some shipment of arms coming to the guerrillas from
Belgium (there is nothing in fact to support this claim). Still, *Baljikiyyih* is
intended to render Palestinian Jordanians foreign — non-Jordanian and non-
Arab — thus denationalizing them. This epithet continues to be used as a
national insult against Palestinian Jordanians today.

More expressions of Palestinian identity emerged in the late 1970s and
1980s leading to confrontations between the Jordanian state and Palestinian
Jordanians. One such example is the case of the Committee for the Annual
Palestinian Folklore Day, which was established in 1981 by Nimr Sarhan in
conjunction with other Palestinian institutions. Sarhan, a specialist in Palestinian folklore, was detained and later imprisoned by the government. His
passport was confiscated, and he was prevented from returning to his job.
His folklore exhibits and other cultural events were canceled by the police
or were the objects of police harassment.[146]

Other expressions of Palestinian-Jordanian and Transjordanian solidarity
with Palestinians outside Jordan were also muted. During Israel's 1978 invasion of Lebanon, many Palestinian Jordanians and Transjordanians volunteered to go to Lebanon to fight with the PLO. Large demonstrations
were held to push the government to permit the volunteers to go to Lebanon.
The government responded with bullets, killing a number of demonstrators
(mostly students and one teacher) and arresting a large number of them.
Many Transjordanians participated in these demonstrations, especially from
the town of Sahab, a neighbor of the Wihdat refugee camp southeast of
Amman. The king intervened, chastising the police and ordering the release
of those arrested, while at the same time the government issued directives
against the holding of any public demonstrations.[147] The situation repeated
itself after Israel's 1982 invasion of Lebanon, when many of the volunteers
were sent home by the Jordanian government after their passports were con-

fiscated and after being subject to intense interrogations by the Mukhabarat (Jordan's ubiquitous and highly efficient intelligence service).[148]

Moreover, as a number of cultural groups (dancing troupes and singing bands) were formed in the late 1970s at local initiative in the Palestinian and Transjordanian communities, the state sought to co-opt them with new initiatives. It was in this context that the state launched its project of the annual Jerash Festival of Culture (Mahrajan Jarash), which was inaugurated in the summer of 1981.[149] Despite the commercialism endemic to the festival, not to mention the privileging of foreign performers over Jordanian artists regardless of geographic origins, a number of local bands began to emerge on the national scene, while others were discouraged by not being granted permits to perform. The emerging groups include the talented and now popular al-Fuhays Band or Firqat al-Fuhays (formed in 1982), from the Christian Transjordanian town of al-Fuhays near Amman. The festival, whose head was Michel Hamarnah (a Transjordanian from Madaba), was criticized by many for its elitism.[150] Still, the Jerash Festival pushed for certain cultural performances over others. Bedouin male line-dancing, or Dabkah, and Bedouin songs were always featured. Although, outside of Samirah Tawfiq's "Bedouin" songs, few state-sponsored songs were ever popular, a new Bedouin singer emerged in the early 1990s with a song that came to be the most popular song sung by a Jordanian ever. The singer is 'Umar al-'Abdallat and his song was "Hashmi Hashmi" or "Hashemite Hashemite," whose refrain "our Jordan, the Hashemite" (Urdunna ya Hashmi) combined allegiance to the new Jordan and its king with an affirmation of Jordan's Hashemiteness. Al-'Abdallat followed with another popular "Bedouin" song called "Ya Sa'd" which, along with "Hashmi," is still played at wedding receptions (including those of middle- and upper-class Palestinian Jordanians) throughout the country as well as at night clubs. Palestinian-Jordanian groups, however, are still denied such backing by the state's cultural commissars.

Another battle that has raged in the country from the 1970s to the present is the football (soccer) battle. As in other nations, sports have come to play an important role in nationalist mobilization, both domestically and internationally. Jordan is not an exception in this regard. As in many ex-British colonies and mandates, football came to play an important role in the life of Jordanians.[151] It is said that two brothers (Husni and 'Ali Sidu al-Kurdi, of Iraqi Kurdish background, residing in Amman) brought the game back to Amman from Jerusalem in 1922, where they attended high school.[152] The Palestinians, of course, had been introduced to the game through the British

and through European missionary schools, which have a longer history in
Palestine than in Transjordan. The first football team was formed in 1926
and used to play against British teams stationed in Markah, outside Amman.
In 1943, King 'Abdullah took an interest in the different teams (many of
which were Circassian teams[153]) and instituted an annual competition (da-
wri) beginning in 1944.[154] That year, a Circassian club (the Ahli Sports
Club) was founded by young Circassian men who were fleeing the control
of their community elders, who controlled the Circassian Charity Association (founded in 1932).[155] The young men wanted to call their club the
Circassian Sports Club, but the governor of Amman objected to the name.
One of the members of the club was Amir 'Abdullah's driver. He brought
the matter before the amir, who told the young man, "My son, you are my
family [Ahl], so call it the Ahli club." [156] The Ahli club included Arab players
in it also.

In the early 1950s, football received a boost. The annexation of the West
Bank brought a number of Palestinian football teams to join the annual
competitions, in addition to the many Palestinian football players who joined
the East Bank teams, such as Jabra al-Zarqa' and Marcus Da'das, who joined
the Ahli club for a period.[157] Al-Zarqa' had played in the 1934 World Cup
football games.[158] Moreover, in the 1950s, the United Nations Relief and
Works Agency (UNRWA) set up some youth clubs in the refugee camps on
both banks, some of which (e.g., in the Wihdat refugee camp in the eastern
part of Amman) became major sports clubs in the 1970s.[159]

By the early 1960s, King Husayn launched the project of building a sports
city with a football stadium, as the country still did not have a single stadium.
Most of the teams used to play in the al-Husayni Mosque plaza downtown,
the Kuban playground in a Circassian neighborhood west of the city, a
number of playgrounds in Jabal 'Amman (including that of the Bishop
School for boys), and finally, from the late 1940s until 1968 when construction on the football stadium was completed, in the playground of al-Kulliyah
al-'Ilmiyyah al-Islamiyyah school in Jabal 'Amman. The first match played
in the new stadium was between the Jordanian and the Egyptian national
teams, and the outcome was 6 to 1 in favor of the Egyptians. Mu'nis al-
Razzaz, Jordan's well-known contemporary novelist, states that most of the
Jordanian youth in the country, who were Arab nationalists, rooted for the
Egyptian team. There were only a minority of Jordanian nationalists who
rooted for Jordan's team.[160]

To organize athletic activities in the country and to set a new plan in
motion for Jordan's youth, the government issued in 1968 the Law of the

Foundation of Care for the Youth.[161] In 1977, the foundation was placed under the institutional rubric of the ministry of culture and youth.[162] Jordanian government philosophy governing the kind of athletes Jordanians were supposed to be included the following: "The Jordanian athlete is a citizen who is loyal to his homeland, loving toward his parents, his family, his neighbors, and his co-citizens, brothers and sisters. He defends the honor of the homeland and of its soil, and seeks, as much as he is able, to improve his psychological, spiritual, physical and ethical abilities. . . . The Jordanian Athlete is a citizen whose manliness is strong [Qawiyy al-Rujulah], an adorer of heroism . . . who believes that Jordan is one cohesive family and that the Arab nation [al-Ummah al-ʿArabiyyah] is one big loving family."[163]

As is clear, sports here is staged as an arena for the performance of gendered citizenship by the nation-state, and, as will become clear shortly, by citizen-nationals themselves. Moreover, a Jordanian athlete, by definition, is said to be a nationalist who adheres to national unity ("one cohesive family") and is inhabited by a strong manliness in support of it. This coupling of gendered citizenship with sports is meant to nationalize sports and masculinity, and to render all sports activity a national performance, which is the supreme function that sports have within the modality of the nation-state.

With the waning of Arab nationalism after the death of ʿAbd al-Nasir, Jordanian football did not encounter much politics until the mid to late 1970s. UNRWA funding cuts deprived the refugee youth centers of paid staff to direct their activities. As a result, club members assumed responsibility for activities such as fund-raising, and they formed sports leagues that competed with each other annually in football, volleyball, basketball, and boxing. In 1975, the camp teams decided to compete with other Jordanian East Bank clubs and their teams.[164] The situation became explosive in 1980 when the Wihdat team won the annual competition (al-Dawri), defeating the Ramtha team. This gave a boost to refugee Palestinian Jordanians, especially of the Wihdat camp, who had taken a heavy human casualty toll during the civil war.[165] Supporting the Wihdat or the Ramtha team became a national act of loyalty to one's Palestinianness or Jordanianness, respectively. Absent any other legal political expression, these matches occasioned Palestinian protests and assertion of national identity. Many fights and brawls broke out between the Transjordanian and the Palestinian-Jordanian fans, leading to police intervention and the arrest of many. As Laurie Brand puts it, "For many fans, Palestinian and Transjordanian alike, each time a refugee camp team locked horns with an East Bank squad, it was, on a very basic and emotional level, as if the civil war were being fought again."[166]

After a particularly bloody confrontation in 1986, the Ministry of the Occupied Territories' Affairs asked UNRWA to surrender control of the youth centers. The ministry moved in and dissolved the administrative councils of the centers, replacing them with new councils consisting of many high-ranking government officials. Crown Prince Hasan renamed the Wihdat Youth Center, Nadi al-Diffatayn or "the Two Banks Club." Transjordanians were included in the administration of the club, in line with the Ministry of Youth's recommendation. With government pressure and the reorganized administrative council, a majority voted in favor of the crown prince's bid to rename the center. The situation lasted only a short time, as people continued to refer to the club and the team as Wihdat. In 1988, following the disengagement from the West Bank, administrators of the government and the center restored the original name of the club and the team—Nadi al-Wihdat. It is notable that in addition to Wihdat and other camp teams, most of the East Bank "Jordanian" teams include a large number of Palestinian-Jordanian players.

Football serves not only to divide the population, but, as happened more recently, also to unify them. At the Arab football championship held in Beirut in the summer of 1997, the Jordanian national team (composed of the best players from all Jordanian clubs including Wihdat) won the championship, defeating the Syrian national team. At the end of the game, which most of the people of Jordan watched on satellite television at home or in cafes, thousands of people and cars crowded the streets of Jordan's cities and towns, especially Amman, where cars stopped in the middle of the streets and young men and women danced, bringing traffic to a complete halt for hours. King Husayn chartered a plane to bring the players home from Beirut. On arrival, the team toured Amman's streets in a massive convoy, with supporters (men and women) lining all the major thoroughfares. Many Jordanian news columnists saw this as a sign of Palestinian-Jordanian unity under one Jordanian identity. Fahd al-Fanik, Jordan's most outspoken exclusivist Jordanian nationalist, stressed that this unity was certain, because it did not express itself against a non-Arab foreign team but against an *Arab* team, affirming that Palestinian Jordanians and Transjordanians inhabit the same national identity, at least in an international context.[167] When the games were held in Amman in August 1999, the Jordanian team played against the first Palestinian national team, which was formed under the Palestinian Authority. West Bank Palestinians, who had traditionally rooted for the Jordanian team, were now rooting for the new Palestinian team. The Palestinian team lost to the Jordanians, 4 to 1. Some clashes among fans ensued in the streets but were contained by the heavy police presence. It is interesting that eight of the eleven members of the Jordanian team are Palestinian Jordanians. During the game, the crowds chanted a rhyming couplet: "This is what al-Husayn taught us, one people, not two."[168] By all accounts, most Palestinian Jordanians, like their Transjordanian compatriots, supported the Jordanian team, especially because they were heavily represented in its ranks.

Contracting the Nation: The Road to "The Severing of Ties"

As the seventies proceeded, relations between the Jordanian state and the PLO remained at odds until Anwar Sadat's trip to Jerusalem in 1977. Attempts to disengage from the West Bank were put forth by Prime Minister Mudar Badran (a Transjordanian) in 1976 when he proposed that the Jordanian government cut off the salaries of West Bank Jordanian citizens who were state employees. Palestinian-Jordanian loyalists in the West Bank opposed the measure, and the proposal was not pursued. Although such tactics were used early in the seventies, their use in 1976 was signaling Jordan's realization that the Jordanianness of West Bankers could no longer be ascertained. That year, the mayoral elections that took place under Israeli occupation resulted in PLO mayors in all major cities except one. In Jordan, the proportion of Palestinian Jordanians in the cabinet was dropped from one half to one quarter, with many Palestinian-Jordanian government personnel dismissed and replaced by Transjordanians.[169] It was around the same time that Jordanian universities began an unofficial quota system for employing Transjordanian professors. Whereas Palestinian Jordanians, by virtue of their disproportionately high level of educational attainment, had dominated most faculties at the University of Jordan in the 1960s and 1970s, the new quota system drastically transformed these demographics. This situation, which proceeded more belligerently after 1989 and to the present, has resulted in emptying Jordan's state universities of Palestinian faculty, as few if any new positions go to Palestinian Jordanians.[170]

Following Sadat's move in 1977, Jordan and the PLO experienced a rapprochement. Relations in fact warmed up so much that the PNC, the Palestinian parliament-in-exile, was convened in Amman on November 21, 1984, and was addressed by none other than King Husayn himself. The king saluted the PNC with "an effusion of happy and loving feelings. . . . On Jordan's soil and in its name, I welcome you; and from the heights overlooking [masharif] Palestine, I send a salute of loyalty to the people of Palestine, and through you, the representatives of the Palestinian people, I salute every Palestinian. [We] welcome you in Amman, among its people, or rather, [we] welcome you among your people, your tribe ['Ashirah], your brethren and family, your brothers and your brothers-in-law; [we] welcome you in the vastness [rihab] of the twin brother [of Palestine], we welcome you in Jordan, the lighthouse of men and the castle of steadfastness."[171] The king proceeded to review Palestinian-Jordanian relations, with no mention of the civil war, stressing that Jordan had done its utmost to "prove to our Palestinian brethren Jordan's recognition of their national identity, and that Jordan has no ambitions on their land. . . . Your meeting here today under the umbrella of your National Council testifies to the victory of the Palestinian will, Palestinian legitimacy, Palestinian decision, and Palestinian determination to uphold one loyalty toward one goal, that of Palestine and the people of Palestine."[172]

Less than three months later, on February 11, 1985, Jordan and the PLO reached an agreement on Jordanian-Palestinian coordination. The rapprochement, however, did not last long. As Jordan and Syria (the latter considered by the PLO to be its archenemy in the Arab camp at the time) were restoring warm relations, Jordan began to move away from the PLO in February 1986, particularly because the United States was not responsive to Jordan's initiatives based on the February 11 agreement.

Jordan proceeded to make changes in its relationship to the West Bank, and in certain cases toward Palestinian Jordanians residing in East Bank refugee camps. This manifested itself in the new election law of 1986, where parliamentary seats were increased to 142, with each Bank assigned 71 seats. The change, however, was in the law's consideration of East Bank camps as West Bank districts, thus having eleven seats (one per camp) out of the seventy-one assigned to the West Bank reserved to the East Bank camps. This juridical rearrangement of geography and demography, wherein people who reside in actuality on the East Bank are considered West Bankers, was an Orwellian move designed to decrease alleged Palestinian political "influence" on the East Bank. In addition, the actual districting of the camps as separate from the districts within which they were located was a juridical act of separation of Palestinian-Jordanian refugees from Palestinian and Transjordanian Jordanians living outside the camps. This was an unprecedented move, as the 1960 election law did not include any such provisions.[173] This sentiment of separatism was shared by some in Parliament. For example, Zuhayr Dhuqan al-Husayn, a Transjordanian parliamentarian representing the northern city of Salt, proposed during parliamentary discussions of the law that East Bank Palestinian Jordanians not be permitted to vote for

East Bank candidates, and that they be allowed to vote only for West Bank candidates. He was heavily criticized by West Bank deputies, who asked that his proposal be removed from the minutes. Parliament voted against Mr. al-Husayn's measure and approved its removal from the minutes. However, Parliament approved a proposal banning West Bank Palestinians from nominating themselves for East Bank seats (which no candidate had ever done in the past), and vice versa.[174] Still, many opposed the new districting measures. Prominent among these was Jordan's former prime minister, and, until recently, member of the senate, Ahmad 'Ubaydat. 'Ubaydat saw the measures as creating divisions between Palestinian Jordanians and Transjordanians.[175]

With the eruption of the intifada in the West Bank and Gaza in December 1987, and its increasing militancy against Israeli occupation and for Palestinian independence, the Jordanian government opted to take its thirteen-year rhetoric and political measures (pursued since its recognition of the PLO in 1974 as the sole legitimate representative of the Palestinian people wherever they are) to their logical conclusion. Four months into the intifada, beginning in late April 1988, King Husayn delivered a number of speeches to tribal conventions in the country in which he stressed Jordan's support for the PLO as the sole legitimate representative of the Palestinian people and his support for the end of Israeli occupation and for an international peace conference at which the PLO would be represented.[176] In his speech to the tribal leaders of the Mafraq governorate, for example, the king stressed, "As for here, on this land [East Bank], everyone is equal, for we have inherited from our fathers and our forefathers the principles of the Great Arab Revolt . . . its purposes and its goals. . . . [F]or every Arab is a patriot [watani] regardless of the place from which his father or forefather came . . . he is a Jordanian with full rights but also one who has duties to respect the constitution and the [Jordanian] family to which he belongs. . . . My talk [of this] is for the purpose of strengthening national unity. . . . As for Palestine and our Jordanian brethren of Palestinian origins, we are with them and to them as we have always been and their rights there will be restored."[177]

Another important speech was delivered internationally in Algiers on June 7, 1988, at the opening of the Arab summit, in which the king affirmed Jordan's commitment to support the PLO and chastised critics of Jordan, who claimed that the help some Jordanian institutions were extending to the intifada was intended to achieve Jordanian hegemony on the West Bank to the detriment of the PLO.[178] These series of speeches were the dress rehearsal for what came to be known as the decision to sever legal and administrative ties between the East Bank and the West Bank, or Qarar Fakk al-Irtibat, which was announced in a now famous speech that the king delivered on July 31, 1988, thus ending, by royal decree, the Jordanian unity between the West Bank and the East Bank that had lasted thirty-eight years.[179] The day before the "severing" of ties, the king had dissolved Parliament.[180]

Indeed, as the king affirmed in his speech addressing the Jordanian people, "in your cities, villages, camps, tribal areas [fi madaribikum], factories, schools, offices and institutions," the severing of ties between the West and the East Banks "will not surprise you as many among you have been expecting it, and some of you have demanded it some time before it was made."[181] The king stressed that after a long and deep study of the issue, his government decided to undertake a series of measures aiming to "support the Palestinian national direction and to render prominent [ibraz] Palestinian identity, aiming [to achieve] through them the interests of the Palestinian Cause and the Palestinian Arab people."[182] These measures, which will help the PLO "to concretize Palestinian identity on Palestinian national soil," will result in the "*separation* of the West Bank from the Hashemite Jordanian Kingdom [emphasis added]."[183] The king stressed,

> It must be understood clearly, without any confusion or ambiguity, that our measures which are related to the West Bank only deal with the occupied Palestinian land and its people, and, naturally, not with Jordanian citizens of Palestinian origins in the Hashemite Jordanian Kingdom. All of these have full citizenship rights and duties exactly like any other citizen, irrespective of origin. They are a part, that cannot be subdivided [juz' la yatajazza'], of the Jordanian state to which they belong and on whose land they live and in whose life and entire activities they participate, for Jordan is not Palestine, and the Palestinian state will be established on the occupied Palestinian land after its liberation, God willing. . . . [T]hus, the preservation of national unity is a sacred matter with which we will not be lax [la tahawun fihi] and any attempt to manipulate ['abath] it under any slogan or title, will only be assisting the enemy in executing his expansionist policies at the expense of Palestine and Jordan equally. Hence, supporting and buttressing it [national unity] is true patriotism [wataniyyah] and authentic nationalism [qawmiyyah]. Thus, it is everyone's responsibility to preserve it so that there will not be among us any room for a misleading informer, or a traitor with ulterior motives, for we shall not be,

with God's help, except as we have always been, one cohesive family whose members are characterized by brotherhood, love and consciousness, and with combined patriotic and nationalist goals.[184]

As the link between the West Bank and the East Bank was severed, the government moved to denationalize Palestinian Jordanians residing in the West Bank. They were issued temporary, two-year Jordanian passports to facilitate their international travel, it being understood that these passports do not signify any national belonging to Jordan.[185] The decision to sever ties, however, was never published in the *Official Gazette* and thus it does not have the status of law, nor was it ever issued in a legal form, although many provisions based on it were (e.g., amendments to the election law, the passports law). Because the unity of both Banks is enshrined in Jordan's constitution, the decision to "separate" the West Bank from the kingdom, as many of its critics have pointed out, is in fact unconstitutional and therefore illegal. Until the present, no constitutional amendment has been issued or even contemplated by the regime or by Parliament. Cases against the government questioning the constitutionality of the denationalization of the West Bank and its Jordanian citizens are still pending in Jordan's courts.

Whereas the "unification" of Jordan and central Palestine in 1949 and 1950, like the establishment of Transjordan in 1921, was legitimated politically by appeals to Hashemite Arab nationalism and was effected through juridical measures, the "separation" of the West Bank from the East Bank in 1988 was carried out by appeals to regionally based Palestinian and Jordanian nationalisms and the repudiation of Hashemite Arab nationalism, and it was effected by new juridical measures (although the actual separation was carried out extra-juridically, as already mentioned, all commensurate measures to denationalize the West Bank and its Jordanian citizens were carried out juridically). The state's official adoption of an East Bank–based Jordanian nationalism as the new ideology (although central Palestine had been incorporated into Jordanianness in 1949–1950, the regime still insisted oxymoronically that, in that context, Jordanianness stood for Hashemite Arabness, which included both Banks) gave a strong push to societal forces, which the state and the regime had encouraged since the 1940s; these forces were calling for a separation between citizenship and nationality and asserting an exclusivist nationalism that excluded large segments of the citizen population as non-Jordanian. The societal forces were unleashed in 1989 after the partial democratic opening liberalized the press and the political process. They took the denationalization of the West Bank Jordanians as their cue and evidence that not all Jordanian citizens belong to the Jordanian nation, and that, as foreigners, they must therefore be excluded from it.

Who Is Jordanian?

Many East Bank Palestinian Jordanians are content to be both Jordanians and Palestinians; they realize that their Palestinian identity is thoroughly inflected by its development in the national context of Jordan, and for the majority among them Jordan is the only physical home they ever knew. They vehemently reject the recent attempts to de-Palestinize them by an exclusivist Jordanian nationalism. Moreover, although a large number of Palestinians supported the PLO in 1970, many others did not, evidenced by those who served the regime. In fact, only 5,000 (among them, Transjordanians) out of tens of thousands of military personnel actually defected to the guerrillas, and as Palestinians they have not staged any revolts against Jordan, not even during the 1970 civil war or in its aftermath (the 1986 University of Yarmuk student uprising, which was put down violently by Bedouin military units, was mostly composed of Palestinian Jordanians but also included Transjordanians—Communists, Islamists, and many others).[186] If anything, all internal military threats to the regime, as we saw in the last chapter, came from Transjordanian elements in the military. The more recent popular uprisings took place in southern, almost exclusively Transjordanian cities with no Palestinian-Jordanian participation whatsoever. The facts that after 1970 many Palestinian men, like Transjordanian urban men, began to speak in a hybrid accent of Palestinian and Jordanian; that since 1970, *mansaf*, Jordan's invented national dish, is cooked as often by urban Palestinians (who, unlike southern rural and Bedouin Palestinians, did not know it before) as by Transjordanians, and is served on certain occasions (e.g., weddings and funerals) as it is in the Transjordanian community; and that intermarriage between the two communities is so high in the cities that it would be difficult to disentangle the national "origins" of the offspring except through paternalist conceptions of nationality (as we saw in chapter 1), all attest to the conclusion that these aspects of state-sponsored Jordanian national identity are not repudiated but rather are adopted and internalized, and that they are not taken as substitutes for or competitive with Palestinian national identity but rather as complementary.

In fact, urban and rural Palestinian Jordanians, like urban non-Bedouin Transjordanians, have been susceptible to the state's Bedouinization of Jordanian identity, especially after 1970. They also use aspects of tribal law to resolve many social disputes (especially deaths resulting from car accidents and intentional or unintentional shootings) and to inaugurate important social occasions (such as the *Jahat al-Tulbah*, the man's family delegation asking for a woman's hand in marriage, which was practiced only among the rural and Bedouin but not the urban Palestinian population before). Indeed, Jordan's football victory in the summer of 1997 over Syria was seen as a victory by Palestinian Jordanians, too, because they recognize themselves as Jordanians in this inter-Arab context, wherein many of the Jordanian players are Palestinian Jordanians. This situation became even clearer when Palestinian Jordanians supported the Jordanian national team against the Palestinian national team in 1999. Transjordanian exclusivist nationalists were watching the crowds with a hawk's eye for any signs of national "disloyalty." This litmus test that the exclusivists require is predicated on their belief that the Jordanian national team represents "Jordan" as defined by their exclusivist terms. Palestinian Jordanians, however, view it clearly as inclusivist and thus as reflective of *their* own national presence in the country and therefore see no contradiction in supporting it. What the exclusivists demand as a litmus test, however, is for the Palestinian Jordanians to view the team as Jordanian in an exclusivist way and still support it. It is unclear if similar tests would be required of Transjordanian Christian or Muslim nationalists, or Transjordanian Arab or Circassian nationalists, or Transjordanian northern or southern nationalists, if members of one community were competing against members of the other, or of the Chechen community if the Jordanian national team were playing against the Chechen national team. If the results of these tests reveal the limits of Jordanian national identity and its constitutive parts, then, for the sake of consistency, they should be required of all of Jordan's varied communities. The fact that it is Palestinian Jordanians who are the main group subjected to this inquisition shows how much their recent production as an "other" has become the organizing principle of constituting the new Jordanian "self."

Following an uprising in the south protesting Jordan's economic austerity measures imposed by the International Monetary Fund (IMF) in mid April 1989, the Jordanian government decided to liberalize its political system. This resulted in the expansion of debates in the Jordanian public sphere, and media outlets, mainly independent newspapers, began to emerge from all corners of the political spectrum. One of the most pressing of the debates that occupied the Jordanian public sphere since then has been the question of Jordanian national identity and whether East Bank Palestinian Jordanians can be part of it.[187] The tone of these debates became much more acrimonious following the signing of the Oslo Accords between Yasir 'Arafat and Israel on September 13, 1993, with Transjordanian Christian voices being some of the loudest (although many Transjordanian Christians actually fought on the side of the PLO against the Jordanian army during the civil war,[188] and some of them, such as Nayif Hawatmah, head of the Democratic Front for the Liberation of Palestine, became leaders in the Palestinian movement[189]). Fahd al-Fanik and Nahid Hattar stand out as two of the most exclusivist voices in the Transjordanian Christian community (Hattar in fact faced a lawsuit for his editorial "Who is a Jordanian?"[190]). They are paralleled in the Muslim community by Ahmad 'Uwaydi al-'Abbadi[191] (also facing a lawsuit) and former director of public security and current speaker of Parliament 'Abd al-Hadi al-Majali, to list just two.[192] Hattar, in an infamous newspaper article, marvels at how the Jordanian political regime was able to invert the "historical formula" that stresses that "the people are constant while regimes of government change" into a new formula whereby "in Jordan, the regime of government is constant while the people change."[193] For Hattar, those who are Jordanians include those living in the three Ottoman Mutasarrifiyyahs that became Transjordan, added to whom are the Syrians, Palestinians, Hijazis (in reference to the Hashemites), Circassians, and Chechens who were "Jordanized in a natural manner and were dissolved into this country's flesh and greatness." Hattar stresses that "Jordanians . . . do not increase except through natural reproduction and not through élite political decisions." He proceeds to depict Palestinians who were Jordanized after 1948 as playing the same role in Jordan that the Zionists play in Palestine. Hattar, uses his vehement support for the establishment of a Palestinian state on Palestinian land to stress that it is "the right of Palestinians—the refugees and the displaced ["Laji'in wa Nazihin," those made refugees in 1948 and 1967, respectively]—indeed their duty is to return to their lands and homes." This call for the expulsion of post-1948 Palestinian Jordanians is the core of Hattar's ideology of returning Jordan to a pre-Palestinian past as a way of asserting the Jordanians' "full and non-lacking sovereignty over their land." For him, the Palestinians' presence in Jordan is a triumph for Zionism. Therefore, "Jordanizing the Palestinians means the Judaization of Palestine." Hattar concludes that, for all these reasons, "the Jordanian, precisely, specifically and exclusively, *is the non-Palestinian* [emphasis added]." Hattar is quite clear that the marks of modern Jordanian culture and cultural heritage are fabricated by the state and the regime. He sees Jordanians who support the regime and its policy of Jordanizing Palestinians as not real Jordanians but as fabrications by the regime and by the state, although they may speak "in the name of Jordan, Jordani-anness, the [Bedouin] coffee pot, the [Bedouin] tent and that leftover dish [al-Tabkhah al-Ba'itah Iyyaha in reference to mansaf]."[194] Hattar's reference to the three original Mutasarrifiyyahs demonstrates his confusion. As we saw in chapter 2, these three Mutasarrifiyyahs included parts of Syria and Pal-estine and excluded the southern third of the country from Ma'an to 'Aqaba (although Ma'an had been part of the Karak Mutasarrifiyyah for a while before its inclusion in the Hijaz and later annexation to Transjordan in 1925, 'Aqaba shuttled between Egypt and the Hijaz of which it remained part until the 1925 annexation). Moreover, it is unclear why these so-called res-idents of the Mutasarrifiyyahs are considered the real Jordanians. Many among those residents were themselves recent arrivals from Palestine, Syria, Iraq, Egypt, and the Caucasus, who had been residents for no more than four to five decades before the establishment of the state. If their length of stay in the country is the operative criterion, then this would apply equally to Palestinian Jordanians who arrived in the country in 1948 and who, by now, have lived in Jordan for just as many decades. Hattar's views were not unique: Marwan al-Sakit, a Muslim Transjordanian nationalist, proposed that Palestinian Jordanians answer the Palestinian Authority's call to accept Palestinian passports, give up their Jordanian citizenship, and work in the country as foreign labor, as other Palestinians do in the Gulf.[195]

To be sure, the discourse of exclusivist Jordanian nationalists has a ma-terial basis, which is in turn interpreted through a nationalist interpretive grid. This goes back to the dawn of the Transjordanian-Palestinian relation-ship in the country. To begin with, they view the arrival of Palestinian ref-ugees in the country in 1948 as having had a negative impact on Jordan's economic situation. As state financial resources were stretched to their limits, Transjordanians suffered measurably. Many Transjordanian exclusivist na-tionalists point to that period as important, wherein the Palestinian refugees, as recipients of UNRWA largesse, were better off than the poorer Transjor-danians who had to compete with the Palestinians for meager state resources without access to UNRWA benefits. Moreover, the influence of the mer-chant class (composed largely of Palestinians and Syrians and a small num-ber of Transjordanians) on the regime was seen as detrimental to the majority of Transjordanians, who were heavily employed in the public sector (in both the military and the state bureaucracy). The failure of the economy in the late 1980s and the IMF-induced drive for privatization was viewed by exclu-sivist Jordanian nationalists as detrimental to the economic welfare of Transjordanians, as the beneficiaries of privatization would inevitably be the country's merchant class and foreign capital at the expense of the bureaucracy. To these nationalists, this signaled a loss of bureaucratic power, which, as mentioned earlier, was one of the mainstays (along with the military) of Transjordanian influence in the country.

What these exclusivist nationalists fail to account for, however, is that privatization, in addition to benefiting the existing merchant class, was in fact expanding the ranks of the Transjordanian bourgeoisie by accelerating a Transjordanian exodus from the overinflated bureaucracy to the private sector through preferential treatment. Most of the new bids solicited by the state and its bureaucracy were given to Transjordanians (albeit of settled origins or of northern Bedouin origins), who are also the beneficiaries of bureaucratic favoritism on account of Transjordanian hegemony in the bureaucracy. Members of the existing merchant class (who are mostly of Palestinian and Syrian origins) have complained privately of loss of business to this new class of Transjordanians, as well as of bureaucratic discrimination by state institutions. Some see privatization as a sort of "affirmative action" redistribution of wealth from the ranks of the existing business class to the new bureaucratic-cum-business class composed of Transjordanians. The difficulties facing the Palestinian-Jordanian business elite are such that they have recently "resorted to employing Transjordanians whose job it is to ensure that their company's official transactions get through the obstructive bureaucracy."[196] Adnan Abu ʿAwdah, who recently served as advisor to King ʿAbdullah II, states in a recent book, "Some Palestinian-Jordanian businesspeople who returned to Jordan in the wake of the Iraqi invasion of Kuwait and the Gulf War (1990–1991) have adopted the Gulf states' model, in which one cannot start a business without an indigenous partner. When such business people do not find a willing Transjordanian with whom to start a business, they resort to seducing one with free shares. The higher the Transjordanian's official connections the better. Ironically, then, the discriminatory attitude of the Transjordanian bureaucracy has generated new jobs and perhaps a different means of redistributing income."[197]

After the U.S. publication of his book, which details discrimination against Palestinian Jordanians in the country, a major campaign in the press was launched against Abu ʿAwdah by, among others, the Christian Transjordanian nationalists Fahd al-Fanik and Tariq Masarwah. In April 2000, Abu ʿAwdah was asked by the king to submit his resignation, which he immediately did. ʿUrayb Rantawi, a Palestinian-Jordanian columnist, spoke of how Jordanian society had a division of labor, wherein Palestinian Jordanians (who are mostly employers and employed in the private sector) pay state taxes while Transjordanians (mostly employed in the bureaucracy and the military) consume them.[198] These nationalist discourses completely elide the class differentiation in both communities. The reality of the matter is that the southern, poorer part of the country, like the urban poor throughout Jordan's cities, is suffering disproportionately, as most southern Transjordanians are more dependent on the state for employment. As the state bureaucracy contracts, so do their incomes. As for the poor urban Palestinian Jordanians, thanks to IMF and World Bank policies, they can no longer eke out a living in a globalized economy.

Concomitant with these developments was the second Gulf war, which led to the arrival of between 200,000 and 300,000 Palestinian-Jordanian refugees from Kuwait and other Gulf states, further stretching state resources and worsening an already weakened economy. This led to more impoverishment of Jordan's poor population (both Palestinian and Transjordanian). Exclusivist nationalists saw this as "drowning" Transjordanians deeper in a "sea" of Palestinians that only gets bigger with time. The protests of these exclusivist nationalists became even louder.

What is problematic, however, in this nationalist discourse of nation-class is that the exclusivist nationalists positing it see the Palestinian segment of the merchant class as representing *all* the Palestinians in the country. Whereas the Transjordanian section of the merchant class has increased measurably in the last two decades (capital accumulation in this sector resulted from profits made during the 1970s land speculation drive, as most of the country's land is owned by Transjordanians, and from IMF-induced privatization since 1989), these accounts ignore such developments. In fact, conspiracy theories among these exclusivist nationalists abound. One conspiracy theory sees any Palestinian land purchases in the country as attempts to transfer lands from Transjordanians to Palestinians as part of a larger project of transforming Jordan into a Palestinian state.

Jordanian Christians have come to play a very important role in these debates, ranging from the Communist left to the neo-liberal right. Figures such as Jamal al-Sha'ir, Tariq Masarwah, Mustafa Hamarnah, Marwan Mu'ashshir, and Ya'qub Zayyadin occupy very different positions on the Jordanian political spectrum, although, with the exception of Zayyadin, they remain within the official establishment (Hamarnah's more recent fall from grace with al-Rawabdah's government notwithstanding). Zayyadin, the celebrated head of the underground Jordanian Communist Party for decades, has come out recently claiming that the PLO was the one who "destroyed the relationship between Palestinians and Jordanians [in 1970]," and also as a supporter of the cause for the rehabilitation of the right-wing anti-Palestinian Wasfi al-Tall, Jordan's late prime minister, among the Trans-jordanian left—an increasingly popular cause among Transjordanian nationalists in recent years.[199] This cause is espoused equally by Christian and Muslim Transjordanian nationalists, and increasingly by erstwhile leftists such as the novelist Mu'nis al-Razzaz (a Muslim whose father is Syrian-born and whose mother is Palestinian-born), who continues to be critical of the regime, albeit mildly.[200] Conferences honoring Wasfi al-Tall's contributions to Jordan's history as well as those of the late Prime Minister Hazza' al-Majali were recently sponsored by the ministry of culture and the Jordanian Center for Studies and Information (headed by Bilal Hasan al-Tall). Al-Tall and al-Majali have become canonical figures for Transjordanian nationalism, a choice that is hardly mitigated by the belief that Palestinians or their cohorts are blamed for assassinating both of them.[201]

Following the signing of the peace agreement with Israel, the Jordanian government contemplated three candidates for the position of the country's first ambassador to the Jewish state. These candidates, Aktham al-Qusus, Kamil Abu Jabir, and Marwan al-Mu'ashshir, are all Transjordanian Christians. Mu'ashshir was finally chosen. Many Transjordanian nationalists (although certainly not all) are as committed to an anti-Palestinian-Jordanian chauvinism as they are to supporting the establishment of a Palestinian state and to opposing the Jordanian peace agreement with Israel (Nahid Hattar stands out in this group). Their international support for non-Jordanian Palestinians is not in contradiction with their national anti-Palestinian positions, as the two can be complementary—if Palestinians have a state to go to, they will no longer have to be in Jordan. This position, in fact, is neither unique nor new. Since the nineteenth century, European anti-Semites (including subsequently the Nazis for a time) have always supported Zionism while attacking Jews in their communities, as anti-Semites and Zionists were equally committed to emptying Europe of Jews and transporting them elsewhere. This comparison is not to suggest that exclusivist Jordanian nationalists are necessarily like the Nazis (as the most extreme among them have never called for anything beyond "repatriating" the Palestinians) but simply to illustrate that there are non-Jordanian precedents to such arguments.[202]

This new anti-Palestinian exclusivist nationalism should be contrasted with the support Transjordanians had given to the Palestinians after the 1920s and especially in the second half of the 1930s, when the Palestinians staged their now famous anticolonial revolt. During that period, as explained in chapter 1, anticolonial Jordanian nationalism saw itself as Arab, and British colonialism as its "other." Although some groups attempted to build on the nativist struggle of 1920s, their attempt to build an exclusivist Jordanian nationalism in the 1930s failed. It was this Arab dimension of the Jordanian nationalism of the 1930s that propelled it to support the Palestinians. Immediately after the declaration of the Palestinian revolt, Jordanian anticolonial nationalists held a conference at Umm al-'Amad in June 1936 and called for the collection of money and arms, which they sent with hundreds of Jordanian volunteers to Palestine to fight alongside the Palestinians. At the time, the government, which could not stop them, opted to open up the Arab Legion for volunteers. Later, the Amir 'Abdullah prevented Transjordanians from traveling to Palestine. The government also responded to the Umm al-'Amad conference by banning all political meetings, and it threatened its attendants with arrest. When many of them attended the solidarity conference in Bludan, Syria, in September 1937, they were arrested on returning to the country. In addition, many Palestinian rebels who sought refuge in Transjordan were hidden in people's homes and treated by Jordanian physicians. This was in addition to massive demonstrations that were held in Amman in solidarity with the Palestinians. Jordanian rebels, furthermore, undertook a campaign of sabotage of British installations in the country, including cutting off telephone lines and bombing petroleum pipelines going from Iraq to Haifa. Moreover, by early 1937, Jordanian rebels attacked government buildings throughout the country (in Irbid, Salt, Madaba, 'Ajlun, and Tafilah, and even in small towns such as Kafr Najd, Umm al-Rumman, and Karimah, where they attacked police stations). The rebellion continued until the spring of 1939. The Arab Legion under Glubb and the British air force were sent in hot pursuit of the rebels, cornering them in 'Ajlun and killing many of them. Ten airplanes were used to strafe the positions of the rebels. With the defeat of the Palestinian revolt, the Jordanian rebels were also defeated. They fled to the Syrian border where they engaged in a battle with Glubb's forces. Many were killed and injured. Some fled into Syria, and others were caught and tried.[203]

The Arab dimension of Jordanian anticolonial nationalism continued in the forties, with the rise of the Group of al-Shabab al-Ahrar, or the Free Youth, who were influenced by Subhi Abu-Ghanimah of national congress fame. This group was suppressed, leading to the exile of many of its leaders. Those who remained continued to attack the mandate and the colonial relations that continued after independence was nominally granted in 1946. They formed a new party called the Jordanian Arab Party, which the recently self-declared King 'Abdullah refused to license. The king was able to co-opt some party members, however, by including them as ministers in the government. These included Sulayman al-Nabulsi and what was called at the time the Damascus intellectuals (in reference to Jordanians who obtained their high school or university education in Damascus); some among them were close to the regime but opposed British presence in the country.[204]

Whereas in the 1920s, Jordanian national identity was initially formed representing nativist interests against a foreign British-Hashemite state staffed by the British and by a coterie of Arabs from neighboring countries, it later adopted a pan-Arab nationalist vision, which manifested itself in the 1930s through active solidarity with the neighboring Palestinians' struggle against the British and the Zionists, and during the 1940s through its continued opposition to the British and their presence in Jordan after independence in 1946. Its pan-Arab vision was further strengthened in the 1950s through 'Abd al-Nasir's Arab unionist nationalism. Concomitant with the Arab nationalist identity that was solidified during the 1950s, however, a particularist/exclusivist Jordanian nationalist trend was emerging. The arrival of Palestinians in 1948, along with the annexation of the West Bank, inaugurated this trend, which was given a push after the assassination of King 'Abdullah by a Palestinian in 1951. Exclusivist nationalists attempted to draw comparisons between their post-1948 exclusivist nationalism and the nativist opposition in the 1920s to the colonial and Hashemite apparatus. This trend continued during the 1950s, albeit checked by Arab nationalism until the end of the decade, and it acquired momentum in the 1960s after the failure of the Egypto-Syrian union, which signaled a major blow to unionist Arab nationalism. The trend was further strengthened by the emergence of the Palestinian guerrilla groups that threatened Jordanian regime claims to represent Palestinian lands (the West Bank) and the Palestinian people (those who became Jordanian citizens after 1948), and by the *coup de grâce* delivered to Unionist Arab nationalism by the 1967 June War. This particularist/exclusivist Jordanian nationalist trend was finally solidified in 1970 during and after the civil war between the Jordanian armed forces and the Palestinian guerrillas.

Whereas the Jordanian nativist identity, and subsequently Jordanian Arab nationalist identity, saw foreign colonial powers as the *other* against whom they defined themselves, the particularist/exclusivist Jordanian national identity that was developing since the 1950s, and that was solidified after 1970, saw Palestinian Jordanians as the *other* against whom it defined itself. Following the 1988 disengagement from the West Bank and the 1989 liberalization of the regime, exclusivist Jordanian nationalists emerged in the open as enemies of Palestinian Jordanians. For them, the very presence of Palestinian Jordanians in Jordan had placed Jordanian national identity in jeopardy. Mustafa Wahbah al-Tall's 1920s nativist cry "Jordan for the Jordanians" was appropriated and mobilized by these exclusivist nationalists against the Palestinians. However, their discourse of exclusivist nationalism not only is based on the internal history of Jordan vis-à-vis its Palestinian-Jordanian citizens, but also results from increasing Israeli claims since the 1970s that Jordan *is* the real Palestine and thus should be converted into a Palestinian state. With the recent impasse in the Arab-Israeli peace process and recent claims made by Israeli Likud leaders, and even by Labor leader Haim Ramon, the second man in the Israeli Labor Party, who claimed in 1999 that Jordan will certainly be transformed into a Palestinian state in a few years, Jordanian exclusivist nationalists have increased their attacks on the Palestinian *other*.[205]

With the increase of the anti-Palestinian exclusivist discourse in the press, King Husayn, in exasperation, asserted on September 19, 1993, in response to those who were fostering national disunity in the country, that "here, we must concentrate on national unity; and as for anyone who hurts a brother with an injurious word or with harm, or expresses a sense of superiority [yuzayid], I shall be his enemy till Judgment Day."[206] The king reiterated similar sentiments in October, affirming that "our national unity is too strong for it to be harmed . . . and he who harms it is not of us."[207] He continued to call for equality for all Jordanians "of all origins and birthplaces" ("min jami' al-usul wa al-manabit") until his death, as does his son, King 'Abdullah II.[208]

Jordan's journey of expansion and contraction, however, did not end with the 1988 "severing of ties." Jordan's territorial and demographic expansion of 1949 to 1950 was only partially reversed, as the Palestinian population interpellated as Jordanian in 1949, a major segment of which continues to reside on the East Bank, remains Jordanian. Whereas Jordan fully reversed its territorial expansion of 1950 by renouncing sovereignty over the West Bank in 1988, the denationalization of West Bank Palestinian Jordanians was only a partial demographic contraction. Although 1988 acted as the inaugural moment for the release of the new and exclusivist Transjordanian nationalism in light of this contraction, much of this new and eruptive nationalist exclusivism was not directed at the parts of the nation that had just been severed but rather at an internal part whose status remains tenuous, namely Palestinian Jordanians who were nationalized after 1948 and who are residents of the East Bank.

Jordan as a territory and as a people has proved to be quite elastic, expanding and contracting while retaining an unchanging territorial core, the Jordan of 1925, and a demographic core, the various peoples who lived in the country until 1948. This expansion and contraction were produced both politically and juridically. Still, it is not only post-1948 Palestinian Jordanians who are being targeted—although they remain the easiest and most frequently chosen target: many nationalists question the Jordanianness of many other groups in the country, Syrians, Circassians, Chechens, and even some of the Bedouin tribes themselves. Fahd al-Fanik launched a campaign beginning in 1994, assailing Jordanian Chechens for being active in providing help to the Chechen republic besieged by Russian troops, and calling on them to choose one identity, Jordanian or Chechen, as if the two need to be mutually exclusive.[209] No one has yet joined al-Fanik's anti-Chechen inquisition. Ahmad 'Uwaydi al-'Abbadi, the well-known author of books on the Bedouins and a current member of Parliament, until recently considered the indigenous Jordanian al-'Adwan tribe "non-Jordanian."[210] Many in the new camp of exclusivist nationalists, such as al-'Abbadi and Hattar, are also questioning the Jordanianness of the Hashemites themselves, and consequently, the latter's right to rule the country.[211] These debates continue to rage in Jordan. Increasing divisions between northerners and southerners, present since the inception of the state, are also evident. The king's use of prime ministers hailing from the south in recent years (Majali is from Karak and Kabariti is from Aqaba) is further aggravating the problem, especially because the military has always been the mainstay of southern power. The more recent appointment of 'Abd al-Ra'uf al-Rawabdah and 'Ali Abu al-Raghib (both northerners) by King 'Abdullah II seems to have restored the balance. Moreover, the continuing backward economy of the south compared to the more prosperous north is making the south (historically perceived as more loyal to the regime) the hotbed of instability, as evidenced by uprisings in 1989, 1996, and 1998, all of which erupted in southern cities.

The recent uprising in February 1998 in the southern city of Ma'an is important to note in this regard, especially in relation to the way the regime dealt with it. Because of the increased threat of a U.S. military attack on Iraq in February 1998, demonstrations opposed to U.S. aggression against an Arab country began to rage throughout the Arab world. This also included Jordan, where demonstrations took place in a number of cities, from Irbid in the north to Ma'an in the south. The Ma'an demonstrations turned violent as the police and the Special Forces (headed at the time by the king's eldest son, Prince 'Abdullah) intervened violently to quell the demonstrations, which the government had outlawed. One person was killed and twenty-five injured, including a number of police officers. It is said that Saudi flags were flown by the demonstrators. The king ordered the deployment of the army in the city, which was immediately placed under curfew. The government also cut off all phone lines connecting Ma'an to the outside world. The king, in full military uniform, flew in his chopper to Ma'an and met with army units as well as with Ma'an's tribal leaders in an attempt to placate (some say chastise) them. The regime was distressed over the assertion by Ma'anis of their Arab identity, whose *other* is colonialism/imperialism. As Jordanians felt besieged by colonial/imperialist powers again, their Arab identity reasserted itself, manifesting its other as the colonial and imperialist powers, as it had done on numerous other occasions before (especially in the 1950s). The king's strategy was to remind Ma'anis that they are Jordanians first. In light of the events in Ma'an, he stressed that the "riots" were an insult to Jordan and to Ma'an and that they were the work of foreign infiltrators. He spoke to army officers, telling them that some "infiltrators and those with ulterior motives" have fomented discord in "Ma'an from which the beginning of the foundation of the kingdom was launched."[212] The king is referring to the fact that Ma'an had been the launching point of 'Abdullah's nation-state project back in 1921. The king also spoke of "Ma'an the origin" and "Ma'an the history."[213] He further added that Jordan might be engulfed with refugees as a result of a U.S. attack on Iraq and a possible expulsion of the Palestinians eastwards by Israel, thus "realizing the alternative-homeland [project] wherein Jordan would be finished."[214] In doing so, the king was attempting to shift the attention of Jordanians and Ma'anis from their larger Arab identity, whose other is colonialism, to their exclusivist Jordanian identity, whose other is the Palestinians, an identity, despite its attendant risks, that is safer for regime survival.[215]

Whereas the Jordanian state effectively used the post-1948 Palestinian Jordanians as an *other* to consolidate a Jordanian national identity, of which it was the initial architect and subsequent sponsor, it could no longer control the independent momentum that this identity later acquired, and which, if anything, could turn against the monarchy itself, thus redefining the Jordanian state that had been organized around the monarchy since its inception. In fact, the state's attempt to Jordanize Palestinians was always in contradiction to its express policy at many moments since 1948 to foster divisions between Transjordanians and Palestinians (especially in the late 1960s and early 1970s) in order to prevent any class alliances between the two groups that might turn against the monarchy itself.[216] However, whereas the Palestinians' presence in the country was a *sine qua non* for the consolidation of an exclusivist Jordanianness, it no longer plays that role exclusively. Jordanian national identity, like all national identities, is in flux today. As a reactive identity—and indeed all identities are reactive—it seems to have a better idea of what it is not than of what it actually is. Whereas the exclusivist nationalists insist on a further contraction of the nation into yet smaller and smaller segments and tribes, Palestinian Jordanians, in defense of their national citizenship rights, insist on their status as Palestinians and Jordanians simultaneously. Although the current trends in the country range from an ambivalent state policy that hovers between exclusivism and inclusivism to Palestinian Jordanians, torn between Jordanian and Palestinian national identities, to exclusivist Transjordanians, who want to subdivide the nation into smaller and more parochial groupings, Jordanian national identity (which includes in it Palestinianness and Transjordanianness) is waiting for a new definition. What that will be will depend on the ultimate victor or victors in these raging battles. Indeed, this political and juridical national journey, which, as we saw in chapter 1, began as a debate between British colonial officials on whether Transjordan should have a "nationality" at all, or if its population should be called, in the words of Winston Churchill, "Transjordanian Palestinians," has been a productive one.[217] What started as a British-Hashemite idea has exceeded its architects' intentions, their designs, and, most of all, their control. As we have seen through the course of this book, this was to be achieved through a series of juridical and military procedures and measures and the cultural productions they generated. These not only repressed existing identities and cultural practices but also produced a Transjordanian national identity and the national culture this identity came to constitute.

Unless the new Jordanian nationalism reconstitutes itself in terms that are not oppositional to and exclusive of Palestinian Jordanians and redefines itself in an inclusive manner to include all those who are citizens of the state, the future of Jordan and its Palestinian-Jordanian citizens will be far from stable. By charting the inclusivist history of Jordanian national identity, its new exclusivist manifestation is shown to be contingent on specific historical conditions, and on juridical and military strategies that are far from permanent. Through inclusive policies (especially juridical and military) and an inclusive nationalist discourse, the Jordanian government and Jordanian nationalists might be able to unify the country under identities that are not mutually exclusive, thus averting a second civil war in which all Jordanians, no matter what their geographic origins might be, will be the losers.

Concluding Remarks

This study has demonstrated how the colonial institutions of law and the military play both a repressive and a productive role in the constitution of postcolonial national identity and national culture. This is accomplished through the institutionalization of a juridical-disciplinary dyad, which constitutes the colonial and postcolonial modes of governance.

Transjordan, a territory carved from the Ottoman Empire, was rearranged territorially and demographically by British colonialism and the Hashemite Amir ʿAbdullah and ushered into a new age, the age of the nation-state. To render the new order permanent, a number of strategies were created that led to the imposition of a new identity, called *national*, on a population that adhered to a different set of identities. The new identity began as a juridical invention. Through a number of juridical and military strategies, this identity was generalized, normalizing and unifying a disparate population.Even what came to constitute Jordanian national culture, a set of practices identified as "traditional" and "national," was produced through these institutions, which in the process repressed and destroyed existing cultural practices while generating new processes that produced new cultural practices and identities. The new identity and the new national culture were then deployed not as the new products, which they in fact were, but as eternal essences that had always existed. Jordanian popular nationalism, like its postcolonial counterparts in the rest of Asia and Africa, was to internalize the new identity and its culture without any acknowledgment of their recent juridical and military genealogy. In fact, Jordanian nationalism today is predicated on the denial of this genealogy, and it posits instead a "national" history throughout which Jordanian identity is said to have always existed.

The production of national identity and national culture was also shown to be a gendered project. Women and men occupy different discursive positions within it. Masculinity and femininity are nationalized and given "national" valuations as reflective of "past traditions." These "traditions," which were produced as such by the juridical-disciplinary state, determine the status of men and women within the nation-state and guide the behavior of citizen-nationals today.

Conventional studies of national identity have not paid much attention to law and the military as "nationalizing" institutions. The extent to which some studies posited the military as an organ of nationalization at all, they failed to explicate how the military played that role internally within its ranks and externally vis-à-vis society. In this study, I have introduced a mode of inquiry that helped unravel the complicated roles that the law and the military have played in constructing national identity and national culture in a colonized and a postcolonial context, namely Jordan. Whereas the results of this inquiry may be specific to Jordan, the questions it asks are not. In using this mode of inquiry, students of nationalism will be able not only to answer questions that traditional methods have not, but also to formulate new questions that conventional approaches could not pose.

This study has described the different strategies used by the nation-state of Jordan to create an identity that is crucial to the reproduction of the nation-state itself. The result is a Jordanian national identity and national culture that think of themselves in essentialist terms. Like other postcolonial national identities, Jordanian national identity and Jordanian national culture are products and effects of colonial institutions. Perhaps anticolonial nationalism's main manifestation of its agency was its opposition to colonial rule and colonial racial hierarchies that denied the colonized their agency. However, the ontological status of anticolonial nationalism changes with the historical moment. By appropriating colonial discourse, anticolonial nationalism was able to subvert it and resist it, leading to the end of colonial rule. Its subsequent refusal, however, to question colonial modes of governance and the very precepts of colonial epistemology, except for its place in them, meant its abdication of agency to colonial law and discipline. Instead of understanding their anticolonial nationalism as a *strategic* essentialism to fight colonial power, anticolonial nationalists mistook their nationalism for an absolute essence.[1]

After the end of formal colonialism, national identities and cultures in the postcolonies are not only modes of resistance to colonial power, they are also the proof of colonialism's perpetual victory over the colonized. The irony of this is in having us believe that this colonial subjection and subjectivation *is* anticolonial agency.

Notes

Introduction

1. See Ernest Gellner, *Nations and Nationalism* (Ithaca, NY: Cornell University Press, 1983).

2. See Benedict Anderson, *Imagined Communities, and Reflections on the Origin and Spread of Nationalism* (London: Verso, 1991), originally published in 1983.

3. See Partha Chatterjee's important criticisms of these approaches in his *Nationalist Thought and the Colonial World: A Derivative Discourse* (Minneapolis: University of Minnesota Press, 1993), pp. 1–35.

4. Frantz Fanon, *The Wretched of the Earth* (New York: Grove Press, 1968), pp. 148–205.

5. On the Indian case, see Partha Chatterjee, *The Nation and Its Fragments: Colonial and Postcolonial Histories* (Princeton, NJ: Princeton University Press, 1993), p. 15.

6. Michel Foucault, *Discipline and Punish: The Birth of the Prison*, translated by Alan Sheridan (New York: Vintage Books, 1979), p. 82.

7. Ibid., p. 128.

8. Ibid., pp. 128–129.

9. Ibid., p. 216.

10. Michel Foucault, "Governmentality," in *The Foucault Effect: Studies in Governmentality, with Two Lectures by and an Interview with Michel Foucault*, edited by Graham Burchell, Colin Gordon, and Peter Miller (Chicago: University of Chicago Press, 1991), pp. 87–104.

11. Foucault, "Governmentality," p. 102.

12. Michel Foucault, *The History of Sexuality*, vol. I: *An Introduction*, translated by Robert Hurley (New York: Vintage Books, 1980), p. 89.
13. Antonio Gramsci, "The Intellectuals," in *Selections from the Prison Notebooks*, edited and translated by Quintin Hoare and Geoffrey Nowell Smith (New York: International, 1971), p. 12.
14. Nicos Poulantzas, *State, Power, Socialism*, translated by Patrick Camiller (London: NLB, 1978), p. 77.
15. Louis Althusser, "Ideology and Ideological State Apparatuses (Notes Toward an Investigation)," in *Lenin and Philosophy and Other Essays* (New York: Monthly Review Press, 1971), p. 165.
16. See Joseph Massad, "Conceiving the Masculine: Gender and Palestinian Nationalism," *Middle East Journal* 49, no. 3 (summer 1995): 467–483.
17. Chatterjee, *The Nation*, p. 6.
18. See Andrew Parker, Mary Russo, Doris Summer, and Patricia Yaeger, eds., *Nationalisms and Sexualities* (New York: Routledge, 1992). See also George Mosse, *Nationalism and Sexuality: Respectability and Abnormal Sexuality in Modern Europe* (New York: Howard Fertig, 1985).
19. Chatterjee, *The Nation*, p. 10.
20. Ibid., p. 5.
21. Ibid., p. 6.
22. See Abdulla Laroui, *The Crisis of the Arab Intellectual: Traditionalism or Historicism?* (Berkeley: University of California Press, 1976).
23. See, for example, Abraham F. Lowenthal and J. Samuel Fitch, eds., *Armies and Politics in Latin America*, revised edition (New York: Holmer and Meier, 1986). See also Anthony Giddens, *The Nation-State and Violence*, vol. 2 of *A Contemporary Critique of Historical Materialism* (Berkeley: University of California Press, 1987). See also Charles Tilly, *Coercion, Capital and European States, AD 990–1992* (Cambridge, MA: Blackwell, 1992).
24. Samuel P. Huntington, *Political Order in Changing Societies* (New Haven: Yale University Press, 1968), p. 195.
25. Alfred Stepan, *Rethinking Military Politics: Brazil and the Southern Cone* (Princeton, NJ: Princeton University Press, 1988).
26. Timothy Mitchell, "The Limits of the State: Beyond Statist Approaches and Their Critics," *American Political Science Review* 85, no. 1 (March, 1991).
27. Antonio Gramsci, "The Modern Prince," in *Selections*, pp. 180–185.
28. Chatterjee, *Nationalist Thought*, pp. 50–52.
29. This does not necessarily mean that the new colonially planned state structure expands bureaucracies and institutions, as French colonialism had done in Tunisia, for example; it could just as easily destroy existing ones, as Italian colonialism had done in Libya. On the cases of Tunisia and Libya, see Lisa Anderson, *The State and Social Transformation in Tunisia and Libya, 1830–1980* (Princeton, NJ: Princeton University Press, 1986).

30. Sulayman Nusayrat, *Al-Shakhsiyyah al-Urduniyyah, Bayna al-Bu'd al-Watani wa al-Bu'd al-Qawmi* (Amman: Manshurat Wizarat al-Thaqafah, 1997).

31. Yusuf Darwish Ghawanmah, *Al-Tarikh al-Siyasi Li-Sharqiyy al-Urdunn Fi al-'Asr al-Mamlukiyy: Al-Mamalik al-Bahriyyah* (Amman: Dar al-Fikr lil-Nashr wa al-Tawzi', 1982).

32. Mahmud 'Ubaydat, *al-Urdunn Fi al-Tarikh: Min al-'Asr al-Hajariyy Hatta Qiyam al-Imarah*, part I (Tripoli, Lebanon: Jarrus Bars, 1992).

1. Codifying the Nation: Law and the Articulation of National Identity in Jordan

1. See Benedict Anderson, *Imagined Communities: Reflections on the Origin and Spread of Nationalism* (London: Verso, 1991), and Partha Chatterjee, *Nationalist Thought and the Colonial World, A Derivative Discourse* (Minneapolis: University of Minnesota Press, 1993). See also Ernest Gellner, *Nations and Nationalism* (Ithaca, NY: Cornell University Press, 1983), and Eric Hobsbawm, *Nations and Nationalism Before 1780: Programme, Myth, Reality* (Cambridge: Cambridge University Press, 1990).

2. I rely in this chapter on Louis Althusser's notion of "interpellation." Althusser borrows the notion from French parliamentary procedure, where the act of verifying the attendance of parliamentarians by hailing them is called *interpellation* or *interpeller*. For Althusser, interpellation is the act by which hailing someone *identifies* them and *subjectifies* them: "[I]t transforms the individuals into subjects." This hailing operation, called interpellation, is the way ideology "acts" and "functions." See Louis Althusser, "Ideology and Ideological State Apparatuses (Notes Toward an Investigation)," in *Lenin and Philosophy and Other Essays* (New York: Monthly Review Press, 1971), p. 174.

3. Louis Althusser, "Ideology," p. 143, note.

4. Antonio Gramsci, "State and Civil Society, Observations on Certain Aspects of the Structure of Political Parties in the Period of Organic Crisis," in *Selections from the Prison Notebooks of Antonio Gramsci*, edited and translated by Quintin Hoare and Geoffrey Nowell Smith (New York: International, 1971), pp. 206–275.

5. Jacques Derrida, "Force of Law: The Mystical Foundation of Authority," in *Cardozo Law Review* 11, nos. 5–6 (1990): 941; all emphases in the original.

6. Jacques Derrida "Devant la Loi," in *Kafka and the Contemporary Critical Performance: Centenary Readings*, edited by Ulan Udoff (Bloomington: Indiana University Press, 1987), p. 145.

7. *The Organic Law of Transjordan*, published in *Al-Jaridah al-Rasmiyyah* (*Official Gazette*), #188 (April 24, 1928). In the remainder of the book, I will refer to *Al-Jaridah al-Rasmiyyah* as the *Official Gazette*.

8.   Homi Bhabha, "DissemiNation: Time, Narrative, and the Margins of the Modern Nation," in *Nation and Narration*, edited by Homi Bhabha (New York: Routledge, 1990), p. 297.

9.   *The Nationality Law of Transjordan*, published in the *Official Gazette* #193 (June 1, 1928).

10. Jacques Derrida, "Declarations of Independence," in *New Political Science*, no. 15 (summer, 1986), p. 10.

11. Jacques Derrida, "Force of Law," p. 963.

12. See, for example, Jabir Ibrahim al-Rawi, *Sharh Ahkam al-Jinsiyyah Fil-Qanun al-Urduni, Dirasah Muqarinah* (Amman: Al-Dar al-'Arabiyyah Lil-Tawzi' wa al-Nashr, 1984), pp. 83–89, and Hasan al-Hiddawi, *Al-Jinsiyyah wa Ahkamuha Fi al-Qanun al-Urduni* (Amman: Dar Majdalawi lil-Nashr wa al-Tawzi', 1993), pp. 71–75.

13. The Ottoman Law of Nationality had been in effect since January 19, 1869, when it was originally enacted, until the signing of the Treaty of Lausanne in 1923 ceding the erstwhile Ottoman territories to the Allies, which was effective within a year of signing.

14. On the Tanzimat and the influence of European laws, see Stanford Shaw and Ezel Kural Shaw, *History of the Ottoman Empire and Modern Turkey*, vol. II, *Reform, Revolution and Republic: The Rise of Modern Turkey, 1808–1975* (Cambridge: Cambridge University Press, 1977), pp. 118–119.

15. See the Treaty of Lausanne, signed on July 24, 1923, between the Allies (the British Empire, France, Italy, Japan, Greece, Roumania and the Serb-Croat-Slovene state) and Turkey, reproduced in *The Treaties of Peace 1919–1923*, vol. II (New York: Carnegie Endowment for International Peace, 1924), p. 969.

16. See articles 32 and 33 of the Treaty of Lausanne, p. 238.

17. *The Statutes*, 2nd revised edition, vol. XII, from the Session of the Thirty-First and Thirty-Second to the Session of the Thirty-Fourth and Thirty-Fifth Years of Queen Victoria, A.D. 1868–1871 (London: 1896), pp. 679–686.

18. *The Statutes Revised*, Great Britain, vol. 23, nos. 2, 3 GEO V to 6, 7 GEO V, 1912–1916 (London: Wymans & Sons, 1929), pp. 282–297.

19. *The Statutes Revised*, Great Britain, vol. 24, nos. 6, 7 GEO V to 10, 11 GEO V, 1917–1920 (London: Wymans & Sons, 1929), pp. 366–367.

20. Letter from John Shuckburgh, assistant secretary to the Colonial Office to the undersecretary of state at the Foreign Office, FO371/6372 (May 18, 1922), p. 26, and Despatch no. 280 from Acting High Commissioner of Palestine W. H. Deedes to Winston Churchill, the secretary of state for the colonies, FO371/6372 (April 28, 1922), p. 27, and Foreign Office to the undersecretary of state, Colonial Office, FO371/6372 (June 9, 1922), p. 29.

21. "Official Designation of Trans Jordania," FO 371/6372 (April 28, 1921), p. 41.

22. *The Law of Foreigners* (Qanun al-Ajanib) was signed on July 3, 1927, and published in the *Official Gazette* #162 (August 1, 1927).

23. *Agreement Between His Britannic Majesty and His Highness the Amir of Trans-Jordan*, Jerusalem (February 20, 1928), with ratifications exchanges on October 31, 1929, article 9.

24. CO 831/41/7 #77058, Acting High Commissioner Battershill to Secretary of State, Ormsby Gore, 14 October 1937, Ref. TS/37/33, cited by Abla Amawi, *State and Class in Transjordan: A Study of State Autonomy*, doctoral dissertation (Washington, DC: Georgetown University, 1993), p. 238.

25. Etienne Balibar, "The Nation Form," in *Race, Nation, Class, Ambiguous Identities*, edited by Etienne Balibar and Immanuel Wallerstein (London: Verso, 1991), p. 94.

26. In this vein, women as residents of the private domestic sphere, and Bedouins as residents of the nonurban desert, signify through their spatial locations a temporal location—that of tradition. However, men, considered as residents of the public sphere, and urbanites, through their spatial locations, signify the temporal location of modernity. More on this in chapter 2.

27. Sigmund Freud, "Leonardo da Vinci and a Memory of His Childhood," in *The Standard Edition of the Complete Psychological Works of Sigmund Freud* (London: Hogarth Press, 1953–1974), vol. XI, pp. 83–84, published originally in 1927.

28. See Munib Madi and Sulayman Musa, *Tarikh al-Urdunn Fi al-Qarn al-'Ishrin* (Amman: Maktabat al-Muhtasib, 1959); see also 'Ali Mahafzah, *Tarikh al-Urdunn al-Mu'asir, 'Ahd al-Imarah, 1921-1946* (Amman: Markaz al-Kutub al-Urduni, 1973), Sulayman Musa, *Ta'sis al-Imarah al-Urduniyyah, 1921–1925, Dirasah Watha'iqiyyah* (Amman: Maktabat al-Muhtasib, 1971), Sulayman Musa, *Imarat Sharq al-Urdunn, 1921-1946, Nash'atuha wa Tatawwuruha fi Rub'i Qarn* (Amman: Lajnat Tarikh al-Urdunn, 1990). Also see Kamal Salibi, *The Modern History of Jordan* (New York: I. B. Tauris, 1998), pp. 49 and 91. These views were also articulated by British officials as well as by Prince (later King) 'Abdullah in his writings.

29. Michel Foucault, "Governmentality," p. 102.

30. On British-Hashemite relations, see 'Abdullah al-Tall, *Karithat Filastin, Mudhakkarrat 'Abdullah al-Tall, Qa'id Ma'rakat al-Quds*, part I (Cairo: Dar al-Qalam, 1959), Avi Shlaim, *Collusion Across the Jordan* (London: Oxford University Press, 1989), Mary Wilson, *King Abdullah, Britain and the Making of Jordan* (Cambridge: Cambridge University Press, 1989), John Bagot Glubb, *A Soldier with the Arabs* (London: Hodder and Stoughton, 1957). For two recent attempts addressing the national question, see Linda Layne, *Home and Homeland: The Dialogics of National and Tribal Identities in Jordan* (Princeton, NJ: Princeton University Press, 1994), and Schirin Fathi, *Jordan: An Invented Nation?* (Hamburg: Deutsches Orient-Institut, 1994).

31. Cited by King 'Abdullah in his memoirs, or *Al-Mudhakkarat*, included in 'Abdullah Ibn al-Husayn, *Al-Athar al-Kamilah Lil Malik 'Abdullah*, 3rd edition (Beirut: Al-Dar al-Muttahidah Lil-Nashr, 1985), p. 175.

32. See Kamil Mahmud Khillah, *Al-Tatawwur al-Siyasi Li-Sharq al-Urdunn, Maris 1921–Maris 1948* (Tripoli, Libya: Al-Munsha'ah al-'Ammah Lil-Nashr wa al-Tawzi' wa al-I'lan, 1983), pp. 126–128.

33. Munib Madi and Sulayman Musa, *Tarikh al-Urdunn*, pp. 210–220.

34. The initial border demarcation with Saudi Arabia was not ratified until 1965 (see later), although the two governments had established relations with each other in May 1933. Also, the border demarcations with Syria were not ratified until both governments signed an agreement in October 1931. Although the borders with Iraq had been agreed on by the two countries in April 1928, they were finally demarcated in the summer of 1932. See Ali Mahafza, *Tarikh al-Urdunn al-Mu'asir, 'Ahd al-Imarah, 1921-1946* (Amman: Markaz al-Kutub al-Urduni, 1973), pp. 62, 112, 119–121. See also Riccardo Bocco and Tareq Tell, "Frontière, Tribus et État(s) en Jordanie Orientale à l'Époque du Mandat," in *Maghreb-Machrek*, no. 147, January-February, 1995, pp. 26–47.

35. See Kamil Mahmud Khillah, *Al-Tatawwur*, pp. 274–277.

36. August/September 1923 was the date of the al-'Adwan uprising. Also, the end of 1923 saw the Kuwait conference, in which the Saudi and Jordanian governments were attempting to delineate their borders, which were finally agreed on in the Hida' agreement in November 1925, stressing that Hijazi and East Jordanian tribes ('Asha'ir) cannot cross the border between the two countries "as armed groups" without proper documents issued "by their government and certified by the consul of the government into whose territory entry is sought." See Madi and Musa, *Tarikh al-Urdunn*, pp. 221, 254.

37. Khillah, *Al-Tatawwur*, p. 277; Musa and Madi, *Tarikh al-Urdunn*, pp. 321–323.

38. John Bagot Glubb was to expel a number of different branches of the tribe to the Hijaz after finding them guilty of conspiring with the Hashemite government to launch raids against the Saudis. Riccardo Bocco states, "[L]es membres de ces sections des Bani 'Atiyah ont été expulsés en masse, escortés avec leur famille par les jundi [Bedouin soldiers] de la DPF [Desert Patrol Force], vers le Hijaz." in Bocco, *Etat et tribus bedouines en Jordanie, 1920-1990, Les Huwaytat: Territoire, changement économique, identité politique*, doctoral dissertation, Institut d'Etudes Politiques de Paris, 1996, pp. 143, 170n–171n.

39. Quoted in Khillah, *Al-Tatawwur*.

40. On the membership of this party, see Madi and Musa, *Tarikh al-Urdunn*, pp. 326–328.

41. For the history of all these parties, see Khillah, *Al-Tatawwur*, pp. 277–287, and Madi and Musa, *Tarikh al-Urdunn*, pp. 321–334.

42. In 1965, the Saudi and Jordanian governments signed an agreement for border rectification and demarcation, which expanded the area around Aqaba from 6 to 25 km for the benefit of the Jordanians with other border rectifications in other areas. The agreement was signed on August 9, 1965. Final demarcation was concluded on January 29, 1967, after the two parties had hired a Japanese

survey company to finalize the placement of border posts. See *Official Gazette*, no. 1868, August 26, 1965. See also Sulayman Musa, *Tarikh al-Urdunn Fi al-Qarn al-'Ishrin, 1958–1995*, vol. II (Amman: Maktabat al-Muhtasib, 1996), pp. 92–94. In 1990, there was another border rectification with the Saudis around the Jabal Tubayq area.

43. Balibar, "The Nation Form," p. 95.

44. See Michael Fischbach, "British Land Policy in Transjordan," in *Village, Steppe and State: The Social Origins of Modern Jordan*, edited by Eugene Rogan and Tareq Tell (London: British Academic Press, 1994). According to Fischbach's research, two thirds of Transjordan's village lands were musha' (or communally owned) lands, p. 83, note.

45. John Bagot Glubb, *Britain and the Arabs: A Study of Fifty Years 1908–1958* (London: Hodder and Stoughton, 1959), pp. 173–174.

46. Fischbach, "British Land Policy," p. 105.

47. Frederick Engels, *The Origin of the Family, Private Property and the State* (Peking: Foreign Language Press, 1978), p. 206.

48. On the modern conceptions of space, see Neil Smith, *Uneven Development, Nature, Capital and the Production of Space* (Cambridge, MA: Basil Blackwell, 1984). See also Edward Soja, *Postmodern Geographies: The Reassertion of Space in Critical Social Theory* (London: Verso, 1989).

49. Engels, *The Origin*, p. 138.

50. Francesca Klug, " 'Oh to Be in England': The British Case Study," in Nira Yuval-Davis and Floya Anthias, eds., *Woman-Nation-State* (London: Macmillan, 1989), p. 21.

51. Ibid.

52. On other aspects of Jordanian law that followed the French and the British examples, see E. Theodore Mogannam, "Developments in the Legal System of Jordan," *Middle East Journal* 6, no. 2 (spring 1952): 194–206.

53. Agency is established if the state's subject is of legal age (defined as eighteen solar years according to article 18) and the time of his/her choice (August 6, 1926), in which case she or he can remain Jordanian as interpellated by article 1, choose another nationality (articles 2 and 3), or choose Jordanian nationality as in article 5. Whereas articles 2 and 5 are clearly targeting the erstwhile Ottomans, it is unclear whether article 3 also does so, given its mention of race (this article is lifted verbatim from the Treaty of Lausanne—see earlier). Because Jordan was/is for the most part "racially" homogeneous, it is unclear if race here is conflated with national affiliation in the sense of the Arab race, the Turkish race, and so forth.

54. See *British Nationality and Status of Aliens Law of 1914*, article 1, pp. 285–286.

55. Law #6 for the Year 1954, *The Law of Jordanian Nationality*, published in the *Official Gazette*, no. 1171 (February 16, 1954).

56. Articles 4 and 5 of Law #7 for the Year 1963, *An Amendment Law to Jordanian Nationality Law,* signed on March 7, 1963.

57. Ibid.

58. However, these aspects of the law were changed significantly in the 1980s. See "The Women, Immigration and Nationality Group," in *Worlds Apart, Women Under Immigration and Nationality Law,* edited by Jacqueline Bhabha, Francesca Klug, and Sue Shutter, (London: Pluto Press, 1985), and Ann Dummett and Andrew Nicol, *Subjects, Citizens, Aliens and Others, Nationality and Immigration Law* (London: Weidenfeld and Nicholson, 1990).

59. A foreigner, according to article 18 of *The Law of Foreigners,* means "anyone who is not Jordanian."

60. Article 2 of the *British Nationality and Status of Aliens Law of 1914,* p. 287, states the following: "(a) that he have either resided in His Majesty's dominions for a period not less than five years in the manner required by this section. . . . (b) that he be of good character and have an adequate knowledge of the English language; and (c) that he intend, if his application is granted, either to reside in His Majesty's dominions or to enter or continue in the service of the Crown."

61. See article 27 of the *British Nationality and Status of Aliens Law of 1914,* p. 296, which states, "The expression 'disability' means the status of being a married woman, a minor, a lunatic, or idiot."

62. Article 2 of Law #6 for the Year 1954.

63. *An Addendum to Nationality Law,* Law #56 for the Year 1949, published in the *Official Gazette* (December 20, 1949).

64. Article 7 of the British Mandate for Palestine (which came into operation on 29 September, 1923) stipulated the enactment of a nationality law, which took the form of the Palestinian Nationality Order, 1925, and was effective on August 1 of that year. See the text of both in *A Survey of Palestine: Prepared in December 1945 and January 1946 for the Information of the Anglo-American Committee of Inquiry,* vol. I. (Washington, DC: Institute for Palestine Studies, 1991), pp. 5–6, 206.

65. Article 2 of this law introduces two new definitions of two new terms relevant to the text of this law. These words are *Arab* and *émigré* (Mughtarib). An Arab, according to this law, "means any person whose father is of Arab origin and who [the father] holds one of the nationalities of the Arab League." For the purposes of this law, "the word 'Mughtarib' means every Arab who was born in the Hashemite Kingdom of Jordan or in the usurped part of Palestine and who has emigrated outside the country or fled it, and this term also refers to the children of that person regardless of where they were born."

66. The reading and writing parts were added in the 1963 amendment. The original text required only "knowledge of Arabic" without any specifications.

67. See Hasan al-Hiddawi, *Al-Jinsiyyah,* pp. 44–46.

68. Article 1 of the 1952 Jordanian constitution as published in the *Official Gazette* no. 1093 (January 8, 1952).
69. Article 2 of the 1952 constitution.
70. The 1946 constitution was passed by the legislative council on November 28, 1946, and was published in the *Official Gazette*, no. 886 (February 1, 1947).
71. Article 15 of the 1946 constitution.
72. *The Organic Law of Transjordan*, published in the *Official Gazette*, no. 188 (April 24, 1928), article 1.
73. Article 10 of *The Organic Law*.
74. Article 15 of *The Organic Law*.
75. Article 6-1 of the 1952 constitution.
76. Article 6 of the 1946 constitution, emphasis added.
77. Article 5 of *The Organic Law*.
78. Ironically and in contradiction with article 4, article 13 asserts that the "Council of Ministers has the prerogative to waive the condition requiring four years of residency if the applicant was an Arab or if special circumstances existed which would result in the general public interest." The point, however, is that unlike a non-Arab, an Arab *is* required to reside in the country for fifteen, not four, years!
79. Article 13, section 4 of the 1954 law attempts to restrict access to Jordanian nationality to foreigners who demonstrate lack of loyalty to the privilege of being accorded Jordanian nationality: "A nationality certificate is not granted to a person who had acquired Jordanian nationality through naturalization and then lost it by his choice through acquiring another foreign nationality."
80. The regulations for applying for Transjordanian nationality stipulated that Bedouin applicants must swear allegiance in writing to the Amir 'Abdullah, his descendents, and successors. See *Official Gazette*, no. 228, May 16, 1929, cited in Bocco, *Etat et tribus*, pp. 144–145.
81. See Mazin Salamah, "Al-Fashal Yulahiq Mu'tamarat al-Mughtaribin," in *Al-Urdunn al-Jadid*, no. 10 (spring 1988), pp. 70–73.
82. Qanun al-Intikhab al-Mu'aqqat Li Majlis al-Nuwwab, no. 24, 1960, *Official Gazette*, no. 1494 (June 11, 1960), article 17-A. Hasan al-Haddawi is mistaken in his assertion that the 1987 amendments to Nationality Law introduced restrictions on naturalized citizens for the first time, as the election law of 1960 had already done that. What is new is the inclusion of these restrictions and their expansion within Nationality Law itself; see Al-Haddawi, *Al-Jinsiyyah*, pp. 152–154.
83. Qanun al-Intikhabat Li Majlis al-Nuwwab, no. 22, 1986, *Official Gazette*, no. 3398 (May 17, 1986), article 18-A.
84. The Temporary Law no. 18 for the Year 1969, the *Law Amending the Jordanian Nationality Law*, signed on May 21, 1969.

85. This amendment was added by Law no. 50 for the Year 1958, *An Amendment Law to the Law of Jordanian Nationality*, article 2, signed on December 21, 1958, by King Husayn.

86. One more condition for loss of nationality deals with Jordanians who acquired their nationality though article 6. The law claims that they can petition to give up their Jordanian nationality within a year of reaching legal age if they had been born and had taken up residence outside Jordan. According to the law, a Jordanian who loses his nationality will not be considered free of duties related to actions that "he" may have undertaken while still a national.

87. *The Law of Exile and Deportation*, published in the *Official Gazette*, no. 206 (October 15, 1928). This law was imposed by the British despite the opposition of many members in the executive and the legislative councils. See Abla Amawi, *State and Class in Transjordan: A Study of State Autonomy*, p. 340.

88. *The Law of Exile and Deportation*, article 3-1.

89. Jordan's king announced the severing of all Jordanian legal and administrative ties from the West Bank (Fakk al-Irtibat, literally, "the untying of ties") on July 31, 1988, by royal decree, thus nullifying the 1950 annexation of central Palestine to Jordan by his grandfather, King 'Abdullah. Note that the Fakk al-Irtibat decree was never published in the *Official Gazette* (although commensurate regulations were), which deprived it of the status of law. All binding laws in Jordan must be published in the *Official Gazette*.

90. On the denationalization of West Bank Jordanians and the views of the Jordanian high court in relation to such denationalization, see Ibrahim Bakr, *Dirasah Qanuniyyah 'an A'mal al-Siyadah wa Qararat Naz' al-Jinsiyyah al-Urduniyyah wa Sahb Jawazat al-Safar al-'Adiyyah* (Amman: Maktabat al-Ra'y, 1995).

91. *British Nationality and Status of Aliens Law of 1914*, p. 291. The influence of British nationality law on the Treaty of Lausanne is everywhere in evidence. Article 36 of the treaty, in line with British law, stipulates, "For the purposes of the provisions of this Section, the status of a married woman will be governed by that of her husband, and the status of children under eighteen years of age by that of their parents." See *The Treaties of Peace*, p. 970.

92. *British Nationality and Status of Aliens Law of 1914*, article 10, p. 291: "The wife of a British subject shall be deemed to be a British subject, and the wife of an alien shall be deemed to be an alien."

93. Law #3 amending the Jordanian Law of Nationality signed on January 30, 1961.

94. Law #7 amending the Jordanian Law of Nationality signed on March 7, 1963.

95. "[O]r who married a non-Jordanian" as amended in 1963.

96. Amended to two years in 1963.

97. Law #22 for the Year 1987, the Law Amending Jordanian Nationality Law, signed on July 27, 1987.

98. Decision no. 4 for the year 1992 issued by the Special Office [Diwan] for the Explication of Laws, May 21, 1992.

99. *British Nationality and Status of Aliens Law of 1914*, article 12, p. 292.

100. Article 13 of the 1963 law.

2. Different Spaces as Different Times: Law and Geography in Jordanian Nationalism

1.   See Qanun no. 26 for the Year 1947, Qanun Huquq al-ʿAʾilah al-Muʾaqqat, signed on June 29, 1947, and published in the *Official Gazette*, no. 915 (August 2, 1947).

2.   Qanun Huquq al-ʿAʾ ilah, Law no. 92 for the Year 1951, published in the *Official Gazette*, no. 1081 (August 16, 1951). This law replaced both the 1947 temporary law and Qarar Huquq al-ʿAʾilah al-ʿUthmani of 1917.

3.   "Qanun Muʾaqqat Raqam (61) Li-Sanat 1976, Qanun al-Ahwal al-Shakhsiyyah," *Official Gazette*, no. 2668 (January 1, 1976).

4.   See Khadijah al-Habashnah Abu-ʿAli, "Qanun al-Ahwal al-Shakhsiyyah al-Urduni, Waraqat ʿAmal," presented at the conference Al-Marʾah al-Urduni-yyah fi Zill al-Qawanin wal Tashriʿat al-Haliyyah, sponsored by the General Jordanian Women's Union, Amman, March 23–25, 1992.

5.   The 1924 law that was supposed to be published in the *Official Gazette*, which at the time was called *Al-Sharq al-ʿArabi*, was never actually published, although its amendments were. See for example amendments to the law in *Official Gazette*, no. 148 (January 15, 1927), no. 151 (March 1, 1927), and no. 231 (July 1, 1929). For the text of the 1924 law, see *Turath al-Badu al-Qadaʾiyy, Nazariyyan wa ʿAmaliyyan*, by Muhammad Abu Hassan (Amman: Daʾirat al-Thaqafah wa al-Funun, 1987), pp. 463–466.

6.   Uriel Dann, *Studies in the History of Transjordan, 1920–1949: The Making of a State* (Boulder, CO: Westview Press, 1984), p. 88.

7.   Ibid., p. 88.

8.   See Saʿd Abu Dayyah and Abdul-Majid al-Nasʿah, *Tarikh al-Jaysh al-ʿArabi fi ʿAhd al-Imarah, 1921–1946, Dirasah ʿIlmiyyah Tahliliyyah Wathaʿiqiyyah* (Amman: n.p., 1990), pp. 69, 81.

9.   Quoted in Major C. S. Jarvis, *Arab Command: The Biography of Lieutenant-Colonel F. G. Peake Pasha* (London: Hutchinson & Co., 1942), p. 61.

10. See Munib Madi and Sulayman Musa, *Tarikh al-Urdunn Fi al-Qarn al-ʿIshrin, 1900–1959* (Amman: Maktabat al-Muhtasib, 1959), p. 221, pp. 253–255.

11. This law was published in the *Official Gazette*, no. 230, June 16, 1929. The updated Qanun al-Ishraf ʿala al-Badu was published in the *Official Gazette*, no. 516 (February 16, 1936). Ahmad ʿUwaydi al-ʿAbbadi argues that the origi-

nal laws were written in English and the official Arabic versions were mere translations: See his *Al-Qada' 'Ind al-'Asha 'ir al-Urduniyyah*, part 4 of "Silsilat Man Hum al-Badu?" (Amman: Dar al-Bashir Lil-Nashr wal-Tawzi', 1982), p. 127, note 4.

12.　See Qanun Ilgha' al-Qawanin al-'Asha'iriyyah, Qanun Mu'aqqat Raqam (34) li Sanat 1976, published in the *Official Gazette*, no. 2629 (June 1, 1976), p. 1299.

13.　Article 6 of the 1952 constitution, "Dustur al-Mamlakah al-Urduniyyah al-Hashimiyyah," *Official Gazette*, no. 1093 (January 8, 1952), p. 6.

14.　See article 6 of "Al-Dustur al-Urduni," enacted on November 28, 1946, and published in the *Official Gazette*, no. 886 (February 1, 1947), and article 5 of "Al-Qanun al-Asasi li Sharq al-Urdunn," *Official Gazette*, no. 188 (April 19, 1928).

15.　See "La'ihat Qanun Intikhab al-Nuwwab Fi Mintaqat al-Sharq al-'Arabi," published in the annex of *Al-Sharq al-'Arabi Gazette*, no. 52 (1923), articles 2, 4, 9, and 15.

16.　See Emily Naffa', "Dawr al-Mar'ah al-Urduniyyah Fi al-Nidal al-Siyasi," presented at *Al-Mar'ah al-Urduniyyah Fi Zill al-Qawanin wal Tashri'at al-Haliyyah* conference held in Amman, March 23–25, 1992.

17.　"Qanun Intikhab A'da' al-Majlis al-Tashri'i" was initially published as a project for a law in the *Official Gazette*, no. 195 (June 2, 1928) and was announced as an enacted law in the *Official Gazette*, no. 199 (August 15, 1928).

18.　See article 2 of the 1928 law.

19.　See "Nizam Intikhab 'Udwayn Li-Yumaththila Badu al-Imarah," *Official Gazette*, no. 216 (January 28, 1929).

20.　See article 2 of "Qanun Raqam (9) Li Sanat 1947, Qanun al-Intikhab li Majlis al-Nuwwab," published in the *Official Gazette*, no. 898 (April 16, 1947).

21.　See articles 3, 30, 31, 32.

22.　See article 3, subsections B–F.

23.　See Suhayr Salti al-Tall, *Muqaddimah Hawl Wad'iyyat al-Mar'ah wa al-Harakah al-Nisa'iyyah Fi al-Urdunn* (Beirut: Al-Mu'assassah al-'Arabiyyah lil-Dirasat wal-Nashr, 1985), p. 116.

24.　"Qanun al-Intikhab al-Mu'aqqat li Majlis al-Nuwwab," Law no. 24 for the Year 1960, published in the *Official Gazette*, no. 1494 (June 11, 1960). See articles 2-a and 3-1, 17-A–E. Article 17-A stresses that candidates should have been Jordanian for at least five years.

25.　See Paul A. Jureidini and R. D. McLaurin, *Jordan: The Impact of Social Change on the Role of the Tribes* (Washington, DC: Praeger, 1984), p. 15.

26.　See article 5.

27.　This letter was dated April 21, 1966.

28.　See Qanun 8 for the Year 1974, "Qanun Mu'addil li Qanun al-Intikhab li Majlis al-Nuwwab," *Official Gazette*, no. 2481 (April 1, 1974).

29. See Law no. 22 for the Year 1986, "Qanun al-Intikhab li Majlis al-Nuwwab," *Official Gazette*, no. 3398 (May 17, 1986). See articles 2, 3-a, and 5. This law was amended twice in 1989 prior to the country's first democratic elections in decades—see the *Official Gazette*, no. 3622 (April 16, 1989), and no. 3638 (July 8, 1989).

30. See Munib Madi and Sulayman Musa, *Tarikh al-Urdunn*, pp. 7–9.

31. See Sulayman Musa, *Ta'sis al-Imarah al-Urduniyyah, 1921–1925, Dirasah Watha'iqiyyah* (Amman: Maktabat al-Muhtasib, 1971), pp. 188–189.

32. See Hani Hurani's classic *Al-Tarkib al-Iqtisadi al-Ijtima'i Li Sharq al-Urdunn* (Beirut: Markaz al-Abhath, Munazzamat al-Tahrir al-Filastiniyyah, 1978), p. 67. On general population surveys in the country, see A. Konikoff, *Transjordan: An Economic Survey* (Jerusalem: Economic Research Institute of the Jewish Agency for Palestine, 1946), pp. 16–19.

33. See article 3 of the "Qanun al-Ishraf 'ala al-Badu li Sanat 1929," *Official Gazette*, no. 230 (June 16, 1929).

34. Article 4, A–F.

35. Article 6.

36. See "Qanun al-Ishraf 'ala al-Badu," *Official Gazette*, no. 516 (February 16, 1936).

37. See Ricardo Bocco and Tariq M. M. Tell, "Pax Britannica in the Steppe: British Policy and the Transjordan Bedouin," in *Village Steppe and State: The Social Origins of Modern Jordan*, edited by Eugene Rogan and Tariq Tell (London: British Academic Press, 1994), p. 120.

38. See Al-'Abbadi, Ahmad 'Uwaydi, *Al-Qada' 'Ind al-'Asha'ir al-Urduniyyah*, no. 4 of "Silsilat Man Hum al-Badu,"(Amman: Dar al-Bashir lil-Nashr wal-Tawzi', 1988), pp. 54–55.

39. See article 2-B of "Qanun Mahakim al-'Asha'ir li Sanat 1936," *Official Gazette*, no. 516 (February 16, 1936).

40. "Qanun al-Amn al-'Am al-Mu'aqqat," Temporary Law #29 for the Year 1958, signed on June 16, 1958, *Official Gazette*, no. 1388, p. 641–643.

41. "Qanun Mu'aqqat Bi Fasl al-Shurtah wa al-Darak 'an al-Jaysh al-'Arabi al-Urduni," Temporary Law #27 for the Year 1956, signed on July 12, 1956, *Official Gazette*, no. 1285 (July 14, 1956), pp. 1763–1764. On the revoking of this law, see the *Official Gazette*, no. 1661 (May 16, 1957), p. 429.

42. Circassians were the second favorite group for employment in the Iraq Petroleum Company; see Seteney Shami, *Ethnicity and Leadership: The Circassians in Jordan*, doctoral dissertation, Department of Anthropology (Berkeley: University of California, 1982), p. 81.

43. See Abla Amawi, *State and Class in Transjordan: A Study of State Autonomy*, doctoral dissertation (Washington, DC: Georgetown University, 1993), p. 369.

44. Christians, who numbered 6.9 percent of the population, received 18.7 percent of the seats, whereas Circassians, who numbered 5.2 percent of the population,

received 12.5 percent of the seats. See Ma'an Abu Nowar, *The History of the Hashemite Kingdom of Jordan*, vol. 1, *The Creation and Development of Transjordan: 1920–1929* (Oxford: The Middle East Center, Ithaca Press, 1989), p. 211.

45. CO 831/27/2 #37226, high commissioner to secretary of state, 20 October 1934, #TC/101/34, cited by Amawi, *State and Class*, pp. 366–367.

46. CO 831/5/69421/31, high commissioner to L. S. Amery, 31 May 1929, cited by Amawi, *State and Class*, p. 367.

47. See Hani Hurani, *Al-Tarkib al-Iqtisadi al-Ijtima'i Li Sharq al-Urdunn*, p. 138.

48. Ibid., p. 140.

49. The council was set up juridically through enacting the Temporary Law no. 52 of the Year 1971, "Qanun Majlis Shuyukh Al-'Asha'ir," which became permanent on July 31, 1972, through the enactment of Law #4. See Law 52, *Official Gazette*, no. 2317 (August 16, 1971), p. 1273, and Law #4 of the Year 1972, *Official Gazette*, no. 2351 (March 16, 1972), p. 457. The council's operations were governed by internal statutes; see *Official Gazette*, no. 2339 (December 30, 1971), p. 2089.

50. Wizarat al-Thaqafah wa al-I'lam, *Al-Urdunn Fi Khamsin 'Am, 1921–1971* (Amman: Da'irat al-Matbu'at wal-Nashr, 1972), pp. 49–50. Also see article 15 of the law.

51. See al-'Abbadi, *Al-Qada' 'Ind al-'Asha'ir*, pp. 61–64.

52. See Law #25 for the Year 1973, "Qanun Ilgha' Qanun Majlis Shuyukh al-'Asha'ir," *Official Gazette*, no. 2426 (June 16, 1973), p. 1119.

53. See al-'Abbadi, *Al-Qada' 'Ind al-'Asha'ir*, pp. 441–442.

54. Ibid., p. 441.

55. See articles 2 and 4.

56. For a summary of these organizations' plans and programs regarding sedentarization of nomadic populations, see Riccardo Bocco, *Etat et tribus bedouines en Jordanie, 1920-1990, Les Huwaytat: Territoire, changement économique, identité politique*, doctoral dissertation, Institut d'Etudes Politiques de Paris, 1996, pp. 211–225.

57. Ibid., p. 210.

58. See the Law Canceling Tribal Laws (Qanun Ilgha' al-Qawanin al-'Asha'iriyyah), Temporary Law #34 for the Year 1976, signed on May 23, 1976, *Official Gazette*, no. 2629 (June 1, 1976), p. 1299.

59. Bedouin Police Files, #MA/22/1102, September 5, 1961. The proposal was dated September 20, 1959, cited by 'Abbadi, *Al-Qada' 'Ind al-'Asha'ir*, p. 112. 'Abbadi, who served in 1976 as editor of the police magazine and as police director of public relations, had access to police files, which remain closed to the public.

60. Order #148, dated 1962, cited ibid., p. 112.

61. Files of the Karak Police #12/8/1634, June 4, 1964, cited ibid., p. 114.

62. Files of the Directorate of Public Security, #MA/22/700. July 7, 1962, cited by al-'Abbadi, *Al-Qada' 'Ind al-'Asha'ir*, p. 112. A similar appeal was made in 1964 by the head of the police of the city of Ma'an, wherein he called on the government to abolish the Bedouin Supervision Law of 1936, as it was incompatible with present circumstances, see Files of the Ma'an Police, #MM/12/private/1562, November 16, 1964, cited by 'Abbadi ibid., p. 113.

63. Files of the Directorate of Public Security #MA/22/456, July 28, 1966, cited ibid., p. 113.

64. Ibid., p. 113.

65. Files of the Ministry of Interior #214/12554, July 17, 1966, cited ibid., p. 113.

66. King Husayn, speech delivered on June 9, 1976, cited ibid., p. 121.

67. See Anne Sinai and Allen Pollak, eds., *The Hashemite Kingdom of Jordan and the West Bank: A Handbook* (New York: American Academic Association for Peace in the Middle East, 1977), p. 35.

68. See Robert Satloff, *Troubles on the East Bank: Challenges to the Domestic Stability of Jordan* (New York: Praeger, 1986), p. 19.

69. See al-'Abbadi, *Al-Qada' 'Ind al-'Asha'ir*, pp. 118–119.

70. Seteney Shami, *Ethnicity and Leadership*, pp. 122–123.

71. See Robert Satloff, *Troubles*, p. 66.

72. Ibid.

73. Ibid. Note that Mudar Badran, a former director of the Mukhabarat (Jordan's Intelligence Services), was not a friend of Palestinian Jordanians, who, in fact, consider him hostile to them as a group.

74. For example, Nabil al-Sharif, the editor of *Al-Dustur*, in a veiled editorial called for an "objective" assessment of this "historical moment" so that Jordanians can learn from these "mistakes"; see *Al-Dustur* (March 13, 1984).

75. Mahmud al-Kayid, "Al-'Atwah wa al-Qanun," "Al-'Atwah and law," in *Al-Ra'y* (December 4, 1984), p. 1.

76. Abdul-Latif al-Subayhi, "Al-'Atwah wa al-Qanun," "Al-'Atwah and law," in *Al-Ra'y* (December 6, 1984), p. 2.

77. Ghassan al-Tall, "Hal Yastati' al-Mujtma' al-Urduni An La Yakun 'Asha'iriyyan?" "Can Jordanian society afford not to be tribalist?" *Al-Ra'y* (December 30, 1984).

78. Hussayn Taha Mahadin, "'Asha'iriyyat al-Nasab La 'Asha'iriyyat al-Dawr," "The tribalism of descent, not the tribalism of role," *Al-Ra'y* (January 13, 1985), p. 14. See also Ghazi Salih al-Zabn, "Haqa'iq La Budda Min Dhikriha Fi al-'Adat al-'Asha'iriyyah," or "Facts that must be mentioned about Tribal traditions," in *Al-Ra'y* (January 13, 1984), p. 15. Al-Zabn insists that "a majority of the people of Jordan in both banks [East and West] are tribal groupings," and therefore their tribal traditions must be respected. Also see Yahya Salim al-Aqtash, who suggested that the Islamic Shari'ah replace all the laws of the land, tribal and civil alike: "Al-Badil al-Amthal Lil A'raf al-'Asha'iriyyah," "The most ideal alternative to tribal conventions," in *Al-Ra'y* (January 27, 1985).

79. 'Abdullah al-Khatib, "Nusaffiq Li-Ilgha' al-'Asha'iriyyah al-Idariyyah," in Al-Ra'y (January 24, 1985), last page.

80. For the views of the different senators, including al-Rifa'i, expressed during the senate debate, see Al-Dustur (January 8, 1985), p. 12.

81. Tatawwur is often mistakenly translated as development instead of evolution. Although tatawwur is used at times in the sense of development, in Arabic development is Tanmiyah.

82. Marwan Muasher, "Detribalization: Towards the Rule of One Law," Jordan Times (January 19, 1985).

83. Al-Ra'y (January 28, 1985), pp. 1, 20.

84. For a short biography of Sharaf, see Al-Mar'ah al-Urduniyyah, Ra'idat Fi Maydan al-'Amal, compiled by 'Umar al-Burini and Hani al-Hindi (Amman: Matabi' al-Safwah, 1994), pp. 63–65.

85. Al-Ra'y (January 29, 1985), also see Jordan Times (January 29, 1985). The newspapers made the announcement of Sharaf's resignation with no comment whatsoever.

86. On these developments, see Linda Layne, Home and Homeland: The Dialogics of Tribal and National Identities in Jordan (Princeton, NJ: Princeton University Press, 1994), pp. 103–105.

87. Quoted in Middle East International (February 8, 1985), p. 11.

88. Quoted in Arthur R. Day, East Bank/West Bank: Jordan and the Prospects of Peace (New York: Council on Foreign Relations, 1986), p. 35.

89. Schirin Fathi, Jordan: An Invented Nation? Tribe-State Dynamics and the Formation of National Identity (Hamburg: Deutsches Orient-Institut, 1994), p. 210.

90. On the results of sedentarization and the different development projects launched by the state, see Kamal Abu Jaber, Fawzi Gharaibeh, and Allen Hill, eds., The Badia of Jordan: The Process of Change (Amman: University of Jordan Press, 1987), pp. 107–125. Also see Peter Gubser's important study of Karak and its environs in Peter Gubser, Politics and Change in al-Karak, Jordan: A Study of a Small Arab Town and Its District (New York: Oxford University Press, 1973).

91. Paul Jureidini and R. D. McLaurin, The Impact, pp. 31–36.

92. Ibid., p. 35.

93. Salwa's husband Jamil al-'As, of Palestinian origin from Jerusalem, was Jordan radio's most important song and music composer in the sixties and seventies.

94. Karl Marx, The German Ideology, reproduced in Robert C. Tucker, ed., The Marx-Engels Reader (New York: Norton Press, 1978), p. 163.

95. Ibid., p. 176.

96. On the Western invention of African "tribalism," see Nelson Kasfir, "Explaining Ethnic Political Participation," World Politics 31, no. 3 (1979): 365–388; also

see Terrence Ranger, "The Invention of Tradition in Colonial Africa," in *The Invention of Tradition*, edited by Eric Hobsbawm and Terrence Ranger (Cambridge: Cambridge University Press, 1983), pp. 211–262.

97. On Israeli claims that "Jordan is Palestine," see Sheila Ryan and Muhammad Hallaj, *Palestine Is, But Not in Jordan* (Belmont, MA: The Association of Arab-American University Graduates Press, 1983).

98. This representation has become so pervasive that a Palestinian scholar chose a picture of Petra's famous "Khaznah" as a cover for his book on Jordan and the Palestinians. The "Palestinian" white-and-black hatta was superimposed on the Khaznah representing the book's theme; see Yazid Yusuf Sayigh, *Al-Urdunn wa al-Filastiniyyun, Dirasah Fi Wihdat al-Masir Aw al-Sira' al-Hatmi* (London: Riyad al-Rayyis Press, 1987).

99. The fascination expressed by most Israeli Jews with Petra is enshrined in Zionist mythology, wherein stories of daredevil Israeli Jews illegally crossing the border between Jordan and Israel (between 1948 and 1994) in disguise (it is said that they prefer the Bedouin disguise) risking their lives to see Petra are prevalent. It is said many were killed making the trip. One could see this mythology translated into action following the 1994 peace treaty signed between Jordan and Israel, which was followed by a flood of Israeli and American Jews descending on Petra. Most were uninterested in visiting Amman or any other "living" city in the country, or even in staying in hotels in Petra itself, as they would visit Petra for a few hours and return to Israel at the end of the day. The Jordanian government was so concerned about the lack of Israeli tourist benefits that it instituted a policy wherein border crossings would be open for only a few hours every day to prevent tourists from visiting Petra and returning in the same day without spending any money in the country. In addition, stories of Israeli tourists defacing some of Petra's ruins and scribbling on them statements like "this belongs to Israel," or "this is the land of Israel," became embarrassing to the Israeli and Jordanian governments after the press reported the incidents. Other stories concerning Israeli tourists bringing their own food and sandwiches with them were reacted to negatively by the Jordanian government and Petra's restaurateurs and hotel managers, not to mention stories of Israeli tourists stealing hotel property, which were also reported in the Israeli press. Such stories had been reported before in Turkey about Israeli tourists stealing, among other things, hotel bathroom sinks! As for King Husayn's popularity in the country, the Israeli press was consistently reporting stories about the king being so popular among Israeli Jews that he would be able to defeat any Israeli candidate running for prime minister of Israel without much competition!

100. Walter Benjamin, "The Work of Art in the Age of Mechanical Reproduction," in Walter Benjamin, *Illuminations: Essays and Reflections*, edited by Hannah Arendt (New York: Schocken Books, 1969), pp. 217–251.

101. Benedict Anderson, *Imagined Communities*, p. 181.
102. Jordan is hardly unique in this regard, as many postcolonial states were to adopt such colonially constructed "national" ruins as national monuments. For other examples, see Anderson, ibid., pp. 178–185. Note that Jerusalem, which was part of Jordan and under Jordanian control from 1950 to 1967, was also prominent in posters and other representations of Jordan. The Dome of the Rock was used most commonly as a stand-in for Jerusalem, which in turn was a stand-in for Jordan. Jerusalem, however, played a role different from that of Petra, in that it partook of the religious discourse that the regime used to legitimize itself (see chapter 4).
103. Linda Layne, *Home and Homeland*, p. 102.
104. Layne observes how the Jordanian national airline ALIA used to offer its passengers "a pair of painted wooden Bedouin dolls packaged in a bag made from the *traditional* red-and white checkered headdress," emphasis added (Layne, *Home and Homeland*, p. 103). The invention of national tradition has become so institutionalized that even an observer such as Layne fails to realize that the red-and-white checkered headdress is not traditional at all. As we will see in chapter 3, it was produced by John Glubb as "traditional."
105. See the magazine *Jordan* (Washington, DC: Jordan Information Bureau). The bureau is run by the Jordanian ministry of information. See, for example, the following issues: winter 1981/1982, spring/summer 1984, winter 1984/1985, and spring/summer 1986.
106. On the history of traditional Bedouin forms of songs and their early transformation for radio listeners, see Tawfiq al-Nimri, "Al-Musiqa wa al-Ghina'," in Da'irat al-Thaqafah wa al-Funun (Jordanian Department of Culture and Arts), *Thaqafatuna fi Khamsin 'Am* (Amman: Da'irat al-Thaqafah wa al-Funun, 1972), pp. 369–395. Also see Ahmad al-Muslih, *Malamih 'Ammah Lil-Hayah al-Thaqafiyyah Fi al-Urdunn (1953–1993)* (Amman: Manshurat Lajnat Tarikh al-Urdunn, 1995), pp. 57–61.
107. Hani al-'Amad, "Al-Fulklur Fi al-Diffah al-Sharqiyyah," in Da'irat al-Thaqafah wa al-Funun, *Thaqafatuna Fi Khamsin 'Am* (Amman: Da'irat al-Thaqafah wa al-Funun, 1972), p. 303.
108. Such books included the three-volume *Dictionary of Jordanian Traditions, Dialects and Unusual Events*, by Ruks Za'id al-'Uzayzi. See his *Qamus al-'Adat, al-Lahajat wa al-Awabid al-Urduniyyah* (Amman: Da'irat al-Thaqafah wa al-Funun, 1973–1974), vols. I, II, III.
109. Da'irat al-Thaqafah wa al-Funun, *Thaqafatuna fi Khamsin 'Am* (Amman: Da'irat al-Thaqafah wa al-Funun, 1972).
110. This is an adaptation of Johannes Fabian's critique of the structuralist anthropology of Claude Lévi-Strauss in his classic *Time and the Other: How Anthropology Makes Its Object* (New York: Columbia University Press, 1983), p. 61.
111. Ibid., p. 18.

112. Ibid., pp. 25, 31.

113. The Layathnah are enduring a different kind of transformation through the development by Amman developers of the nineteenth-century village of Taybah into a resort village renamed Taybat Zaman or "the Taybah of long ago." The new five-star hotel resort boasts of nineteenth-century village-residences converted into luxurious hotel rooms, equipped with Bani-Hamidah rugs covering the floors and with Bani-Hamidah quilts (Bani Hamidah is a tribe in northern Jordan, some 300 kilometers north of Taybah), as well as satellite television showing CNN, Israeli satellite channels, and other Arab satellite channels including the Jordanian satellite channel. The resort hotel advertises itself as environmentally conscious and claims that it has not disturbed the ecology of the area. Furthermore, it claims that it has benefited the Layathnah economically by employing many of them—its opinion of itself, however, is not shared by most Layathnah members living in the area and subjected to the total transformation of their environment, the least of which is the music blasting from the hotel garden dining hall and its live band in the middle of the night. The Taybat Zaman management assures its guests, in posters hanging in its lobby, that their "village" will transport the guests to a past time of long ago.

114. John Shoup, "The Impact of Tourism on the Bedouin of Petra," *Middle East Journal* 39; no. 2 (spring 1985): 283.

115. For the history of the Bidul, see John Shoup, "The Impact of Tourism," pp. 277–291. Also see Ahmad ʿUwaydi al-ʿAbbadi, *Fi Rubuʿ al-Urdunn, Jawlat wa Mushahadat*, part 1 (Amman: Dar al-Fikr, 1987), p. 313. Al-ʿAbbadi lists the Bidul as part of the Huwaytat tribe; see Ahmad ʿUwaydi al-ʿAbbadi, *Al-ʾAshaʾir al-Urduniyyah, al-Ard wal Insan Wal Tarikh* (Amman: Al-Dar al-ʿArabiyyah lil Nashr wal Tawziʿ, 1988), p. 633.

116. See Anna Ohannessian-Charpin, "Strategic Myths: Petra's B'doul," in *Middle East Report*, no. 196 (September/October 1995), pp. 24–25. Note that whereas many Bidul continued to work in the Petra tourist industry, in 1995 the government moved again to disrupt their lifestyle. Because of the bad ventilation in the Siq, which constitutes the entryway to Petra and which is crossed by Layathnah- and Bidul-owned and operated horses, horse dung was said to render the air unbreathable, leading the ministry of tourism to outlaw the use of horses, putting many Bidul out of business.

117. See Jürgen Habermas, *The Structural Transformation of the Public Sphere: An Inquiry into a Category of Bourgeois Society*, translated by Thomas Burger (Cambridge, MA: MIT Press, 1991).

118. Aziz al-Azmeh, *Islam and Modernities* (London: Verso, 1993), p. 12.

119. See Jamil Nasir, *The Islamic Law of Personal Status* (London: Graham and Trotman, 1986), p. 29.

120. See Enid Hill, "Islamic Law as a Source for the Development of a Comparative Jurisprudence: The modern Science of Codification (1): Theory and Practice

in the Life and Work of 'Abd al-Razzaq Ahmad al-Sanhuri (1895–1971)," in *Islamic Law: Social and Historical Contexts*, edited by Aziz al-Azmeh (London: Routledge, 1988), pp. 155, 164.

121. Sanhuri wrote this in a 1938 article quoted by Hill, ibid., p. 165.

122. Kumari Jayawardena, *Feminism and Nationalism in the Third World* (London: Zed Press, 1986).

123. Ibid., pp. 11–12.

124. Ibid., p. 15.

125. This law was published in the *Official Gazette*, no. 1081 (August 16, 1951).

126. The Temporary Personal Status Law, #61, *Official Gazette*, no. 2668 (January 1, 1976).

127. This decree was published in the *Official Gazette*, no. 3 (June 11, 1923).

128. Qanun Huquq al-'A'ilah al-Mu'aqqat (the Temporary Law of Family Rights), no. 26 for the Year 1947, *Official Gazette*, no. 915 (August 2, 1947). This was the first such law promulgated by an independent Arab state, soon to be followed by Syria, Iraq, Tunisia, and Morocco.

129. J. N. D. Anderson, "Recent Developments in Shari'a Law VIII: The Jordanian Law of Family Rights 1951," *Muslim World* 42 (1952): 190. Anderson goes through every article, tracing its legal basis in Ottoman and Egyptian laws as well as the Hanafi tradition and identifying Jordanian innovations.

130. See article 62 of the 1947 Temporary Family Rights Law, and article 64 of the 1951 Law of Family Rights. Note that the 1951 law grants a woman the right to leave the marital home without her husband's approval in cases where the husband has beaten her, harmed her (verbally), or harmed her family (verbally). In these cases, her moving out of the marital home cannot be used to exempt the husband from supporting his wife financially.

131. See article 68 of the 1976 Personal Status Law.

132. See Lynn Welchman, "The Development of Islamic Family Law in the Legal System of Jordan," in *International and Comparative Law Quarterly* 37, part 4 (October 1988): 876. Also see 'A'ishah al-Faraj al-'Atiyyat, "Al-Mar'ah Fi Zill Qanun al-Ahwal al-Shakhsiyyah al-Urduni," paper available from the Office of Advisory Services for Women (Maktab al-Khadamat al-Istishariyyah lil-Mar'ah), Amman, 1984. Also, for some of the suggested amendments to the 1976 law, see Raja' Abu Nuwwar, "Al-Mar'ah al-Urduniyyah Fi Nihayat al-'Aqd al-Dawli Lil-Mar'ah," in *Al-Urdunn al-Jadid*, nos. 3–4 (spring/summer 1985), Nicosia, Cyprus, pp. 176–177.

133. For similarities and differences in the way the Egyptian state dealt with married women, see Mervat Hatem, "The Enduring Alliance of Nationalism and Patriarchy in Muslim Personal Status Laws: The Case of Egypt," in *Feminist Issues* 6, no. 1 (spring 1986): 19–43.

134. For example, according to official statistics, whereas Jordanian women constituted 7.7 percent of the wage-earning workforce in 1979, their numbers in-

creased to 12.5 percent in 1985 and to 15 percent in 1993, cited by Suhayr al-Tall, "Dirasah Hawl Awda' al-Mar'ah al-Urduniyyah," paper presented at the Arab Institute for Human Rights in Tunis, 1994, p. 5. With the increasing unemployment levels in Jordan since the late 1980s, educated Jordanian women have been some of the worst-affected sections of the population. In 1991, the unemployment of women was 34.2 percent (compared to 14.5 percent of men); 90 percent of those unemployed women were between the ages of 20 and 40, and 70.2 percent of them held at least an associate university degree. See al-Tall, pp. 9–10.

135. Article 23-1, The Constitution of the Hashemite Kingdom of Jordan, *Official Gazette*, no. 1093 (January 8, 1952). On women's labor rights, see Jordanian Labor Laws, the last of which was enacted in 1996, see *Official Gazette*, no. 4113 (April 16, 1996).

136. Article 12 of the Passport Law no. 2, *Official Gazette*, no. 2150 (February 16, 1969).

137. On the 1990 draft law project, see Khadijah Habashnah Abu-'Ali, Center of Woman's Studies, untitled paper presented to the special panel The Jordanian Woman in the Shadow of Contemporary Laws and Legislations, Amman, March 1992.

138. For a brief but comprehensive overview of gender discrimination in Jordanian laws, see Fatimah Qassad, "Al-Mar'ah wa Ba'd al-Tashri'at," unpublished paper, Amman, n.d.

139. On Jordanian women and labor laws, see Asma' Khadir, "Al-Mar'ah al-'Amilah Fi al-Urdunn Waqi'an wa Tashri'an," unpublished paper, Amman, October 1983; see also Khalil Abu Kharmah, "Al-Mar'ah Fil Naqabat al-'Ummaliyyah," paper presented at the panel Working Women, sponsored by the Women's Committee in the Journalists Union, Amman, December 1987.

140. See the Penal Laws or Qanun al-'Uqubat no. 16, 1960, *Official Gazette*, no. 1487 (May 1, 1960), especially articles 96, 97, 283, 340.

141. See al-Tall, "Dirasah Hawl," pp. 40–41. See also Lama Abu-Odeh, *Crimes of Honor and the Construction of Gender in Arab Societies*, doctoral dissertation (Cambridge, MA: Harvard Law School, 1995).

142. See "'Amman: Qanun Jara'im al-Sharaf fi Muwajahah Bayn al-Hukumah wa al-Islamiyyin," in *Al-Hayah*, 15 February 2000, pp. 1, 6.

143. Carole Pateman, *The Sexual Contract* (Stanford, CA: Stanford University Press, 1988).

144. Ibid., p. 5.

145. Ibid., pp. 5–6.

146. Ibid., p. 7.

147. Ibid., p. 11.

148. Ibid., p. 221.

149. Ibid., p. 222.

150. Al-Mithaq al-Watani al-Urduni, article 8, text published by the Ministry of Information in December 1991. The actual charter was signed on June 9, 1991, after fourteen months of deliberations and massive press coverage, culminating in the Jordanian National Conference for the Charter, which took place on June 9, 1991. A draft of the charter was published by the Jordanian daily press (*Al-Ra'y* and *Al-Dustur*) on December 31, 1990.

151. Emily Naffa', "Dawr al-Mar'ah al-Urduniyyah Fi al-Nidal al-Siyasi," paper presented at the Jordanian Women in the Shadow of Contemporary Legislation conference held in Amman, March 23–25, 1992, p. 8.

152. Catharine Mackinnon, *Toward a Feminist Theory of the State* (Cambridge, MA: Harvard University Press, 1989).

153. Ibid., p. 163.

154. Ibid., p. 169.

155. Ibid., p. 170.

156. The manifesto is reproduced by 'Abdullah in his memoirs, *Al-Mudhakkarat*, published as part of all of 'Abduallh's works, *Al-Athar al-Kamilah Lil-Malik 'Abdullah*, 3rd edition (Beirut: Al-Dar al-Muttahidah Lil-Nashr, 1985), p. 158.

157. See Qanun Man' Buyut al-Bagha' (The Law Banning Houses of Prostitution), *Official Gazette*, no. 165 (September 1, 1927).

158. See *Al-Jazirah*, "Ghirat al-Amir al-Mu'azzam 'ala al-Taqalid wa al-Akhlaq al-'Ammah," (January 4, 1939).

159. *Al-Jazirah*, "Ra'y 'Alim Dini Kabir Fi Mushkilat al-Mar'ah al-Muslimah wa Mas'alat Sufuriha" (The Opinion of a Major Religious 'Alim About the Problem of the Muslim Woman and the Question of Her Unveiling) (February 1, 1940).

160. 'Abdullah's attitude was reportedly the same toward European women. James Lunt reports that "King Abdullah was a stickler for protocol and woe betide the European woman who entered the royal presence short-sleeved and short-skirted." in James Lunt, *Glubb Pasha: A Biography* (London: Harvill Press, 1984), p. 175.

161. *Al-Jazirah*, "Hirs Sumuw al-Amir al-Mu'azzam 'ala al-Akhlaq al-'Ammah wa al-Mazahir al-Islamiyyah" (The Avidity of his Majesty the Prince about Public Ethics and Islamic Appearances) (March 20, 1940). Note that this concern with women teachers' public appearance was not peculiar to 'Abdullah but was more of a universal phenomenon. Three decades earlier, in a Massachusetts town, in the United States, the school board issued "Rules for Female Teachers," which included that women teachers "not dress in bright colors," "not dye [their] hair," and "not wear any dress more than two inches above the ankle," as well as "not keep company with men," "not smoke," "be home between the hours of 8 p. m. and 6 a. m." The "Rules" are reproduced in Howard Zinn, *A People's History of the United States* (New York: Harper & Row, 1980), p. 330.

162. The amir's decree, the prime minister's letter, and the judge's manifesto were all published in *Al-Jazirah*, "Al-Iradah al-Saniyyah Bi Man' al-Tabarruj," (March 27, 1940).

163. *Al-Jazirah*, "Al-Raghbah al-Saniyyah Fi Ittikhadh al-Mula'ah Libasan Lil-Mar'ah al-Muslimah Kharij Baytiha" (The Exalted Desire that the Muslim Woman Don *Al-Mula'ah* as Her Dress Outside Her Home) (July 27, 1940).

164. See his *Al-Mudhakkarat*, p. 44.

165. See for example *Al-Jazirah*, August 7, 1940, p. 2, and August 24, 1940; these articles were written by Fathi Mustafa al-Mufti.

166. See "Man Yuthir Harakat al-Fasad Fil Madinah? Al-Tilmidhah Aw al-Mu'alli- mah?" (Who Provokes the Movement of Corruption in the City? The Girl- Student or the Woman-Teacher?) *Al-Jazirah* (August 17, 1940).

167. *Al-Jazirah* (October 10, 1940).

168. *Al-Jazirah* (August 24, 1940).

169. 'Awni Jaddu' al-'Ubaydi, *Jama'at al-Ikhwan al-Muslimin Fi al-Urdunn was Fi- lastin 1945—1970, Safahat Tarikhiyyah* (Amman: n.p., 1991), pp. 40–41.

170. *Al-Jazirah* (February 6, 1945).

171. "Ayyatuha al-Mar'ah al-Mutabarrijah,"*Al-Jazirah* (January 25, 1946). In his poem, al-Shanqiti expresses his horror that with this kind of appearance, men cannot tell who among such women are "virgins" and who are "'Awani" (which literally means middle-aged but in this context means nonvirgins) or between "adulteresses" and those who might be considered their "equals."

172. See for example Taysir Zibyan, *Al-Malik 'Abdullah Kama 'Araftahu* (King 'Abdullah as I Knew Him), 2nd edition (Amman: n.p., 1994), pp. 63–67. See also 'Awni Jaddu' al-'Ubaydi, *Jama'at al-Ikhwan al-Muslimin*, pp. 38–41.

173. John Bagot Glubb, *A Soldier with the Arabs* (London: Hodder and Stoughton, 1957), p. 214.

174. Interview with Taysir Zibyan on August 3, 1951, cited in his *Al-Malik 'Abdullah Kama 'Araftahu*, p. 67.

175. The law was signed on July 17, 1951, see *Official Gazette*, no. 1081, August 16, 1951.

176. Wizarat al-I'lam, *Al-Mar'ah al-Urduniyyah* (Amman: Ministry of Information's Department of Press and Publications, 1979), p. 20.

177. Ibid.

178. On the merchant class, see Abla Amawi, *State and Class in Transjordan*.

179. Wizarat al-I'lam, *Al-Mar'ah al-Urduniyyah*, p. 21. It is unknown why the so- ciety was dissolved or on whose initiative it was dissolved.

180. Ibid., p. 22.

181. See Suhayr al-Tall, *Muqaddimah*, p. 122–123.

182. The research center for women's studies was founded in 1990. This club or- ganizes conferences for business women, has a consultative office offering legal advice to women on women's issues, and publishes a number of informative

brochures on a variety of subjects including women and social security, women and labor laws, tenancy laws, retirement laws, civil service, personal status laws, and divorce.

183. *Business and Professional Women Newsletter*, no. 1 (May 1992).

184. Al-Ittihad al-Nisa'i al-'Arabi was founded on June 17, 1954, at a meeting of over 100 Jordanian women at the Philadelphia Hotel in downtown Amman (the owners of the hotel, Antoine Nazzal and his wife, donated the hotel hall-room and services for the meeting). Among those attending were Samihah al-Majali, Faridah Shubaylat, Emily Bisharat, Widad Bulus, Lam'a al-Razzaz, Salwa Dajani, Fayruz Sa'd, Zaha Manko, and Faridah Ghanma. See *Al-Difa'* (June 18, 1954); see also *Filastin* (June 16, 1954). For press coverage of the subsequent internal developments within al-Ittihad, see *Al-Difa'* (June 22, 1954 and June 26, 1954). On support for the Ittihad from other cities and towns, see the letter sent to the prime minister by the women of Ramallah in *Al-Jihad* (December 3, 1954). For the history of this period, see Suha Kamil 'Id, "Tarikh Nidal al-Mar'ah Fi al-Urdunn Fi Wajh al-Mukhattatat al-Suhyuniyyah," (The History of Women's Struggle in Jordan in the Face of Zionist Schemes), un-published paper, October 1983, Ministry of Social Development.

185. For the history of the Union, see Da'id Mu'adh, "Tajribat al-Ittihad al-Nisa'i (1974–1981)," in *Al-Urdunn al-Jadid* no. 7 (spring 1986): 59–64.

186. See al-Tall, *Muqaddimah*, pp. 125–165. For a critique of the record of the new official union, see Majidah al-Masri, "Al-Azmah al-Rahinah Lil-Harakah al-Nisa'iyyah fi al-Urdunn," in *Al-Urdunn al-Jadid*, no. 7 (spring 1986): 65–69.

187. For a list of all members of the council, see Sa'id Darwish, *Al-Marhalah al-Dimuqratiyyah al-Jadidah Fil Urdunn, Tafasil al-Munaqashat wa Hukumat al-Thiqah* (Beirut and Amman: Dana, a subsidiary of Al-Mu'assasah al-'Arabiyyah Lil Dirasat wa al-Nashr, 1990), pp. 160–161.

188. Ibid., p. 162.

189. Ibid., p. 164.

190. Al-Tall, *Muqaddimah*, p. 117–118. About the union, see chapter 6.

191. See *Al-Mar'ah al-Urduniyyah*, pp. 147–154. For media coverage of women and women's issues in this period, see Suhayr al-Tall, "Al-Siyasah al-I'lamiyyah wa Qadayah al-Mar'ah," in *Al-Urdunn al-Jadid*, no. 7 (spring 1986), pp. 70–73.

192. *Al-Muqawamah al-Sha'biyyah*, no. 10 (June 1951), cited by Emily Naffa', "Dawr al-Mar'ah al-Urduniyyah Fi al-Nidal al-Siyasi," Paper presented at the Jordanian Women in the Shadow of Contemporary Legislation conference held in Amman, March 23–25, 1992, p. 3. Also see Suha Kamil 'Id, "Tarikh Nidal al-Mar'ah Fi al-Urdunn Fi Wajh al-Mukhattatat al-Suhyuniyyah," Oc-tober 1983, Ministry of Social Development, pp. 9–10.

193. *Al-Difa'* (November 30, 1954).

194. Documents of the Women's Awakening League cited by Emily Naffa', "Dawr al-Mar'ah," p. 4.

195. "Nuridu Haqqana Kamilan," *Filastin* (October 10, 1955).

196. *Filastin* (October 12, 1955).

197. *Al-Mithaq*, the Jordanian Socialist Party mouthpiece, 1956, cited by Emily Naffa', "Dawr al-Mar'ah," p. 4.

198. See *Filastin* (March 30, 1956, April 19, 1956). Around the same time, Queen Zayn, King Husayn's mother, donated a gold watch to be raffled (by the Ittihad) for the benefit of the National Guard. See *Filastin* (March 19, 1956). The raffle brought a profit of 500 Jordanian dinars. See *Filastin* (April 1, 1956).

199. See *Filastin*, April 12, 1956, and April 18, 1956.

200. See " Raja' Abu 'Ammashah . . . Fi Damir al-Sha'b wa al-Watan," in *Al-Tali'ah*, a Amman weekly, no. 94 (January 1, 1956), reprinted in *Al-Urdunn al-Jadid*, no. 7 (spring 1986), p. 160, and see Suhayr al-Tall, *Muqqadimah*, p. 113n.

201. Ibid., pp. 113–116.

202. See Hayfa' al-Bashir and Hiyam Najib al-Shuraydah, "Al-Musharakah al-Siyasiyyah lil Mar'ah al-Urduniyyah wa Ittijahat al-Qita' al-Siyasi Nahwa 'Amaliha Fi Nafs al-Majal" (Political Participation of Jordanian Women and the Direction of the Political Sector Toward Her Work in the Same Field), paper presented at the National Conference on Jordanian Women, Reality and Vision (al-Mu'tamar al-Watani lil Mar'ah al-Urduniyyah, Waqi' wa Tatallu'at) held in Amman, May 14–16, 1985, p. 6.

203. Ibid.

204. 'Ablah Mahmud Abu 'Ulbah, "Al-Mar'ah al-Urduniyyah wa al-Nidal al-Siyasi" (Jordanian Women and Political Struggle), paper presented at the Jordanian Women in the Shadow of Contemporary Legislation, a conference sponsored by the General Federation of Jordanian Women, held in Amman on 23–25 March, 1992, p. 2.

205. See *Intikhabat 1993: Dirasah Tahliliyyah wa Raqamiyyah* (The 1993 Elections: An Analytical and a Numerical Study) (Amman: Markaz al-Urdunn al-Jadid, February 1994).

206. *Al-Hayah* (November 5, 1997), p. 7.

207. *Al-Hayah* (October 22, 1997), p. 4.

208. *Al-Hayah* (November 6, 1997), p. 1.

209. Zionist ideology has always been ambivalent about the Middle East. On the one hand, it portrays European Jews as having originated historically in the Middle East (to lay its suspect colonial claim to Palestine), while simulta-neously portraying them as modern gentile Europeans carrying gentile enlight-enment European achievements to a desolate Asian outpost (the implication being that the couple of millennia of Jewish residence in Europe forced them to shed their uncivilized Middle-Eastern roots, adopting instead civilized gentile European norms). This ambivalence about being *in* but not *of* the Middle East continued in Israeli culture after the settler-colony was established. While mod-ern Jewish Israelis are presented as indistinguishable from gentile Europeans

in terms of lifestyle and technoaesthetic culture, Zionist theft of Palestinian Arab food (e.g., hummus, falafil) and dance (dabkah), Palestinian Armenian pottery, and Yemeni and other Arab jewelry making (now coded as "Yemenite-Jewish" as if Yemeni Jews were living in complete isolation) is engineered to give a "Middle Eastern" flavor to an otherwise gentile European, Hebrew-speaking people. For an examination of Zionist and Israeli cultural forms, see Joseph Massad, "The 'Post-Colonial' Colony: Time, Space and Bodies in Palestine/Israel," in *The Pre-Occupation of Post-Colonial Studies*, edited by Fawzia Afzal-Khan and Kalpana Seshadri-Crooks (Durham, NC: Duke University Press, 2000).

3. Cultural Syncretism or Colonial Mimic Men: Jordan's Bedouins and the Military Basis of National Identity

1. Chandra Talpade Mohanty, "Introduction: Cartographies of Struggle: Third World Women and the Politics of Feminism," in Chandra Talpade Mohanty, Ann Russo, and Lourdes Torres, eds., *Third World Women and the Politics of Feminism* (Bloomington, IN: Indiana University Press, 1991), pp. 1–49.

2. Ibid., p. 16.

3. Timothy Mitchell, *Colonising Egypt* (Berkeley, CA: University of California Press, 1991), p. xi.

4. On Western cultural cross-dressing, see Marjorie Garber's essay "The Chic of Araby: Transvestism and the Erotics of Cultural Appropriation," in her *Vested Interests: Cross-Dressing and Cultural Anxiety* (New York: Harper Perennial, 1993), pp. 304–352.

5. See Eric Hobsbawm and Terence Ranger, eds., *The Invention of Tradition* (Cambridge: Cambridge University Press, 1983).

6. Louis Althusser, "Ideology and Ideological State Apparatuses (Notes Toward an Investigation)," in *Lenin and Philosophy and Other Essays* (New York: Monthly Review Press, 1971), p. 169.

7. The following historical review is based on Munib Madi and Sulayman Musa, *Tarikh al-Urdunn Fi al-Qarn al-'Ishrin 1900–1959* (Amman: Maktabat al-Muhtasib, 1959); Benjamin Shwadran, *Jordan A State of Tension* (New York: Council for Middle Eastern Affairs, 1959); Uriel Dann, *Studies in the History of Transjordan, 1920–1949: The Making of a State* (Boulder, CO: Westview Press, 1984); Sa'd Abu-Dayyah and 'Abd al-Majid Mahdi, *Al-Jaysh al-'Arabi wa Diblumasiyyat al-Sahra', Dirasah Fi Nash'atihi wa Tatawwur Dawr al-Thaqafah al-'Askariyyah* (Amman: Mudiriyyat al-Matabi' al-'Askariyyah, 1987); Ma'an Abu Nowar, *The History of the Hashemite Kingdom of Jordan*, vol. I: *The Creation and Development of Transjordan 1920–1929* (Oxford: Ithaca Press, 1989); Abla Amawi, *State and Class in Trans-Jordan: A Study of State Autonomy*, doctoral dissertation (Washington, DC: Georgetown University, 1993); P. J. Vatikiotis, *Politics and the Military in Jordan: A Study of the Arab*

Legion, 1921–1957 (New York: Frederick A. Praeger, 1967); and Sa'd Abu-Dayyah and 'Abd al-Majid Mahdi, *Tarikh al-Jaysh al-'Arabi Fi 'Ahd al-Imarah, 1921–1946, Dirasah 'Ilmiyyah Tahliliyyah* (Amman: Al-Matabi' al-'Askariyyah, 1989).

8. F. G. Peake, "Transjordan," *Journal of the Royal Central Asian Society* XXVI, part III (July 1939): 388.

9. Frederick G. Peake, unpublished autobiography, Imperial War Museum, F. G. Peake (Peake Pasha) Papers, DS/Misc/16, Reel 1, cited by George S. Dragnich, *The Bedouin Warrior Ethic and the Transformation of Traditional Nomadic Warriors into Modern Soldiers within the Arab Legion, 1931–1948*, masters thesis in history (Washington, DC: Georgetown University, 1975), p. 61, note 1.

10. Bernard Vernier adds that this appellation bestowed on this force "faisait entrevoir que cette troupe modèle pourrait un jour devenir le noyau de l'armée unifieé de l'arabisme," in Bernard Vernier, *Armée et Politique au Moyen-Orient* (Paris: Payot, 1966), p. 83.

11. Benjamin Shwadran, *Jordan*, p. 159. Ma'an Abu Nowar states that aside from a few Transjordanians, the TJFF included Circassians, Chechens, Armenians, Jews, Palestinian Arabs, Sudanese, Lebanese, Syrians, Egyptians, and Druze Arabs. In addition, the TJFF enlisted British officers and N.C.O.s of ex–Black and Tans, previously used by the British against Irish nationalists. See Ma'an Abu Nowar, *The History*, p. 174. Note how Abu Nowar does not consider Circassians and Chechens "Transjordanian."

12. Article 10, *Agreement Between the United Kingdom and Trans-Jordan*, signed in Jerusalem on February 20, 1928. This agreement was never ratified by the Trans-Jordanian legislature.

13.. *Official Gazette* (June 17, 1944), p. 796.

14. C. S. Jarvis, *Arab Command: The Biography of Lieutenant-Colonel F. G. Peake Pasha* (London: Hutchinson & Co., 1942), p. 59.

15. Quoted in Jarvis, *Arab Command*, p. 59.

16. Uriel Dann, *Studies in*, p. 88.

17. See Sa'd Abu Dayyah and 'Abd al-Majid al-Nas'ah, *Tarikh al-Jaysh, al-'Arabi fi 'Ahd al-Imarah, 1921–1946, Dirasah 'Ilmiyyah Tahliliyyah Watha'iqiyyah* (Amman: n.p., 1990), pp. 69, 81.

18. Quoted in Jarvis, *Arab Command*, p. 61.

19. On the need to control the desert and the increasing tension between the Saudis and the Transjordanian governments, see Ricardo Bocco and Tariq M. M. Tell, "Pax Britannica in the Steppe: British Policy and the Transjordan Bedouin," in *Village Steppe and State: The Social Origins of Modern Jordan*, edited by Eugene Rogan and Tariq Tell (London: British Academic Press, 1994), pp. 116–120.

20. Quoted in Jarvis, *Arab Command*, p. 62.

21. Quoted ibid., p. 62.

22. Quoted ibid., p. 83.

23. Quoted ibid., p. 88.

24.. Ibid., pp. 107–109.

25. Peter Young, *Bedouin Command: With the Arab Legion 1953–1956* (London: William Kimber, 1956), pp. 24–25.

26. Young, *Bedouin Command*, p. 37.

27. James Lunt, *Glubb Pasha: A Biography* (London: Harvill Press, 1984), p. 94.

28. John Bagot Glubb, *A Soldier with the Arabs* (London: Hodder and Stoughton, 1957), pp. 369–370.

29. Lunt, *Glubb Pasha*, pp. 98–99. Lunt adds to his defense of Glubb a quote from Albert Hourani: "Although Glubb was far too intelligent to dismiss city-dwellers out of hand, he was much happier in the society of bedouins and villagers." See also p. 168.

30. Syed Ali El-Edroos, *The Hashemite Arab Army, 1908–1979: An Appreciation and Analysis of Military Operations* (Amman: Publishing Committee, 1980), pp. 213–214. El-Edroos is of Pakistani nationality. It is interesting that, aside from some memoirs and a few unimpressive period histories, there is no single Jordanian historian who wrote a comprehensive history of the armed forces. Also, not only is the Pakistani connection a state-to-state military alliance, but also it extends to the royal family, as former crown-prince Hasan, Husayn's brother, is married to a Pakistani, Princess Servat, or as she is known in Jordan, Princess Tharwat.

31. El-Edroos, *The Hashemite Arab Army*, p. 214.

32. Glubb, *A Soldier*, p. 261.

33. Lunt, *Glubb Pasha*, p. 97.

34. Great Britain, Colonial Office, *Report by His Majesty's Government in the United Kingdom of Great Britain and Northern Ireland to the Council of the League of Nations on the Administration of Palestine and Trans-Jordan for the Year 1933* (London: His Majesty's Stationary Office, 1934), p. 318.

35. Nicos Poulantzas, *State, Power, Socialism*, translated by Patrick Camiller (London: NLB, 1978), p. 77.

36. John Bagot Glubb, *The Story of the Arab Legion* (London: Hodder and Stoughton, 1948), p. 22.

37. Ibid., p. 37.

38. Edward Said, *Orientalism* (New York: Vintage Books, 1979), p. 96.

39. *Al-Istiqlal*, November 16, 1928, cited by James Lunt, *Glubb Pasha*, p. 60. Lieutenant-Colonel G. E. Leachman (1880–1920) was a soldier, explorer, traveler, and administrator in Mesopotamia, where he was murdered near Falluja by members of the Ramadi tribe on August 12, 1920. He traveled among the Bedouins in disguise. See Lunt, p. 60, note.

40. Thomas Henry Thornton, *Colonel Sir Robert Sandeman: His Life and Work on an Indian Frontier: A Memoir, with Selections from His Correspondence and*

Official Writings (London: John Murray, 1895). I would like to thank Riccardo Bocco for directing me to Sandeman's biography.

41. Monthly Reports on the Administration of the Transjordan Deserts, A Sandeman Policy, March 1935, cited in Riccardo Bocco, *État et Tribus Bedouines en Jordanie, 1920–1990, Les Huwaytat: Territoire, Changement Économique, Identité Politique*, doctoral dissertation, Institut d'Études Politiques de Paris, 1996, p. 135.

42. *Journal of the Royal Society of Asian Affairs* XVII, part III (October 1986): 357.

43. John Bagot Glubb, "Relations Between Arab Civilization and Foreign Culture in the Past and To-day," *Journal of the Royal Central Asian Society* XXIV (July 1937): 417.

44. John B. Glubb, "The Conflict Between Tradition and Modernism in the Role of Muslim Armies," in *The Conflict of Traditionalism and Modernism in the Middle East*, edited by Carl Leiden (Austin: University of Texas Press, 1966), pp. 9–21.

45. Ibid., p. 9.

46. Glubb, "Relations Between," p. 418.

47. Ibid., p. 419.

48. Ibid., p. 419.

49. John Bagot Glubb, *The Changing Scenes of Life, An Autobiography* (London: Quarter Books, 1983), pp. 212–214.

50. Glubb, "The Conflict," p. 17.

51. See Edward Said, *Orientalism*, p. 172.

52. Glubb, *The Story*, p. 147.

53. Ibid., p. 42.

54. Glubb, *A Soldier*, p. 347.

55. Ibid., p. 401.

56. Glubb, *The Changing*, p. 175.

57. Glubb, *A Soldier*, p. 370.

58. Glubb, *The Changing*, p. 81.

59. Glubb, "The Conflict," p. 18.

60. Ibid., p. 18.

61. Glubb, "Relations Between," p. 421.

62. John Bagot Glubb, *Britain and the Arabs: A Study of Fifty Years 1908–1958* (London: Hodder and Stoughton, 1959), p. 171.

63. Glubb, "Relations Between," p. 421.

64. Ibid., p. 422.

65. Ibid., p. 422.

66. Ibid., p. 424.

67. Ibid., p. 424.

68. Glubb, "The Conflict," p. 15. See also Glubb, *The Story*, p. 38.

69. Glubb, "Relations Between," p. 424.

70. Glubb, *The Story*, p. 199.
71. Michel Foucault, *Discipline and Punish: The Birth of the Prison*, translated by Alan Sheridan (New York: Vintage Books, 1977), p. 139.
72. Glubb, "Relations Between," pp. 424–425.
73. Ibid., p. 425.
74. Glubb, *The Story*, p. 103.
75. Jarvis, *Arab Command*, p. 129.
76. Timothy Mitchell, *Colonising Egypt*, pp. xiii, xiv.
77. Ibid., p. xv.
78. Guy Debord, *The Society of the Spectacle* (New York: Zone Books, 1994), p. 26.
79. See Karl Marx, "The Fetishism of Commodities and the Secret Thereof," in *Capital*, vol. 1: *A Critical Analysis of Capitalist Production*, edited by Frederick Engels (New York: International Publishers, 1967), pp. 71–83.
80. As T. E. Lawrence explains: "All the subject provinces of the Empire were not worth one dead English boy," quoted in Stephen Ely Tabachnick, "The Two Veils of T. E. Lawrence," *Studies in the Twentieth Century*, no. 16 (fall 1975), p. 97.
81. Glubb, *The Changing*, pp. 102–103.
82. Great Britain, Colonial Office, *Report*, p. 281. Note that since 1923, Peake contracted a recent Armenian immigrant, Haïg Peltékian, to become the tailor for the Arab Legion. Haïg Pasha (or, more precisely, Hayk Pasha), as he became known after 'Abdullah bestowed on him this Ottoman title, became also the personal tailor for 'Abdullah. Until 1940, Haïg employed thirty Armenian workers and became "the supplier of army uniforms." See Anna Ohannessian-Charpin, "Les Arméniens à Amman: La Naissance d'une Communauté," in Jean Hannoyer and Seteney Shami, eds., *Amman: The City and Its Society* (Beirut: CERMOC, 1996), pp. 333–334.
83. Shelagh Weir, *Palestinian Costume* (Austin: University of Texas Press, 1989), p. 68. Palestinian peasants before the 1930s mostly wore the *Tarbush Maghribi* or the *Laffah*. Before the 1930s, only Palestinian Bedouins wore the *hatta*, see ibid., pp. 58–66. See also Walid Khalidi, *Before Their Diaspora: A Photographic History of the Palestinian People 1876–1948* (Washington, DC: Institute for Palestine Studies, 1991), especially the pictures on the following pages: 198, 208, 209, 219, 221, 226. See also Sarah Graham-Brown, *Palestinians and Their Society 1880–1946: A Photographic Essay* (London: Quartet Books, 1980), pp. 166, 169, 174–176, 181.
84. Sir Gawain Bell, *Shadows on the Sand: The Memoirs of Sir Gawain Bell* (New York: St. Martin's Press, 1983), pp. 141–142.
85. Musa 'Adil Bakmirza Shirdan, *Al-Urdunn Bayna 'Ahdayn* (Amman: n.p., 1957?), p. 24.

86. I would like to thank Dr. Ma'n Abu Nuwwar for the information he provided me regarding this point. Also, on the modifications in clothing during this period, see Dragnich, *The Bedouin Warrior*, p. 159.

87. Glubb, *The Story*, p. 335.

88. Glubb, *The Changing*, p. 106.

89. Letter, February 13, 1980, cited by Lunt, *Glubb Pasha*, p. 169.

90. Ibid., p. 169.

91. Said, *Orientalism*, p. 160.

92. Ibid., p. 160.

93. Glubb, *A Soldier*, p. 19.

94. On performatively constituted identities, see Judith Butler, *Gender Trouble: Feminism and the Subversion of Identity* (New York: Routledge, 1990).

95. Glubb, *A Soldier*, p. 419.

96. Ibid., p. 419. In his autobiography, Glubb identifies the Arab diplomat as Lebanon's president. See *The Changing*, p. 169

97. Ghalib Halasa, *Zunuj, Badu, wa Fallahun* (Beirut: Dar al-Masir, 1980), p. 6.

98. Glubb, *The Changing*, p. 83.

99. Glubb, *The Story*, p. 248.

100. Glubb reveled in these titles and writes of them glowingly. See Glubb, *A Soldier*, p. 372.

101. Glubb, *The Changing*, p. 115.

102. Glubb, *A Soldier*, p. 264.

103. Lunt, *Glubb Pasha*, p. 176. On another occasion, Lunt asserts that "Unlike T. E. Lawrence or St. John Philby, he never dressed as an Arab, but always wore the uniform of the Arab Legion. . . . He was of course enormously helped by his fluency in Arabic, reading and writing it with equal ease," p. 81.

104. John Glubb, *War In the Desert, An R.A.F. Frontier Campaign* (New York: W. W. Norton, 1961), p. 146.

105. Glubb, *A Soldier*, p. 51.

106. Glubb, *The Changing*, p. 129.

107. Quoted in Larry Collins and Dominique Lapierre, *O Jerusalem* (New York: Simon & Schuster, 1972), p. 198.

108. J. Glubb "The Bedouins of Northern Iraq," *Journal of the Royal Central Asian Society* XXII, part I (January 1935): 13.

109. Lunt, *Glubb Pasha*, pp. 185–186.

110. Young, *Bedouin Command*, p. 33.

111. Extract from a circular letter from Glubb to British officers, no. A:CO/1/3, cited by Lunt, *Glubb Pasha*, p. 117.

112. T. E. Lawrence, "Twenty-Seven Articles," first published in the *Arab Bulletin*, #60, August 20, 1920, reproduced in John E. Mack, *A Prince of Our Disorder* (London: Weidenfeld and Nicolson, 1976), p. 467.

113. Gawain Bell, *Shadows*, pp. 144–145.
114. Glubb, *The Changing*, p. 106.
115. Lunt, *Glubb Pasha*, p. 117.
116. *Monthly Report*, July 1933, cited by Lunt, *Glubb Pasha*, p. 84.
117. Glubb, *A Soldier*, p. 414.
118. Lunt, *Glubb Pasha*, p. 90.
119. See Trevor Royle, *Glubb Pasha* (London: Little Brown, 1992), p. 297. When I wrote my dissertation, I had not read Royle's account and had to rely on erroneous information claiming that Naomi was of Palestinian origins. Royle's account based on interviews with Naomi Glubb puts the matter to rest. A picture of Naomi and her mother, Rosemary Glubb, can be seen in Lunt, *Glubb Pasha*, between p. 110 and p. 111.
120. Royle, *Glubb Pasha*, pp. 321–322.
121. Glubb, *A Soldier*, pp. 414–415.
122. John Glubb, *Arabian Adventures: Ten Years of Joyful Service* (London: Cassell, 1978), p. 24.
123. Glubb, *A Soldier*, p. 6.
124. Ibid., p. 419.
125. Ibid., p. 445.
126. Ibid., p. 194. For the actual collusion between the Jordanian government, Glubb, and Mr. Bevin, see Avi Shlaim, *Collusion Across the Jordan: King Abdullah, the Zionist Movement, and the Partition of Palestine* (New York: Columbia University Press, 1988), pp. 134–138. For more information on the loss of Ramlah and Lydda, see ibid., pp. 261–267.
127. See, for example, Riyad Ahmad Bunduqji, *Al-Urdunn Fi 'Ahd Klub* (Amman: Matabi' al-Safadi, circa 1957).
128. Gustave Schlumberger describes the creation of Outre-Jourdain as follows: "Aussi les rois chrétiens de Jérusalem avaient-ils dès longtemps reconnu la nécessité de constituter ces divers territoires avec leurs grands châteaux en une seigneurie unique, sorte de marche frontière d'importance capitale, avant-garde du royaume s'avançant par delà la mer Morte jusqu'à la mer Rouge, éperon audacieux projeté entre les deux grandes divisions du monde sarrasin avoisinant: l'Égypte et la Syrie. Du nom de ces deux principales forteresses, aussi de celui de la ville d'Hébron, près de la rive occidentale du lac Asphaltite, qui en faisait partie, cette seigneurie si fameuse dans l'histoire des guerres de la Croisade avait pris le nom de seigneurie de Karak et Montréal, ou simplement du Karak et Montréal, ou encore d'Hébron, de Karak et Montréal, plus souvent même du Karak, ou par corruption du Krak, tout court. On l'appelait aussi, en raison de sa situation *au delà du Jourdain*, ou encore des terres bibliques ou antiques dont elle occupait l'étendue, seigneurie de *la terre d'outre Jourdain*, ou seigneurie de la terre Moab et d'Idumée." *Renaud de Chatillon, Prince D'Antioche, Seigneur de la Terre d'Outre-Jourdain*, by Gustave Schlumberger,

Plon-Nourrit, Paris, 1923, p. 147, emphases added. He also states that "On l'appelait encore 'Terre d'Oultre le Jourdain,' " p. 152. He adds that "Ce qui faisait que les chrétiens attachaient tant de prix à la conservation de ces puissants châteaux d'Outre-Jourdain, que les Sarassins, d'autre part, s'efforçaient sans cesse de s'en emparer, c'était . . . la situation incomparable qu'ils occupaient sur les routes militaires et commerciales conduisant de l'Égypte en Syrie et en Arabie, et sur celle du Hadj, ou du pèlerinage aux villes saintes," p. 163.

129. Glubb, *The Story*, pp. 187–188.

130. For more information about Renaud De Chatillon, see Gustave Schlumberger, *Renaud de Chatillon*.

131. Glubb, *The Story*, p. 248.

132. Edward Gibbon, *The History of the Decline and Fall of the Roman Empire*, edited by J. B. Bury, vol. VI (London: Methuen, 1912), p. 325. On de Bouillon, also see Frederick G. Peake, *History and Tribes of Jordan* (Coral Gables: University of Miami Press, 1958).

133. Royle, *Glubb Pasha*, p. 322.

134. Glubb, "Relations Between," p. 425.

135. Glubb, "The Conflict," p. 17.

136. Glubb, *A Soldier*, p. 6.

137. Homi Bhabha, "Of Mimicry and Man: The Ambivalence of Colonial Discourse," *October*, no. 28 (spring 1984), p. 126.

138. J. B. Glubb, "The Mixture of Races in the Eastern Arab Countries," The J. L. Myers Memorial Lecture was delivered at New College, Oxford, on 25th April, 1967.

139. Glubb, *A Soldier*, p. 32.

140. Ibid., p. 151.

141. Ibid., p. 152.

142. Ibid., pp. 164–165.

143. Glubb, *A Soldier*, p. 335.

144. Ibid., p. 385.

145. Ibid., p. 388.

146. Glubb, *The Changing*, p. 172.

147. Ibid.

148. Ibid.

149. Ibid., p. 176.

150. Glubb, *A Soldier*, p. 37.

151. Glubb, *Periodic Report*, February-May 1942, cited by Lunt, *Glubb Pasha*, p. 107.

152. Glubb, *The Story*, p. 253–254.

153. Ibid., p. 355.

154. Ibid., p. 181.

155. Glubb, *A Soldier*, p. 265.

156. Glubb, *The Story*, p. 20.
157. Ibid., p. 325.
158. Ibid., pp. 103–104. Glubb even tells us how Bedouin soldiers made bread for lunch, ibid., pp. 104–105.
159. Lunt, *Glubb Pasha*, p. 102. Also see Peter Young, *The Arab Legion* (Berkshire: Osprey Publishing, 1972), p. 30.
160. I would like to thank Dr. Ma'n Abu Nuwwar for the information he provided me on this matter.
161. Musa 'Adil Bakmirza Shirdan, *Al-Urdunn Bayna 'Ahdayn*, pp. 24–25.
162. Glubb, *The Story*, p. 96. Contrast these descriptions of women with the noble descriptions of the Shammar tribe on pp. 20–21.
163. Ibid., p. 42.
164. Ibid., p. 160.
165. Ibid.
166. Ibid., p. 161.
167. Ibid.
168. Glubb, *Britain and*, p. 171.
169. Glubb, *The Story*, p. 87.
170. Ibid., pp. 149–150.
171. Glubb, *The Changing*, p. 60. On how Arabs imparted to Europeans chivalrous behavior, see J. B. Glubb, "Arab Chivalry," *The Journal of the Royal Central Asian Society* XXIV, part I (January 1937).
172. Edward Said, *Orientalism*, p. 104.
173. Ibid., p. 67.
174. Glubb, *The Story*, p. 150.
175. Glubb, *A Soldier*, p. 188.
176. On filiation and affiliation, see Edward Said, *The World: The Text and the Critic* (Cambridge, MA: Harvard University Press, 1983).
177. Glubb, *The Changing*, p. 114.
178. Ibid., p. 113.
179. Ibid., p. 108.
180. Ibid., p. 114.
181. Glubb, *The Story*, p. 37.
182. Ibid., p. 45.
183. Ibid., pp. 58–59.
184. Godfrey Lias, *Glubb's Legion* (London: Evans Brothers, 1956), p. 88.
185. Glubb, *The Story*, pp. 92–93.
186. On Glubb's earliest Iraqi recruits into the Legion, see Sa'd Abu Dayyah and 'Abd al-Majid Mahdi, *Al-Jaysh al-'Arabi*, pp. 103–107.
187. See Ricardo Bocco and Tariq M. M. Tell, "Pax Britannica in the Steppe," p. 122.

188. Great Britain, *Report . . . for the Year 1933*, p. 283.
189. See George S. Dragnich, *The Bedouin Warrior*, p. 110.
190. Dragnich, *The Bedouin Warrior*, p. 111.
191. See article 2b and article 16 of The Law of Tribal Courts for the Year 1936, published in the *Official Gazette*, no. 516 (February 16, 1936). Note that these powers were given the head of the Arab Legion over *nomadic* Bedouins. Also, the administrative structure of the government also changed in 1939. The Organic Law was amended so that the Executive Council was replaced by the Council of Ministers, and a Defense Ministry was created that soon merged with the Ministry of the Interior with one minister (Rashid al-Madfaʿi) presiding over both.
192. Glubb, *The Story*, p. 102.
193. Ibid., p. 113.
194. Ibid., p. 177.
195. Ibid., p. 165.
196. J. B. Glubb, "The Economic Situation of the Trans-Jordan Tribes," *Journal of the Royal Central Asian Society* XXV, part III (July 1938): 458.
197. Glubb's Monthly Reports on the administration of the Transjordan deserts, Arab Legion Headquarters, April 1940, cited by Riccardo Bocco, *État et Tribus*, p. 303n.
198. Cited in Bocco, *État et Tribus*, p. 198.
199. Glubb, *The Story*, p. 219.
200. Ibid., pp. 363–364.
201. Ibid., p. 82.
202. Ibid., pp. 82–83.
203. Ibid., p. 83.
204. Ibid., p. 99.
205. Glubb's Monthly Reports on the Administration of the Transjordan Desert, The Desert Medical Unit, February 1940, cited by Bocco, *Etat et Tribus*, pp. 201, 304n.
206. ʿAdil Ziyadat, "Al-Khadamat al-Tibbiyyah Lil-Jaysh al-ʿArabi fi ʿAhd al-Imarah, 1921–1946," *Abhath al-Yarmuk* 7, no. 2 (1991): 180–181.
207. Louis Althusser, "Ideology," p. 145.
208. Glubb, *The Changing*, p. 65.
209. Ibid., p. 105.
210. Ibid., p. 145.
211. Lunt, *Glubb Pasha*, p. 80. More information on the forts with the Transjordan flags fluttering from them connecting the desert and acting as reconnaissance stations fit with wireless connected to Amman can be found on pp. 80–81.
212. On military schools set up by Glubb, see Saʿd Abu Dayyah and ʿAbd al-Majid Mahdi, *Al-Jaysh al-ʿArabi*, pp. 119–145, 162–166.

213. Glubb, A *Soldier*, p. 263.
214. Ibid., p. 263.
215. Ibid.
216. Ibid., p. 265. The word *Watan*, which Glubb translated as nation, actually means homeland.
217. Letter from Glubb to de Chair, in Somerset de Chair, *The Golden Carpet* (New York: Harcourt, Brace, 1945), p. 244.
218. Ibid., p. 368.
219. He speaks derisively of Jordan's defense minister for making such queries concerning the educational level of officers. See Glubb, *The Changing*, p. 160.
220. Glubb, A *Soldier*, p. 153.
221. Glubb, *The Story*, p. 244.
222. Glubb, *Britain*, p. 171.
223. Great Britain, Colonial Office, *Report . . . for the Year 1938*, p. 353.
224. Glubb, *The Story*, p. 172.
225. *Annual Report*, 1928, p. 112, quoted by Amawi, *State and Class*, p. 309.
226. Lunt, *Glubb Pasha*, p. 175.
227. Dragnich, *The Bedouin Warrior*, p. 118.
228. Young, *Bedouin Command*, p. 49.
229. Ibid., pp. 59–60.
230. Althusser, "Ideology" p. 154.
231. Lunt, *Glubb Pasha*, pp. 185–186.
232. Young, *Bedouin Command*, p. 42.
233. Ibid., p. 41.
234. Ibid., p. 77.
235. Sir Gawain Bell, *Shadows*, p. 157.
236. Naji al-Zuʿbi, Chief Officer of the Musical Massed Bands, "Lamhah Tarikhi-yyah ʿan Musiqat al-Quwwat al-Musallahah al-Urduniyyah," (Amman, unpublished paper, 1994). For a list of the names of the musicians, see p. 1.
237. F. G. Peake, "Trans-Jordan," *Journal of the Royal Central Asian Society* XXVI, part III (July 1939): 387–388.
238. Interview with Maʿn Abu Nuwwar, Amman, January 30, 1995. The royal anthem has no reference whatsoever to the nation. The brief one-verse lyrics read as follows:

    Long live the young king
    Long live the young king
    His status is paramount
    His banners are fluttering up on high.

239. See Nizam Rusum Jawqat Musiqa al-Jaysh al-ʿArabi Li Sanat 1936 (The Statute of the Fees of the Arab Army's Massed Band for the Year 1936) published in the *Official Gazette*, no. 520 (April 4, 1936), p. 135.

240. Seteney Shami, *Ethnicity and Leadership*, p. 85.

241. Young, *Bedouin Command*, p. 44.

242. Young, *The Arab Legion*, p. 19. Young provides pictures and detailed descriptions of the uniforms worn by the armed bands.

243. It should be mentioned here that the Bedouins have their own musical instrument, namely, the Rababah, a one-string instrument played with a bow. On the importance of the Rababah in Bedouin life, see Yasin Suwaylih, *Al-Rababah Fi Hayat al-Badiyah* (Damascus: Dar al-Hasad, 1994).

244. Naji al-Zu'bi, "Lamhah," p. 2.

245. Young, *The Arab Legion*, p. 21.

246. Glubb, *A Soldier*, p. 384.

247. Theodor W. Adorno, *Introduction to the Sociology of Music* (New York: Continuum, 1976), p. 155.

248. Bell, op. cit., p. 156.

249. Ibid., pp. 156–157.

250. Young, *Bedouin Command*, p. 35. Several cases of Bedouin resistance to the wrongs they felt they had received by the Legion are also mentioned by Young, ibid., pp. 33–36.

251. J. B. Glubb, "The Economic," pp. 451–452. On the importance of coffee in Bedouin culture, see Muhammad Abu Hassan, "Al-Qahwah wa Atharuha fi Hayat al-Badu al-Ijtima'iyya," *Al-Funun al-Sha'biyyah*, no. 2, Amman (April 1974). Also see Ahmad Abu Khusah, *Al-'Asha'ir al-Urduniyyah wal Filastiniyyah wa Washa'ij al-Qurbah Baynaha* (Amman: n.p., 1989), pp. 153–156, and Ahmad 'Uwaydi al-'Abbadi, *Min al-Qiyam wa al-Adab al-Badawiyyah*, part 2 of "Silsilat Man Hum al-Badu," (Amman: Da'irat al-Matbu'at wa al-Nashr, 1976), pp. 189–253.

252. Godfrey Lias, *Glubb's Legion*, p. 109.

253. Sami Zubaida, "National, Communal and Global Dimensions in Middle Eastern Food Cultures," in Sami Zubaida and Richard Tapper, eds., *Culinary Cultures of the Middle East* (London: I. B. Tauris, 1994), p. 41.

254. The word *mansaf* originally referred to a large dish used to serve food to guests.

255. See Nina Jamil, *Al-Ta'am Fi al-Thaqafah al-'Arabiyyah* (London: Riyad al-Rayyis Lil-Kutub wa al-Nashr, 1994), p. 153. I also would like to thank Dr. Hasan Jum'ah Hammad for the information he shared with me about Bedouin mansaf and about jamid.

256. Ahmad 'Uwaydi al-'Abbadi, *Min al-Qiyam*, pp. 169–174. Al-'Abbadi describes the variations of mansaf cooking in different regions of Jordan.

257. See Ruks Bin Za'id al-'Uzayzi, *Qamus al-'Adat, al-Lahjat wa al-Awabid al-Urduniyyah*, vol. 3 (Amman: Da'irat al-Thaqafah wa al-Funun, 1973), p. 201, Also see al-'Abbadi, *Min al-Qiyam*, pp. 170–171.

258. In fact, the word "laban," which for village folks meant yogurt, for the Bedouins meant milk; see ibid., p. 157.

259. See Nimr Sarhan, "Ta'am al-Mansaf Fil Ma'thurat al-Sha'biyyah al-Filasti-niyyah," in *Al-Turath al-Sha'bi* (Baghdad) 9, no. 9 (1978): 79–84.

260. Kamel Abu Jaber, Fawzi Gharaibeh, Allen Hill, eds., *The Badia of Jordan: The Process of Change* (Amman: University of Jordan Press, 1987), p. 67. Foreign anthropologists claiming a nuanced understanding of Bedouin life in the age of the nation-state make similar faulty claims. Andrew Shryock, for example, identifies mansaf as "the traditional feast dish," without noting the process through which mansaf had been traditionalized by the Hashemite state. He describes mansaf ahistorically as consisting of "piles of rice heaped on sheets of unleavened bread, drenched in fatty broth and topped off with boiled lamb and almonds," without noting that many of mansaf's current ingredients were introduced by the Mandatory-Hashemite state and by the postindependence Hashemite state more recently, and that the new mansaf was repackaged as "traditional" and then, and only then, nationalized. See Shryock's *Nationalism and the Genealogical Imagination: Oral History and Textual Authority in Tribal Jordan* (University of California Press, Berkeley, 1997), p. 47. Linda Layne was only slightly more careful in describing mansaf. She states that it is "an 'arab [Bedouin] speciality consisting of lamb or goat meat served over a bed of rice with a sauce prepared from dried yoghurt and clarified goat butter" (p. 85). On another occasion, she identifies mansaf as a "traditional Bedouin feast," (p. 103), and, finally, states that "*mansaf* (an 'arab speciality of rice and lamb), . . . has come to be known as Jordan's national dish," (p. 147). While Layne registers the appropriation of mansaf by the Hashemite state, she does not seem to realize that the dish had been repackaged and reintroduced by the state to the Bedouins as *their* traditional dish (which has by now been nationalized) in a form that differs substantially from the form it had had before the Mandatory and the postindependence Hashemite state altered it. See Linda Layne, *Home and Homeland: The Dialogics of Tribal and National Identities in Jordan* (Princeton, NJ: Princeton University Press, 1994).

261. Abu Jaber, et al., *The Badia*, p. 69.

262. Ibid., p. 69. Although this has become the case recently because of the colonial introduction of tea to Jordan and the ease and speed with which tea can be prepared compared to Bedouin coffee, the authors mention this phenomenon as if it exists today as it always has! On Bedouin coffee, see footnote 251.

263. See Eliahu Epstein, "The Bedouin of Transjordan: Their Social and Economic Problems," *Journal of the Royal Central Asian Society* XXV, part II (April 1938). Epstein recommended that foreign capital be introduced to the country to improve the worsening lot of the tribes. His was a barely veiled Zionist attempt to introduce European Jewish colonial settlers to the country.

264. Glubb, "The Economic," p. 457.

265. Lias, *Glubb's Legion*, pp. 109. The only variation was the star that was added to the original flag design. Note that the flags of neighboring Syria, Iraq, and the Palestinians are also based on Sykes' original design.

266. Ibid., pp. 89–90.

267. Said, *Orientalism*, p. 95.

268. On catachresis, see Gayatri Chakravorty Spivak, *Outside in the Teaching Machine* (New York: Routledge, 1993), pp. 64–65, 298.

269. Guy Debord, *The Society of the Spectacle* (New York: Zone Books, 1994), p. 23.

270. On double-mimesis and T. E. Lawrence, see Kaja Silverman's essay "White Skin, Brown Masks: The Double Mimesis, or With Lawrence in Arabia," in her *Male Subjectivity at the Margins* (New York: Routledge, 1992), pp. 299–338.

271. Freud actually sees the fetish as a substitute for the loss of the mother's penis, which the boy-child believed she possessed. The boy's inability to deal with the perceived "castration" of his mother leads him to fetishize an object as a substitute for the absence of a penis in a woman, short of which, Freud tells us, he would have become a homosexual! See Sigmund Freud, "Fetishism," in *The Standard Edition of the Complete Psychological Works of Sigmund Freud*, vol. XXI (London: Hogarth Press, 1953–1974), originally published in 1927.

272. Glubb, *A Soldier*, p. 49.

273. Ibid., p. 49.

274. Ibid., p. 445.

275. Ibid.

276. Lunt, *Glubb Pasha*, p. 120.

277. Glubb, *A Soldier*, p. 426.

278. Ibid., p. 427. These claims are confirmed by the account of Musa ʿAdil Bakmirza Shirdan, a pro-Glubb Jordanian officer, in his memoirs, *Al-Urdunn Bayna ʾAhdayn*, pp. 136–137.

279. Glubb, *The Changing*, p. 58.

280. Glubb, *A Soldier*, p. 428.

281. Ibid.

282. Timothy Mitchell, *Colonising Egypt*, p. xii.

4. Nationalizing the Military: Colonial Legacy as National Heritage

1. Timothy Mitchell, *Colonising Egypt* (Berkeley: University of California Press, 1991), p. xi.

2. On this and on the early development of what came to be the Free Officers in the Jordanian Arab Army, see the memoirs of Shahir Abu Shahut, *Qissat Harakat al-Dubbat al-Urduniyyin al-Ahrar (1952–1957)*, unpublished manuscript, to be published as part of Silsilat Ihyaʾ al-Dhakirah al-Tarikhiyyah, New Jordan Studies Center, edited by Hani Hurani, Amman, Jordan, p. 34. I would like to thank Hani Hurani for providing me with a copy of the draft manuscript.

3. Ibid., p. 35, note.

4. Ibid., p. 36.

5. Ibid., pp. 36–37.

6. See John Bagot Glubb's account in his A *Soldier with the Arabs* (London: Hodder and Stoughton, 1957), pp. 255–257. Glubb analogizes king 'Abdullah's promise to promote al-Tall to colonel, to King Herod's promise to grant Salome's wishes. In Herod's case, the price was the head of John the Baptist, in 'Abdullah's, according to Glubb, it was 'Abdullah's own head.

7. 'Abdullah al-Tall, *Karithat Filastin, Mudhakkarat 'Abdullah al-Tall Qa'id Ma-'rakat al-Quds*, vol. I (Cairo: Dar al-Qalam, 1959), pp. 584–586.

8. See P. J. Vatikiotis, *Politics and the Military in Jordan: A Study of the Arab Legion, 1921–1957* (New York: Frederick A. Praeger, 1967), pp. 98–108.

9. Al-Tall, *Karithat Filastin*, pp. 581–582, 592.

10. Ibid., p. 587. The date stated in the book is December 1949, which is clearly an error, as al-Tall had left the country by then.

11. Ibid., p. 587. In his memoirs, published in 1990, 'Ali Abu-Nuwwar mentions the names of other officers who worked with al-Tall, including Mahmud al-Rusan and Qasim Nasir, as well as Shahir Abu-Shahut and Mahmud Ma'ayta. See 'Ali Abu-Nuwwar, *Hina Talashat al-'Arab, Mudhakkarat Fi al-Siyasah al-'Arabiyyah, 1948–1964* (London: Dar al-Saqi, 1990), p. 112.

12. Al-Tall, *Karithat Filastin*, p. 589.

13. Ibid., p. 591.

14. Ibid., p. 593. Al-Tall's use of the term *Free Officers* here is anachronistic, as the group had not formed yet, although its subsequent members were already active.

15. 'Ali Abu-Nuwwar, *Hina*, p. 114. Abu-Nuwwar states that he dismissed all these officers from the army upon becoming chief of staff in 1956.

16. Al-Tall, *Karithat Filastin*, p. 597.

17. Defenders of King 'Abdullah's armistice deal with the Israelis at Rhodes counter al-Tall's accusations by accusing him (al-Tall) of responsibility for that deal in which the Jordanian government relinquished control over the large Palestinian area known as the Triangle to the Israelis and which became proof to King 'Abdullah's enemies of his "treason." See, for example, Hazza' al-Majali, *Mudhakkarati* (Amman: n.p., May 1960), pp. 89–92.

18. On 'Abdullah's assassination and the ensuing trial, see chapter 5.

19. Glubb, *A Soldier*, p. 281.

20. The official Jordanian line continued to consider al-Tall the head of the conspiracy until the mid sixties, when King Husayn pardoned him. See for example, Munib Madi and Sulayman Musa, *Tarikh al-Urdunn Fi al-Qarn al-'Ishrin, 1900–1959* (Amman: Maktabat al-Muhtasib, 1988), p. 558. To my knowledge, he was only pardoned but never exonerated officially. In his book, 'Ali Abu-Nuwwar defends al-Tall and asserts that he had nothing to do with the assassination, in *Hina*, pp. 128–129. See also the new two-volume biography of al-Tall written by his brother Ahmad Yusuf al-Tall, *'Abdullah al-Tall, Batal Ma'rakat al-Quds* (Amman: Dar al-Furqan, 1999).

21. For an assessment of al-Tall's role, see Vatikiotis, *Politics*, pp. 98–108, and 'Abbas Murad, *Al-Dawr al-Siyasi Lil-Jaysh al-'Arabi, 1921–1973* (The Political Role of

the Arab Army, 1921–1973) (Beirut: Munazzamat al-Tahrir al-Filastiniyyah, Markaz al-Abhath, 1973), pp. 65–68.

22. See Kamil Mahmud Khillah, *Al-Tatawwur al-Siyasi Li Sharq al-Urdunn, Maris 1921–Maris 1948* (Tripoli, Libya: Al-Munsha'ah al-'Amah Lil-Nashr wal Tawzi' wal I'lan, 1983), pp. 300–305.

23. Abu Shahut, *Qissat al-Dubbat*, pp. 49–50.

24. Ibid., p. 50.

25. Ibid., p. 51.

26. Ibid., p. 55.

27. See Abu Shahut for a list of the committed members, pp. 60–61.

28. Abu-Shahut reports that Muhammad Ma'ayta pledged to support the group, while 'Ali al-Hiyari was more cautious and ambivalent in his support. Mahmud al-Rusan disappointed the officers, as he proposed that he would join the group as its leader. The Free Officers, shocked at his opportunism, decided not to pursue him as a result; in Abu-Shahut, *Qissat al-Dubbat*, pp. 62–64.

29. 'Ali Abu-Nuwwar's mother arrived in Jordan with her family as a little girl at the beginning of the century (her father is Shahm Shirdan) from the Caucasus and settled in the small town of Suwaylih, near Amman. She married 'Abd al-Qadir Abu-Nuwwar, of Salt, who lived in Suwaylih at the time. See Musa 'Adil Bakmirza Shirdan, *Al-Urdunn Bayna 'Ahdayn* (Amman: n.p., 1957?), pp. 10–11. In his memoirs, 'Ali Abu-Nuwwar mentions briefly that he grew up among his Circassian uncles and cousins in Suwaylih. See *Hina*, p. 9.

30. Abu-Nuwwar, *Hina*, p. 64.

31. Ibid., pp. 134–136.

32. It is said that in one such argument, the king slapped Glubb on the face and dismissed him from the palace. It is unclear, assuming this happened, if it was over the Hannun incident. Other incidents were reported, but their veracity cannot be ascertained. See Ribhi Jum'ah Hallum, *Ha'ula'A'da' al-Taharrur Fi al-Urdunn*, Silsilat Kutub Qawmiyyah (Cairo: Al-Dar al-Qawmiyyah Lil-Tiba'ah wa al-Nashr, 1962), p. 11.

33. *Mudhakkarat al-Malik Talal*, prepared by Mamduh Rida, and edited by Subhi Tuqan (Cairo: Al-Zahra' Lil-I'lam al-'Arabi, 1991). This is the second printing of the memoirs, which were initially published in the Egyptian magazine Ruz al-Yusif, in 1960, followed by their publication in book form by Ruz al-Yusif Lil-Nashr, in 1961. This book was part of the continuing Nasirist propaganda campaign against the Hashemites, as it was published shortly after the memoirs of 'Abdullah al-Tall and followed by Ribhi Hallum's book, and others. It is still unverifiable whether these memoirs are real or forged, especially as they contain a number of errors and inaccuracies.

34. John Bagot Glubb, *The Story of the Arab Legion* (London: Hodder and Stoughton, 1948), p. 248.

35. See Glubb, *A Soldier*, pp. 284, 288, 292–296.

36. Abu Shahut, *Qissat al-Dubbat*, pp. 64–65.

37. Abu-Nuwwar, *Hina*, p. 115.

38. See Glubb, *A Soldier*, pp. 291–292. Note that Abu-Nuwwar had had a public argument with Glubb on political and military strategies as early as 1949. According to Glubb, Abu-Nuwwar was seeking an audience with King Talal through the king's barber, for the purpose of conspiring with the mentally unstable king against Glubb himself. It was then that he sought to exile him to Paris.

39. Abu-Nuwwar, *Hina*, p. 141. Also see Peter Snow, *Hussein* (Washington: Robert B. Luce, 1972), p. 44, for a slightly different story. Also see Musa 'Adil Bakmirza Shirdan, *Al-Urdunn*, pp. 84–85, who claims that Abu-Nuwwar was interested in overthrowing Glubb for his own selfish reasons, not because of his nationalism, as he (Abu-Nuwwar) is alleged to have been a heavy drinker and "woman-hungry." This book was part of a progovernment propaganda campaign to discredit Abu-Nuwwar after 1957.

40. Abu-Nuwwar, *Hina*, pp. 144–146.

41. See Abu-Shahut, *Qissat al-Dubbat*, pp. 69–70. Abu-Nuwwar makes no mention whatsoever of this meeting.

42. Abu-Nuwwar, *Hina*, pp. 146–151. Whereas Abu-Nuwwar claims that the king invited him to Amman to ask him about developments in the Algerian Revolution, Abu-Shahut claims that Abu-Nuwwar was called to Amman to advise the king on the recent fate of the Moroccan king, Muhammad V, who had just been deposed by the French; see Abu-Shahut, *Qissat al-Dubbat*, p. 85.

43. Abu-Nuwwar, *Hina*, p. 158.

44. Ibid., pp. 158–159. Glubb's expression "Aquss 'Umrak" literally means to cut your life, as in the English expression "to cut someone's life short."

45. Abu-Shahut, *Qissat al-Dubbat*, p. 77.

46. Ibid., pp. 77–79.

47. See Hani Hurani and Salim Tarawnah, "Hakadha Saqata Hilf Baghdad fi 'Amman," in *Al-Urdunn al-Jadid*, no. 7 (spring 1986), pp. 112–163.

48. See Shirdan, *Al-Urdunn*, pp. 121–124. Shirdan, who was an officer in the Jordanian Arab Army with the rank of ra'is awwal (a rank in between captain and major), also served as aide-de-camp to several Jordanian prime ministers as well as (briefly) to King 'Abdullah. Although he mentions discrimination against him in the army, he is unwavering in his support for the government's pro-British and anticolonial nationalist line, espousing instead a pro-British nationalist line, in that the British are seen as "friends" of Jordan whose welfare he seeks.

49. Abu-Nuwwar tries to exonerate Hazza' al-Majali from supporting the Baghdad Pact venture and the army killings, when in fact al-Majali was the prime minister heading the campaign to join the pact at the time (his premiership lasted only five days in the face of public pressure). See Abu-Nuwwar, *Hina*, pp. 161–162. For al-Majali's own account, see Hazza' al-Majali, *Mudhakkarati* (Am-

man? n.p., 1960), pp. 171–174. He claims to have opposed the use of force in quelling the demonstrations. On the actual negotiations with Sir Gerald Templer on joining the pact, see Hazza' al-Majali, *Hadha Bayanun Lil-Nas, Qissat Muhadathat Timblar* (Amman: n.p., 1956).

50. See Abu-Shahut, *Qissat al-Dubbat*, p. 87.
51. On the army role in repressing the population, see Peter Young, *Bedouin Command: With the Arab Legion 1953–1956* (London: William Kimber, 1956), pp. 119–158.
52. Ibid., pp. 140, 154.
53. Ibid., p. 158. Rumors had it that one Yusuf al-Harbid, a communist, declared an independent republic of Ramtha. I would like to thank Mr. Salti al-Tall for this piece of information.
54. They named a number of collaborating officers, such as 'Abd al-Rahman al-Sahin and Khalid al-Sahin, as well as Muhammad Suhaymat. See pamphlet #36 reproduced in Murad, *Al-Dawr*, pp. 78–79, and in Young, *Bedouin Command*, pp. 173–174.
55. Young, *Bedouin Command*, pp. 142, 146.
56. Ibid., p. 146.
57. Ibid., pp. 150–151, 153.
58. Ibid., p. 151.
59. Ibid., p. 161.
60. Ibid., pp. 134–135.
61. Ibid., p. 175.
62. Ibid. On Rashdan's tribal affiliation, see Young, *Bedouin Command*, p. 202.
63. Quoted by Abu-Shahut, *Qissat al-Dubbat*, p. 86.
64. Ibid., p. 86.
65. King Husayn reports the incident without mentioning the meeting with Abu-Shahut or any other officer, see King Hussein, *Uneasy Lies the Head: The Autobiography of King Hussein I of the Hashemite Kingdom of Jordan* ((New York: Bernard Geis Associates, Random House, 1962), p. 140.
66. 'Ali Abu-Nuwwar insists in his memoirs that no such group existed in the Jordanian army and concurs with Glubb's assessment that these were circulated by the Egyptian embassy in Amman. Abu-Nuwwar's "ignorance" of the group, however, seems less than genuine given his earlier meetings with Abu-Shahut—although his being away in Paris made him ignorant of the development of the group during the years when its ranks were expanded. See Abu-Nuwwar, *Hina*, p. 163. Note that as a result of the London meeting with Abu-Nuwwar and the king, Abu-Shahut was heavily censured by his fellow officers and was almost dismissed from the group. See Abu-Shahut, *Qissat al-Dubbat*, pp. 70–71.
67. See Glubb, *A Soldier*, pp. 386–387.
68. Murad, *Al-Dawr*, pp. 73–74.

69. On the new education facilities and the new education section and philosophy in the army, see Sa'd Abu-Dayyah and 'Abd al-Majid Mahdi, *Al-Jaysh al-'Arabi wa Diblumasiyyat al-Sahra'*, *Dirasah fi Nash'atihi wa Tatawwur Dawr al-Thaqafah al-'Askariyyah* (Amman: Mudiriyyat al-Matabi' al-'Askarriyah, 1986).

70. P. J. Vatikiotis, *Politics*, p. 83.

71. Ibid., pp. 83–84.

72. Abu-Nuwwar, *Hina*, p. 166.

73. Ibid., p. 145.

74. On the Bedouin composition of the army, see Young, *Bedouin Command*, pp. 201–202. The non-Jordanian tribes included the 'Unayzah tribe, the Ruwalah, and the Shammar, as well as Bani 'Atiyyah.

75. Vatikiotis, *Politics*, p. 82. The Bedouin regiments were the First, Second, Third, Seventh and Ninth Infantry and the First and Second Armored Cars, see Peter Young, *Bedouin Command*, p. 194.

76. Ibid., pp. 78, 81; see also Glubb, *A Soldier*, p. 386. Glubb puts the number at 23,000 men.

77. Glubb, *A Soldier*, p. 386.

78. Ibid., p. 412.

79. Ibid., pp. 412–413.

80. Young, *Bedouin Command*, pp. 172–175.

81. I am referring here to the memoirs of Abu-Shahut and Abu-Nuwwar. As for historical accounts that do not distinguish among the different nationalist trends among the army officers, see, for example, Benjamin Shwadran's brief account of the period in his *Jordan: A State of Tension* (New York: Council for Middle Eastern Affairs Press, 1959), p. 349; also see Sulayman Musa and Munib Madi's account in their *Tarikh al-Urdunn*, pp. 669–875; see also Vatikiotis's confused account of the Free Officers in *Politics*, pp. 100–101, note. The only exception is Robert Satloff's *From Abdullah to Hussein, Jordan in Transition* (Oxford: Oxford University Press, 1994), pp. 138–139. Satloff relies on Abu-Shahut's memoirs but does not consult with Abu-Nuwwar's.

82. See Madi and Musa, *Tarikh al-Urdunn*, pp. 628–629. The nucleus for what later became the Jordanian air force was born in July 1948, when the army purchased seven transport planes. King 'Abdullah inaugurated officially the new air force in July 1951. Still, however, by 1955, very little expansion had taken place. For more details on the early development of the air force, see Sahar 'Abd al-Majid al-Majali, *Al-Jaysh al-'Arabi, 1921–1951, Dawruhu fi al-Sira' al-'Arabi-al-Suhyuni* (Amman: n.p., 1992), pp. 181–183.

83. King Husayn, speech delivered on May 25, 1955, reproduced in Sultan al-Hattab, *Al-Thawrah al-Kubra wa al-Jaysh al-'Arabi kama Yarahuma al-Husayn, Qira'at wa Nusus, 1953–1992* (Amman: Dar al-'Urubah Lil-Dirasat, 1993), p. 71.

84. King Hussein, *Uneasy*, p. 131. Husayn was twenty-seven when he wrote this autobiography.

85. Ibid., pp. 131–132.
86. Ibid., p. 132.
87. Glubb, A Soldier, pp. 387–388.
88. King Hussein, Uneasy, p. 132.
89. Ibid., pp. 132–133.
90. Ibid., pp. 135–136.
91. Ibid., p. 136.
92. Ibid., p. 132.
93. Ibid., p. 137.
94. Ibid., p. 138.
95. Ibid.
96. Ibid., p. 133.
97. Ibid., pp. 133–134.
98. Ibid., p. 140.
99. Ibid., pp. 140–141.
100. Ibid., p. 139.
101. Ibid., p. 141.
102. Ibid., p. 142.
103. Ibid.
104. Glubb, A Soldier, p. 424.
105. Abu-Nuwwar, Hina, p. 179. The Bedouin's officer name is Dhuqan al-Sha'lan.
106. King Hussein, Uneasy, pp. 143–145.
107. Glubb, A Soldier, p. 428.
108. Ibid., pp. 425–426.
109. Ibid., p. 427.
110. King Hussein, Uneasy, p. 138.
111. Faruq Nawwaf al-Surayhin, Al-Jaysh al-'Arabi al-Urduni, 1921–1967 (Amman: n.p., 1990), p. 333.
112. King Hussein, Uneasy, p. 146.
113. Ibid.
114. Ibid., pp. 148–149.
115. For the texts of a number of poems and songs written on the occasion of Glubb's expulsion and its subsequent anniversaries, see Hashim Isma'il al-Luqyani, Ta'rib Qiyadat al-Jaysh al-'Arabi (Amman, n.p.,1993), pp. 92–95.
116. Abu-Nuwwar, Hina, p. 165.
117. Ibid., p. 171.
118. Abu-Shahut, Qissat al-Dubbat, pp. 91–92. Abu-Nuwwar seems to want to score a point against Abu-Shahut by asserting that he was absent the day of Glubb's dismissal; see Abu-Nuwwar, Hina, pp. 177, 189.
119. For a list of the new appointments, see Abu-Shahut, Qissat al-Dubbat, p. 94, and Abu-Nuwwar, Hina, pp. 192–193.
120. Young, Bedouin Command, p. 193.

121. Abu-Nuwwar, op. cit., p. 194. There is very little information about "Al-Jaysh al-Maryami" or "the Mary-ite Army" It is said that a number of sectarians in Palestine had submitted a request before the 1948 war to the British high commissioner to form a Christian military battalion. The request is said to have been forwarded to the Pope, who recommended its implementation to the British so that Christian "rights" could be safeguarded from alleged Muslim discrimination. As a result, a small military group formed and was called al-Jaysh al-Maryami. The group disintegrated following the 1948 war. It re-emerged in 1955 again in Jordan as a special palace guard (modeled after King ʿAbdullah's Circassian guards). Its reemergence seems to have precipitated a rare sectarian massacre that took place in the predominantly Christian Jorda-nian town of Madaba, in which a number of Christians were killed. It was said that the Ikhwan al-Muslimun and the Islamist Tahrir Party were the instigators. The riot began after a brawl between a Christian taxi driver and a Muslim taxi driver. This seems to have followed an attack on a monastery in Salt by the Tahrir Party. Samir al-Tandawi claims that Parliament member Muhammad Salim Abu al-Ghanam, representing Madaba, was behind the transformation of the brawl into an outright sectarian riot. See Samir al-Tandawi, *Ila Ayna Yattajihu al-Urdunn?* (Cairo: Al-Dar al-Misriyyah Lil-Kutub, 1958?), pp. 76–77. Ribhi Hallum claims that the Jordanian Christian army officer Salim Kar-adshah and a number of Christians and Muslims were behind the riots to push the issue for the reconstitution of al-Jaysh al-Maryami. Karadshah and the prominent Turkish-born Palestinian Armenian officer in the Jordanian army, Karim Uhan, are said to have cooperated with Prince Muhammad (Husayn's brother and successor to the throne at the time) and sent another petition to Pope John XXIII, requesting of him that he ensure Christian rights in Jordan. In his account, Hallum claims that the prince became the secret head of al-Jaysh al-Maryami, with Uhan as his assistant and Karadshah as chief of opera-tions. Jordanian army officers are said to have been contacted secretly to train the new force (see Hallum, *Haʾulaʾ*, pp. 34–35). ʿAbbas Murad, who is a more credible source than the propagandistic Hallum, claims that the band of Chris-tian youth who were organized by Uhan as "Al-Jaysh al-Maryami" within the Jordanian army began asking that homes of worship and Christian sermons be made available in their units as is the case with Muslim soldiers—a request that created much sectarianism, fed at the time by the proregime Muslim Broth-ers and the antiregime Islamist Tahrir Party. Members of al-Jaysh al-Maryami included, in addition to the Palestinian Armenian Uhan and the Jordanian Karadshah, Iskandar Najjar (a Palestinian Jordanian officer who was director of wireless operations), Jubran Hawwa (a Palestinian Jordanian officer who was director of provisions), Jamil Qaʿwar (a Jordanian officer), and Imil Jumayʿan and Shafiq Jumayʿan (Jordanian officers). See ʿAbbas Murad, *Al-Dawr*, p. 72. What is interesting about this brief affair is the state's continuing uncertainty about its own nationalist project manifested in its encouragement of religious

identities at the expense of national ones. For the biography of Uhan and the subsequent positions he occupied in Jordan's security apparatuses, see Mudiriyyat al-Amn al-'Am, *Al-Amn al-'Am al-Urduni Fi Sittin 'Aman, Min 1920 Ila 1980* (Amman: n.p., 1981), pp. 352–353.

122. Young, *Bedouin Command*, p. 186.
123. Ibid., p. 179.
124. Ibid.
125. Abu-Nuwwar, *Hina*, pp. 204–205.
126. Cited in Young, *Bedouin Command*, p. 195.
127. Ibid.
128. Vatikiotis, *Politics*, p. 110.
129. Ibid., p. 128.
130. Abu-Shahut, *Qissat al-Dubbat*, p. 98.
131. For details, see ibid., pp. 95–96.
132. On the allegation of Salti control, see Abu-Nuwwar, *Hina*, p. 183.
133. Abu-Shahut, *Qissat al-Dubbat*, p. 97.
134. Ibid., p. 98.
135. Ibid., pp. 99–100. Abu-Shahut speaks of Abu-Nuwwar's alleged paranoia that Abu-Shahut would replace him through a coup; see pp. 100–101.
136. Ibid., p. 105.
137. See Aqil Hyder Hasan Abidi, *Jordan: A Political Study, 1948–1957* (New Delhi: Asia Publishing House, 1965), pp. 134–137.
138. King Husayn, speech delivered on March 6, 1957, reproduced in Hattab, *Al-Thawrah*, pp. 81–82.
139. Sulayman al-Nabulsi, speech delivered on March 1, 1957, published in *Al-Mithaq*, March 7, 1957, and reproduced in *Al-Urdunn al-Jadid*, no. 7 (spring 1986), pp. 209–210.
140. Abidi, *Jordan*, p. 142.
141. Ibid., p. 148. The recommendations also included the establishment of relations with the former USSR and with the People's Republic of China to express Jordan's gratitude over the stance taken by both countries during the tripartite invasion.
142. See Madi and Musa, *Tarikh al-Urdunn*, pp. 651–660.
143. The text of the letter is reproduced in King Hussein, *Uneasy*, pp. 159–160.
144. Ibid., p. 153.
145. Abu-Nuwwar, *Hina*, p. 250.
146. Abu-Shahut, *Qissat al-Dubbat*, p. 112.
147. King Hussein, *Uneasy*, pp. 155–156.
148. Ibid., pp. 156–157.
149. Ibid., pp. 114–115.
150. Robert Satloff claims that the list included twenty-seven officials to be retired. See Satloff, *From Abdullah*, p. 164.
151. Abu-Shahut, *Qissat al-Dubbat*, p. 116.

152. Ibid., p. 113.
153. See Glubb, *A Soldier*, pp. 433–434. For arguments exposing Glubb's conspiracy theory, see Abidi, *Jordan*, pp. 155–157, and Erskine Childers, *The Road to Suez* (London: MacGibbon & Kee, 1962), n. 58, p. 397, cited by Abidi.
154. Abu-Nuwwar, *Hina*, pp. 318, 323. Note that Abu-Nuwwar was very much disliked by the exiled officers after 1957, including ʿAli al-Hiyari, all of whom refused to work or coordinate political activities with him. Many of the Free Officers, including ʿAli al-Hiyari, blamed him for the palace coup, alleging that his leadership methods were characterized by regionalist chauvinism (for his town of Salt), his arrogance (despite his humiliating collapse in front of the king, which became known to everyone), his young age, and his greed and ambition. These allegations were communicated by Free Officers to ʿAbdullah al-Tall in 1958 in Damascus, where al-Tall had come (from his Cairo residence) to meet them. See Ahmad Yusuf al-Tall, *ʿAbdullah al-Tall*, pp. 928–931.
155. Ibid., pp. 317–319.
156. The United States, following its first major international military intervention after World War II in Korea, had just helped topple the Iranian nationalist prime minister, Dr. Muhammad Mossadegh, in 1953, and restored the shah. It also overthrew the Guatemalan nationalist president Jacobo Arbenz in 1954, launching in Guatemala a civil war that continued through the early 1990s. Its role in Jordan at the time was part of its new international policy of interventionism.
157. King Hussein, *Uneasy*, p. 162.
158. Ibid., pp. 163–164.
159. Abu-Shahut, *Qissat al-Dubbat*, p. 117.
160. Ibid., p. 118.
161. See Murad, *Al-Dawr*, p. 91.
162. See King Hussein, *Uneasy*, p. 173.
163. King Husayn, speech delivered on April 14, 1957, reproduced in Hattab, *Al-Thawrah*, p. 84.
164. Glubb, *A Soldier*, p. 435, and Murad, *Al-Dawr*, p. 92.
165. King Hussein, *Uneasy*, p. 179.
166. Abu-Nuwwar, *Hina*, pp. 322–324.
167. Ibid., p. 326.
168. See Naseer Aruri, *Jordan: A Study in Political Development (1921–1965)* (The Hague: Martinus Nijhoff, 1972), pp. 143–144.
169. *New York Times*, April 17, 1957, cited by Aruri, *Jordan*, p. 144n.
170. See Murad, *Al-Dawr*, p. 95, and Satloff, *From Abdullah*, p. 170.
171. Al-Baʿth, Syrian newspaper, August 12, 1957, cited by Murad, *Al-Dawr*, p. 96.
172. Murad, *Al-Dawr*, p. 96.
173. For details, see Abu-Shahut, *Qissat al-Dubbat*, pp. 120–126.
174. Aruri, *Jordan*, p. 144.
175. Cited in Satloff, *From Abdullah*, p. 171.

176. For the specifics of martial law, see the Martial Law instructions published in the *Official Gazette*, no. 1327 (April 27, 1957), pp. 410–414. For the declaration of martial law throughout the kingdom, see the *Official Gazette*, no. 1328 (May 4, 1957), pp. 415.

177. Abidi, *Jordan*, p. 163.

178. The initial law separating the two forces was issued in 1956, "Qanun Mu'aqqat bi-Fasl al-Shurtah wa al-Darak 'an al-Jaysh al-'Arabi al-Urduni," Temporary Law #27 for the Year 1956, signed on July 12, 1956, *Official Gazette*, no. 1285 (July 14, 1956), pp. 1763–1764. On the revoking of this law, see the *Official Gazette*, no. 1661 (May 16, 1957), p. 429.

179. "Qanun al-Amn al-'Am al-Mu'aqqat," Temporary Law #29 for the Year 1958, signed on June 16, 1958, *Official Gazette*, no. 1388 (July 1, 1958), pp. 641–643. See also Mudiriyyat al-Amn al-'Am, *Al-Amn al-'Am al-Urduni Fi Sittin 'Aman, Min 1920 Ila 1980*, p. 28.

180. Satloff, *From Abdullah*, p. 171.

181. Murad, *Al-Dawr*, p. 97.

182. King Hussein, *Uneasy*, p. 159.

183. Ibid., p. 166.

184. King Husayn, speech delivered on August 22, 1957, reproduced in Hattab, *Althawrah*, p. 89.

185. *The Arab Federation Agreement* was published in the *Official Gazette*, no. 1371 (February 19, 1958), pp. 235–238. Also see Naseer Aruri, *Jordan*, pp. 151–164.

186. *The Arab Federation Agreement*, article 4-b, p. 237.

187. See Dustur al-Ittihad al-'Arabi, *Official Gazette*, no. 1377 (March 31, 1958), pp. 402–413.

188. Ibid., see article 4-A of the constitution.

189. See Murad, *Al-Dawr*, p. 102; see also King Hussein, *Uneasy*, p. 205.

190. The pamphlet is cited in Murad, *Al-Dawr*, p. 101.

191. King Hussein, *Uneasy*, p. 206.

192. See Murad, *Al-Dawr*, p. 101.

193. For a list of arrested officers, see ibid., pp. 101–102.

194. Ibid., p. 102.

195. Actually, al-Shar' belongs to a Palestinian family who settled in the northern Jordanian town of Irbid before Transjordan was formed.

196. For a list of the accused, see Murad, *Al-Dawr*, p. 103.

197. On these defections, see ibid., p. 107.

198. King Husayn, speech delivered on April 15, 1961, reproduced in Hattab, *Al-Thawrah*, p. 120.

199. Murad, *Al-Dawr*, p. 147.

200. For attempts on the king's life, see King Hussein, *Uneasy*, pp. 209–216.

201. For the assassination attempts and the names of arrested officers, see Murad, *Al-Dawr*, pp. 105–106.

202. Murad, *Al-Dawr*, p. 108.
203. Ibid.
204. Abu-Shahut, *Qissat al-Dubbat*, p. 161. Abu-Shahut states how he was invited by then Prime Minister Wasfi al-Tall to his office. The prime minister paid Abu-Shahut a debt that he owed to Abu-Shahut's father and found a job for him in the civil service.
205. Ibid., p. 163.
206. Ibid., pp. 164–172.
207. Murad, *Al-Dawr*, p. 115.
208. Adnan Abu-Odeh, *Jordanians, Palestinians and the Hashemite Kingdom in the Middle East Peace Process* (Washington, DC: United States Institute of Peace Press, 1999), p. 119.
209. Ibid., p. 118.
210. As late as 1962, King Husayn still claimed that "Abu-Nuwwar has certainly been an active enemy ever since [he left the country in 1957]," in King Hussein, *Uneasy*, p. 178.
211. Murad, *Al-Dawr*, pp. 115–116. More recently, Mr. al-Kilani participated in the interrogation of the young Jordanian officer, Ahmad al-Daqamsah, from northern Jordan, who was accused of shooting seven Israeli schoolgirls who mocked and ridiculed him when he was performing his prayers. The shooting occurred in March 1997 at the Baqura border area.
212. See the extensive list provided by Murad, *Al-Dawr*, pp. 116–117.
213. Al-Tall had already met with King Husayn in Cairo on February 26, 1955, during the latter's visit to Egypt. They met in Ma'adi at the home of the Sharif 'Abd al-Hamid, father of Husayn's first-wife-to-be, Dina. Husayn's uncle, the Sharif Nasir, was also present at the meeting during which al-Tall assured the young king of his innocence of King 'Abdullah's assassination. See Ahmad Yusuf al-Tall, *'Abdullah al-Tall*, vol. II, p. 913. On another occasion, Wasfi al-Tall, a cousin of 'Abdullah's, conveyed an oral message in July 1959 from Prime Minister Hazza' al-Majali to 'Abdullah al-Tall asking him to write a letter exonerating himself of the assassination of King 'Abdullah. Al-Tall refused to write the letter, asserting that a full amnesty for all political prisoners and exiles was in order. He also understood al-Majali's offer to be an attempt on the part of the latter to split the exiled nationalist opposition. See Ahmad Yusuf al-Tall, *'Abdullah al-Tall*, vol. II, p. 943.
214. Ibid, p. 970.
215. See Murad, *Al-Dawr*, p. 117n.
216. Ahmad Yusuf al-Tall, *'Abdullah al-Tall*, vol. II, p. 971.
217. The text of the letter was published on the front page of the Jordanian newspaper *Al-Manar* (January 25, 1967), pp. 1, 4. It is said that when al-Tall was in Egypt, he became close to the Ikhwan al-Muslimun, which is why he became alienated from 'Abd al-Nasir, prompting him to send him his famous letter. In

fact, al-Tall's Islamist direction led him to prepare for a doctorate at al-Azhar. His dissertation (the topic was the "struggle between the Torah and the Qur'an") was not finished, as it was interrupted by the Jordanian amnesty and his return to Jordan. In 1964, he had published a book titled *Khatar al-Yahudiyyah al-'Alamiyyah 'Ala al-Islam wa al-Masihiyyah* (The Danger of World Judaism on Islam and Christianity). See Ahmad Yusuf al-Tall, *'Abdullah al-Tall*, vol. II, pp. 753–754.

218. See, for example, al-Tall, *Karithat Filastin*, p. 581.

219. See 'Abdullah al-Tall's prefatory letter published in Taysir Zibyan, *Al-Malik 'Abdullah Kama 'Ariftuhu* (Amman: Majallat al-Shari 'ah, 1994), pp. 13–16. The book was originally published in 1967.

220. Ahmad Yusuf al-Tall, *'Abdullah al-Tall*, vol. II, p. 973.

221. Murad, *Al-Dawr*, p. 117.

222. Ibid.

223. See his recent memoirs in which he mentions all his appointments without making any reference to the plot of which he was accused or to his imprisonment. See Sadiq al-Shar', *Hurubuna ma' Isra'il, 1947–1973, Ma'arik Khasirah wa Intisarat Da'i'ah, Mudhakkarat wa Mutala 'at Al-Liwa' al-Rukn al-Mutaqa'id Sadiq al-Shar* ('Amman: Dar al-Shuruq Lil-Nashr, 1997), jacket back.

224. For a list of the arrested officers, see Muard, *Al-Dawr*, pp. 119–120.

225. Ibid., p. 120.

226. See "Qanun al-Haras al-Watani," Law no. 7 for the Year 1950, signed on January 17, 1950, *Official Gazette*, no. 1010 (February 9, 1950), pp. 71–72. The law stipulated that all Jordanians between the ages of twenty and forty years should serve (or be trained) up to 150 hours a year, which essentially amounts to one month, according to Glubb. See articles 2 and 3 of the law. See also Glubb, *A Soldier*, p. 290. On the National Guard, see also Avi Plascov, *The Palestinian Refugees in Jordan, 1948–57* (London: Frank Cass, 1981), pp. 92–96. Plascov mistakenly reports that Jordanians between the ages of eighteen and forty were to serve in the National Guard (p. 92). Also see P. J. Vatkiotis, *Politics*, pp. 79–81.

227. Al-Surayhin, *Al-Jaysh al-'Arabi*, p. 318.

228. Glubb, *A Soldier*, p. 290. Note that the law refers to "all Jordanians" without specifying gender, although in reality only males were recruited and/or volunteered. This conflation of "all Jordanians" with "all male Jordanians" is characteristic of such laws.

229. Glubb, *A Soldier*, p. 289.

230. Ibid. Glubb later added that the purpose was "to bring Palestinians into a larger share of the defense of their country," cited in Vatikiotis, *Politics*, p. 80.

231. Al-Husayn Ibn Talal, *Mihnati Ka Malik*, translated by Ghalib A. Tuqan (Amman: n.p., 1978), p. 112. The book initially appeared in French in 1975 under the title *Mon Métier de Roi*.

232. Glubb, *A Soldier*, p. 369.
233. Vatikiotis, *Politics*, p. 80.
234. Avi Plascov, *The Palestinian*, p. 93.
235. Ibid.
236. Ibid. Plascov mentions erroneously that 1965 was the year of integration. See also Vatikiotis, *Politics*, p. 110.
237. Plascov, *The Palestinian*, p. 96.
238. Vatikiotis, *Politics*, p. 81.
239. For other government efforts undertaken in the sixties to Jordanize the Palestinians, see Clinton Bailey, *The Participation of the Palestinians in the Politics of Jordan*, doctoral dissertation, Department of Political Science (New York: Columbia University, 1966), pp. 248–256.
240. Vatikiotis, *Politics*, p. 111.
241. Shwadran, *Jordan*, pp. 336–337.
242. In reality, the term "all Jordanians" in the law refers to "all male Jordanians" as women were never conscripted into Jordan's military, although some were to join its professional and service sections. See "Qanun al-Khidmah al-Wataniyyah al-Ijbariyyah," Temporary Law #102 for the Year 1966, *Official Gazette*, no. 1966 (November 27, 1966), pp. 2464–2466, articles 2 and 16. This law was signed on November 23, 1966, ten days after the raid on Samu'. Note that compulsory conscription was being instituted also in response to the Arab League's formation of the PLO in 1964, and the PLO was recruiting and commanding Palestinian guerrillas; see Vatikiotis, *Politics*, p. 30.
243. Vatikiotis, *Politics*, p. 27.
244. Ibid., p. 28.
245. Ibid., pp. 28–29.
246. Ibid., p. 29.
247. See Plascov, *The Palestinian*, pp. 96–103.
248. On nationalism and sexuality, see Andrew Parker, Mary Russo, Doris Sommer, and Patricia Yaeger, eds., *Nationalisms and Sexualities* (New York: Routledge, 1992), as well as George Mosse, *Nationalism and Sexuality: Respectability and Abnormal Sexuality in Modern Europe* (New York: Howard Fertig, 1985).
249. For a review of these rumors, see Sa'id al-Tall, *Al-Urdunn wa-Filastin, Wujhat Nazar 'Arabiyyah* (Amman: Dar al-Liwa' Lil-Sahafah wa al-Nashr, 1986), pp. 41–64.
250. Ibid., p. 51.
251. See Hani Hurani, "'Al-Ittihad al-Watani' wa al-Shakl al-Rahin Lil-Sultah Fi al-Urdunn," in *Shu'un Filastiniyyah*, no. 14 (October 1972).
252. Mudiriyyat al-Tawjih al-Ma'nawi, *Al-Fida 'iyyun Bayna al-Riddah wa al-Intihar* (Amman: Mudiriyyat al-Tawjih al-Ma'nawi, 1973), p. 26.
253. Speech cited in Mudiriyyat al-Tawjih al-Ma'nawi, *Al-Fida 'iyyun*, p. 61.

254. King Husayn, speech delivered on July 8, 1958, reproduced in al-Hattab, *Al-Thawrah*, p. 100.

255. Here, the soldier is reciting the *Surah of al-Fatihah*, traditionally the first surah in the Qur'an; *The Koran Interpreted*, translation by Arthur J. Arberry (New York: Collier Book, 1955), p. 29.

256. Here, the soldier is reciting the *Surah of al-Nas*, traditionally the last surah of the Qur'an; ibid., p. 354.

257. *Al-Aqsa* (the newspaper of the Jordanian army), August 26, 1970, cited in "Hamlat al-Ta'bi'ah Did al-Muqawamah," in Khalil Hindi, Fu'ad Bawarshi, Shihadah Musa, and Nabil Sha'ath, *Al-Muqawamah al-Filastiniyyah wa al-Nizam al-Urduni, Dirasah Tahliliyyah Li Hajmat Aylul* (Beirut: Munazzamat al-Tahrir al-Filastiniyyah, Markaz al-Abhath, 1971), p. 123.

258. Mudiriyyat al-Tawjih al-Ma'nawi, *Al-Fida'iyyun*, p. 40.

259. Ibid., p. 78.

260. Ibid., p. 125.

261. Cited in David Hirst, *The Gun and the Olive Branch: The Roots of Conflict in the Middle East* (London: Faber and Faber, 1984), p. 306.

262. Shirdan, *Al-Urdunn*, p. 238.

263. Ibid., pp. 92–93.

264. Ibid., p. 276.

265. Ibid., pp. 195–197. Al-Halabi is cited by Shirdan as allegedly saying that one of the things that stood out for him when he accompanied the Syrian president to the former USSR was the beauty of a young Russian man, a situation that reminded him of a Damascene man who fell in love with his handsome Lebanese male barber in Beirut.

266. The story is reported by David Hirst, *The Gun*, p. 308.

267. This version of the story is reported by the king's biographer, James Lunt, in his biography *Hussein of Jordan: A Political Biography* (London: Macmillan, 1989), p. 134.

268. Ibid.

269. *Al-Aqsa* (October 10, 1970), p. 1.

270. Ibid., p. 6.

271. Cited in Khalil Hindi, "Al-Ta'bi'ah al-Urduniyyah Did al-Muqawamah al-Filastiniyyah Qabl Hajmat Sibtimbar 1970," in *Shu'un Filastiniyyah*, no. 4 (September 1971), p. 41.

272. Ibid., p. 40.

273. Interview with Ma'n Abu-Nuwwar, reproduced in Khalil Hindi et al., *Al-Muqawamah*, p. 480.

274. See Abu Iyad with Eric Rouleau, *My Home, My Land: A Narrative of the Palestinian Struggle* (New York: Times Books, 1981), p. 76. Also see the interview with Ma'n Abu-Nuwwar, reproduced in Khalil Hindi et al., *Al-Muqawamah*, p. 481.

275. Murad, *Al-Dawr*, p. 143–144.
276. King Husayn, speech delivered on November 11, 1957, reproduced in Hattab, *Al-Thawrah*, p. 91.
277. See Seteney Shami, *Ethnicity and Leadership: The Circassians in Jordan*, doctoral dissertation, Department of Anthropology (Berkeley: University of California, 1982), pp. 42, 128.
278. Ibid., p. 128.
279. Seteney Shami, "The Circassians of Amman: Historical Narratives, Urban Dwelling and the Construction of Identity," in Jean Hannoyer and Seteney Shami, eds., *Amman: The City and Its Society* (Beirut: CERMOC, 1996), p. 315.
280. The king's name was changed in the early years. Although he referred to himself as Husayn al-Awwal, or Husayn the First, he signed his name as Al-Husayn Bin Talal; see *Official Gazette*, no. 1187 (July 17, 1954), p. 552. Earlier, he used to sign his name as Husayn Bin Talal; see *Official Gazette*, no.1143 (May 6, 1953), p. 691. Finally, by August 1954, he began referring to himself as Al-Husayn al-Awwal and also signing as Al-Husayn Bin Talal; see *Official Gazette*, no. 1191 (August 18, 1954), p. 607.
281. No formal decrees were issued to add "al" to the name of the prince; rather, it was done informally. While the king was abroad in September 1986, newspapers began referring inconsistently to the prince (on September 10 and 11, 1986) as "Prince al-Hasan" and as "Prince Hasan." The hesitation was resolved by September 14, after which the name of the prince would always appear in newspapers as "al-Hasan." See *Al-Dustur* and *Al-Ra'y* (September 10, 11, and 14, 1986). In the *Official Gazette*, the name al-Hasan began to appear intermittently after 1969. See the *Official Gazette*, no. 2144 (January 16, 1969), p. 5, for the use of al-Hasan, and the *Official Gazette*, no. 2174 (May 27, 1969), p. 532, referring to him as "Hasan." Since then, however, he has been referred to consistently as "al-Hasan."
282. On the establishment of the University of Mu'tah, see al-Luqyani, *Ta'rib Qiyadat*, p. 77.
283. See 'Umar Sulayman Badran, *Hakadha Yakun al-Intima' Lil-Watan* (Amman: Mudiriyyat al-Matabi' al-'Askariyyah, 1989).
284. See Sami al-Khazendar, *Jordan and the Palestine Question: The Role of Islamic and Left Forces in Foreign Policy-Making* (Berkshire: Ithaca Press, 1997), p. 149.
285. Murad, *Al-Dawr*, p. 146.
286. For the names of the military government's members and their tribal affiliations, see ibid., p. 146.
287. See *Al-Dustur* (February 4, 1971), cited by Murad, *Al-Dawr*, p. 147.
288. Interview with Ma'n Abu-Nuwwar, head of the army's Department of Spiritual Guidance, reproduced in Khalil Hindi et al., *Al-Muqawamah*, p. 480.

289. Murad, *Al-Dawr*, pp. 148–149.

290. Ibid., pp. 152–153.

291. For the new law imposing military service, see the *Official Gazette*, no. 2599 (January 1, 1976). This law was replaced by a new law of compulsory military service in 1986. See the *Official Gazette*, no.3402 (June 1, 1986).

292. Wizarat al-I'lam, *Al-Mar'ah al-Urduniyyah* (Amman: Department of Press and Publications, 1979), p. 86.

293. Ibid., p. 95.

294. Ibid., pp. 87–88.

295. In the late 1980s, a scandal broke out in the country regarding the discovery of a major prostitution ring involving a high-ranking officer in the Women's Police Force and a female university professor. The story entered every household in the country until it finally petered out. The police officer in question was subsequently retired. Rumors had it that she had been demoted first.

296. See Suhayr al-Tall, *Muqaddimah Hawla Qadiyyat al-Mar'ah wa al-Harakah al-Nisa'iyyah Fi al-Urdunn* (Beirut: Al-Mu'assasah al-'Arabiyyah Lil-Dirasat wa al-Nashr, 1985), pp. 84–85.

297. In 1952, the Hashemite Band was renamed the Second Massed Band. In 1953, a third Band was formed and was attached to the First Infantry Regiment. Finally in 1954, a fourth band was set up.

298. Naji al-Zu'bi (chief officer of the Musical Massed Bands), "Lamhah Tarikhiyyah 'an Musiqat al-Quwwat al-Musallahah al-Urduniyyah," (Amman: unpublished manuscript, 1994), p. 3.

299. In 1958, two more Bands were formed, one of which was led by the Egyptian Isma'il 'Askar, who was later granted Jordanian nationality. See ibid.

300. Ibid., p. 4.

301. They performed in Egypt in 1956, Lebanon in 1957 and 1966, Kuwait in 1964, Oman in 1972, Syria in 1972 to 1974, Yemen in 1976, Libya in 1979, Iraq in 1990, Turkey in 1960, Iran in 1962 and 1971, see ibid., pp. 5–6.

302. They performed in Italy in 1959, Scotland in 1962, the United States in 1964, 1976 and 1986, England in 1966 and 1985, France in 1981 and 1993, Switzerland in 1987 and Spain in 1992, see ibid., pp. 5–6.

303. Ibid., p. 2.

304. Ibid., p. 6.

305. Ibid.

306. Timothy Mitchell, *Colonising Egypt*, p. xi, emphasis in original.

307. Seteney Shami, *Ethnicity*, p. 110.

308. Paul A. Jureidini and R. D. McLaurin, *Jordan: The Impact of Social Change on the Role of the Tribes* (New York: Praeger, 1984), p. 61.

309. Ibid.

310. Ibid., pp. 62–63.

311. Ibid., p. 63.

312. King Husayn, speech delivered on July 12, 1980, reproduced in Hattab, *Al-Thawrah*, p. 200.

313. See *Official Gazette*, no. 796 (June 17, 1944).

314. *Official Gazette*, no. 912 (July 1, 1947), p. 853.

315. *Official Gazette*, no. 1410 (January 1, 1959).

316. *The Arab Federation Agreement*, article 4-b, p. 237.

317. *Official Gazette*, no. 753 (April 16, 1964).

318. *Official Gazette*, no. 1948 (September 15, 1966).

319. *Official Gazette*, no. 2189 (August 16, 1969).

320. King Hussein, *Uneasy*, p. 150.

321. *Journal of the Royal Society of Asian Affairs* XVII, part III (October 1986), pp. 357–358.

322. Abu-Shahut, *Qissat al-Dubbat*, p. 85.

323. See Murad, *Al-Dawr*, pp. 155–157.

5. The Nation as an Elastic Entity: The Expansion and Contraction of Jordan

1. On 'Abdullah's schemes to rule over Syria and Iraq and unify them with Trans-jordan, see, for example, Kamil Mahmud Khillah, *Al-Tatawwur al-Siyasi Li Sharq al-Urdunn, Maris 1921—Maris 1948* (Tripoli, Libya: Al-Munsha'ah al-'Amah Lil-Nashr wa al-Tawzi' wa al-I'lan, 1983), pp. 346–428. On his plans for taking over Palestine, see, for example, Anis Sayigh, *Al-Hashimiyun wa Qadiyyat Filastin* (Beirut: Al-Maktabah al-'Asriyyah wa Jaridat al-Muharrir, 1966), 'Abdullah al-Tall, *Karithat Filastin, Mudhakkarat 'Abdullah al-Tall, Qa 'id Ma 'rakat al-Quds,* part I (Cairo: Dar al-Qalam, 1959), Sulayman al-Bashir, *Judhur al-Wisayah al-Urduniyyah, Dirasah fi Watha 'iq al-Arshif al-Suhyuni* (Beirut: Dar al-Farabi, 1982), and Avi Shlaim, *Collusion Across the Jordan: King 'Abdullah, the Zionist Movement, and the Partition of Palestine* (New York: Columbia University Press, 1988).

2. Annex to the *Official Gazette*, Parliamentary Minutes (Mulhaq al-Jaridah al-Rasmiyyah, Mudhakkarat Majlis al-Nuwwab) no. 3 (May 13, 1950), p. 7.

3. Ibid.

4. "Khitab al-'Arsh," in al-Hukumah al-Urduniyyah, *Wihdat Diffatay al-Urdunn: Waqa 'i ' wa Watha 'iq* (The Unity of Both Banks of Jordan: Events and Documents) (Amman: Idarat al-Sahafah wa al-Nashr, June 1950), p. 3.

5. "Rad Majlis al-A'yan 'Ala Khitab al-'Arsh," in *Wihdat Diffatay*, p. 15.

6. Ibid., p. 15.

7. "Khitab al-'Arsh," in *Wihdat Diffatay*, pp. 3–4.

8. Ibid., p. 4.

9. Ibid., p. 5.

10. Ibid., p. 6.

11. Ibid.

12. "Rad Majlis al-Nuwwab 'Ala Khitab al-'Arsh," in *Wihdat Diffatay*, p. 18.

13. Such tendencies can also be found in Arab nationalism as well as in the individual nationalisms of other Arab countries and peoples. For similar tendencies in post-WWII Palestinian nationalism, see Joseph Massad, "Conceiving the Masculine: Gender and Palestinian Nationalism," in the *Middle East Journal* 49, no. 3 (summer 1995).

14. For the Jordanian government's annexation of central Palestine to Jordan, see 'Isam Sakhnini, "Damm Filastin al-Wusta Ila Sharqiyy al-Urdunn," *Shu'un Filastiniyyah*, no. 40 (December 1974), pp. 56–83; see also Munib Madi and Sulayman Musa, *Tarikh al-Urdunn Fi al-Qarn al-'Ishrin, 1900–1959* (Amman: Maktabat al-Muhtasib, 1988), pp. 533–546, and Muhammad Mahafzah, *Al-'Ilaqat al-Urduniyyah al-Filastiniyyah, al-Siyasiyyah, al-Iqtisadiyyah wa al-Ijtima'iyyah, 1939–1951* (Amman: Dar al-Furqan wa Dar 'Ammar, 1983), pp. 197–223.

15. See the proposal in *Al-Athar al-Kamilah Lil-Malik 'Abdullah*, 3rd edition (Beirut: Al-Dar al-Muttahidah Lil-Nashr, 1985), pp. 390.

16. See, for example, Anis Sayigh, *Al-Hashimiyun*, p. 244.

17. See Sakhnini, "Damm Filastin," p. 59.

18. On the Amman conference, see Sakhnini, "Damm Filastin," pp. 56–57; see also Benjamin Shwadran, *Jordan: A State of Tension* (New York: Council for Middle Eastern Affairs Press, 1959), p. 280. Shwadran mistakenly reports the number of delegates as 5,000, when the real number was 500; see Sayigh, *Al-Hashimiyyun*, pp. 272–274, and also Madi and Musa, *Tarikh al-Urdunn*, pp. 535–536.

19. A number of telegrams sent by Palestinian delegates to the Palestine government explaining the repressive measures used by the Jordanian government are cited by Sakhnini, "Damm Filastin," p. 60.

20. See Sakhnini, "Damm Filastin," p. 60.

21. See Shwadran, *Jordan*, p. 280.

22. See Sayigh, *Al-Hashimiyyun*, p. 272.

23. See 'Abdullah al-Tall, *Karithat Filastin*, pp. 375–376.

24. 'Arif al-'Arif, *Al-Nakbah, Nakbat Bayt al-Maqdis wa al-Firdaws al-Mafqud, 1947–1955*, part IV (Sidon-Beirut: Al-Matba'ah al-'Asriyyah, 1959), p. 877.

25. 'Abdullah al-Tall, *Karithat Filastin*, p. 376.

26. Ibid.

27. Ibid., pp. 378–379.

28. *Al-Ruwwad*, December 3, 1948, cited by Sakhnini, "Damm Filastin," p. 63. There were in fact three different versions of the conference resolutions, the one signed by the attendees and two subsequent versions modified and doctored by 'Abdullah; see Avi Plascov, *The Palestinian Refugees in Jordan, 1948–57* (London: Frank Cass, 1981), pp. 13–14.

29. See Sakhnini, "Damm Filastin," p. 64.
30. See Abidi, *Jordan*, pp. 55–56.
31. Ordinance (Amr) no. 21 for the Year 1949, issued according to the Defense Ordinance (Nizam) no. 6 for the Year 1939, published in the *Official Gazette*, no. 1002 (December 1, 1949).
32. "Qanun Dhayl Qanun Jawazat al-Safar number 11 for the Year 1949," *Official Gazette*, no. 970 (February 14, 1949).
33. *Official Gazette*, no. 1012 (March 1, 1950), p. 92.
34. John Bagot Glubb, *A Soldier with the Arabs* (London: Hodder and Stoughton, 1957), p. 237.
35. *Official Gazette*, no. 1132 (February 1, 1953), p. 518.
36. See Sakhnini, "Damm Filastin," pp. 69–70.
37. See "Qanun al-Idarah al-'Amah Fi Filastin #17 for the Year 1949," published in the *Official Gazette*, no. 975 (March 16, 1949).
38. See Sakhnini, "Damm Filastin," pp. 70–71. Before the position was abolished, Matar had been succeeded by Falah al-Madadhah, another Transjordanian, who was finally replaced by the Palestinian Raghib Nashashibi, an 'Abdullah supporter.
39. Published in the *Official Gazette*, no. 1003 (December 17, 1949).
40. Cited by Sakhnini, "Damm Filastin," p. 71.
41. *Official Gazette*, no. 987 (July 1, 1949). Finally, in June 1950, the Council of Ministers issued a decree by which it gave people still in possession of Palestinian currency, until August 1950 to turn in their money and replace it with Jordanian currency; see *Official Gazette*, no. 1026 (June 17, 1950).
42. See *Al-Sharq al-'Arabi*, no. 174 (December 20, 1927), for "Qanun Ihlal al-Naqd al-Filastini Mahal al-Naqd al-Masri wa al-'Uthmani" or "The Law of Using the Palestinian Currency in Place of the Egyptian and Ottoman currencies."
43. *Official Gazette*, no. 988 (July 16, 1949).
44. Muhammad 'Izzat Darwazah, *Al-Qadiyyah al-Filastiniyyah Fi Mukhtalaf Marahiliha, Tarikh wa-Mudhakkarat wa-Ta'liqat*, vol. II (Sidon: n.p., 1959–1960), p. 307.
45. Quoted in Sakhnini, "Damm Filastin," p. 72.
46. "Addition to the Electoral Law, no. 55, 1949" published in the *Official Gazette*, no. 1004 (December 20, 1949).
47. See Sakhnini, "Damm Filastin," pp. 73–74.
48. Glubb, *A Soldier*, p. 351.
49. See Sakhnini, "Damm Filastin," p. 75.
50. See *Al-Jil al-Jadid*, no. 24, May 1, 1950, cited in Sakhnini, "Damm Filastin," p. 76.
51. See Sakhnini, "Damm Filastin," pp. 77–80.
52. A manifesto issued by the Prime Minister's Office in May 31, 1950, published in *Wihdat Diffatay*, p. 28.

53. This is based on the detailed account of the aftermath of ʿAbdullah's assassi-
    nation in Mary C. Wilson, *King Abdullah: Britain and the Making of Jordan*
    (Cambridge: Cambridge University Press, 1987), pp. 209–215. Also, see a brief
    account in Robert Satloff, *From Abdullah to Hussein: Jordan in Transition* (New
    York: Oxford University Press, 1994), pp. 13–14. John Bagot Glubb gives the
    impression that civilians committed the looting and the destruction in Jerusa-
    lem. He states, "In Jerusalem, a few shops were looted before the troops took
    over," in Glubb, *A Soldier*, p. 278.

54. Mary Wilson, *King Abdullah*, p. 209.

55. For a skeptical account about who was responsible for the assassination of King
    ʿAbdullah, see Nasir al-Din al-Nashashibi, *Man Qatala al-Malik ʿAbdullah*
    (Kuwait: Manshurat al-Anbaʾ, 1980). Al-Nashahibi wants to exonerate the Pal-
    estinian people from the responsibility of killing ʿAbdullah. He tries to uncover
    credible evidence of Egyptian, British, and/or Jordanian parties who were be-
    hind the murder.

56. Ibid., p. 211. Kirkbride served as British resident to Jordan from 1939 to 1946
    when he became minister to Transjordan and later ambassador until December
    1951. Musa ʿAdil Bakmirza Shirdan speaks of angry Jordanians intent on killing
    Palestinian refugees and says that a massacre was averted by deploying the army
    in the streets. See his memoirs *Al-Urdunn Bayna ʿAhdayn* (Amman: n.p.,
    1957?) p. 72.

57. For these demographics, see Yazid Yusuf Sayigh, *Al-Urdunn wa al-Filastiniyyun,
    Dirasah fi Wihdat al-Masir aw al-Siraʿ al-Hatmi* (London: Riyad El-Rayyis
    Books, 1987), pp. 12–14.

58. See ibid. for all demographic calculations cited here.

59. Ibid., pp. 34–35.

60. Ibid., pp. 14–16. Sayigh also provides numbers for the cities of Irbid and Zarqaʾ.

61. For literacy rates, health care standards, level of political participation, number
    of newspapers, and so forth among Palestinians and Jordanians, see Shaul Mishal,
    West Bank/East Bank: The Palestinians in Jordan 1949–1967 (New Haven: Yale
    University Press, 1978), pp. 1–9; also see Naseer Aruri, *Jordan: A Study in Political
    Development, 1921–1965* (The Hague: Nijhoff, 1972), pp. 49–69.

62. See Plascov, *The Palestinian*, pp. 36–37.

63. Shaul Mishal, *West Bank/East Bank*, p. 21. Mishal cites letters of complaints
    sent to the government by the West Bank Chamber of Commerce in this regard.

64. Jamil Hilal, *Al-Diffah al-Gharbiyyah, al-Tarkib al-Ijtimaʿi wa al-Iqtisadi (1948–
    1974)* (The West Bank: Its Economic and Social Composition, 1948–1974)
    (Beirut: Markaz al-Abhath, Munazzamat al-Tahrir al-Filastiniyyah, 1975), pp.
    133–134. Hilal goes on to specify in detail these policies and projects; see
    chapter 3, pp. 77–176.

65. For the extent of emigration, see the comprehensive analysis and statistics pro-
    vided by Hilal, ibid., pp. 82–106.

66. Plascov, *The Palestinian*, p. 37.
67. Quoted ibid., p. 36.
68. Yazid Sayigh, *Al-Urdunn*, p. 17.
69. King Husayn had initially opposed the idea of the PLO or Palestinian entity when it was being proposed by Ahmad Shuqayri after the latter had been appointed as Palestine's representative to the Arab League. King Husayn would insist that there was no need for such an organization, because, according to him, "[W]e are Palestine and we are the Palestinian Cause. . . . [And] Jordan, as a state, as an army, and as a people will attend to the Palestinian Cause, and [therefore,] there is no need for anything more than this." See Shuqayri's account of their initial talks in the fall of 1963 in Ahmad Shuqayri, *Min al-Qimmah Ila al-Hazimah: Ma' al-Muluk wa al-Ru'asa' al-'Arab* (Beirut: Dar al-'Awdah, 1971), pp. 20–21.
70. See Yazid Sayigh, *Al-Urdunn*, pp. 22–25.
71. Article 24 of the Palestinian Nationalist Charter, Al-Mithaq al-Qawmi al-Filastini, reproduced in Faysal Hurani, *Al-Fikr al-Siyasi al-Filastini, 1964–1974, Dirasah Lil-Mawathiq al-Ra'isiyyah Li-Munazzamat al-Tahrir al-Filastiniyyah* (Beirut: Markaz al-Abhath, Munazzamat al-Tahrir al-Filastiniyyah, 1980), p. 231; for similar statements and commitments made by the PLO, see Mishal, *West Bank*, pp. 66–69.
72. *Al-Ahram*, January 21, 1964, cited in 'Isa al-Shu'aybi, *Al-Kiyaniyyah al-Filastiniyyah, al-Wa'i al-Dhati wa al-Tatawwur al-Mu'assasati, 1947–1977* (Beirut: Markaz al-Abhath, Munazzamat al-Tahrir al-Filastiniyyah, 1979), p. 117; for an excellent overview of PLO–Jordanian relations in this period, see ibid., pp. 116–127.
73. See Letter of Designation of the Prime Minister, Kitab Taklif Wizarat Wasfi al-Tall, February 13, 1965, published in the *Official Gazette* and reproduced in Sa'd Abu-Dayyah, *Al-Fikr al-Siyasi al-Urduni, Namudhaj fi Dirasat al-Fikr al-Siyasi al-Urduni min Khilal Kutub al-Taklif allati Wajjahaha al-Malik Husayn Bin Talal ila Ru'asa' al-Wizarat* (Amman: Dar al-Bashir, 1989), p. 154.
74. *Al-Kitab al-Sanawi Lil-Qadiyyah al-Filastiniyyah li-'Am 1964* (Beirut: Mu'assasat al-Dirasat al-Filastiniyyah, 1966), pp. 10–11, cited in Shu'aybi, *Al-Kiyaniyyah*, p. 118.
75. *Al-Jihad*, June 4, 1965, cited in Shu'aybi, *Al-Kiyaniyyah*, p. 120.
76. Speech delivered on October 4, 1965, in the Diwan of the royal palace, reproduced in *Khamsah wa 'Ishrun 'Am min al-Tarikh, 1952–1977, Majmu'at Khutab Jalalat al-Malik al-Husayn Bin Talal al-Mu'azzam, Malik al-Mamlakah al-Urduniyyah al-Hashimiyyah*, vol. II (London, Amman: Samir Mutawi' Lil-Nashr, 1978), p. 368.
77. King Husayn's letter to President Jamal 'Abd al-Nasir, October 18, 1965, reproduced in Mundhir Fa'iq 'Anabtawi, editor, *Al-Watha'iq al-Filastiniyyah al-'Arabiyyah Li-'Am 1966* (Beirut: Mu'assasat al-Dirasat al-Filastiniyyah, 1967), pp. 568–571.

78. Shuʿaybi, *Al-Kiyaniyyah*, p. 121.

79. King Husayn's speech at the graduation ceremony of the ʿAjlun Teachers College, June 14, 1966, reproduced in *Khamsah wa ʿIshrun*, pp. 441–443.

80. Yazid Sayigh, *Al-Urdunn*, pp. 25–27.

81. For more elaborate statistics, see Yazid Sayigh, *Al-Urdunn*, pp. 34–35.

82. For the official Jordanian version of events at al-Karamah where the guerrillas are cursorily mentioned and where credit is given wholesale to the Jordanian Arab army, see Maʿn Abu-Nuwwar, *Maʿrakat al-Karamah, March 21, 1968*, 3rd edition (Amman: n.p., 1970). For a Palestinian account, see, for example, Abu Iyad with Eric Rouleau, *My Home, My Land: A Narrative of the Palestinian Struggle*, translated by Linda Butler Koseoglu (New York: Times Books, 1981), pp. 57–60. For another official Jordanian military account that attempts to be slightly less partial, see El-Edroos, Syed Ali, *The Hashemite Arab Army, 1908–1979: An Appreciation and Analysis of Military Operations* (Amman: Publishing Committee, 1980), pp. 438–442. Also see "Shihadat Min Maʿrakat al-Karamah," (Testimonies from the Battle of al-Karamah) in *Shuʾun Filastiniyyah*, no. 8 (April 1972), pp. 197–210, especially the testimony of the Jordanian army officer Saʿd Sayil, who speaks of an immediate interest shown by the king and his coterie to underestimate the contribution of the Fidaʾiyyin in the fighting at al-Karamah, pp. 209–210. Sayil, of Palestinian origins, defected to the PLO during Black September.

83. For an analysis of the importance of the battle of al-Karamah for the Palestinian guerrilla movement, see Munir Shafiq, "Maʿrakat al-Karamah," in *Shuʾun Filastiniyyah*, no. 19 (March 1973), pp. 103–110.

84. Text of the interview is reproduced in *Al-Wathaʾiq al-Urduniyyah 1968* (Amman: Daʾirat al-Matbuʿat wa al-Nashr, 1973), pp. 152–156. A similar quote is reproduced in El-Edroos, *The Hashemite*, p. 442, wherein El-Edroos reports that the king, in response to "a demand by East Bank and Army leaders to crack down on the undisciplined and over-assertive Commandos," stated, "I try to exert control. . . . [W]hat do you expect me to do? What should I do to a people who have lost everything—who were driven out of their country? Shoot them? I think we have come to a point where we are all Fedayeen." Moreover, at a press conference held in Amman on March 23, 1968, and in response to a question about the guerrillas, the king expressed a similar sentiment and in exasperation asked the journalists if "you expect us to kill them [the Fidaʾiyyin] and destroy their abilities?" reproduced in *Al-Wathaʾiq al-Urduniyyah 1968*, p. 99.

85. More recently, Robert Satloff, an operative of the Washington Institute for Middle East Policy, the unofficial academic arm of the pro-Israel lobby in the United States, began propagating a fabrication that "East Bankers" refer to Black September as "White September." See Robert Satloff, "From Hussein to Abdullah: Jordan in Transition," Research memorandum, published by the Washington Institute for Middle East Policy, Washington, DC, no. 38, April 1999, p. 2. Although he did not quote any "East Banker" as saying or writing

this expression, this fabrication has become "fact," not only for the Israel lobby but also for the *New York Times*. In an article on King Abdullah II, the *Times* reporter mentions casually how Transjordanians refer to Black September as "White September." "Facts," for *the New York Times*, it would seem become such through its peremptory power to repeat them. It was Joseph Goebbels, after all, who asserted that the first rule of propaganda is endless repetition. See Jeffrey Goldberg, "Suddenly a King," *New York Times Magazine*, February 6, 2000. On the European scene, Paul Lalor partakes of spreading the new fabrication in a paper called "Black September/White September," presented at a symposium sponsored by the Center d'Études et de Recherches sur le Moyen-Orient Contemporain, Paris, June 24–25, 1997, cited by Adnan Abu-Odeh, *Jordanians, Palestinians, and the Hashemite Kingdom in the Middle East Peace Process* (Washington, DC: United States Institute of Peace Press. 1999), p. 290n. Perhaps Transjordanian nationalists will soon learn of the new fabrication in the Unites States and Europe and adopt it as their own!

86. On Jordanian agents, see Abu Iyad with Eric Rouleau, *My Home*, p. 75.
87. On tribal conferences, see Olivier Carre, *Séptembre Noir: Refus Arabe de la Resistance Palestinienne* (Brussels: Editions Complexes, 1980), p. 60, and also see Khalil Hindi, Fu'ad Bawarshi, Shihadah Musa, and Nabil Sha'ath, *Al-Muqawamah al-Filastiniyyah wa al-Nizam al-Urduni, Dirasah Tahliliyyah Li Hajmat Aylul* (Beirut: Munazzamat al-Tahrir al-Filastiniyyah, Markaz al-Abhath, 1971), pp. 129–131.
88. For this estimate, see Olivier Carre, *Séptembre Noir*, p. 24.
89. The king gave this statement to *Le Monde*, cited in *Al-Yawmiyyat al-Filastiniyyah*, vol. 4–5, entry date: November 25, 1966 (Beirut: Markaz al-Abhath, Munazzamat al-Tahrir al-Filastiniyyah, 1967), p. 238.
90. This estimate is taken by Sayigh from the testimony of a Jordanian army officer, Sa'd Sayil (of Palestinian origins), who participated in the al-Karamah battle; see "Shihadat," p. 210.
91. See Sayigh, *Al-Urdunn*, p. 39. King Husayn himself may have exaggerated these figures when he stated in 1973 that "Palestinians constitute no less than half of those in the Jordanian armed forces," speech delivered on February 3. 1973, reproduced in *Majmu'at Khutab Jalalat al-Malik al-Husayn Bin Talal al-Mu'azzam, Malik al-Mamlakah al-Urduniyyah al-Hashimiyyah*, vol. III (London, Amman: Samir Mutawi' Lil-Nashr), p. 402.
92. *New York Times*, February 19, 1968, cited in *Al-Muqawamah al-Filastiniyyah wa al-Nizam al-Urduni*, op. cit., p. 35.
93. High-ranking PLO official Abu Iyad admits to such mistakes, especially the failure of the guerrillas to appeal to Transjordanians; see Abu Iyad, *My Home*, p. 76. It should be noted however, that Fath had sought to include many Transjordanian nationalists in its activities, inviting them to attend Palestine National Council meetings as observers. These included many former nationalist politicians and Free Officers, including Sulayman al-Nabulsi. Sa'id al-

Mufti, 'Akif al-Fayiz, Mahmud al-Rusan, Jamal al-Sha'ir, Ja'far al-Shami, Dafi Jam'ani. Mahmud al-Ma'ayta, et al. Court historian Sulayman Musa claims that the popularity of Fath was such that some high-ranking Transjordanian officials in the government would wear Fath uniforms to work. See Sulayman Musa, *Tarikh al-Urdunn fi al-Qarn al-'Ishrin, 1958–1995*, vol. 2 (Amman: Maktabat al-Muhtasib, 1996), p. 365.

94. See "Qanun al-Khidmah al-Wataniyyah al-Ijbariyyah," published in the *Official Gazette*, no. 2069 (January 16, 1968), and which replaced "Qanun al-Khidmah al-Wataniyyah al-Ijbariyyah" of the previous year published in the *Official Gazette*, no. 1988 (March 1, 1967). For the period of service, see article 4-A of the 1968 law stipulating the period of service to be two years, as opposed to article 4-A of the 1967 law, which stipulated that period to be ninety days.

95. "Qanun Ilgha' Qawanin al-Khidmah al-Wataniyyah al-Ijbariyyah," *Official Gazette*, no. 2248 (July 1, 1970). The law was actually signed on June 25, 1970.

96. See "Nizam Munazzamat al-Muqawamah al-Sha'biyyah," in the *Official Gazette*, no. 1305 (November 11, 1956).

97. See *Al-Muqawamah*, pp. 135–137.

98. For an assessment of Palestinian-Jordanian relations by a pro-Palestinian Transjordanian who was part of the Jordanian national movement and the PLO, see 'Isam Ahmad al-Fayiz, *Al-Nizam al-Hashimi wa al-Huquq al-Wataniyyah lil Sha'b al-Filastini* (Beirut: Dar Ibn Khaldun, 1974). Al-Fayiz (whose last name indicates his belonging to the Bani-Sakhr tribe) identifies the Jordanian regime as the party responsible for creating divisions between the two people and accuses the regime of fostering *iqlimiyyah*, or nationalist chauvinism. In fact, al-Fayiz turns out to be a pseudonym used by Hani Hurani, a Jordanian born to a Palestinian-Jordanian mother and a Syrian father, who was a DFLP activist (from an interview with Hani Hurani, August 2000).

99. See "Nizam al-Jaysh al-'Arabi," *Official Gazette*, no. 2272 (January 2, 1970).

100. Hindi et al., *Al-Muqawamah*, p. 135.

101. Quoted ibid.

102. See Khalil Hindi, "Al-Ta'bi'ah al-Urduniyyah Did al-Muqawamah al-Filastiniyyah Qabl Hajmat Sibtimbar 1970," or "Jordanian Mobilization Against the Palestinian Resistance Before the September 1970 Onslaught," in *Shu'un Filastiniyyah*, no. 4 (September 1971), pp. 31–54.

103. See Carre, *Séptembre Noir*, p. 60. Carre quotes the chiefs as having pressed the king to "frapper avec le fer ceux qui défient la loi Jordanienne," while assuring him of their "soutien total pour faire appliquer les lois de l'Etat," ibid.

104. Reported in the Lebanese newspaper *Al-Muharrir*, May 5, 1970, cited in *Al-Muqawamah al-Filastiniyyah*, p. 130.

105. *Al-Muqawamah al-Filastiniyyah*, p. 130.

106. The communiqué is quoted in *Al-Muqawamah al-Filastiniyyah*, pp. 130–131.

107. Adnan Abu-Odeh, *Jordanians, Palestinians*, p. 177.

108. Ibid.
109. For events in the south, see the important essay of Mahjub ʿUmar, "Aylul fi Junub al-Urdunn" (September in the South of Jordan), in *Shuʾun Filastiniyyah*, no. 71 (October 1977), p. 124.
110. Ibid., p. 131.
111. See Mahjub ʿUmar, "Aylul," for arguments refuting PLO accounts of southern Jordanian tribes and their relationship to the monarchy.
112. James Lunt follows the Jordanian government's assessment of the number of casualties, see James Lunt, *Hussein of Jordan: Searching for a Just and Lasting Peace: A Political Biography* (New York: William Morrow, 1989), p. 142. El-Edroos, in his official history of the Jordanian army, was to later revise the number of dead, citing the number of casualties to be 5,000 to 10,000 between dead and wounded, including 600 Jordanian army soldiers and over 1,500 wounded. El-Edroos, *The Hashemite Arab Army*, p. 459.
113. See *Black September* (Beirut: PLO Research Center, 1971), pp. 131–138; see also *Newsweek* October 12, 1970. On mass graves, see Eric Pace, *New York Times* (September 29, 1970); see also Abu Iyad, *My Home*, pp. 95–96, where he cites the number of casualties to be 7,000 to 8,000 dead.
114. On these desertions, see El-Edroos, *The Hashemite*, p. 459.
115. See ʿAbbas Murad, *Al-Dawr al-Siyasi Lil-Jaysh al-Urduni, 1921–1973* (Beirut: Markaz al-Abhath, Munazzamat al-Tahrir al-Filastiniyyah, 1973), p. 130.
116. See the Lebanese newspaper, *Al-Nahar* (November 11, 1971) cited by Murad, *Al-Dawr*, p. 130.
117. Muna told her father, "I am ashamed of what you are doing. . . . I cannot believe that Amman, Salt and Zarqa are burning. The lackey authorities are setting them on fire. Fire is burning the youth, the women, the children and the old people. I wish I had never been born; I wish I had never seen you so that no one could say that I was your daughter—the daughter of the executioner Mohammed Daoud. . . . Father, I will join the ranks of the fighters to liberate Amman and Palestine. Goodbye father. You may find me among the debris caused by the napalm bombs—your bombs. Revolution Until Victory. [Signed] Your daughter." Muna's letter is cited in *Black September*, p. 77, and in Carre, *Séptembre Noir*, p. 48. On Dawud's resignation as prime minister and as army officer on September 24 and his request for asylum in Libya, see *Black September*, p. 78, and Lunt, *Hussein of Jordan*, p. 143.
118. See *Black September*, p. 5.
119. On the trial of the four Palestinian assassins, see Ahmad Shuqayri, *Al-Nizam al-Urduni Fi Qafas al-Ittiham, Asrar wa Khafaya Masraʿ Wasfi al-Tall* (The Jordanian Regime in the Cage of the Accused: The Secrets and Hidden Facts of the Death of Wasfi al-Tall) (Cairo: Dar Hardot, 1972). This book was republished in Beirut as *Inni Attahim* (I Accuse) (Beirut: Dar al-ʿAwdah, 1973). The title of the second edition is presumably an echo of Emile Zola's famous evocative state-

ment in condemnation of French anti-Semitism manifested in the Dreyfus Affair at the end of the nineteenth century, which began with "J'accuse."

120. For PLO reassessment of its own role in the Jordanian civil war, see Khalil al-Hindi, "Al-Muqawamah wa al-As'ilah al-Masiriyyah ba'da Aylul," in *Al-Muqawamah*, pp. 255–279; also see Haytham al-Ayyubi, "Waqfah Naqdiyyah Amam al-Muqawamah Qabla Ahdath Aylul wa Khilalaha wa Ba'daha," in *Al-Muqawamah al-Filastiniyyah*, pp. 280–290, and Fath, "Al-Thawrah Ma' al-Tajribah wa al-Khata'," *Al-Muqawamah*, pp. 309–315. Also, for the views and reassessment of the Democratic Front for the Liberation of Palestine (DFLP), see al-Jabhah al-Dimuqratiyyah Li Tahrir Filastin, *Hamlat Aylul wa al-Muqawamah al-Filastiniyyah: Durus wa Nata 'ij* (The September Campaign and the Palestinian Resistance: Lessons and Results) (Beirut: Dar al-Tali'ah, February 1971).

121. See, for example, the book published by the Jordanian armed forces' Mudiriyyat al-Tawjih al-Ma'nawi, *Al-Fida 'iyyun Bayna al-Riddah wa al-Intihar* (Amman: Mudiriyyat al-Tawjih al-Ma'nawi, 1973). The only exception is the Jordanian Sa'id al-Tall (brother of the late prime minister Wasfi al-Tall), *Al-Urdunn wa Filastin, Wujhat Nazar 'Arabiyyah* (Amman: Dar al-Liwa' Lil-Sahafah wa al-Nashr, 1986), p. 67, where, in addition to holding the PLO mostly responsible, he claims that "from the start, one must admit that the Jordanian government must shoulder part of the responsibility for exacerbating the situation that led to the clash, wherein it did not develop an equation that rendered its responsibilities, its duties and its sovereignty, on the one hand, compatible with the responsibilities and the duties of the resistance, on the other."

122. On the conditions of the arrests and of Jordanian prisons, see the memoirs of Ghazi al-Khalili, *Shihadat 'ala Judran Zinzanah, Yawmiyyat Mu 'taqal fi al-Sujun al-Urduniyyah* (Testimonies on the Walls of a Prison Cell: The Memoirs of a Detainee in Jordanian Prisons) (Beirut: Ittihad al-Kuttab wa al-Sahafiyyin al-Filastiniyyin, 1975).

123. On the massive purges, see Asher Susser, *On Both Banks of the Jordan: A Political Biography of Wasfi al-Tall* (Essex: Frank Cass, 1994), pp. 156–160; on the massive arrests and trials of "subversives," see Yazid Sayigh, *Al-Urdunn*, pp. 58–60.

124. The king's speech, September 7, 1971, in *Majmu 'at Khutab*, vol. III, p. 301. Note that the literal translation of this sentence is "the need for the establishment of a general organization that includes all the people's sons and daughters," a figure of speech referring to *all* Jordanian men and women.

125. Hani Hurani, " 'Al-Ittihad al-Watani' wa al-Shakl al-Rahin Lil-Sultah Fi al-Urdunn," ("The National Union" and the Current Form of Authority in Jordan), in *Shu 'un Filastiniyyah*, no. 14 (October 1972), p. 55.

126. Sulayman Musa, *A 'lam Min al-Urdunn, Safahat min Tarikh al- 'Arab al-Hadith, Hazza' al-Majali, Sulayman al-Nabulsi, Wasfi al-Tall* (Amman: Dar al-Sha'b, 1986), p. 98.

127. Sulayman Musa, "Wasfi al-Tall: Surah Shakhsiyyah," (Wasfi al-Tall: A Personal Portrait), an introduction to Wasfi al-Tall, *Kitabat Fi al-Qadaya All-'Arabiyyah* (Amman: Dar al-Liwa', 1980), pp. 64–65.

128. King's speech opening the National Union Conference, November 25, 1971, in *Al-Watha'iq al-Urduniyyah, 1971* (Amman: Da'irat al-Matbu'at wa al-Nashr, n.d.), p. 247.

129. The royal decision was published ibid., pp. 291–292.

130. On Dudin's role in the village leagues, see David Hirst, *The Gun and the Olive Branch: The Roots of Violence in the Middle East* (London: Faber and Faber, 1984), p. 390.

131. See Adnan Abu-Odeh, *Jordanians, Palestinians*, p. 201.

132. See Hurani, " 'Al-Ittihad al-Watani' wa al-Shakl al-Rahin Lil-Sultah Fi al-Urdunn," p. 54.

133. Sa'diyyah al-Jabiri was the daughter of the Syrian leader Ihsan al-Jabiri. Before marrying Wasfi al-Tall, she had been married to the Palestinian political figure Musa al-'Alami. It is said that she and Wasfi fell in love while she was married, which led to her divorce from her husband. She married Wasfi al-Tall a year later in 1950. See Sulayman Musa, *A'lam Min al-Urdunn*, p. 115; see also Sulayman Musa, "Wasfi al-Tall, Surah Shakhsiyyah," in Wasfi al-Tall, *Kitabat Fi al-Qadayah al-'Arabiyyah*, p. 33.

134. See list of members in *Al-Watha'iq al-Urduniyyah, 1971*, p. 291.

135. Asher Susser, *On Both Banks of the Jordan*, p. 163. Sulayman Musa claims that it was dissolved in 1973; see his "Wasfi al-Tall, Surah Shakhsiyyah," p. 65.

136. See Yazid Sayigh, *Al-Urdunn*, pp. 64–65. For the PLO's conception of a future Palestinian state and its response to King Husayn's project, see 'Isa al-Shu'aybi, *Al-Kiyaniyyah al-Filastiniyyah*, p. 163; see also Clinton Bailey, *Jordan's Palestinian Challenge, 1948–1983: A Political History* (Boulder, CO: Westview Press, 1984), p. 63.

137. Yazid Sayigh, *Al-Urdunn*, p. 65.

138. "Rad Majlis al-Nuwwab 'ala Khitab al-'Arsh al-Sami" (The Response of the People's Assembly to the Speech from the Paramount Throne), December 8, 1971, published in *Al-Watha'iq al-Urduniyyah, 1971*, p. 281.

139. For the 1973 to 1974 developments, see 'Isam Sakhnini, "Al-Kiyan al-Filastini," in *Shu'un Filastiniyyah*, nos. 41, 42 (January/February 1975), pp. 70–72.

140. King Husayn, speech delivered on November 30, 1974, reproduced in *Khamsah wa 'Ishrun 'Aman* vol. 3, p. 497. 'Adnan Abu 'Awdah claims that the king began to use the Muslim analogy after Black September. See Abu-Odeh, *Jordanians, Palestinians*, p. 211.

141. Hani al-'Amad, "Al-Fulklur Fi al-Diffah al-Sharqiyyah," in Da'irat al-Thaqafah wa al-Funun, *Thaqafatuna Fi Khamsin 'Am* (Amman: Da'irat al-Thaqafah wa al-Funun, 1972), p. 303. For the result of government efforts to collect data on Jordanian cultural songs, see Hani al-'Amad, *Aghanina al-Sha'biyyah Fi al-*

Diffah al-Sharqiyyah Min al-Urdunn (Amman: Da'irat al-Thaqafah wa al-Funun, 1969). On the similarities between the music and singing cultures of the West Bank and East Bank, which vary no more than the southern and northern parts of the East Bank itself, see Tawfiq Abu al-Rubb, *Dirasah Fi al-Fulklur al-Urduni* (Amman: Wizarat al-Thaqafah wa al-Shabab, 1980), pp. 55–102, and 'Abd al-Latif al-Barghuthi, *Al-Aghani al-'Arabiyyah al-Sha'biyyah fi Filastin wa al-Urdunn* (Jerusalem: Matba'at al-Sharq al-'Arabi, 1979). On the history of Tawfiq al-Nimri and his early contributions to "Jordanian" songs, see *Al-Ra'y*, September 23, 1998.

142. Hani al-'Amad, "Al-Fulklur," p. 307.

143. Contrast, for example, the pre-1970 pictures of the king included in his autobiography, *Uneasy Lies the Head: The Autobiography of His Majesty King Hussein I of the Hashemite Kingdom of Jordan* (New York: Bernard Geis and Random House, 1962), and in Vick Vance and Pierre Lauer, *Hussein de Jordanie: Ma "Guerre" Avec Israël* (Paris: Editions Albin Michel, 1968), where the red-and-white *hatta* is nowhere in sight, with the post-1970 pictures in and on the cover of, James Lunt, *Hussein of Jordan: A Political Biography* (London: Macmillan, 1989), and on the jacket of the Arabic edition of Husayn, *Malik al-Mamlakah al-Urduniyyah al-Hashimiyyah, Mihnati KaMalik*, translated by Ghalib 'Arif Tuqan (Amman: n.p., 1978), where the *hatta* is ubiquitous.

144. For example, in words such as *katlah*, meaning a beating, or *wakit*, meaning time, the qaf is pronounced as a *ka*, not a *ga*. Other words include *qum* and *qut*, which are pronounced *kum* and *kut*, respectively, by Karakis and Madabites. For the different pronunciations of *qaf* and *kaf* in Jordan, see Ruks Za'id al-'Uzayzi, *Qamus al-'Adat, al-Lahajat wa al-Awabid al-Urduniyyah*, vol. I (Amman: Da'irat al-Thaqafah wa al-Funun, 1973–1974), pp. 15–16.

145. On the code-switching of accents among the children of Palestinian refugees of peasant background in poor East Amman, see Aseel Sawalha, "Identity, Self and the Other Among Palestinian Refugees in East Amman," in Jean Hannoyer and Seteney Shami, eds., *Amman: The City and Its Society* (Beirut: CERMOC, 1996), pp. 353–354.

146. Laurie Brand, *Palestinians in the Arab World: Institution Building and the Search for a State* (New York: Columbia University Press, 1988), pp. 181–182. Among Sarhan's publications is *Al-Hikayah al-Sha'biyyah al-Filastiniyyah* (Beirut: Al-Mu'assasah al-'Arabiyyah Lil-Dirasat wa al-Nashr, 1988).

147. See Ghanim Zurayqat, "Al-Taharruk al-Jamahiri Fi al-Urdunn Khilal Harb al-Junub" (Popular Mobilization in Jordan During the War in the South), in *Shu'un Filastiniyyah*, no. 78 (May 1978), pp. 190–193.

148. Brand, *Palestinians in the Arab World*, pp. 181–182.

149. On the Jordanian state's efforts to plan the festival, see Ahmad Muslih, *Malamih 'Ammah Lil-Hayah al-Thaqafiyyah fi al-Urdunn, 1953–1993* (Amman: Manshurat Lajnat Tarikh al-Urdunn, 1995), pp. 98–101. The festival has been held

every year since 1981, with the exceptions of 1982 and 1991, as a result of the
Israeli invasion of Lebanon and the second Gulf war, respectively.

150. See Fu'ad 'Alim, "Mahrajan Jarash al-Khamis, Min Ajl Jamahiriyyat al-Mahrajan
. . . wa Tathbit Hawiyyatihi al-Thaqafiyyah," in *Al-Urdunn al-Jadid*, nos. 8–9 (fall/
winter 1986), pp. 124–130, and Fu'ad 'Alim, "Mahrajan Jarash 87: Bila Lawn
. . . wa la Hawiyyah," in *Al-Urdunn al-Jadid*, no. 10 (spring 1988), pp. 73–75.
In 1988, the festival had an independent committee headed by Akram Masarwah, a Christian Transjordanian.

151. For the importance of cricket and football in other British colonies, see C. L. R.
James's classic *Beyond a Boundary* (Durham, NC: Duke University Press, 1993).
The book was originally published in 1963.

152. Kan'an 'Izzat and 'Umar Bishtawi, *Kurat al-Qadam al-Urduniyyah Fi Nisf
Qarn* (Jordanian Football Across Half a Century) (Amman: n.p., 1986), chapter
1, "Nubdhah Tarikhiyyah." The book is not paginated.

153. Husni Sido al-Kurdi, who later on founded the Bank of Jordan, or "Bank al-
Urdunn," was married to a Circassian woman of the Shuqum family.

154. See chapter 2, "Qissat al-Dawri," ibid. Also, for the poor conditions under
which these clubs labored, see Muhammad Hamdan, "Al-Riyadah wa al-
Shabab," in Hani Hurani and Hamid al-Dabbas, eds., *'Amman, Waqi' wa
Tumuh, Qadayah al-Thaqafah, al-Bi'ah wa al-'Imran* (Amman: Markaz al-
Urdunn al-Jadid Lil-Dirasat, 1996), pp. 75–78. For the popularity that football
achieved among teenage boys in Amman, see 'Abd al-Rahman Munif's memoirs of his childhood and youth in Amman in *Sirat Madinah* (Biography of
a City) (Beirut: Al-Mu'assasah al-'Arabiyyah Lil-Dirasat wa al-Nashr, 1994),
pp. 120–125.

155. Seteney Shami, *Ethnicity and Leadership: The Circassians in Jordan*, doctoral
dissertation, Department of Anthropology (Berkeley, CA: University of California, 1982), p. 86.

156. Ibid.

157. Kan'an 'Izzat and 'Umar Bishtawi, *Kurat al-Qadam al-Urduniyyah Fi Nisf
Qarn*, chapter 1, "Nubdha Tarikhiyyah."

158. I would like to thank Jihad Yahya and Salim Hamdan of the Wihdat Club for
information about both players.

159. See the entry on the Wihdat team in 'Izzat and Bishtawi, *Kurat al-Qadam*.
"Wihdat" is in fact an abbreviation of widhat sakaniyyah (housing units), which
referred initially to the refugee camp but later became abbreviated as "wihdat"
or "units."

160. Mu'nis al-Razzaz informed me of this during a number of conversations that
I had with him between 1988 and the present. He also states in his novel *Al-
Shazaya wa al-Fusayfisa'* (Fragments and Mosaics) (Beirut: Al-Mu'assasah al-
'Arabiyyah Lil-Dirasat wa al-Nashr, 1994), that "the Jordanian public supported
the Egyptian Zamalik [team] against the Jordanian Faysali [team] . . . for the
sake of 'Abd al-Nasir, Umm Kulthum, and Taha Husayn," p. 36. Al-Razzaz

makes another implicit reference to such support in his despairing novel *Mud-hakkarat Dinasur* (Memoirs of a Dinosaur) (Beirut: Al-Mu'assasah al-'Arabiyyah Lil-Dirasat wa al-Nashr, 1994), p. 79.

161. "Qanun Mu'assasat Ri'ayat al-Shabab," Law #13 for the Year 1968, published in the *Official Gazette*, no. 2076 (February 15, 1968).

162. Qarar #8 for the Year 1978, issued by the Special Office for the Interpretation of Laws, article 3, reproduced in Wizarat al-Thaqafah wa al-Shabab (Jordanian Ministry of Culture and Youth), *Al-Siyasah al-Urduniyyah Lil-Shabab wa al-Riyadah, Nahwa Jil al-Intima' wa al-I'tizaz al-Watani* (Jordanian Policy toward Youth and Sports, Toward A Generation of National Belonging and Pride) (Amman: Publications of the Ministry of Culture and Youth, 1983), p. 38.

163. Ibid., pp. 26–27.

164. Laurie Brand, *Palestinians in the Arab World*, p. 183.

165. In fact, following the civil war, during which the camp was almost leveled by army bombardment, the government had gone into the camp and widened the streets, or more precisely alleys, to allow tanks to move in should the need arise in the future, as tanks were unable to enter the camp's narrow alleys during the 1970 confrontation.

166. Brand, *Palestinians in the Arab World*, p. 183.

167. Fahd al-Fanik expressed this opinion in a discussion of a lecture I gave at the New Jordan Studies Center in Amman on August 4, 1997.

168. "Hik 'allamna al-Husayn, sha'b wahad la sha'bayn."

169. Arthur Day, *East Bank/West Bank: Jordan and the Prospects for Peace* (New York: Council on Foreign Relations, 1986), pp. 61–62.

170. See Abu-Odeh, *Jordanians, Palestinians*, p. 215.

171. King Husayn's speech at the opening of the Seventeenth Convention of the Palestine National Council in Amman on November 21, 1984, reproduced in *'Ashrat A'wam min al-Kifah wa al-Bina': Majmu'at Khutab Jalalat al-Malik al-Husayn Bin Talal al-Mu'azzam, Malik al-Mamlakah al-Urduniyyah al-Hashimiyyah, Min Sanat 1977 ila Sanat 1987* (Ten Years of Struggle and Construction: The Collection of Speeches of His Majesty King Husayn Bin Talal, the Exalted, King of the Hashemite Jordanian Kingdom, from the Year 1977 to the Year 1987), collected and edited by 'Ali Mahafzah (Amman: Markaz al-Kutub al-Urduni, 1988), p. 590.

172. Ibid., pp. 593, 596.

173. On the 1986 election law, see Hani Hurani's important and thorough analysis in "Mashru' Qanun al-Intikhab al-Jadid li Majlis al-Nuwwab, Riddah Kabirah lil-Wara' 'ala Sa'id al-Damanat al-Dimuqratiyyah wa Ikhlal Sarih bi-Iltizamat al-Urdunn al-Qawmiyyah," (The Project of the New Election Law for Parliament: A Retreat Backwards at the Level of Democratic Guarantees and a Clear Violation of Jordan's [Arab] Nationalist (Qawmiyyah) Commitments), in *Al-Urdunn Al-Jadid*, no. 7 (spring 1986), pp. 27–50.

174. Cited in a report published in the *Journal of Palestine Studies*, no. 60 (summer 1986): 177.

175. His statement in Parliament is reproduced in the *Journal of Palestine Studies*, no. 61, Autumn 1986: 214–219; also see Laurie Brand, *Palestinians in the Arab World*, pp. 174–175.

176. His speeches on April 24, 1988, to the tribal leaders of the Irbid governorate; on April 27, 1988, to the tribal leaders of the Zarqa' governorate; on May 2, 1988, to the tribal leaders of the Balqa' governorate; on May 3, 1988, to the tribal leaders of the governorate of the capital (Amman); on May 4, 1988, to the tribal leaders of the Mafraq governorate; on May 8, 1988, to the tribal leaders of the Karak governorate; on May 11, 1988, to the tribal leaders of the Ma'an governorate; and on May 18, 1988, to the people of the southern city of Tafilah, are reproduced in *Majmu'at Khutab Jalalat al-Qa'id al-A'la, Khilal al-Fatrah 1/1/1987—1/1/1990*, edited and compiled by Qasim Muhammad Salih and Qasim Muhammad al-Duru' (Amman: n.p., n.d.), pp. 179–227.

177. Speech delivered on May 4, 1988 to the tribal leaders of the Mafraq governorate, ibid., p. 207.

178. Speech delivered on June 7, 1988 at the Arab summit, in *Majmu'at Khutab Jalalat al-Qa'id al-A'la, Khilal al-Fatrah 1/1/1987—1/1/1990*, pp. 229–248.

179. Speech reproduced ibid., pp. 253–258.

180. For a discussion of the different measures undertaken by the Jordanian government following the July 31 speech, see Asher Susser, *In Through the Out Door: Jordan's Disengagement and the Middle East Peace Process* (Washington, DC: The Washington Institute for Near East Policy, 1990), pp. 25–30.

181. Ibid., p. 253.

182. Ibid.

183. Ibid.

184. Ibid., p. 256.

185. On the court cases that citizens brought against the government for denationalizing them, see Ibrahim Bakr, *Dirasah Qanuniyyah 'an A'mal al-Siyadah, wa Qararat Naz' al-Jinsiyyah al-Urduniyyah wa Sahb Jawazat al-Safar al-'Adiyyah* (A Study about the Workings of Sovereignty, and the Decisions to Remove Jordanian Nationality and the Withdrawal of Regular Passports) (Amman: Maktabat al-Ra'y, 1995). In November 1995, the government restored to West-Bank Palestinians their 5-year passports (but not their nationality), as a gesture of good will, until they received Palestinian citizenship once the Palestine National Authority achieved its hoped-for "independence."

186. See Laurie Brand, *Palestinians in the Arab World*, pp. 219–220.

187. It is beyond the scope of this book to delve into the intricate details of this lively period of Jordanian history. For an informative overview of the debates about national identity in the post-1988 period, see Marc Lynch, *Contested Identity and Security: The International Politics of Jordanian Identity*, political

science dissertation (Ithaca, NY: Cornell University, 1997), chapter 3. See also Laurie Brand, "Palestinians and Jordanians: A Crisis of Identity," *Journal of Palestine Studies*, no. 96 (summer 1995): 54–60. Also see Schirin Fathi, *Jordan: An Invented Nation? Tribe-State Dynamics and the Formation of National Identity* (Hamburg: Deutsches-Orient Institut, 1994), pp. 201–239, and Adnan Abu-Odeh, *Jordanians, Palestinians*, pp. 235–261.

188. These included Jihad Hattar. See her memoirs: Jihad Hattar, *Dhikrayat ʿan Maʿrakat Aylul: al-Urdunn 1970* (Memoirs from the September Battle: Jordan 1970) (Beirut: Al-Ittihad al-ʿAm Lil-Kuttab wa al-Sahafiyyin al-Filastiniyyin, 1977).

189. Other prominent Transjordanian Christians working within the Palestinian national movement include Ghanim Zurayqat, part of the PLO's writer's union and Ghalib Halasa, Jordan's most illustrious late novelist, who worked with Fath in Beirut in the late 1970s until 1982, when the PLO was evicted from Beirut by Israel's invasion of that country. He moved to Syria, where he continued to work with Fath on cultural issues. Halasa, an exile since 1955, died in Syria in December 1989. His brilliant novels and short stories remain banned in Jordan as they are considered "immoral" because of their explicit, albeit tasteful, sexual and political content. His writings on the Palestinian question include *Azmat Thawrah Am Azmat Qiyadah*, a collection of essays initially published in the magazine *Al-Taʿmim* in the years 1983 to 1984 (n.p: Manshurat al-Intifadah, circa 1992), and *Naqd al-Adab al-Suhyuni, Dirasah Aydiyulujiyyah wa Naqdiyyah li-Aʿmal al-Katib al-Suhyuni ʿAmus ʿUz* (Beirut: Al-Muʾassasah al-ʿArabiyyah Lil-Nashr, 1995). Both books were published posthumously.

190. See Nahid Hattar, "Man Huwa al-Urduni?" in *Al-Hadath* (November 1, 1995), p. 9.

191. See al-ʿAbbadi's articles in *Shihan*. For example, see his "Al-Urduniyyun wa al-Jinsiyyah al-Filastiniyyah," in *Shihan* (February 25, 1995), and his article "Wathiqat al-Milyun Tawqiʿ," in *Al-Hadath* (November 11, 1995). On al-ʿAbbadi, see also Abu-Odeh, *Jordanians, Palestinians*, pp. 244–246.

192. ʿAbd al-Hadi al-Majali, who is also head of the ultranationalist al-ʿAhd Party (the Covenant), seeks to formally distinguish between Palestinians seeking a Palestinian state in the occupied territories and those who renounce such a goal in favor of "national unity" in Jordan. He insists that those who seek a Palestinian state should not be allowed to work in Jordanian political institutions (see *Al-Dustur*, May 11, 1993). See also Marc Lynch's discussion of al-Majali's views in "A Very Public Separation: Jordanian and Palestinian Identities in the New Jordan," a paper presented at the Middle East Studies Association, in Washington, DC, December 1995.

193. Hattar, "Man Huwa al-Urduni?" p. 9.

194. See also Hattar's response to the heavy barrage of attacks on him in Jordanian newspapers, "Filastin lil-Filastiniyyin wa al-Urdunn Lil-Urduniyyin" *Al-Hadath*

(November 15, 1995). Hattar calls all his detractors "the Pseudo-intellectuals of the Alternative Homeland Idea," as, in his opinion, they all support Jordan becoming the Palestinian homeland!

195. See Marwan al-Sakit, "Muttafiqun Am Mukhtalifun," in *al-Hadath*, December 6, 1995.

196. Abu-Odeh, *Jordanians, Palestinians*, p. 197.

197. Ibid.

198. ʿUrayb Rantawi, "Qiraʿah fi al-Buʿd al-Dakhili lil ʿIlaqah al-Urduniyyah al-Filastiniyyah," *Al-Dustur*, October 3, 1995.

199. *Al-Mithaq* (July 9, 1997), pp. 22–23.

200. Muʾnis al-Razzaz expressed this view to me during a conversation in July 1997 at his office at the Ministry of Culture where he works as an advisor to the minister. The regime's attempt to revive the cult of Wasfi al-Tall was symbolized by its renaming the 1980s new Amman Garden's Boulevard as the Wasfi al-Tall Boulevard. Despite the erection of signs to that effect and the official media's reference to the street by its new official name, most Ammanis persist in referring to it as the "Garden's Boulevard."

201. The conferences were held in 1996. See *Wasfi al-Tall, Fikruhu wa Mawaqi-fuhu*, Waqaʿiʿ al-Nadwah allati Nazzamaha al-Markaz al-Urduni wa al-Islami Lil-Dirasat wa al-Maʿlumat bil Taʿawun maʿ Wizarat al-Tahaqafah (Amman: al-Markaz al-Urduni wa al-Islami Lil-Dirasat wa al-Maʿlumat bil Taʿawun maʿ Wizarat al-Tahaqafah, 1996), and *Hazzaʿ al-Majali, Qiraʿah Fi Siratihi wa Tajribatihi Zaʿid al-Mudhakkarat*, Waqaʿiʿ al-Nadwah allati Nazzamaha al-Markaz al-Urduni Lil-Dirasat wa al-Maʿlumat bil Taʿawun maʿ Wizarat al-Tahaqafah (Amman: al-Markaz al-Urduni Lil-Dirasat wa al-Maʿlumat bil Taʿawun maʿ Wizarat al-Tahaqafah, 1996). Note that the Jordanian Center for Studies and Information sometimes calls itself the Jordanian and *Islamic* Center for Studies and Information.

202. See Lenni Brenner, *Zionism in the Age of the Dictators: A Reappraisal* (London: Lawrence Hill, 1983).

203. On the Jordanian revolt from 1936 to 1939, see Kamil Mahmud Khillah, *Al-Tatawwur al-Siyasi Li Sharq al-Urdunn, Maris 1921—Maris 1948* (Tripoli, Libya: Al-Munshaʾah al-ʿAmah Lil-Nashr wal Tawziʿ wal Iʿlan, 1983), pp. 300–305.

204. Khillah, *Al-Tatawwur*, pp. 305–310. Also see the official documents of al-Shabab al-Ahrar in *Maʿrakat al-Huriyyah Fi Sharq al-Urdunn, wa Aqwal Rijal al-Siyasah Fi Surya al-Kubra*, edited and written by Muhammad Sayf al-Din al-ʿAjluni (Damascus: Matbaʿat Judat Babil, 1947).

205. For an interesting discussion of Israeli claims and the ideological collusion of Jordanian exclusivist nationalists, see Salamah Niʿmat, "Al-Urdunn wa Maqulat ʿAl-Watan al-Badilʾ lil-Filastiniyyin," *Al-Hayah*, April 4, 2000: 4.

206. This was expressed at a press conference, see *Al-Raʾy* (September 19, 1993): 14.

207. *Al-Ra'y* (October 13, 1993): 1, 23.

208. On 'Abdullah II's recent rule, see Lamis Andoni, "King Abdallah: In His Father's Footsteps?" *Journal of Palestine Studies*, no. 115, spring 2000: 77–90.

209. Al-Fanik wrote a number of editorials to that effect and repeated these assertions at conferences, as he did in October 1994 at a Center for Strategic Studies Conference on the Jordanian Press, held in Amman at the University of Jordan.

210. Al-'Abbadi is quoted in Andrew Shryock, *Nationalism and the Genealogical Imagination: Oral History and Textual Authority in Tribal Jordan* (Berkeley, CA: University of California Press, 1997), p. 325.

211. Al-'Abbadi was taken to court because of an anti-Hashemite editorial he published in *Shihan*, July 1996.

212. *Al-Dustur*, electronic edition (February 22, 1998), p. 1.

213. Middle East Broadcasting Corporation, televised news, London (February 22, 1998).

214. *Al-Hayah* (February 23, 1998): 1, 6.

215. On February 22, the day after the king's visit to Ma'an, most of the mayors of southern towns and cities that constitute the governorate of Tafilah of which Ma'an is part met and sent a communiqué to the king pledging their allegiance to him and to the Hashemite leadership, stressing that Jordanians must be united with their regime internally to face external threats. Most mayors were represented, but with the notable exception of Ma'an's mayor. See the text of the communiqué in *Al-Dustur*, electronic edition (February 23, 1998).

216. See Laurie Brand's discussion in *Palestinians in the Arab World*, pp. 180–185, and Brand's "Palestinians and Jordanians," pp. 59–60.

217. Letter from John Shuckburgh, assistant secretary to the Colonial Office to the undersecretary of state at the Foreign Office, FO371/6372, p. 26, May 18, 1922, and Despatch no. 280 from Acting High Commissioner of Palestine W. H. Deedes to Winston Churchill, the secretary of state for the colonies, FO371/6372, p. 27, April 28, 1922, and Foreign Office to the Undersecretary of State, Colonial Office, FO371/6372, p. 29, June 9, 1922.

Concluding Remarks

1. On the strategic uses of essentialism, see Gayatri Chakravorty Spivak, "Subaltern Studies: Deconstructing Historiography," in *In Other Worlds: Essays in Cultural Politics* (New York: Methuen, 1987), p. 205.

Works Cited

Government Archives

Public Record Office, London, United Kingdom

International Documents

Treaties of Peace 1919–1923, vol. II (New York: Carnegie Endowment for International Peace, 1924)

Newspapers and Periodicals

Al-Difa', Amman, Jordan
Al-Dustur, Amman, Jordan
Filastin, Amman, Jordan
Al-Hadath, Amman, Jordan
Al-Hayah, London, United Kingdom
Al-Jaridah al-Rasmiyyah Li-Hukumat Sharq al-Urdunn, Amman, Transjordan, 1926–1946
Al-Jaridah al-Rasmiyyah Lil-Mamlakah al-Urduniyyah al-Hashimiyyah (Official Gazette), Amman, Jordan, 1946–1998
Al-Jazirah, Amman, Transjordan
Al-Jihad, Amman, Jordan
Jordan, Jordan Information Bureau, Washington, DC

Jordan Times, Amman, Jordan
Journal of the Royal Society of Asian Affairs, London, United Kingdom
Al-Manar, Amman, Jordan
Al-Mithaq, Amman, Jordan
New York Times, New York
Al-Ra'y, Amman, Jordan
Sahibat al-A'mal wa al-Mihan, Nashrah Dawriyyah (Business and Professional
    Women's Newsletter), Amman, Jordan
Shihan, Amman, Jordan
Al-Urdunn al-Jadid, Nicosia, Cyprus
Al-Sharq al-'Arabi, 1921–1926, Amman, Transjordan

Arabic Sources

Al-'Abbadi, Ahmad 'Uwaydi, *Al-Qada' 'Ind al-'Asha'ir al-Urduniyyah*, part 4 of "Sil-
    silat Man Hum al-Badu?" (Amman: Dar al-Bashir Lil-Nashr wal-Tawzi', 1982).
———, *Fi Rubu' al-Urdunn: Jawlat wa Mushahadat*, part 1 (Amman: Dar al-Fikr,
    1987).
———, *Al-'Asha'ir al-Urduniyyah, al-Ard wal Insan Wal Tarikh* (Amman: Al-Dar al-
    'Arabiyyah Lil Nashr wal Tawzi', 1988).
———, *Min al-Qiyam wal Adab al-Badawiyyah*, part 2 of "Silsilat Man Hum al-
    Badu," (Amman: Da'irat al-Matbu'at wal Nashr, 1976).
Abu Dayyah, Sa'd, and 'Abd al-Majid al-Nas'ah, *Tarikh al-Jaysh al-'Arabi fi 'Ahd al-
    Imarah, 1921–1946, Dirasah 'Ilmiyyah Tahliliyyah Watha'iqiyyah* (Amman:
    n.p., 1990).
———, and 'Abd al-Majid Mahdi, *Al-Jaysh al-'Arabi wa Diblumasiyyat al-Sahra',
    Dirasah Fi Nash'atihi wa Tatawwur Dawr al-Thaqafah al-'Askariyyah* (Amman:
    Mudiriyyat al-Matabi' al-'Askariyyah, 1987).
———, *Al-Fikr al-Siyasi al-Urduni, Namudhaj fi Dirasat al-Fikr al-Siyasi al-Urduni
    min Khilal Kutub al-Taklif allati Wajjahaha al-Malik Husayn Bin Talal ila
    Ru'asa' al-Wizarat* (Amman: Dar al-Bashir, 1989).
Abu Hassan, Muhammad, *Turath al-Badu al-Qada'iyy, Nazariyyan wa 'Amaliyyan*
    (Amman: Da'irat al-Thaqafah wal Funun, 1987).
———, "Al-Qahwah wa Atharuha fi Hayat al-Badu al-Ijtima'iyya," *Al-Funun al-
    Sha'biyya*, no.2, Amman (April 1974).
Abu Kharmah, Khalil, "Al-Mar'ah Fil Naqabat al-'Ummaliyyah," paper presented at
    the panel; "Working Women," sponsored by the Women's Committee in the
    Journalists Union, Amman (December 1987).
Abu Khusah, Ahmad, *Al-'Asha'ir al-Urduniyyah wal Filastiniyyah wa Washa'ij al-
    Qurbah Baynaha* (Amman: n.p., 1989).
Abu-Nuwwar, 'Ali, *Hina Talashat al-'Arab, Mudhakkarat Fi al-Siyasah al-'Arabiyyah,
    1948–1964* (London: Dar al-Saqi, 1990).

Abu-Nuwwar, Ma'n, *Ma'rakat al-Karamah, March 21, 1968*, 3rd edition (Amman: n.p., 1970).

Abu Nuwwar, Raja', "Al-Mar'ah al-Urduniyyah Fi Nihayat al-'Aqd al-Dawli Lil-Mar'ah," in *Al-Urdunn al-Jadid*, nos. 3, 4 (spring/summer 1985), Nicosia, Cyprus, pp. 176–177.

Abu al-Rubb, Tawfiq, *Dirasah Fi al-Fulklur al-Urduni* (Amman: Wizarat al-Thaqafah wa al-Shabab, 1980).

Abu Shahut, Shahir, *Qissat Harakat al-Dubbat al-Urduniyyin al-Ahrar (1952-1957)*, unpublished manuscript, 1993 (to be published as part of Silsilat Ihya' al-Dhakirah al-Tarikhiyyah, New Jordan Center for Studies, edited by Hani Hurani, Amman, Jordan).

Abu-'Ulbah, 'Ablah Mahmud, "Al-Mar'ah al-Urduniyyah wa al-Nidal al-Siyasi," paper presented at "Jordanian Women in the Shadow of Contemporary Legislation," a conference sponsored by the General Federation of Jordanian Women, held in Amman on March 23–25, 1992.

Al-'Ajluni, Muhammad Sayf al-Din, *Ma'rakat al-Huriyyah Fi Sharq al-Urdunn, wa Aqwal Rijal al-Siyasah Fi Surya al-Kubra* (Damascus: Matba'at Judat Babil, 1947).

'Alim, Fu'ad, "Mahrajan Jarash al-Khamis, Min Ajl Jamahiriyyat al-Mahrajan . . . wa Tathbit Hawiyyatihi al-Thaqafiyyah," in *Al-Urdunn al-Jadid*, nos. 8, 9 (fall/winter 1986), pp. 124–130.

———, "Mahrajan Jarash 87: Bila Lawn . . . wa la Hawiyyah," in *Al-Urdunn al-Jadid*, no. 10 (spring 1988).

Al-'Amad, Hani, "Al-Fulklur Fi al-Diffah al-Sharqiyyah," in Da'irat al-Thaqafah wa al-Funun, *Thaqafatuna Fi Khamsin 'Am* (Amman: Da'irat al-Thaqafah wa al-Funun, 1972).

———, *Aghanina al-Sha'biyyah Fi al-Diffah al-Sharqiyyah Min al-Urdunn* (Amman: Da'irat al-Thaqafah wa al-Funun, 1969).

'Anabtawi, Mundhir Fa'iq, ed., *Al-Watha'iq al-Filastiniyyah al-'Arabiyyah Li-'Am 1966* (Beirut: Mu'assasat al-Dirasat al-Filastiniyyah, 1967).

Al-'Arif, 'Arif, *Al-Nakbah, Nakbat Bayt al-Maqdis wa al-Firdaws al-Mafqud, 1947–1955*, part IV (Sidon-Beirut: Al-Matba'ah al-'Asriyyah, 1959).

Al-'Atiyyat, 'A'ishah al-Faraj, "Al-Mar'ah Fi Zill Qanun al-Ahwal al-Shakhsiyyah al-Urduni," paper available from the Office of Advisory Services for Women (Maktab al-Khadamat al-Istishariyyah Lil-Mar'ah), Amman, 1984.

Badran, 'Umar Sulayman, *Hakadha Yakun al-Intima' Lil-Watan* (Amman: Mudiriyyat al-Matabi' al-'Askariyyah, 1989).

Bakr, Ibrahim, *Dirasah Qanuniyyah 'an A'mal al-Siyadah wa Qararat Naz' al-Jinsiyyah al-Urduniyyah wa Sahb Jawazat al-Safar al-'Adiyyah* (Amman: Maktabat al-Ra'y, 1995).

Al-Barghuthi, 'Abd al-Latif, *Al-Aghani al-'Arabiyyah al-Sha'biyyah fi Filastin wa al-Urdunn* (Jerusalem: Matba'at Al-Sharq al-'Arabi, 1979).

Al-Bashir, Hayfa', and Hiyam Najib al-Shuraydah, "Al-Musharakah al-Siyasiyyah Li al-Mar'ah al-Urduniyyah wa Ittijahat al-Qita' al-Siyasi Nahwa 'Amalaha Fi Nafs al-Majal," paper presented at Al-Mu'tamar al-Watani Li al-Mar'ah al-Urduniyyah, Waqi' wa Tatallu'at (the National Conference on Jordanian Women, Reality and Vision), held in Amman, May 14–16, 1985.

Al-Bashir, Sulayman, *Judhur al-Wisayah al-Urduniyyah, Dirasah fi Watha 'iq al-Arshif al-Suhyuni* (Beirut: Dar al-Farabi, 1982).

Bunduqji, Riyad Ahmad, *Al-Urdunn Fi 'Ahd Klub* (Amman: Matabi' al-Safadi, circa 1957).

Al-Burini, 'Umar, and Hani al-Hindi, *Al-Mar'ah al-Urduniyyah, Ra 'idat Fi Maydan al-'Amal* (Amman: Matabi' al-Safwah, 1994).

Da'irat al-Thaqafah wa al-Funun, *Thaqafatuna fi Khamsin 'Am* (Amman: Da'irat al-Thaqafah wa al-Funun, 1972).

Darwazah, Muhammad 'Izzat, *Al-Qadiyyah al-Filastiniyyah Fi Mukhtalaf Marahi-liha: Tarikh wa-Mudhakkarat wa-Ta 'liqat*, vol. II (Sidon: n.p., 1959–1960).

Darwish, Sa'id, *Al-Marhalah al-Dimuqratiyyah al-Jadidah Fil Urdunn, Tafasil al-Munaqashat wa Hukumat al-Thiqah* (Beirut and Amman: Dana, a subsidiary of Al-Mu'assasah al-'Arabiyyah Lil Dirasat wa al-Nashr, 1990).

Al-Fayiz, 'Isam Ahmad, *Al-Nizam al-Hashimi wa al-Huquq al-Wataniyyah lil Sha 'b al-Filastini* (Beirut: Dar Ibn Khaldun, 1974).

Ghawanmah, Yusuf Darwish, *Al-Tarikh al-Siyasi Li-Sharqiyy al-Urdunn Fi al-'Asr al-Mamlukiyy: Al-Mamalik al-Bahriyyah* (Amman: Dar al-Fikr lil-Nashr wa al-Tawzi', 1982).

Al-Habashnah Abu-'Ali, Khadijah,"Qanun al-Ahwal al-Shakhsiyyah al-Urduni, Wa-raqat 'Amal," presented at the conference "Al-Mar'ah al-Urduniyyah fi Zill al-Qawanin wal Tashri'at al-Haliyyah," sponsored by the General Jordanian Women's Union, Amman, March 23–25, 1992.

————, Untitled paper presented to the special panel, "The Jordanian Woman in the Shadow of Contemporary Laws and Legislations," Center for Woman's Studies, Amman, March 1992.

Halasa, Ghalib, *Zunuj, Badu, wa Fallahun* (Beirut: Dar al-Masir, 1980).

————, *Azmat Thawrah Am Azmat Qiyadah*, Manshurat al-Intifadah, (n.p, circa 1992).

————, *Naqd al-Adab al-Suhyuni, Dirasah Aydiyulujiyyah wa Naqdiyyah li-A 'mal al-Katib al-Suhyuni 'Amus 'Uz* (Beirut: Al-Mu'assasah al-'Arabiyyah Lil-Nashr, 1995).

Hallum, Ribhi Jum'ah, *Ha 'ula ' A 'da ' al-Taharrur Fi al-Urdunn*, Silsilat Kutub Qaw-miyyah (Cairo: Al-Dar al-Qawmiyyah Lil-Tiba'ah wa al-Nashr, 1962).

Hamdan, Muhammad, "Al-Riyadah wa al-Shabab," in Hani Hurani and Hamid al-Dabbas, eds., *'Amman, Waqi' wa Tumuh, Qadayah al-Thaqafah, al-Bi'ah wa al-'Imran* (Amman: Markaz al-Urdunn al-Jadid Lil-Dirasat, 1996).

Al-Hattab, Sultan, *Al-Thawrah al-Kubra wa al-Jaysh al-'Arabi kama Yarahuma al-Husayn, Qira'ah wa Nusus, 1953-1992* (Amman: Dar al-'Urubah Lil-Dirasat, 1993).

Hattar, Jihad, *Dhikrayat 'an Ma'rakat Aylul, al-Urdunn 1970* (Beirut: Al-Ittihad al-'Am Lil-Kuttab wa al-Sahafiyyin al-Filastiniyyin, 1977).

Al-Hiddawi, Hasan, *Al-Jinsiyyah wa Ahkamuha Fi al-Qanun al-Urduni* (Amman: Dar Majdalawi lil-Nashr wa al-Tawzi', 1993).

Hilal, Jamil, *Al-Diffah al-Gharbiyyah, al-Tarkib al-Ijtima'i wa al-Iqtisadi (1948–1974)* (Beirut: Markaz al-Abhath, Munazzamat al-Tahrir al-Filastiniyyah, 1975).

Hindi, Khalil, "Al-Ta'bi'ah al-Urduniyyah Did al-Muqawamah al-Filastiniyyah Qabl Hajmat Sibtimbar 1970," in *Shu'un Filastiniyyah*, no. 4 (September 1971).

Hindi, Khalil, Fu'ad Bawarshi, Shihadah Musa, and Nabil Sha'ath, *Al-Muqawamah al-Filastiniyyah wa al-Nizam al-Urduni, Dirasah Tahliliyyah Li Hajmat Aylul* (Beirut: Munazzamat al-Tahrir al-Filastiniyyah, Markaz al-Abhath, 1971).

Al-Hukumah al-Urduniyyah, *Wihdat Diffatay al-Urdunn, Waqa'i' wa Watha'iq* (Amman: Idarat al-Sahafah wa al-Nashr, June 1950).

———, *Al-Watha'iq al-Urduniyyah 1968* (Amman: Da'irat al-Matbu'at wa al-Nashr, 1973).

———, *Al-Watha'iq al-Urduniyyah, 1971* (Amman: Da'irat al-Matbu'at wa al-Nashr, n.d.).

Hurani, Faysal, *Al-Fikr al-Siyasi al-Filastini, 1964–1974, Dirasah Lil-Mawathiq al-Ra'isiyyah Li-Munazzamat al-Tahrir al-Filastiniyyah* (Beirut: Markaz al-Abhath, Munazzamat al-Tahrir al-Filastiniyyah, 1980).

Hurani, Hani, *Al-Tarkib al-Iqtisadi al-Ijtima'i Li Sharq al-Urdunn* (Beirut: Markaz al-Abhath, Munazzamat al-Tahrir al-Filastiniyyah, 1978).

———, " 'Al-Ittihad al-Watani' wa al-Shakl al-Rahin Lil-Sultah Fi al-Urdunn," in *Shu'un Filastiniyyah*, no. 14 (October 1972).

———, "Mashru' Qanun al-Intikhab al-Jadid li Majlis al-Nuwwab, Riddah Kabirah lil-Wara' 'ala Sa'id al-Damanat al-Dimuqratiyyah wa Ikhlal Sarih bi-Iltizamat al-Urdunn al-Qawmiyyah," in *Al-Urdunn al-Jadid*, no. 7 (spring 1986), pp. 27–50.

Hurani, Hani, and Salim Tarawnah, "Hakadha Saqata Hilf Baghdad fi 'Amman," in *Al-Urdunn al-Jadid*, no. 7 (spring 1986), pp.112–163.

Ibn 'Abdullah, Talal, *Mudhakkarat al-Malik Talal*, prepared by Mamduh Rida and edited by Subhi Tuqan (Cairo: Al-Zahra' Lil-I'lam al-'Arabi, 1991).

Ibn al-Husayn, 'Abdullah, *Al-Athar al-Kamilah Lil Malik 'Abdullah*, 3rd edition (Beirut: Al-Dar al-Muttahidah Lil-Nashr, 1985).

Ibn Talal, al-Husayn, *Mihnati Ka Malik*, translated by Ghalib A. Tuqan (Amman: n.p., 1978).

———, *Khamsah wa 'Ishrun 'Am min al-Tarikh, 1952–1977, Majmu'at Khutab Jalalat al-Malik al-Husayn Bin Talal al-Mu'azzam, Malik al-Mamlakah al-Urduniyyah al-Hashimiyyah* (London, Amman: Samir Mutawi' Lil-Nashr, 1978, vols. I, II, III).

———, *Ashrat A'wam min al-Kifah wa al-Bina', Majmu'at Khutab Jalalat al-Malik al-Husayn Bin Talal al-Mu'azzam, Malik al-Mamlakah al-Urduniyyah al-Hashimiyyah, Min Sanat 1977 ila Sanat 1987*, collected and edited by 'Ali Mahafzah (Amman: Markaz al-Kutub al-Urduni, 1988).

———, *Majmu'at Khutab Jalalat al-Qa'id al-A'la, Khilal al-Fatrah 1/1/1987–1/1/1990*, edited and compiled by Qasim Muhammad Salih and Qasim Muhammad al-Duru' (Amman: n.p., n.d).

'Id, Suha Kamil, "Tarikh Nidal al-Mar'ah Fi al-Urdunn Fi Wajh al-Mukhattatat al-Suhyuniyyah," (The History of Women's Struggle in Jordan in the Face of Zionist Schemes), Ministry of Social Development, Amman, October 1983.

'Izzat, Kan'an, and 'Umar Bishtawi, *Kurat al-Qadam al-Urduniyyah Fi Nisf Qarn* (Amman n.p., 1986).

Al-Jabhah al-Dimuqratiyyah Li Tahrir Filastin, *Hamlat Aylul wa al-Muqawamah al-Filastiniyyah, Durus wa Nata'ij* (Beirut: Dar al-Tali'ah, February 1971).

Jamil, Nina, *Al-Ta'am Fi al-Thaqafah al-'Arabiyyah* (London: Riyad al-Rayyis Lil-Kutub wa al-Nashr, 1994).

Khadir, Asma', "Al-Mar'ah al-'Amilah Fi al-Urdunn Waqi'an wa Tashri'an," unpublished paper (Amman, October 1983).

Al-Khalili, Ghazi, *Shihadat 'ala Judran Zinzanah, Yawmiyyat Mu'taqal fi al-Sujun al-Urduniyyah*, Ittihad al-Kuttab wa al-Sahafiyyin al-Filastiniyyin (Beirut, 1975).

Khillah, Kamil Mahmud, *Al-Tatawwur al-Siyasi Li-Sharq al-Urdunn, Maris 1921–Maris 1948* (Tripoli, Libya: Al-Munsha'ah al-'Ammah Lil-Nashr wa al-Tawzi' wa al-I'lan, 1983).

Al-Luqyani, Hashim Isma'il, *Ta'rib Qiyadat al-Jaysh al-'Arabi* (Amman: n.p., 1993).

Madi, Munib, and Sulayman Musa, *Tarikh al-Urdunn Fi al-Qarn al-'Ishrin* (Amman: Maktabat al-Muhtasib, 1959).

Mahafzah, 'Ali, *Tarikh al-Urdunn al-Mu'asir, 'Ahd al-Imarah, 1921–1946* (Amman: Markaz al-Kutub al-Urduni, 1973).

Mahafzah, Muhammad, *Al-'Ilaqat al-Urduniyyah al-Filastiniyyah, al-Siyasiyyah, al-Iqtisadiyyah wa al-Ijtima'iyyah, 1939–1951* (Amman: Dar al-Furqan wa Dar 'Ammar, 1983).

Al-Majali, Hazza', *Hadha Bayanun Lil-Nas, Qissat Muhadathat Timblar* (Amman: n.p., 1956).

———, *Mudhakkarati* (Amman: n.p., May 1960).

Al-Majali, Sahar 'Abd al-Majid, *Al-Jaysh al-'Arabi, 1921–1951, Dawruhu fi al-Sira' al-'Arabi-al-Suhyuni* (Amman: n.p., 1992).

Al-Markaz al-Urduni wa al-Islami Lil-Dirasat wa al-Ma'lumat bil Ta'awun ma' Wizarat al-Tahaqafah, *Wasfi al-Tall, Fikruhu wa Mawaqifuhu*, Waqa'i' al-Nadwah allati Nazzamaha al-Markaz al-Urduni wa al-Islami Lil-Dirasat wa al-Ma'lumat bil Ta'awun ma' Wizarat al-Tahaqafah (Amman: Al-Markaz al-Urduni wa al-

Islami Lil-Dirasat wa al-Ma'lumat bil Ta'awun ma' Wizarat al-Tahaqafah, 1996).

Al-Markaz al-Urduni Lil-Dirasat wa al-Ma'lumat bil Ta'awun ma' Wizarat al-Tahaqafah, *Hazza' al-Majali, Qira'ah Fi Siratihi wa Tajribatihi Za'id al-Mudhakkarat*, Waqa'i' al-Nadwah allati Nazzamaha al-Markaz al-Urduni Lil-Dirasat wa al-Ma'lumat bil Ta'awun ma' Wizarat al-Tahaqafah (Amman: Al-Markaz al-Urduni Lil-Dirasat wa al-Ma'lumat bil Ta'awun ma' Wizarat al-Tahaqafah, 1996).

Markaz al-Urdunn al-Jadid, *Intikhabat 1993, Dirasah Tahliliyyah wa Raqamiyyah*, Report (Amman: Markaz al-Urdunn al-Jadid Press, February 1994).

Al-Masri, Majidah, "Al-Azmah al-Rahinah Lil-Harakah al-Nisa'iyyah fi al-Urdunn," in *Al-Urdunn al-Jadid*, no. 7 (spring 1986).

Mu'adh, Da'id, "Tajribat al-Ittihad al-Nisa'i (1974–1981)," in *Al-Urdunn al-Jadid*, no. 7 (spring 1986).

Mudiriyyat al-Amn al-'Am, *al-Amn al-'Am al-Urduni Fi Sittin 'Aman, Min 1920 Ila 1980* (Amman: n.p. 1981).

Mudiriyyat al-Tawjih al-Ma'nawi, *Al-Fida'iyyun Bayna al-Riddah wa al-Intihar* (Amman: Mudiriyyat al-Tawjih al-Ma'nawi, 1973).

Munazzamat al-Tahrir al-Filastiniyyah, *Al-Yawmiyyat al-Filastiniyyah*, vols. 4–5 (Beirut: Markaz al-Abhath, Munazzamat al-Tahrir al-Filastiniyyah, 1967).

Munif, 'Abd al-Rahman, *Sirat Madinah* (Beirut: Al-Mu'assasah al-'Arabiyyah Lil-Dirasat wa al-Nashr, 1994).

Murad, 'Abbas, *Al-Dawr al-Siyasi Lil-Jaysh al-'Arabi, 1921–1973* (Beirut: Munazzamat al-Tahrir al-Filastiniyyah, Markaz al-Abhath, December 1973).

Musa, Sulayman, *Ta'sis al-Imarah al-Urduniyyah, 1921–1925, Dirasah Watha'iqiyyah* (Amman: Maktabat al-Muhtasib, 1971).

———, *Imarat Sharq al-Urdunn, 1921–1946, Nash'atuha wa Tatawwuruha fi Rub'i Qarn* (Amman: Lajnat Tarikh al-Urdunn, 1990).

———, "Wasfi al-Tall, Surah Shakhsiyyah," introduction to Wasfi al-Tall, *Kitabat Fi al-Qadaya al-'Arabiyyah* (Amman: Dar al-Liwa', 1980).

———, *A'lam Min al-Urdunn, Safahat min Tarikh al-'Arab al-Hadith* (Amman: Matabi' Dar al-Sha'b, 1986).

———, *Tarikh al-Urdunn fi al-Qarn al-'Ishrin, 1958–1995*, vol. 2 (Amman: Maktabat al-Muhtasib, 1996)

———, *A'lam Min al-Urdunn, Hazza' al-Majali, Sulayman al-Nabulsi, Wasfi al-Tall* (Amman: Dar al-Sha'b, 1986).

Al-Muslih, Ahmad, *Malamih 'Ammah Lil-Hayah al-Thaqafiyyah Fi al-Urdunn (1953–1993)* (Amman: Manshurat Lajnat Tarikh al-Urdunn, 1995).

Naffa', Emily, "Dawr al-Mar'ah al-Urduniyyah Fil Nidal al-Siyasi," presented at *Al-Mar'ah al-Urduniyyah Fi Zill al-Qawanin wal Tashri'at al-Haliyyah* conference held in Amman, March 23–25, 1992.

Al-Nashashibi, Nasir al-Din, *Man Qatala al-Malik 'Abdullah* (Kuwait: Manshurat al-Anba', 1980).

Al-Nimri, Tawfiq, "Al-Musiqa wa al-Ghina'," in Da'irat al-Thaqafah wa al-Funun, *Thaqafatuna fi Khamsin 'Am* (Amman: Da'irat al-Thaqafah wa al-Funun, 1972).

Nusayrat, Sulayman, *Al-Shakhsiyyah al-Urduniyyah, Bayna al-Bu'd al-Watani wa al-Bu'd al-Qawmi* (Amman: Manshurat Wizarat al-Thaqafah, 1997).

Qassad, Fatimah, "Al-Mar'ah wa Ba'd al-Tashri'at," unpublished paper (Amman, n.d.).

Al-Rawi, Jabir Ibrahim, *Sharh Ahkam al-Jinsiyyah Fil-Qanun al-Urduni, Dirasah Muqarinah* (Amman: Al-Dar al-'Arabiyyah Lil-Tawzi' wa al-Nashr, 1984).

Al-Razzaz, Mu'nis, *Al-Shazaya wa al-Fusayfisa'* (Beirut: Al-Mu'assasah al-'Arabiyyah Lil-Dirasat wa al-Nashr, 1994).

———, *Mudhakkarat Dinasur* (Beirut: Al-Mu'assasah al-'Arabiyyah Lil-Dirasat wa al-Nashr, 1994).

Sakhnini, 'Isam, "Damm Filastin al-Wusta Ila Sharqiyy al-Urdunn," *Shu'un Filastiniyyah*, no. 40 (December 1974).

———, "Al-Kiyan al-Filastini," in *Shu'un Filastiniyyah*, nos. 41, 42 (January/February 1975).

Salamah, Mazin, "Al-Fashal Yulahiq Mu'tamarat al-Mughtaribin," in *Al-Urdunn al-Jadid*, no. 10 (spring 1988), pp. 70–73.

Sarhan, Nimr, *Al-Hikayah al-Sha'biyyah al-Filastiniyyah* (Beirut: Al-Mu'assasah al-'Arabiyyah Lil-Dirasat wa al-Nashr, 1988).

———, "Ta'am al-Mansaf Fil Ma'thurat al-Sha'biyyah al-Filastiniyyah," in *Al-Turath al-Sha'bi*, Baghdad, no. 9, vol. 9 (1978), pp. 79–84.

Sayigh, Anis, *Al-Hashimiyun wa Qadiyyat Filastin* (Beirut: Al-Maktabah al-'Asriyyah wa Jaridat al-Muharrir, 1966).

Sayigh, Yazid Yusuf, *Al-Urdunn wa al-Filastiniyyun, Dirasah Fi Wihdat al-Masir Aw al-Sira' al-Hatmi* (London: Riad El-Rayyes Press, 1987).

Sayil, Sa'd, "Shihadat Min Ma'rakat al-Karamah," in *Shu'un Filastiniyyah*, no. 8 (April 1972), pp. 197–210.

Shafiq, Munir, "Ma'rakat al-Karamah," in *Shu'un Filastiniyyah*, no. 19 (March 1973), pp. 103–110.

Al-Shar', Sadiq, *Hurubuna ma' Isra'il, 1947–1973, Ma'arik Khasirah wa Intisarat Da'i'ah, Mudhakkarat wa Mutala'at Al-Liwa' al-Rukn al-Mutaqa'id Sadiq al-Shar'* (Amman: Dar al-Shuruq Lil-Nashr, 1997).

Shirdan, Musa 'Adil Bakmirza, *Al-Urdunn Bayna 'Ahdayn* (Amman: n.p., 1957?).

Al-Shu'aybi, 'Isa, *Al-Kiyaniyyah al-Filastiniyyah, al-Wa'i al-Dhati wa al-Tatawwur al-Mu'assasati, 1947–1977* (Beirut: Markaz al-Abhath, Munazzamat al-Tahrir al-Filastiniyyah, 1979).

Shuqayri, Ahmad, *Min al-Qimmah Ila al-Hazimah, Ma' al-Muluk wa al-Ru'asa' al-'Arab* (Beirut: Dar al-'Awdah, 1971).

———, *Al-Nizam al-Urduni Fi Qafas al-Ittiham, Asrar wa Khafaya Masra' Wasfi al-Tall* (Cairo: Dar Hardot, 1972).

————, *Inni Attahim* (Beirut: Dar al-'Awdah, 1973).

Al-Surayhin, Faruq Nawwaf, *Al-Jaysh al-'Arabi al-Urduni, 1921–1967* (Amman: n.p., 1990).

Suwaylih, Yasin, *Al-Rababah Fi Hayat al-Badiyah* (Damascus: Dar al-Hasad, 1994).

Al-Tandawi, Samir, *Ila Ayna Yattajihu al-Urdunn?* (Cairo: Al-Dar al-Misriyyah Lil-Kutub, 1958?).

Al-Tall, 'Abdullah, *Karithat Filastin, Mudhakkarrat 'Abdullah al-Tall, Qa 'id Ma 'rakat al-Quds*, part I (Cairo: Dar al-Qalam, 1959).

Al-Tall, Ahmad Yusuf, *'Abdullah al-Tall, Batal Ma 'rakat al-Quds* (Amman: Dar al-Furqan, 1999), two volumes.

Al-Tall, Sa'id, *Al-Urdunn wa -Filastin, Wujhat Nazar 'Arabiyyah* (Amman: Dar al-Liwa' Lil-Sahafah wa al-Nashr, 1986).

Al-Tall, Suhayr Salti, *Muqaddimah Hawl Wad 'iyyat al-Mar 'ah wa al-Harakah al-Nisa 'iyyah Fi al-Urdunn* (Beirut: Al-Mu 'assassah al-'Arabiyyah Lil-Dirasat wal-Nashr, 1985).

————, "Dirasah Hawl Awda' al-Mar 'ah al-Urduniyyah," paper presented at the Arab Institute for Human Rights in Tunis, 1994.

————, "Al-Siyasah al-I'lamiyyah wa Qadayah al-Mar 'ah," in *Al-Urdunn al-Jadid*, no. 7 (spring 1986), pp. 70–73.

'Ubaydat, Mahmud, *Al-Urdunn Fi al-Tarikh: Min al-'Asr al-Hajariyy Hatta Qiyam al-Imarah*, part I (Tripoli, Lebanon: Jarrus Bars, 1992).

Al-'Ubaydi, 'Awni Jaddu', *Jama 'at al-Ikhwan al-Muslimin Fi al-Urdunn wa Filastin 1945–1970, Safahat Tarikhiyyah* (Amman: n.p., 1991).

'Umar, Mahjub, "Aylul fi Junub al-Urdunn," in *Shu 'un Filastiniyyah*, no. 71 (October 1977).

Al-'Uzayzi, Ruks Za'id, *Qamus al-'Adat, al-Lahajat wa al-Awabid al-Urduniyyah*, vols. I, II, III (Amman: Da'irat al-Thaqafah wa al-Funun, 1973–1974).

Wizarat al-I'lam, *Al-Mar 'ah al-Urduniyyah* (Amman: Mudiriyyat al-Matbu'at, 1979).

Wizarat al-Thaqafah wa al-Shabab, *Al-Siyasah al-Urduniyyah Lil-Shabab wa al-Riyadah, Nahwa Jil al-Intima ' wa al-I 'tizaz al-Watani* (Amman: Wizarat al-Thaqafah wa al-Shabab, 1983).

Wizarat al-Thaqafah wa al-I'lam, *Al-Urdunn Fi Khamsin 'Am, 1921–1971* (Amman: Da'irat al-Matbu'at wal-Nashr, 1972), pp. 49–50.

Zibyan, Taysir, *Al-Malik 'Abdullah Kama 'Araftahu* (King 'Abdullah as I Knew Him), 2nd edition (Amman: n.p., 1994).

Ziyadat, 'Adil, "Al-Khadamat al-Tibbiyyah Lil-Jaysh al-'Arabi fi 'Ahd al-Imarah, 1921–1946," *Abhath al-Yarmuk* 7, no. 2, 1991, pp. 177–195.

Al-Zu'bi, Naji, "Lamhah Tarikhiyyah 'an Musiqat al-Quwwat al-Musallahah al-Urduniyyah," unpublished paper (Amman, 1994).

Zurayqat, Ghanim, "Al-Taharruk al-Jamahiri Fi al-Urdunn Khilal Harb al-Junub," "Popular Mobilization in Jordan During the War in the South," in *Shu 'un Filastiniyyah*, no. 78 (May 1978), pp. 190–193.

English and French Sources

Abidi, Aqil Hyder Hasan, *Jordan: A Political Study, 1948-1957* (New Delhi: Asia Publishing House, 1965).

Abu Iyad, with Eric Rouleau, *My Home, My Land: A Narrative of the Palestinian Struggle* (New York: Times Books, 1981).

Abu Jaber, Kamal, Fawzi Gharaibeh, and Allen Hill, eds., *The Badia of Jordan: The Process of Change* (Amman: University of Jordan Press, 1987).

Abu Nowar, Ma'an, *The History of the Hashemite Kingdom of Jordan*, vol. 1: *The Creation and Development of Transjordan: 1920–1929* (The Middle East Center, Oxford: Ithaca Press, 1989).

Abu-Odeh, Adnan, *Jordanians, Palestinians, and the Hashemite Kingdom in the Middle East Peace Process* (Washington, DC: United States Institute of Peace Press, 1999).

Abu Odeh, Lama, *Crimes of Honor and the Construction of Gender in Arab Societies*, doctoral dissertation, Harvard Law School, Harvard University, 1995.

Adorno, Theodor W., *Introduction to the Sociology of Music* (New York: Continuum, 1976).

Althusser, Louis, "Ideology and Ideological State Apparatuses (Notes Toward an Investigation)," in Louis Althusser, *Lenin and Philosophy and Other Essays* (New York: Monthly Review Press, 1971).

Amawi, Abla, *State and Class in Transjordan: A Study of State Autonomy*, doctoral dissertation, Department of Government, Georgetown University, 1993.

Anderson, Benedict, *Imagined Communities: Reflections on the Origin and Spread of Nationalism* (London: Verso, 1991).

Anderson, J. N. D., "Recent Developments in Shari'a Law VIII, The Jordanian Law of Family Rights 1951," *Muslim World*, vol. xlii (1952).

Anderson, Lisa, *The State and Social Transformation in Tunisia and Libya, 1830–1980* (Princeton, NJ: Princeton University Press, 1986).

Andoni, Lamis, "King Abdallah: In His Father's Footsteps?" *Journal of Palestine Studies*, no. 115, spring 2000, pp. 77–90.

Anglo-American Committee of Inquiry, *A Survey of Palestine: Prepared in December 1945 and January 1946 for the Information of the Anglo- American Committee of Inquiry*, vol. I. (Washington, DC: Institute for Palestine Studies, 1991).

Arberry, Arthur J., translator, *The Koran Interpreted* (New York: Collier Books, 1955).

Aruri, Naseer, *Jordan: A Study in Political Development (1921–1965)* (The Hague: Martinus Nijhoff, 1972).

Al-Azmeh, Aziz, *Islam and Modernities* (London: Verso, 1993).

———, ed., *Islamic Law: Social and Historical Contexts* (London: Routledge, 1988).

Balibar, Etienne, and Immanuel Wallerstein, eds., *Race, Nation, Class, Ambiguous Identities* (London: Verso, 1991).

Bailey, Clinton, *The Participation of the Palestinians in the Politics of Jordan*, doctoral dissertation, Department of Political Science, Columbia University, New York, 1966.

Bailey, Clinton, *Jordan's Palestinian Challenge, 1948–1983: A Political History* (Boulder, CO: Westview Press, 1984).

Bell, Sir Gawain, *Shadows on the Sand: The Memoirs of Sir Gawain Bell* (New York: St. Martin's Press, 1983).

Benjamin, Walter, "The Work of Art in the Age of Mechanical Reproduction," in Walter Benjamin, *Illuminations, Essays and Reflections*, edited by Hannah Arendt (New York: Schocken Books, 1969).

Bhabha, Homi, *Nation and Narration* (New York: Routledge, 1990).

———, "DissemiNation: Time, Narrative, and the Margins of the Modern Nation," in *Nation and Narration*, edited by Homi Bhabha (New York: Routledge, 1990).

———, "Of Mimicry and Man: The Ambivalence of Colonial Discourse," *October*, no. 28 (spring 1984).

Bhabha, Jacqueline, Francesca Klug, and Sue Shutter, eds., *Worlds Apart: Women Under Immigration and Nationality Law* (London: Pluto Press, 1985).

Bocco, Riccardo, *État et Tribus Bedouines en Jordanie, 1920–1990, Les Huwaytat: Territoire, Changement Économique, Identité Politique*, doctoral dissertation, Institut d'Études Politiques de Paris, 1996.

Bocco, Riccardo, and Tariq M. M. Tell, "Pax Britannica in the Steppe: British Policy and the Transjordan Bedouin," in *Village Steppe and State: The Social Origins of Modern Jordan*, edited by Eugene Rogan and Tariq Tell (London: British Academic Press, 1994).

———, "Frontière, Tribus et État(s) en Jordanie Orientale à l'Époque du Mandat," in *Maghreb-Machrek*, no. 147, January-February, 1995, pp. 26–47.

Brand, Laurie, *Palestinians in the Arab World: Institution Building and the Search for a State* (New York: Columbia University Press, 1988).

———, "Palestinians and Jordanians: A Crisis of Identity," *Journal of Palestine Studies* no. 96 (summer 1995), pp. 54–60.

Brenner, Lenni, *Zionism in the Age of the Dictators: A Reappraisal* (London: Lawrence Hill, 1983).

Butler, Judith, *Gender Trouble: Feminism and the Subversion of Identity* (New York: Routledge, 1990).

Carre, Olivier, *Séptembre Noir: Refus Arabe de la Resistance Palestinienne* (Brussels: Editions Complexes, 1980).

Chair, Somerset De, *The Golden Carpet* (New York: Harcourt, Bruce, 1945).

Chatterjee, Partha, *Nationalist Thought and the Colonial World: A Derivative Discourse* (Minneapolis: University of Minnesota Press, 1993).

———, *The Nation and Its Fragments: Colonial and Postcolonial Histories* (Princeton, NJ: Princeton University Press, 1993).

Collins, Larry, and Dominique Lapierre, *O Jerusalem* (New York: Simon and Schuster, 1972).

Dann, Uriel, *Studies in the History of Transjordan, 1920–1949: The Making of a State* (Boulder, CO: Westview Press, 1984).

Day, Arthur R., *East Bank/West Bank: Jordan and the Prospects of Peace* (New York: Council on Foreign Relations, 1986).

Debord, Guy, *The Society of the Spectacle* (New York: Zone Books, 1994).

Derrida, Jacques, "Force of Law: The Mystical Foundation of Authority," in *Cardozo Law Review*, vol. 11, nos. 5, 6 (1990).

———, "Devant La Loi," in *Kafka and the Contemporary Critical Performance: Centenary Readings*, edited by Ulan Udoff (Bloomington: Indiana University Press, 1987).

———,"Declarations of Independence," in *New Political Science*, no. 15 (summer 1986).

Dragnich, George S., *The Bedouin Warrior Ethic and the Transformation of Traditional Nomadic Warriors into Modern Soldiers Within the Arab Legion, 1931–1948*, masters thesis in history, Georgetown University, Washington, DC, 1975.

Dummett, Ann, and Andrew Nicol, *Subjects, Citizens, Aliens and Others: Nationality and Immigration Law* (London: Weidenfeld and Nicholson, 1990).

El-Edroos, Syed Ali, *The Hashemite Arab Army, 1908-1979, An Appreciation and Analysis of Military Operations* (Amman: The Publishing Committee, 1980).

Engels, Frederick, *The Origin of the Family: Private Property and the State* (Peking: Foreign Language Press, 1978).

Epstein, Eliahu, "The Bedouin of Transjordan: Their Social and Economic Problems," *Journal of the Royal Central Asian Society*, vol. XXV, part II (April 1938).

Fabian, Johannes, *Time and the Other: How Anthropology Makes Its Object* (New York: Columbia University Press, 1983).

Fanon, Frantz, *The Wretched of the Earth* (New York: Grove Press, 1968).

Fathi, Schirin, *Jordan: An Invented Nation?* (Hamburg: Deutsches Orient-Institut, 1994).

Fischbach, Michael, "British Land Policy in Transjordan," in *Village, Steppe and State: The Social Origins of Modern Jordan*, edited by Eugene Rogan and Tareq Tell (London: British Academic Press, 1994).

Foucault, Michel, *Discipline and Punish: The Birth of the Prison*, translated by Alan Sheridan (New York: Vintage Books, 1979).

———, *The History of Sexuality*, vol. I: *An Introduction*, translated by Robert Hurley (New York: Vintage Books, 1980).

———, "Governmentality," in *The Foucault Effect: Studies in Governmentality, With Two Lectures by and an Interview with Michel Foucault*, edited by Graham Burchell, Colin Gordon, and Peter Miller (Chicago: University of Chicago Press, 1991).

Freud, Sigmund, *The Standard Edition of the Complete Psychological Works of Sigmund Freud* (London: Hogarth Press, 1953–1974).

———, *Leonardo da Vinci and a Memory of His Childhood*, in *The Standard Edition of the Complete Psychological Works of Sigmund Freud* (London: Hogarth Press, 1953–1974), vol. XI, pp.83–84.

————, "Fetishism," in *The Standard Edition of the Complete Psychological Works of Sigmund Freud* (London: Hogarth Press, 1953–1974), vol. XXI.

Garber, Marjorie, "The Chic of Araby: Transvestism and the Erotics of Cultural Appropriation," in Marjorie Garber, *Vested Interests: Cross-Dressing and Cultural Anxiety* (New York: Harper Perennial, 1993).

Gellner, Ernest, *Nations and Nationalism* (Ithaca, NY: Cornell University Press, 1983).

Gibbon, Edward, *The History of the Decline and Fall of the Roman Empire*, edited by J. B. Bury, vol. VI (London: Methuen, 1912).

Giddens, Anthony, *The Nation-State and Violence: Volume Two of A Contemporary Critique of Historical Materialism* (Berkeley: University of California Press, 1987).

Glubb, John Bagot, *The Story of the Arab Legion* (London: Hodder and Stoughton, 1948).

————, *A Soldier with the Arabs* (London: Hodder and Stoughton, 1957).

————, *Britain and the Arabs: A Study of Fifty Years 1908–1950* (London: Hodder and Stoughton, 1959).

————, *War in the Desert: An R.A.F. Frontier Campaign* (New York: W.W. Norton, 1961).

————, *Arabian Adventures: Ten Years of Joyful Service* (London: Cassell, 1978).

————, *The Changing Scenes of Life: An Autobiography* (London: Quarter Books, 1983).

————, "Relations Between Arab Civilization and Foreign Culture in the Past and To-day," *Journal of the Royal Central Asian Society*, vol. XXIV (July 1937).

————, "The Conflict Between Tradition and Modernism in the Role of Muslim Armies," in *The Conflict of Traditionalism and Modernism in the Middle East*, edited by Carl Leiden (Austin: University of Texas Press, 1966).

————, "The Bedouins of Northern Iraq," *Journal of the Royal Central Asian Society* vol. XXII, part I (January 1935).

————, "The Mixture of Races in the Eastern Arab Countries," The J. L. Myers Memorial Lecture was delivered at New College, Oxford, on April 25, 1967, Oxford, 1967.

————, "Arab Chivalry," *The Journal of the Royal Central Asian Society*, vol. XXIV, part I (January 1937).

————, "The Economic Situation of the Trans-Jordan Tribes," *Journal of the Royal Central Asian Society*, vol. XXV, part III (July 1938).

Government of the United Kingdom, *The Statutes*, Second Revised Edition, vol. XII, From the Session of the Thirty-First and Thirty-Second to the session of the Thirty-Fourth and Thirty-Fifth years of Queen Victoria A.D., 1868–1871 (London, 1896).

————, *The Statutes Revised*, Great Britain, vol. 23, 2 and 3 GEO V. to 6 and 7 GEO V., 1912–1916 (London: Wymans and Sons, 1929).

————, *The Statutes Revised*, Great Britain, vol. 24, 6 and 7 GEO V. to 10 and 11 GEO V., 1917–1920 (London: Wymans and Sons, 1929).

Graham-Brown, Sarah, *Palestinians and Their Society 1880–1946: A Photographic Essay* (London: Quartet Books, 1980).

Gramsci, Antonio, *Selections from the Prison Notebooks of Antonio Gramsci*, edited and translated by Quintin Hoare and Geoffrey Nowell Smith (New York: International, 1971).

————, "The Intellectuals," in *Selections from the Prison Notebooks*, edited and translated by Quintin Hoare and Geoffrey Nowell Smith (New York: International, 1971).

————, "The Modern Prince," in *Selections from the Prison Notebooks*, edited and translated by Quintin Hoare and Geoffrey Nowell Smith (New York: International, 1971).

————, "State and Civil Society, Observations on Certain Aspects of the Structure of Political Parties in the Period of Organic Crisis," in *Selections from the Prison Notebooks of Antonio Gramsci*, edited and translated by Quintin Hoare and Geoffrey Nowell Smith (New York: International, 1971).

Gubser, Peter, *Politics and Change in Al-Karak, Jordan: A Study of a Small Arab Town and Its District* (New York: Oxford University Press, 1973).

Habermas, Jürgen, *The Structural Transformation of the Public Sphere: An Inquiry into a Category of Bourgeois Society*, translated by Thomas Burger (Cambridge, MA: MIT Press, 1991).

Hannoyer, Jean, and Seteney Shami, eds., *Amman: The City and Its Society* (Beirut: CERMOC, 1996).

Hatem, Mervat, "The Enduring Alliance of Nationalism and Patriarchy in Muslim Personal Status Laws: The Case of Egypt," in *Feminist Issues* (spring 1986), vol. 6, no. 1, pp. 19–43.

Hill, Enid, "Islamic Law as a Source for the Development of a Comparative Jurisprudence: The Modern Science of Codification (1): Theory and Practice in the Life and Work of ʿAbd al-Razzaq Ahmad al-Sanhuri (1895–1971)," in Aziz al-Azmeh, ed., *Islamic Law: Social and Historical Contexts* (London: Routledge, 1988).

Hirst, David, *The Gun and the Olive Branch: The Roots of Conflict in the Middle East* (London: Faber and Faber, 1984).

Hobsbawm, Eric, *Nations and Nationalism Before 1780: Programme, Myth, Reality* (Cambridge: Cambridge University Press, 1990).

Hobsbawm, Eric, and Terrence Ranger, eds., *The Invention of Tradition* (Cambridge: Cambridge University Press, 1983).

Huntington, Samuel P., *Political Order in Changing Societies* (New Haven, CT: Yale University Press, 1968).

Ibn Talal, Husayn (King Hussein), *Uneasy Lies the Head: The Autobiography of King Hussein I of the Hashemite Kingdom of Jordan* (New York: Bernard Geis, Random House, 1962).

James, C. L. R., *Beyond A Boundary* (Durham, NC: Duke University Press, 1993).

Jarvis, C. S., *Arab Command: The Biography of Lieutenant-Colonel F. G. Peake Pasha* (London: Hutchinson, 1942).

Jayawardena, Kumari, *Feminism and Nationalism in the Third World* (London: Zed Press, 1986).

Jureidini, Paul A., and R. D. McLaurin, *Jordan: The Impact of Social Change on the Role of the Tribes* (Washington, DC: Praeger, 1984).

Kasfir, Nelson, "Explaining Ethnic Political Participation," *World Politics*, vol. 31, no. 3 (1979).

Khalidi, Walid, *Before Their Diaspora: A Photographic History of the Palestinian People 1876-1948* (Washington, DC: Institute for Palestine Studies, 1991).

Al-Khazendar, Sami, *Jordan and the Palestine Question: The Role of Islamic and Left Forces in Foreign Policy-Making* (Berkshire: Ithaca Press, 1997).

Klug, Francesca, " 'Oh to be in England': The British Case Study," in Nira Yuval-Davis and Floya Anthias, eds., *Woman-Nation-State* (London: Macmillan, 1989).

Konikoff, A., *Transjordan: An Economic Survey* (Jerusalem: Economic Research Institute of the Jewish Agency for Palestine, 1946).

Laroui, Abdulla, *The Crisis of the Arab Intellectual: Traditionalism or Historicism?* (Berkeley, CA: University of California Press, 1976).

Lawrence, T. E., "Twenty-Seven Articles," first published in the *Arab Bulletin*, #60, August 20, 1920, reproduced in John E. Mack in *A Prince of Our Disorder* (London: Weidenfeld and Nicolson, 1976).

Layne, Linda, *Home and Homeland: The Dialogics of National and Tribal Identities in Jordan* (Princeton, NJ: Princeton University Press, 1994).

Lias, Godfrey, *Glubb's Legion* (London: Evans Brothers, 1956).

Lowenthal, Abraham F., and J. Samuel Fitch, eds., *Armies and Politics in Latin America*, Revised Edition (New York: Holmer and Meier, 1986).

Lunt, James, *Hussein of Jordan: A Political Biography* (London: Macmillan, 1989).

———, *Glubb Pasha: A Biography* (London: Harvill Press, 1984).

Lynch, Marc, "A Very Public Separation: Jordanian and Palestinian Identities in the New Jordan," paper presented at the Middle East Studies Association, in Washington, DC, December 1995.

———, *Contested Identity and Security: The International Politics of Jordanian Identity*, doctoral dissertation, Department of Political Science, Cornell University, Ithaca, NY, 1997.

Marx, Karl, "The Fetishism of Commodities and the Secret Thereof," in Karl Marx, *Capital, vol. 1: A Critical Analysis of Capitalist Production*, edited by Frederick Engels (New York: International, 1967).

———, *The German Ideology*, reproduced in Robert C. Tucker, ed., *The Marx-Engels Reader* (New York: Norton Press, 1978).

Mackinnon, Catherine A., *Toward a Feminist Theory of the State* (Cambridge, MA: Harvard University Press, 1989).

Massad, Joseph, "Conceiving the Masculine: Gender and Palestinian Nationalism," *Middle East Journal*, vol. 49, no. 3 (summer 1995), pp. 467–483.

———, "The 'Post-Colonial' Colony: Time, Space and Bodies in Palestine/Israel," in *The Pre-Occupation of Post-Colonial Studies*, edited by Fawzia Afzal-Khan and Kalpana Seshadri-Crooks (Durham, NC: Duke University Press, 2000).

Mishal, Shaul, *West Bank /East Bank: The Palestinians in Jordan 1949–1967* (New Haven, CT: Yale University Press, 1978).

Mitchell, Timothy, *Colonising Egypt* (Berkeley, CA: University of California Press, 1991).

———, "The Limits of the State: Beyond Statist Approaches and Their Critics" *American Political Science Review* 85, no. 1 (March, 1991).

Mogannam, E. Theodore, "Developments in the Legal System of Jordan," *Middle East Journal* 6, no. 2 (spring 1952):194–206.

Mohanty, Chandra Talpade, "Introduction, Cartographies of Struggle, Third World Women and the Politics of Feminism," in Chandra Talpade Mohanty, Ann Russo, and Lourdes Torres, eds., *Third World Women and the Politics of Feminism* (Bloomington, IN: Indiana University Press, 1991).

Mosse, George, *Nationalism and Sexuality: Respectability and Abnormal Sexuality in Modern Europe* (New York: Howard Fertig, 1985).

Nasir, Jamil, *The Islamic Law of Personal Status* (London: Graham and Trotman, 1986).

Ohannessian-Charpin, Anna, "Strategic Myths: Petra's B'doul," in *Middle East Report*, no. 196 (September-October 1995), pp. 24–25.

———, "Les Arméniens à Amman: La Naissance d'une Communauté," in Jean Hannoyer and Seteney Shami, eds., *Amman: The City and Its Society* (Beirut: CERMOC, 1996).

Palestine Liberation Organization, *Black September* (Beirut: PLO Research Center, 1971).

Parker, Andrew, Mary Russo, Doris Summer, and Patricia Yaeger, eds., *Nationalisms and Sexualities* (New York: Routledge, 1992).

Pateman, Carole, *The Sexual Contract* (Stanford, CA: Stanford University Press, 1988).

Peake, Frederick G., *History and Tribes of Jordan* (Coral Gables, FL: University of Miami Press, 1958).

———, "Transjordan," *Journal of the Royal Central Asian Society*, vol XXVI, part III (July 1939).

Plascov, Avi, *The Palestinian Refugees in Jordan, 1948–57* (London: Frank Cass, 1981).

Poulantzas, Nicos, *State, Power, Socialism*, translated by Patrick Camiller (London: NLB, 1978).

Ranger, Terrence, "The Invention of Tradition in Colonial Africa," in *The Invention of Tradition*, edited by Eric Hobsbawm and Terrence Ranger (Cambridge: Cambridge University Press, 1983).

Rogan, Eugene, and Tareq Tell, eds., *Village, Steppe and State: The Social Origins of Modern Jordan* (London: British Academic Press, 1994).

Royle, Trevor, *Glubb Pasha* (London: Little Brown, 1992).

Ryan, Sheila, and Muhammad Hallaj, *Palestine Is, But Not in Jordan* (Belmont, MA: The Association of Arab-American University Graduates Press, 1983).

Said, Edward, *Orientalism* (New York: Vintage Books, 1979).

———, *The World, The Text and the Critic* (Cambridge, MA: Harvard University Press, 1983).

Salibi, Kamal, *The Modern History of Jordan* (New York: I. B. Tauris, 1998).

Satloff, Robert, *Troubles On the East Bank: Challenges to the Domestic Stability of Jordan* (New York: Praeger, 1986).

———, *From Abdullah to Hussein: Jordan in Transition* (Oxford: Oxford University Press, 1994).

———, "From Hussein to Abdullah: Jordan in Transition," Research Memorandum, no. 38, April 1999, published by the Washington Institute for Near East Policy.

Sawalha, Aseel, "Identity, Self and the Other Among Palestinian Refugees in East Amman," in Jean Hannoyer and Seteney Shami, eds., *Amman: The City and Its Society* (Beirut: CERMOC, 1996).

Schlumberger, Gustave, *Renaud de Chatillon, Prince d'Antioche, Seigneur de la Terre d'Outre-Jourdain* (Paris: Plon-Nourrit, 1923).

Shami, Seteney, "The Circassians of Amman: Historical Narratives, Urban Dwelling and the Construction of Identity," in Jean Hannoyer and Seteney Shami, eds., *Amman: The City and Its Society* (Beirut: CERMOC, 1996).

———, *Ethnicity and Leadership: The Circassians in Jordan*, doctoral dissertation, Department of Anthropology, University of California, Berkeley, 1982.

Shaw, Stanford, and Ezel Kural Shaw, *History of the Ottoman Empire and Modern Turkey*, vol. II: *Reform, Revolution and Republic: The Rise of Modern Turkey, 1808–1975* (Cambridge: Cambridge University Press, 1977).

Shlaim, Avi, *Collusion Across the Jordan: King Abdullah, the Zionist Movement, and the Partition of Palestine* (New York: Columbia University Press, 1988).

Shoup, John, "The Impact of Tourism on the Bedouin of Petra," *Middle East Journal* 39, no. 2 (spring 1985).

Shryock, Andrew, *Nationalism and the Genealogical Imagination: Oral History and Textual Authority in Tribal Jordan* (Berkeley, CA: University of California Press, 1997).

Shwadran, Benjamin, *Jordan: A State of Tension* (New York: Council for Middle Eastern Affairs, 1959).

Silverman, Kaja, "White Skin, Brown Masks: The Double Mimesis, or With Lawrence in Arabia," in Kaja Silverman, *Male Subjectivity at the Margins* (New York: Routledge, 1992), pp. 299–338.

Sinai, Anne, and Allen Pollak, eds., *The Hashemite Kingdom of Jordan and the West Bank: A Handbook* (New York: American Academic Association for Peace in the Middle East, 1977).

Smith, Neil, *Uneven Development: Nature, Capital and the Production of Space* (Cambridge, MA: Basil Blackwell, 1984).

Snow, Peter, *Hussein* (Washington: Robert B. Luce, 1972).

Soja, Edward, *Postmodern Geographies: The Reassertion of Space in Critical Social Theory* (London: Verso, 1989).

Spivak, Gayatri Chakravorty, *Outside in the Teaching Machine* (New York: Routledge, 1993).

———, *In Other Worlds: Essays in Cultural Politics* (New York: Methuen, 1987).

Stepan, Alfred, *Rethinking Military Politics: Brazil and the Southern Cone* (Princeton, NJ: Princeton University Press, 1988).

Susser, Asher, *On Both Banks of the Jordan: A Political Biography of Wasfi al-Tall* (Essex: Frank Cass, 1994).

———, *In Through the Out Door: Jordan's Disengagement and the Middle East Peace Process* (Washington, DC: The Washington Institute for Near East Policy, 1990).

Tabachnick, Stephen Ely, "The Two Veils of T. E. Lawrence," *Studies in the Twentieth Century*, no. 16 (fall 1975).

Tilly, Charles, *Coercion, Capital and European States, AD 990–1992* (Cambridge, MA: Blackwell, 1992).

Thornton, Thomas Henry, *Colonel Sir Robert Sandeman: His Life and Work on an Indian Frontier: A Memoir, with Selections from His Correspondence and Official Writings* (London: John Murray, 1895).

Vance, Vick, and Pierre Lauer, *Hussein de Jordanie: Ma "Guerre" avec Israël* (Paris: Editions Albin Michel, 1968).

Vatikiotis, P. J., *Politics and the Military in Jordan: A Study of the Arab Legion, 1921–1957* (New York: Frederick A. Praeger, 1967).

Vernier, Bernard, *Armée et Politique au Moyen-Orient* (Paris: Payot, 1966).

Weir, Shelagh, *Palestinian Costume* (Austin: University of Texas Press, 1989).

Welchman, Lynn, "The Development of Islamic Family Law in the Legal System of Jordan" *International and Comparative Law Quarterly* 37, part 4 (October 1988).

Wilson, Mary, *King Abdullah, Britain and the Making of Jordan* (Cambridge: Cambridge University Press, 1989).

Young, Peter, *Bedouin Command: With the Arab Legion 1953–1956* (London: William Kimber, 1956).

———, *The Arab Legion* (Berkshire: Osprey Publishing, 1972).

Yuval-Davis, Nira, and Floya Anthias, eds., *Woman-Nation-State* (London: Macmillan, 1989).

Zinn, Howard, *A People's History of the United States* (New York: Harper and Row, 1980).

Zubaida, Sami, "National, Communal and Global Dimensions in Middle Eastern Food Cultures," in Sami Zubaida and Richard Tapper, eds., *Culinary Cultures of the Middle East* (London: I. B. Tauris, 1994).

Index